THE BEST PLANNED CITY
IN THE WORLD

Olmsted, Vaux, and the Buffalo Park System

FRANCIS R. KOWSKY

University of Massachusetts Press   Amherst and Boston
Library of American Landscape History   Amherst

A volume in the series
Designing the American Park
Edited by Ethan Carr

ISBN 978-1-62534-006-1

Designed by Jonathan D. Lippincott
Set in Granjon
Printed and bound by Thomson-Shore, Inc.

Library of Congress Cataloging-in-Publication Data

Kowsky, Francis R., 1943–
    The best planned city in the world : Olmsted, Vaux, and the Buffalo park system / Francis R. Kowsky.
        pages cm. — (Designing the American park)
    Includes bibliographical references and index.
    ISBN 978-1-62534-006-1 (cloth : alkaline paper) 1. Parks—New York (State)—Buffalo—History—19th century.
2. Parks—New York (State)—Buffalo—Design and construction—History—19th century. 3. City planning—New York
(State)—Buffalo—History—19th century. 4. Landscape design—New York (State)—Buffalo—History—19th century.
5. Olmsted, Frederick Law, 1822–1903. 6. Vaux, Calvert, 1824–1895. I. Library of American Landscape History. II. Title.
    SB482.N72B83 2013
    333.78'3097471—dc23
                                                                                                            2012047390

British Library Cataloguing-in-Publication Data
A catalogue record for this book is available from the British Library.

Photographs by Andy Olenick were specially commissioned for this book and are © Andy Olenick. They include the chapter frontispieces appearing on pages 2, 22, 54, 78, 92, 106, 132, 152, and 184, which show, in order, Chapin Parkway, Forest Lawn Cemetery, Delaware Park, Front Park, Martin Luther King Jr. Park, Gates Circle and Chapin Parkway, the Towers of the Buffalo Psychiatric Center, Niagara Falls from the American side, and Cazenovia Park.

Frontispiece: Map of Buffalo showing the new park and parkway system, prepared by Frederick Law Olmsted in 1876 for display at the Centennial Exhibition in Philadelphia. It was also shown at the Exposition Universelle in Paris in 1878. Courtesy Frederick Law Olmsted National Historic Site.

The photograph of Frederick Law Olmsted near the conclusion of his career, page 216, is from James Terry White, ed., *National Cyclopaedia of American Biography* (1921).

Endpapers: (front) Spire Head House and the Beech Banks on the south shore of Gala Water; (back) the Parade. Both watercolor drawings were commissioned by Olmsted for the 1876 Centennial Exhibition. Courtesy Buffalo and Erie County Historical Society.

Publication of this book was aided by a generous grant from

 Furthermore: a program of the J. M. Kaplan Fund

THE BEST PLANNED CITY
IN THE WORLD

LALH

Library of American Landscape History

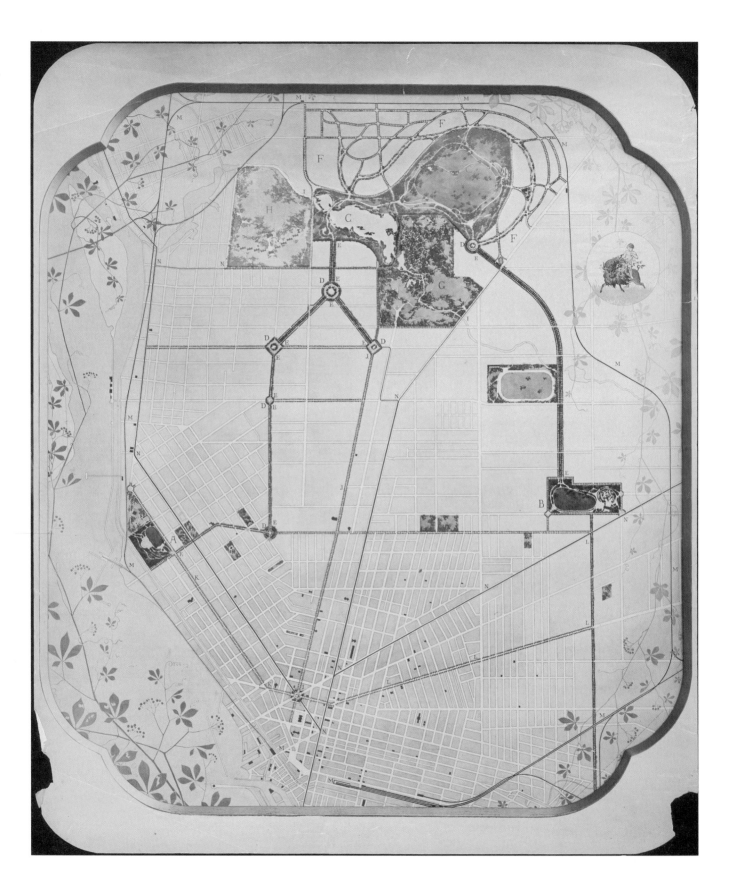

Generous support for the publication of *The Best Planned City in the World*
was provided by the following organizations:

VIBURNUM TRILOBUM FUND OF THE NEW YORK COMMUNITY TRUST

FURTHERMORE: A PROGRAM OF THE J. M. KAPLAN FUND

THE BAIRD FOUNDATION

THE CAMERON AND JANE BAIRD FOUNDATION

THE MARGARET L. WENDT FOUNDATION

ROBERT & PATRICIA COLBY FOUNDATION

FIGURE FOUNDATION

In memory of Charles Capen McLaughlin, who first showed us the way

Contents

Preface

The Buffalo park and parkway system, which Frederick Law Olmsted and Calvert Vaux began planning in 1868, was the first of its type in the United States. Most of the system survives today, remarkably, with great integrity as part of the notable cultural heritage of Buffalo, New York. Historians are often more familiar with the architectural aspects of that city's heritage, from its array of buildings designed by Richardson, Sullivan, and Wright to the imposing grain elevators on the lakeshore. But as Frank Kowsky's important and authoritative research demonstrates, Buffalo's tradition of city planning and its living legacy of parks and parkways constitute a unique monument in American landscape planning, significant not only in the context of the city of Buffalo, but for its place in our national history of urbanization and park design. This history of Buffalo's park and parkway system launches a new series for the Library of American Landscape History and epitomizes much of what the series hopes to achieve. *Designing the American Park* will be dedicated to publishing new research by outstanding scholars on topics and places in North American park history that have remained understudied in proportion to their significance.

Undertaken just a few years after Prospect Park in Brooklyn and while significant portions of Central Park in New York were still under construction, the Buffalo park system has not only been less studied, but it has been less than fully appreciated in terms of its historical significance. When asked by the Buffalo park commissioners for advice for the location for a new park, Olmsted and Vaux proposed instead that they create three parks: the Parade, for recreation and large events; the Front, a smaller park commanding views of Lake Erie at the waterfront entrance to the city; and the Park, a large, pastoral landscape on the city's northern edge. Broad, tree-lined parkways, inspired by contemporary Parisian boulevards, connected the parks and provided the settings for new residences and institutions as the city grew in the 1870s. Building on the existing 1804 radial grid plan of the city (significant in its own right), by 1876 the designers had overseen the development of a diverse and connected system of parks, playgrounds, civic squares, and parkways. That year, in connection with the display of the Buffalo park plan at the Centennial Exposition in Philadelphia, Olmsted remarked that Buffalo could claim to be "the best planned city, as to its streets, public places, and grounds, in the United States, if not in the world."

Francis R. Kowsky, SUNY Distinguished Professor of Fine Arts emeritus at Buffalo State College, is the biographer of Calvert Vaux and a longtime scholar of the life and work of Olmsted as well as a noted historian of American art and architecture. The Library of American Landscape History is pleased to make this important research on the Buffalo park system the inaugural volume of *Designing the American Park* because it achieves a foremost goal of the series: publishing the leading scholars in the field on those topics in the history of American park design with the most potential for expanding and deepening our understanding of this unique form of cultural expression. This series is dedicated, above all, to the idea that parks, as designed public landscapes, offer rich rewards for art and cultural historians who undertake their study. No category of art better deserves to be called "public" art than parks, which derive their meanings and significance largely from the people who use them. Park landscapes express broad themes of social and environmental improvement, while at the same time embodying the political and economic motivations of urbanization and development. If the conflict of progress and nature is a pervasive theme in American culture, where does it find more complete expression and attempted resolution than in park landscapes? The richness of the history of park design deserves the attentions of our finest art historians. The Library of American Landscape History is proud to publish this authoritative work on a vital chapter in early municipal park design history in the United States. The author's unique background and approach, and the powerful narrative he has created, weaving themes of social and political context with those of landscape theory and park design, make his work the first comprehensive history of the Buffalo parks.

The places called parks in American history have ranged from urban playgrounds to wilderness reservations, and their design has involved a similarly wide range of practical concerns and technical skills. The meanings of public parks as well, and their role in defining individual, group, and national identities have also constantly shifted over hundreds of years. In Buffalo, as Kowsky recounts, the interest in creating a municipal park system extended to a concern for the preservation of Niagara Falls and involved many of the same Buffalo park advocates, including Olmsted and Vaux, who produced the plan for the preservation of the falls in 1887. Municipal park making and scenic preservation were always related endeavors, drawing on the same reservoir of picturesque aesthetic theory and compositional ideas. Other parks in the Buffalo system, such as the Parade, embraced the emerging ideals of the neighborhood playground and the benefits of organized recreation. Still others created places of social events and congregation specific to the place and region. The siting of the Front, for example, overlooking the beginning of the Niagara River and Lake Erie, was unique to the city and the region. Our hope is that this series, *Designing the American Park,* will bring the same breadth and diversity to our understanding of its subject.

The Buffalo parks were the first to show how a coordinated system of diverse types of public landscapes could shape a landscape-based form of urbanism in the United States. This volume captures the living heritage of this park system, thanks to the color photography of Andy Olenick, which complements the book's rich program of historical images. The research presented here should be of material assistance in the continued restoration of the Buffalo parks, led by the Buffalo Olmsted Parks Conservancy. We also hope that the book will help assure that the parks receive the recognition they are due, as well as the support they need for their continued survival and success.

We are extremely grateful to Frank Kowsky for his years of research and for the care and broad historical perspective he has brought to this richly illustrated book. The far-ranging program of historical plans and drawings he assembled has been greatly enhanced with new, specially commissioned color photographs by Andy Olenick. This book has also benefited from an excellent editorial team of Sarah Allaback, who patiently managed the project, and copyeditors Amanda Heller and Mary Bellino. The Library of American Landscape History expresses its deepest gratitude to this group for their excellent work, and to Jonathan D. Lippincott for the book's elegant design.

The important work of LALH relies on those organizations and individuals who choose to support education and publishing about landscape architecture and the diverse heritage of North American landscape history. Without their commitment, books such as this one would not exist. We are extremely grateful to the Viburnum Trilobum Fund of the New York Community Trust for supporting this project since its inception, and to Furthermore: a program of the J. M. Kaplan Fund and to the Baird Foundation, the Cameron and Jane Baird Foundation, and The Margaret L. Wendt Foundation of Buffalo, NY, for generous grants.

LALH is overseen by a dedicated, knowledgeable, and committed Board of Directors, who have also helped bring this project to fruition. We thank the Directors, for this and for all the work they do to make LALH the unique organization that it is.

Ethan Carr, FASLA
Series Editor

THE BEST PLANNED CITY
IN THE WORLD

Introduction: Olmsted and Vaux and the Progress of the American Park Movement

If Frederick Law Olmsted had been a painter, Buffalo would have been his canvas. —Lauren Belfer, *City of Light,* 1999

Beginning in 1868, Frederick Law Olmsted (1822–1903) and his British-born partner, Calvert Vaux (1824–1895), created for Buffalo, New York, an assemblage of parks and parkways that attracted national and international attention. Before other American cities, Buffalo endorsed Olmsted and Vaux's pioneering concept of the metropolitan recreational system and introduced the parkway to the American cityscape. Substantially completed by 1874, their scheme augmented the city's original plan, created in the early years of the nineteenth century by Joseph Ellicott, with the addition of three new green spaces. These became known as the Park (in 1896 renamed Delaware Park), the Front (the present Front Park), and the Parade (after 1896 Humboldt Park, the present Martin Luther King Jr. Park). Each of these sites, as their names implied, possessed distinctive attractions and offered special pastimes. Of equal importance to the new public parks were the parkways, which Olmsted and Vaux planned to connect the parks to one another and to the rest of the city. These tributaries of the parks extended through the mostly unbuilt sector of town, an area where many pleasant middle-class residential neighborhoods would come into being distant from the workaday world of commerce and industry. Following the new boulevard route, one might proceed under a canopy of trees throughout the six-mile distance from the Front, which overlooked the waterfront on the West Side, to the Parade, which surveyed the city from high ground on the East Side. In addition to arranging new parkways, Olmsted and Vaux upgraded a number of older streets so that travelers might move from downtown to the new parks and parkways along verdant arterials.

The happy success of this ambitious project rested on foundations laid in 1804, when Joseph Ellicott (1760–1826), agent for the Holland Land Company, the Dutch investors who owned most of the land in western New York, established the original plan for what would become the city of Buffalo. (In deference to the entrepreneurs' Dutch roots, the settlement bore the name New Amsterdam.) Located on the shore of Lake Erie at the origin of the Niagara River, the harbor town stood at the easternmost point for navigation of the Great Lakes and at the western border of New York State, some 450

Joseph Ellicott (1760–1826), the founder of Buffalo.
Harper's New Monthly Magazine (July 1885).

new capital to the lakeshore village. Niagara Square formed the focal point of diagonal thoroughfares, most of which extended inland from Lake Erie through a grid of smaller streets. For their part, Olmsted and Vaux warmly acknowledged the excellence of Ellicott's plan and conceived their own assortment of parks, boulevards, and circles in tandem with it.

The opening of the Erie Canal in 1825, with Buffalo as its western terminus, marked the true beginning of the city's growth and development. One of the first major engineering achievements of the youthful nation, the 450-mile waterway linked the eastern seaboard with the Great Lakes and opened a corridor of travel to the West. Buffalo soon became an important transit point in the country's inevitable expansion. The town's busy waterfront witnessed a steady stream of settlers boarding lake steamers for destinations in the upper Midwest. In 1843 the flow of traffic and goods grew even greater with the construction of the initial railroad parallel to the canal. Many other rail lines were soon built, so that by the end of the century twenty-five lines, many of them trunk lines, converged on the city, where 250 passenger trains arrived and departed daily. Buffalo ranked as one of the largest transportation centers on the continent, a strategic nexus of steamers, trains, and barges. Industry and commerce joined the march of progress, with the grain trade leading the way. From upper midwestern and Canadian fields came boatloads of wheat destined for eastern and foreign markets. The need to store large amounts of grain for transshipment spurred the invention of the grain elevator, the first of which went up in 1842. By the

miles from the docks of Manhattan. In Ellicott's time, the land he surveyed was still little more than wilderness. A former assistant to Pierre L'Enfant in the laying out of Washington, D.C., in the 1790s, Ellicott adapted the French engineer's radiating street pattern for the

View of Lake Erie from Buffalo, 1818. From Frank H. Severance, *Picture Book of Earlier Buffalo* (1912).

THE BEST PLANNED CITY IN THE WORLD

time Olmsted made his first visit to Buffalo, many of these ungainly looking wooden sheds—"as ugly a monster as has yet been produced," Anthony Trollope called them—populated the shore and gave the harbor its distinctive appearance.[1]

The Civil War further promoted the fortunes of the city as a transportation and manufacturing center, and in its wake Buffalo entered an era of industrial prosperity that lasted until the mid-twentieth century. By 1890 Buffalo could boast that it was the world's largest coal and lumber distribution center; its manufacturers turned out fertilizer, soap, railroad cars, milling machinery, refrigerators, carriages, farm implements, iron stoves, bridges, scales, boots and shoes, furniture, and many other commodities.[2] Flush with Gilded Age wealth, the nation's eighth-largest city and the busiest port on earth looked to the dramatic expansion of the Ellicott plan to accommodate an ever-increasing population. Its leaders had the wisdom to seek the counsel of Olmsted and Vaux and the courage to accept their advice.

Before the Civil War, enjoying a day in the park was an experience little known in this country. By the end of the century, the American park movement, which began in earnest in the 1850s, had significantly improved the character of the nation's cities. In the drive to modernize urban life, New York, Brooklyn (not yet part of New York City), and Buffalo held a position of national leadership. In all three of these urban centers, politically

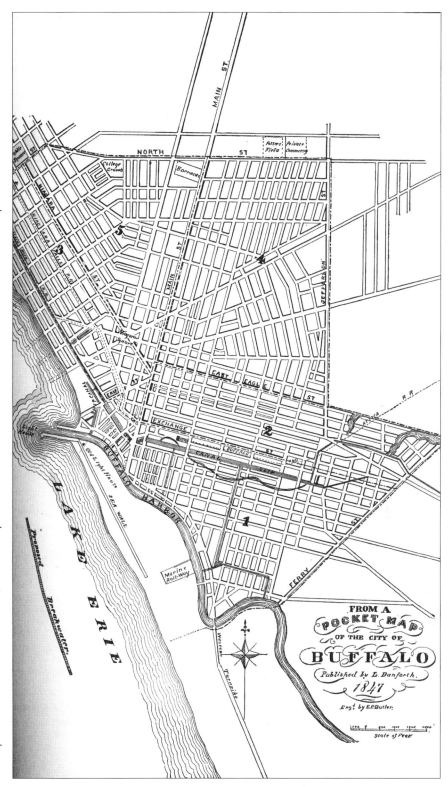

Joseph Ellicott's 1804 plan for the village of New Amsterdam (later Buffalo), as it developed by 1847. From H. Perry Smith, *History of the City of Buffalo and Erie County* (1908).

Erie Canal at Buffalo. Photograph by C. L. Pond, 1869. Courtesy Janice and Dale Rossi.

Buffalo harbor grain elevators. Photograph by C. L. Pond, 1868. Courtesy Janice and Dale Rossi.

powerful park commissions, acting in the name of the public good, directed the construction of large municipal parks. In addition, all three of these places benefited from the extraordinary talents of the men whose achievements dominate the opening pages of the annals of landscape architecture in the United States: Frederick Law Olmsted and Calvert Vaux. In New York and Brooklyn, the partners designed Central Park (1858) and Prospect Park (1865), the first major monuments of the profession they virtually originated; in Buffalo, they fulfilled their desire to create a comprehensive system of parks, parkways, and avenues that mirrored their physical ideal of the modern city. When, at the peak of his career, Olmsted displayed at the 1876 Centennial Exhibition the plan of Buffalo as it had been enlarged and revised under his guidance, he proclaimed Buffalo "the best planned city, as to its streets, public places and grounds, in the United States, if not the world."[3] In 1878 he shared his view with visitors to the Exposition Universelle in Paris, where he again placed his map of Buffalo on display.

To Olmsted and Vaux's way of thinking, public parks laid out in imitation of rural scenery—what they called pastoral landscapes or country parks—provided needed escapes from the push-and-shove competition that characterized life in America's burgeoning cities. Olmsted and Vaux believed that time spent in natural-seeming surroundings could restore equilibrium to the psyches of weary urbanites by inducing an exhilarating sense of freedom. They spoke fondly of "the feeling of relief experienced by those entering [a landscape park] on escaping from the cramped, confined and controlling circumstances of the streets of the town." To those whose daily lives were circumscribed by parallel streets, shoulder-to-shoulder buildings, and tight living spaces, pastoral scenery of the type Olmsted and Vaux artfully created at Central Park and Prospect Park, and which they proposed especially for the Park in Buffalo, was, they contended, the surest way to induce this sense of freedom and to promote the "recuperation of force" in individual minds and bodies. In graceful prose they

THE BEST PLANNED CITY IN THE WORLD

defined such landscapes as consisting "of combinations of trees, standing singly or in groups, and casting their shadows over broad stretches of turf, or repeating their beauty by reflection upon the calm surface of pools"; invoking biblical imagery, they asserted that these places gave rise to "predominant associations" that were "in the highest degree tranquilizing and grateful, as expressed by the Hebrew poet: 'He maketh me to lie down in green pastures; He leadeth me beside the still waters.'"[4] Their parks evoked a timeless existence that had been left behind in the quest for progress and offered a comforting vision of permanence in a rapidly changing world.

Their soul mates in this cause were painters of the so-called Hudson River School and poets and philoso-

phers collectively known as the Transcendentalists. Artists like Thomas Cole, Asher B. Durand, and Frederic Church gazed with reverent eyes upon the natural world and produced canvases that awakened the nation to the beauty enshrined in the New World's outdoor settings. Admiration of the national landscape had become an attribute of the cultivated intelligence. Ralph Waldo Emerson, William Cullen Bryant, and other Transcendentalist thinkers such as Vaux's friend Octavius B. Frothingham reinforced the notion that nature's loveliness was a gift from God that was capable of elevating the receptive mind above profane things and stirring the heart to the love of goodness and beauty. Such noble beliefs could inspire those who devoted themselves to the art of landscape architecture. "Having studied care-

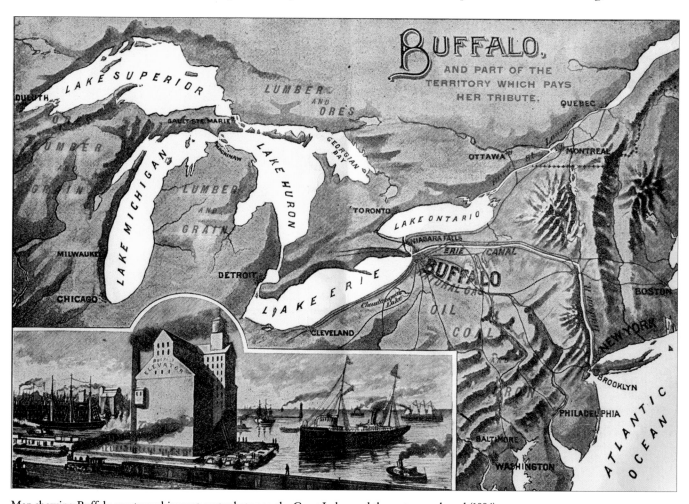

Map showing Buffalo as a transshipment center between the Great Lakes and the eastern seaboard (1894). Courtesy Buffalo and Erie County Historical Society.

fully the works and the method of working of the Creator," Vaux declared, "the designer of a landscape can bring into successful play the great forces of Nature, and subordinating his own personality, can secure for his work an undying vitality which can only follow from such a direct reliance on the resources of the Infinite."[5]

Although the American park movement shared common ground with the visions and thoughts of native painters and philosophers, its design ideals came mainly from the British tradition of landscape architecture. The garden in the British Isles, in the words of the art historian Malcolm Andrews, "became a great laboratory for aesthetic experiments" as the idea that land possessed value as "an aesthetic asset" took hold in the Anglo-Saxon world.[6] In their schemes for extensive grounds—"parks"—of large private estates, English garden designers popularized the notion of "natural" arrangements of plants and topography. Influenced by the spirit of Romanticism, this new style represented a radical departure from the "formal" principles of Renaissance garden design, which imposed symmetrical geometric patterns on the world of the out-of-doors. By the middle of the nineteenth century, the natural style of landscape gardening had become so closely identified with England that on the Continent, where the more formal spirit of design still held sway, French landscape architects referred to the informal style as the *style anglais,* the English style.

In 1845 the well-known British gardener Joseph Paxton transferred the concepts of Romantic landscape design enjoyed by private landowners to the realm of public parks. At Birkenhead, a town across the Mersey

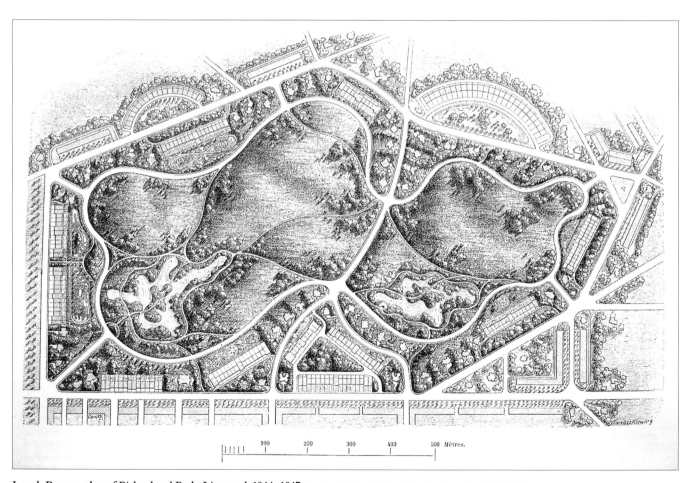

Joseph Paxton, plan of Birkenhead Park, Liverpool, 1844–1847. From Jean-Charles Adolphe Alphand, *Les Promenades de Paris* (1868).

THE BEST PLANNED CITY IN THE WORLD

River from Liverpool, he laid out a 350-acre meadow-land park ringed with meandering pedestrian paths and carriage drives and furnished with attractive pavilions in various historic architectural styles. There were also playgrounds for sports and a bandstand for musical concerts. Many regard Birkenhead Park as the ancestor of the American municipal park. Certainly it had a strong influence on Olmsted's thought. In 1850, long before Olmsted considered becoming a landscape architect and just three years after Paxton's grounds had opened, he visited the new park. He came away impressed by what he saw there. "Besides the cricket and an archery ground," he wrote, "large valleys were made verdant, extensive drives arranged—plantations, clumps, and avenues of trees formed, and a large park laid out." Furthermore, the gates were open to anyone who might wish to enter. "All this magnificent pleasure-ground is entirely, unreservedly, and forever the people's own," Olmsted affirmed to his American readers. "The poorest British peasant is as free to enjoy it in all its parts as the British queen."[7]

Together with its admirable new park, Birkenhead itself made a favorable impression on Olmsted for its progressive attitude toward urban development. For one thing, the city had paid for the construction of the park by the novel idea of selling or renting building lots around its border for new dwellings. Like numerous American towns and cities at the time of Olmsted's visit, Birkenhead was experiencing rapid expansion as a result of the growth of commerce and industry, primarily shipbuilding. Nevertheless, this process was proceeding in an enlightened, orderly fashion. "It seems to me," Olmsted remarked, "to be the only town I ever saw that has been really built at all in accordance with the advanced science, taste, and enterprising spirit that are supposed to distinguish the nineteenth century." In Olmsted's opinion, Birkenhead had much to teach others about city building. It was, he said, "a model town, and may be held up as an example, not only to philanthropists and men of taste, but to speculators and men of business."[8] What Olmsted had learned at Birkenhead would influence his proposals for the rising inland port of Buffalo.

The construction of public parks also assumed an important role in efforts to improve urban life in France in the middle of the nineteenth century. During the years of Emperor Napoleon III, several important public parks came into being in tandem with the great remaking of the city of Paris that began in the autumn of 1853 under the direction of Baron Georges-Eugène Haussmann. This monumental venture to modernize the capital focused the world's attention on the cosmopolitan metropolis that had long been the seat of Francophone culture. Haussmann's audacious plans revised the city's labyrinthine network of narrow streets, which hampered communication between various quarters, with a comprehensive framework of broad boulevards that advanced citywide travel, created dramatic urban vistas, and stirred an enlarged sense of the possibilities of urban life. The age of "circulation" and of the "boulevardier" was born.

The largest of the new Parisian parks was the Bois de Boulogne, a former royal hunting park on the western edge of the city. The plans prepared by Haussmann's close associate Jean-Charles Adolphe Alphand emulated the *style anglais* and provided citizens with a range of leisure-time choices. Moreover, Haussmann sought to link the new public park to the network of boulevards with the most stately of all the new thoroughfares, the Avenue de l'Impératrice. (The flattering name did not survive the reign of Empress Eugénie; today the street is known as the Avenue Foch.) Laid out by another of Haussmann's associates, the engineer Jacques Ignace Hittorf, the mansion-bordered Avenue de l'Impératrice measured an unprecedented 140 meters wide and comprised main and secondary roadways, all shaded beneath multiple rows of trees set in strips of lawn. The grand and dignified thoroughfare conducted Parisians to the Bois de Boulogne from the majestic Place de l'Étoile, home to the Arc de Triomphe, where many major streets converged.

Both Olmsted and Vaux had been to Paris and were well aware of developments there. In 1859 Olm-

Avenue de l'Impératrice and the Arc de Triomphe, Paris. From Jean-Charles Adolphe Alphand, *Les Promenades de Paris* (1868).

sted, during a stay in Paris, had taken a professional's close interest in the new boulevards. He had visited the Bois de Boulogne a number of times and even had met personally with its designer, Alphand. In August 1868, when Olmsted made his first visit to Buffalo, Vaux was pursuing a European tour that took him to the French capital. Modern improvements there would have been fresh in his mind when, back in New York, he sat down with Olmsted to talk over the new Buffalo project. The partners' appreciation of contemporary French urbanism would play an important role in the plan they envisioned for the Great Lakes city.

In this country, the movement to create public parks went hand in hand with the growth of suburban middle-class homeownership. Both of these trends began in earnest in the mid-nineteenth century, when Andrew Jackson Downing (1815–1852), horticulturist, gardener, and general authority on matters of taste, started to promote them. Downing had grown up in Newburgh in the heart of the Hudson Highlands, where the rugged slopes of the Catskills flank the shimmering waters of

the Hudson. Downing shared love of natural scenery with the Romantic artists he admired and the Transcendentalist writers he read, and like them had faith in the spiritually restorative power of nature. In the 1840s he began to publish his own books, such as *A Treatise on the Theory and Practice of Landscape Gardening Adapted to North America* (1841) and *Cottage Residences* (1842) and to write articles in the *Horticulturist.* Addressing both the well-to-do and the expanding middle class, he advised his readers how to design their houses and lay out the grounds around them so that harmony would reign between architecture and nature. Home life, in his view, would be greatly enhanced if the family lived in the midst of a tasteful setting of trees, lawn, flowers, and pretty views.

Downing also saw the need for those who lived in crowded, noisy cities to have access to green space where they could enjoy fresh air and quiet recreation. As early as 1848 his essay "A Talk about Public Parks and Gardens" appeared in the *Horticulturist,* and three years later he called upon the city fathers of New York, a place he

THE BEST PLANNED CITY IN THE WORLD

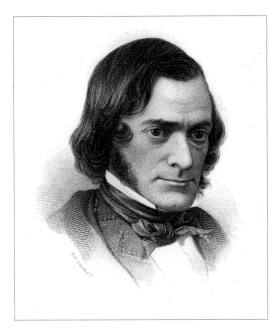

Andrew Jackson Downing (1815–1852). From A. J. Downing,
A Treatise on the Theory and Practice of Landscape Gardening, 8th ed. (1859).

knew well, to create a large public pleasure ground for its citizens.[9] For Downing, the requirement for such a place rested on the claim of democracy as much as it did on aesthetics and health. A large park landscaped in the natural manner, he stated, "is republican in its very idea and tendency. It takes up popular education where the common school and ballot box leave it, and raises up the working-man to the same level of enjoyment with the man of leisure and accomplishment." The shared experience of nature in such idyllic situations, undistracted by commerce and work, would foster, he believed, "a social freedom, and an easy and agreeable intercourse of all classes."[10]

As an earnest young man with an inquisitive mind, Frederick Law Olmsted grew up familiar with Downing's writings and worldview. Moreover, Olmsted's father, a successful businessman in Hartford, enjoyed escorting his son on leisurely tours of the New England countryside in search of picturesque places and inspiring views. These journeys often took father and son through the Connecticut River Valley, a historic area that enjoyed nearly equal renown with the Hudson Valley for the beauty of its pastoral scenery. These agreeable ramblings were a formative influence on Olmsted that confirmed in him a steadfast sense of beauty, especially as it was present in nature and landscape.

Although Olmsted failed to acquire an advanced education, he read his way to enlightenment on many subjects. From such contemporary thinkers as John Stuart Mill, Emerson, John Ruskin, and Thomas Carlyle, he developed a strong social conscience which led him to espouse public institutions that would allow ordinary citizens to acquire knowledge of the arts and sciences. He also came to believe that democratic societies should be based on "communitiveness," a notion which to him meant that each citizen should contribute his talent to sustain the life of the community. In turn, one was entitled to benefit from the skills and services of others. Olmsted also knew well the writings of philosophers of beauty from the previous century whose works still taught men and women of his own time, including Downing, how to appreciate the aesthetic qualities of natural scenery. From Humphry Repton, Uvedale Price, Richard Payne Knight, and William Gilpin came the theory popular in Olmsted and Vaux's day that natural scenery could be divided into three categories: the sublime (landscapes that provoked a sense of awe, such as Niagara Falls), the beautiful (landscapes that were restful and evoked a sense of peace, such as rolling meadows and placid ponds and lakes), and the picturesque (landscapes that were irregular and could stir a pleasant sense of remoteness and mystery, such as mountain valleys and woodland streams). He would frequently employ these concepts in his later work as a landscape architect.

In the late 1840s, at the age of twenty-six, Olmsted purchased rural land on Staten Island, where, a ferryboat ride away from Manhattan, he sought to combine life as a farmer with a career as a writer and journalist. In 1850, with the idea of publishing a book about farming practices and rural life in England, from which his ancestors had emigrated in the seventeenth century,

Olmsted, in the company of two friends, undertook a strenuous walking tour of the English countryside. He also went to Wales and spent a little time on the Continent. It was during this six-month sojourn that Olmsted visited Birkenhead. The result of this agreeable journey was the publication in 1852 of *Walks and Talks of an American Farmer in England.* The book revealed Olmsted to be a keen observer of people and places and received many favorable reviews. Downing, who had been in England at the same time, liked it and printed pre-publication excerpts in the *Horticulturist.* In 1851 Olmsted went to Newburgh and met Downing, with whom he had corresponded and from whose nursery he had purchased fruit trees for his Staten Island farm. Unfortunately, Downing never got to see Olmsted's book, for he was dead by the time it appeared in print. In his memory, Olmsted dedicated the second volume to Downing, whom he continued to hold in high regard throughout his life. Olmsted looked on Downing as "a great benefactor of our race," whose influence he himself wished "almost above all things to do something to extend and prolong." Olmsted would cite Downing as the spiritual progenitor of the Buffalo park system.[11]

The success of Olmsted's volume also prompted the *New York Times* to hire him to make a journey of discovery through the South and to report in a series of articles what he found there. In 1852 he embarked on a tour that took him through a considerable portion of the region that to many northerners was foreign territory. As a correspondent, Olmsted aimed to examine with a critical eye the institution of slavery and its effect on the economy and social life of the South. From this experience came a second book, *A Journey in the Seaboard Slave States,* which appeared in 1854. Olmsted came back from his travels convinced that slavery placed chains on masters as well as on those held in bondage. Controversial at the time, Olmsted's book is regarded today as one of the most thoughtful contemporary accounts of the antebellum South.

The popularity of Olmsted's writings encouraged him to venture further into the world of publishing.

Capitalizing on his literary success, in 1855 he sought and received the editorship of *Putnam's Monthly,* a well-respected periodical that enjoyed a national readership. The same year he also became a partner in an ill-fated publishing house venture.

Before the company failed, however, Olmsted was able to travel for business to Europe, where he took the opportunity to inspect public parks in Paris, Renaissance and Baroque gardens in Italy (the first to make use of panoramic views of landscape), and modern-day public gardens in German cities. Earlier Olmsted had written that on the Continent, especially in Germany, where he had spent much of his time, he had thoroughly enjoyed "the social out-door life." In particular, he appreciated the custom "of taking meals in the gardens and summer houses," for it seemed to him that "the middle classes at least *lived* in the open air more than even the English."[12] More and more, it seems, Olmsted's attention was being drawn toward the way people lived their lives and spent their leisure time in the world's major urban centers.

In New York he followed the progress of the park enthusiasts, and when the city acquired the land for the future Central Park, Olmsted, hard up for money, sought a position on the park staff. With the help of influential friends, he obtained the post of superintendent of the labor force that was readying the ground for construction of the new park. He had little ostensible qualification other than his sense of organization and his ambition to succeed. Nonetheless, the experience introduced him to the embryonic field of landscape architecture and taught him the rudiments of managing men and resources. Even though Olmsted may have failed to realize it at the time, the most important phase of his life had begun.

Olmsted came to know and love the profession with which his name would forever be associated because of the friendship he formed with Calvert Vaux. One of the first professional architects in America, Vaux was the product of quite a different background from that of Olmsted. Born and bred in the heart of London, where his father was a surgeon, Vaux came to maturity having experienced none of the peregrinations that had characterized Olmsted's search for his life's path. After attending the Merchant Taylors' School, Vaux embarked on an architectural career. In 1843 he entered the office of Louis N. Cottingham, a dedicated restorer of medieval church buildings and one of the elders of the Gothic Revival. Following his apprenticeship, Vaux undertook an architectural tour of France and Belgium. During this trip (and at other times), Vaux also made a special study of parks and gardens, for, like Olmsted, he felt a strong attraction to the beauties of nature and of landscape.

In 1850 Vaux was ready to commence practicing his profession in London. At the time, however, scant demand existed for the talents of such bright young architects, and Vaux had limited expectations of attracting clients. That summer he had the good fortune to encounter A. J. Downing, who had come to England to search for someone to join him in a new business venture. With a view to capitalizing on his reputation, Downing hoped to attract clients willing to pay for designs of houses and gardens. At an exhibition of architectural drawings that included works by Vaux, Downing met the young Englishman and fell into a discussion with him concerning his plans. Before long, the two men concluded an agreement. Vaux was soon on his way to America to work with Downing, who would be his passport to transatlantic refined society. At Highland Garden, an English Gothic–style mansion that Downing had built overlooking the Hudson at Newburgh, Vaux began his decades-long career in America. As Downing's architectural collaborator, he guided the design of a number of houses for clients in various parts of the country. Many of these appeared in Downing's 1852 book *The Architecture of Country Houses* and in Vaux's *Villas and Cottages,* which came out in 1857.

The most important project that engaged the two men's attention, however, was the preparation of plans for a landscaped park in Washington, D.C., where they hoped to put in lovely order the untidy land that lay between the White House and the Capitol. In November 1850, shortly after Vaux arrived in America, President Millard Fillmore discussed with Downing the possibility of creating such a model park on federally controlled property. In March of the following year, Downing and Vaux submitted a plan which quickly won congressional approval. Construction of this, the first large-scale publicly financed designed landscape in America, got under way in the summer of 1851. Tragedy, however, was soon to intervene. On one of Downing's visits to Washington to verify the progress of the work, the steamboat on which he was a passenger blew up, killing the country's thirty-six-year-old counselor of good living. With Downing's death and the departure of Fillmore from office early in 1853—the president returned to live in Buffalo, where later he would lend his support to the creation of Olmsted and Vaux's park system—the auspicious project died as well. After four more years in Newburgh, Vaux moved to New York City, some sixty miles downriver. He would live and practice architecture and landscape architecture there until his death in 1895.

A more enduring legacy of Downing's life and thought than the aborted Washington plan was the grand expanse of green in New York that came to be known as Central Park. By 1856 the city had purchased most of the nearly eight hundred acres that would make up the great park in the center of Manhattan Island. Surely if Downing had been alive at the time, he would have been chosen to design it. Therefore, when the city settled on a scheme that many considered a discredit to Downing's memory, Vaux used his influence with civic leaders to persuade them to hold a competition for a new design. Wishing to enter the contest himself, Vaux contacted Olmsted, who was already at work on the site, to propose that they collaborate on the preparation of a competition entry. In April 1858 their plan, submitted under the name "Greensward"—a reference to the open meadowland that formed a significant element of their scheme—prevailed over the other submissions. Construction of the park began soon after under Olmsted's supervision and with Vaux as consulting archi-

Central Park. From Clarence Cook, *Description of the New York Central Park* (1869).

tect. An accomplished designer of landscapes, Vaux also would be responsible for the design of the park's many bridges and numerous structures. Olmsted and Vaux's intention was to create a pastoral environment in the heart of the city—*rus in urbe,* as it was called—that would be available to all classes of society. New York's Central Park demonstrated Olmsted and Vaux's ideal of the art of landscape architecture placed in the service of the people.

Together with aesthetics and leisure, social purpose informed the philosophy behind the Greensward plan and the partners' later municipal parks. A keen observer of modern society, Olmsted had ascertained that life in America's burgeoning cities, while blessed with numerous advantages, could be dehumanizing for many who lived in them. "Every day of their lives they have seen thousands of their fellow-men," he would write, "have met them face-to-face, have brushed against them, and yet have had no experience of anything in common with

them." The modern public park, open to all citizens, was a remedy for the collateral urban evils of personal isolation and ethnic, religious, and class prejudice. Such places, said Olmsted, should provide "gregarious" and "neighborly" recreation.[13]

Gregarious amusement was the sort of phenomenon that one might enjoy on the Mall in Central Park, where people took pleasure in simply being together and being seen by one another—the equivalent of the traditional European promenade. Such neighborly recreation, said Olmsted, was "highly counteractive to the prevailing bias to degeneration and demoralization in large towns." New York's Central Park and Brooklyn's Prospect Park were, he declared, "the only places in those associated cities where . . . you will find a body of Christians coming together, and with evident glee in the prospect of coming together, all classes largely represented, with a common purpose, not at all intellectual, competitive with none, disposing to jealousy and spiritual or intellectual pride toward none, each individual adding by his mere presence to the pleasure of all others, all helping to the greater happiness of each." Enabling people of all backgrounds to congregate "in this way in pure air and under the light of heaven," free from the constraints of the "ordinary hard, hustling working hours of town life," he reasoned, would promote the moral and social well-being of the diverse nation. "Democracy in dirt and trees" was Olmsted and Vaux's corresponding pronouncement to Lincoln's "government of the people, by the people, for the people."

As the first celebrated municipal park in the United States, Central Park would encourage other cities to imitate New York's example. An article in Buffalo's *Courier* in July 1860 called the attention of its readers to the nascent park, which it acknowledged owed its origin "to the lamented Andrew J. Downing—a man who has done more than any other to foster and give direction to the love of the beautiful in Nature." And by way of thinly disguised admonition, the *Courier* informed the residents of its own city that "it is not too much for the tax payers of that city [New York] . . . to provide a retreat for their own citizens and to expend a tithe of their gold in affording an exhibition of the perfection to which the art of Landscape Gardening can be carried." The paper also told its readers that the new park was unlike anything that the people of this country had been accustomed to seeing in their hometowns:

To the American mind the idea of a Park is associated with an iron fence, inclosing sundry

The bandstand on the Mall in Central Park. From Clarence Cook, *Description of the New York Central Park* (1869).

The lake in Central Park. From Clarence Cook, *Description of the New York Central Park* (1869).

rows of stately trees standing sentinels along coarse graveled walks and mutely entreating visitors "to keep off the grass." Such is not the idea of the Central Park. The carriage drives, the walks, the ponds, are disposed to suit the surface of the ground. The roads wind about the hills, and footpaths invite to where roses bloom and flowers in all their various loveliness are domesticated. There is no end of bridges of cut stone that span ravines and lead from one eminence to another. . . . And then there are tunnels under the hills, drives cut out of the solid rock and stone steps leading to declivities.[14]

Here was a fabricated "natural" landscape artistically conceived by up-and-coming masters of their art and realized under their guidance. Already some of the readers of the *Courier* article were seeking to grace their own city with a comparable modern amenity. Joseph Warren, editor of the paper, was one of them.

When Vaux and Olmsted won the Central Park competition in the spring of 1858, they could not have foreseen that the Civil War would cut short immediate prospects for a national park movement. In 1861, shortly after the outbreak of hostilities, Olmsted resigned his post as superintendent of construction at Central Park to become secretary of the United State Sanitary Commission, a nongovernmental organization whose mission was to maintain healthy camp conditions for the Union forces. While Vaux remained behind in New York, Olmsted moved to Washington, D.C., where he labored tirelessly on behalf of the Sanitary Commission. The strain of work and worry, however, soon took its toll on Olmsted's well-being. In 1863 severe fatigue forced him to abandon his post. But rather than return to New York, Olmsted, now with a family to support, headed west in pursuit of the affluence that had so far eluded him. He took up the directorship of the Mariposa Mining Estates, a well-financed operation that was expected to reap abundant profits from the California goldfields. While in California, Olmsted became enthralled with the beauty of the natural scenery there. Of special concern to him was the fear that commercial interests would soon destroy the pristine valley of Yosem-

ite. The imminent threat inspired him to mount a drive to have the State of California purchase the spectacular mountain-ringed meadowland and preserve it for future generations. The Yosemite Valley campaign taught Olmsted lessons that he would afterward apply to saving the great eastern natural wonder, Niagara Falls, an undertaking associated with his work in nearby Buffalo.

Despite his friend's significant achievement in safeguarding Yosemite's natural beauty, Vaux believed that by going west rather than returning to New York and resuming their partnership, Olmsted had made a terrible mistake. In a series of forthright letters laced with

Prospect Park, Brooklyn, c. 1910. Library of Congress, Prints and Photographs Division, Detroit Publishing Company Collection.

THE BEST PLANNED CITY IN THE WORLD

tense exchanges between the two men, Vaux attempted to persuade Olmsted to return to the profession for which, Vaux insisted, God had singularly equipped him. Despite the waning success of the Mariposa venture, Olmsted resisted, saying that there was too little money in park design to maintain him and his family. Nonetheless, Vaux persisted. Finally, when Vaux wrote that he had secured the commission for a new park in Brooklyn, Olmsted relented. Prospect Park—the most fully evolved of their urban parks for the beauty of its scenery and the subtle way that drives and paths enhance one's experience of the landscape—marked the resumption of the Olmsted and Vaux partnership. It also signaled Olmsted's unwavering commitment to making his livelihood as a park planner and landscape architect. "Mr. Olmsted" had become "Olmsted." His career would last until his retirement in 1895, after which his stepson John C. Olmsted and son Frederick Law Olmsted Jr. would continue the historic practice he had established.

With the job in Brooklyn, Olmsted and Vaux's concept of the relation between urban parks and the city took on broader dimensions. They now suggested that in conjunction with Prospect Park, the city lay out a new type of boulevard they called a parkway. Modeled on the Avenue de l'Impératrice in Paris, the parkway was a residential thoroughfare two hundred feet wide, consisting of separate lanes for carriages, equestrians, and pedestrians. The lanes and sidewalks were to be separated by strips of grass, and all would be shaded by multiple rows of trees, preferably the American elm. The parkways they proposed for Brooklyn promised users more than ease of movement; they would have made travel to and from Prospect Park from various parts of town itself a parklike experience. They also envisioned other such roadways joining Prospect Park to Central Park and to other parts of the metropolitan area. Their habit of thought now was to see urban parks as elements of a "comprehensive" urban plan, one that would bind the recreational landscape to the city at large. Yet to Brooklynites the partners' proposal seemed

a risky innovation, and Olmsted and Vaux's aspiration went unfulfilled. After New York and Brooklyn, Olmsted and Vaux touted this new type of street to Chicago, Albany, Newark, and elsewhere. Buffalo, however, in 1869 would become the first place to implement their vision of a metropolitan park system bound together by a series of spacious parkways. The existence of these residential boulevards in conjunction with three new park landscapes was at the heart of Olmsted's contention that Buffalo was the best planned city in the nation.

After 1872, when Olmsted and Vaux parted ways, Olmsted continued to maintain a close association with Buffalo. For more than two decades, progressive political leaders and prominent citizens engaged him to design additional parks, parkways, and public and private sites in the Queen City of the Lakes, as the thriving interior port now fashioned itself. In the 1870s Olmsted furnished plans for Niagara Square, the center of the city plan devised by Ellicott; for the two-hundred-acre property belonging to the Buffalo State Hospital (the present Buffalo Psychiatric Center), a mammoth institution designed by Henry Hobson Richardson (1838–1886); and for the grounds around the new city hall. In the late 1880s and early 1890s, Olmsted in some measure realized his hope of creating parkland in the developing southern neighborhoods with South Park and Cazenovia Park. His office would also stay involved with the evolving plans for the residential community of Parkside, located adjacent to the Park (the present Delaware Park), the largest of the Olmsted and Vaux parks. Like its immediate predecessor, Riverside, Illinois, Parkside was a private venture, but its success was closely tied to the establishment of the municipal park system. As a contiguous group, Parkside, the Park, the preexisting rural cemetery known as Forest Lawn, and the two-hundred-acre Buffalo State Hospital grounds constituted a remarkable instance of nineteenth-century landscape design.

After Olmsted's retirement in 1895, his sons continued to provide landscape and planning services to the city. The most notable contributions of John C. Olmsted, who became his father's partner in 1884, were revisions to the original plan of the Parade and the creation of Riverside Park on the Niagara River, the last of the Buffalo parks to come from the Olmsted office. The Olmsted firm would also be involved with laying out neighborhoods in North Buffalo and serve as consultants, with Daniel H. Burnham, on the selection of a site for the Pan-American Exposition, which took place in Buffalo in 1901.

The first architect with whom Olmsted became closely associated, Vaux furnished many inventive designs for buildings, bridges, and other structures in the parks that he and Olmsted planned, including the original group of Buffalo parks. Chief among Vaux's architectural contributions to Buffalo's parks were a picturesque boathouse and a fanciful summerhouse for the Park and an extraordinary restaurant building located in the Parade. The two men remained lasting friends, and in 1887 they would team up to prepare the plan for the new state reservation at Niagara Falls.

An even closer friendship developed between Olmsted and the young architect H. H. Richardson. Although Olmsted and Richardson never formed an official business partnership as Olmsted had with Vaux, they worked together on many projects. Richardson was a southern plantation owner's son who, like many of his class, had gone north to get an education. After graduating from Harvard in 1859, he spent the years of the Civil War in Paris training to be an architect. The year that Olmsted moved back east from California, Richardson returned to America and chose to begin his professional career in New York, where the two men met. Writing after Richardson's death, Olmsted's friend Mariana Van Rensselaer stated that the architect had "constantly turned to Olmsted for advice, even in those cases where it seemed as though it could have little practical bearing upon his design. And where it could have more conspicuous bearing he worked with him as a brother-artist of equal rank and of equal rights with himself."[15] Olmsted's and Richardson's respective engagements in Buffalo played a role in cementing their friendship.

H. H. Richardson (1838–1886), carte de visite photograph made in Paris, c. 1861. Courtesy National Park Service, Adams National Historical Park.

In October 1868 Richardson received a commission from William Dorsheimer (1832–1888), an up-and-coming Buffalo attorney, to design a house for him on fashionable Delaware Street (after 1879 known as Delaware Avenue). It is not clear from the vantage point of today whether Olmsted had any influence on Dorsheimer's decision to hire Richardson, but soon the three men became fast friends. Dorsheimer, as a person knowledgeable in matters of taste, would surely have been impressed by the young architect's French credentials and would have judged him a man capable of conceiving a dwelling that would turn heads on the avenue that was becoming the city's best address. He was not disappointed. The house still stands at 434 Delaware, a smart red-brick *hôtel particulier* that never fails to surprise those who think that Richardson fashioned all of his architecture in the massive Romanesque style. Richardson began to forge that powerful idiom for the first time in the design of the Buffalo State Hospital, a

William Dorsheimer (1832–1888). Courtesy Buffalo and Erie County Historical Society.

The house designed for William Dorsheimer by H. H. Richardson in 1868. Photograph by Jack E. Boucher, 1965. Courtesy Library of Congress, HABS NY, 15-BUF, 2-1.

commission that may have come his way as a result of Dorsheimer's intervention. One of several large psychiatric hospitals erected by the State of New York after the war, it was Richardson's first major work and the largest building he ever designed. The hospital launched Richardson's career, and later, when Richardson's reputation equaled that of Olmsted, he was sought after for other commissions by Buffalo clients.

Olmsted and Richardson's nascent friendship was certainly fostered by Dorsheimer, the person largely responsible for the creation of the Buffalo park system. He was the son of a German émigré, Phillip Dorsheimer (1797–1868), who had arrived in Buffalo in the mid-1830s after stays in Pennsylvania and central New York. Though well known in Buffalo's German community, he mainly threw in his lot with men who had themselves, or through their forebears, come to western New York from New England and who dominated political and social life in the city. His son William grew up entirely Americanized. After public schooling in Buffalo, he spent the years 1849 to 1852 at Harvard before illness forced him to leave without earning a degree. Nonetheless, he brought away from the experience an enduring fondness for literature, art, and history and a strong sense of public-spiritedness that would lead him to seek a "higher civilization" for his hometown.

In 1854, his health restored, Dorsheimer received an honorary master's degree from Harvard and began his career as a lawyer in Buffalo. During the Civil War, he joined the staff of General John C. Frémont and served with the radical abolitionist during his controversial Missouri campaign. (Dorsheimer later wrote about the experience for *Harper's New Monthly Magazine*.) Like his father, Dorsheimer pursued a robust political life. In 1867, as a leading light of the local Republican Party, he was named United States attorney for northern New York. After 1872, when he went to Cincinnati to support Horace Greeley's presidential candidacy, he became a reformist voice in the Democratic Party. Two years later he won election as lieutenant governor of New York under Samuel Tilden, whose close friend he became. He also shared a friendship with Grover Cleveland, who was a young lawyer in Buffalo during the years when the park system was taking shape.

After 1880 Dorsheimer lived on Park Avenue in New York City, where he edited the *Star* newspaper and served a term in Congress. A stout, six-foot-tall Rabelaisian personage with a reputation as a genial conversationalist and a good after-dinner speaker, he moved among the best society. He also owned property at Newport which Olmsted landscaped. Throughout his long political career Dorsheimer championed progressive causes, among them copyright protection for American and foreign authors, the preservation of the Adirondack forests, and the erection of the Statue of Liberty in New York harbor. But unlike Cleveland, Dorsheimer always felt a warm attachment to his former hometown. When he died in 1888, he was laid to rest in Forest Lawn Cemetery, not far from the spot where, in Dorsheimer's company, Olmsted first laid eyes on the site that would become the Park.

From first meeting Olmsted in Buffalo in the summer of 1868, Dorsheimer became Olmsted's advocate and friend. He worked hard to see that Olmsted and Vaux's ambitious program of parks and parkways for Buffalo became a reality. Later, as the state's lieutenant governor, he used the power of his office to have the Canadian architect Thomas Fuller replaced by Olmsted, Richardson, and Leopold Eidlitz as the designers of the new state capitol then under construction in Albany. This controversial move exposed Dorsheimer and the three men to considerable criticism from powerful voices in the architectural profession. Nearly as audacious was his support for a plan that came to Olmsted's mind in 1869 to remove the commerce and industry that marred the beauty of Niagara Falls and to enshrine the cataract in a public park that would be free to all visitors. A few years later, Lieutenant Governor Dorsheimer championed Olmsted's proposal to have the State of New York purchase Goat Island and other lands surrounding Niagara Falls. In 1883 Cleveland, then governor of New York, helped draft a bill, which the legislature passed, establishing the Niagara Reservation, the name by which the state park was first known.

Niagara Falls by Moonlight. Photograph by George Barker, c. 1885. Courtesy Janice and Dale Rossi.

Dorsheimer became president of the state commission charged with acquiring the land for the reservation.

By the end of the nineteenth century, the concept of the urban park system enjoyed wide acceptance in the United States. Many cities, often with Olmsted's or his successors' involvement, undertook to put together metropolitan park networks. Beginning in the 1870s, Olmsted fashioned the series of linked green spaces in Boston that came to be called the Emerald Necklace, perhaps the most celebrated of all park systems. Other growing cities embarked on aggressive park and boulevard construction programs, including Philadelphia, Rochester, Hartford, Louisville, and Chicago. Olmsted's Buffalo, however, was the premier example of how a comprehensive system of parks and parkways might contribute significantly to the enhancement of life in America's cities.

The American park movement was one of the prin-

Entrance to the Buffalo harbor on Lake Erie. Photograph by Andy Olenick.

cipal achievements of late nineteenth-century reformers who, like Olmsted, strove to cure the ills that expanding commerce, industry, and population inflicted on the nation's cities. The creation of outdoor recreation in tranquil surroundings accessible to all, a residential life apart from business, and the improved design of streets were Olmsted's medicine for the afflictions of congestion and disorder. In the development of a comprehensive physical response to this threat, Olmsted and Vaux's plans for Buffalo were of seminal importance. Drawing on precedents in their own work, as well as with an eye toward the example of Haussmann's Paris, the partners gave form to their full-blown concept of park and urban planning. Here they articulated a plan that Olmsted would hold up to national and international audiences as an example of the well-designed modern city.

ONE

The Creation of the Park System

The artistic eye of Mr. Olmsted discerned at a glance our surpassing advantages. —David Gray, "The Buffalo Park Project," 1868

Beginning in the early 1850s, a number of public-spirited citizens attempted to bring into being a suitable public park in Buffalo. They were driven by discontent with the generally unprepossessing appearance of their community, which was transforming itself from a frontier village into a modern city forty years after having been burned to the ground by the British during the War of 1812. "Their efforts were prompted not only by the desire for a sylvan counterworld, with opportunities for walking and for repose in the midst of the noisy, congested city," the historian David Gerber observes, "but also by an awareness that for all the wealth the city generated, it remained a rough-hewn place without beauty." Visiting the capitals of Europe, Buffalonians had found well-maintained public parks and promenades that were essential elements of modern urban life. Weighing the environment of their hometown against what they had seen abroad, they found it woefully inadequate. Nor did it help to have foreign visitors to the city lament its uninspiring, utilitarian appearance. (Fig. 1.1)

"Of all the thousand and one towns I saw in America, I think Buffalo is the queerest looking," the British travel writer Frances Trollope remarked in 1832, adding that the city's buildings "have the appearance of having been run up in a hurry, though everything has an air of great pretension." Little had changed when her son, the novelist Anthony Trollope, passed through thirty years later. He wrote that "over and beyond the [grain] elevators, there is nothing specially worthy of remark at Buffalo."[1]

Nourished by travel and spurred by criticism of the city's lackluster public image, civic pride eventually took root. By the middle of the nineteenth century, a number of progressive-minded Buffalonians, including several newspaper editors, wished to see the city augment its meager capital of green spaces, a miscellaneous collection of grounds in front of public buildings and modest residential squares. The largest public place was the Terrace, an open area near the lakefront where public gatherings were held and the city's Liberty Pole stood. Prospect Place (the present Prospect and Columbus Park), the land for which had been donated to the city by a former mayor in 1836, formed the nucleus of one of the city's first and most desirable residential neighborhoods. Wadsworth Park (the present Arlington Place)

Fig. 1.1. The city of Buffalo from the waterfront. The city developed inland from Lake Erie and the Niagara River. The new parkland would be in the far distance in this view. *Harper's New Monthly Magazine* (July 1885).

and Days Park were smaller residential squares. These fenced squares followed the model established in 1831 by New York's Gramercy Park.

At the same time that Andrew Jackson Downing was calling for the establishment of a park in New York City and prominent citizens there were agitating to make his dream a reality, park advocates in Buffalo were seeking the same goal for their community. Located at the other end of the state and linked to New York commercially by canal and railroad, Buffalo viewed the grand metropolis as an older, more sophisticated sister to be emulated in matters of culture and urban life. (Early Buffalo directories invariably featured a section on New York City hotels and businesses.) "Now that people all over the country are getting waked up to the comfort and pleasures of parks, public grounds, suburban resorts, etc.," stated an editorial in the *Courier* in the summer of 1851, "we propose to say a word, in addition to what we have already written, touching such an improvement upon our Buffalo bareness." The paper called its readers' attention to two riverside sites that possessed considerable natural beauty. One was near Lake Erie in the vicinity of Buffalo Creek, along whose banks, according to the writer, "the Senecas, with their instinctive good taste," had lived in harmony with their surroundings for generations. The other was the long stretch of the Niagara River from Black Rock

to Grand Island. Equal in its breadth and beauty to the Tappan Zee on the Hudson, this section of the river, according to the paper, had been endowed by nature with "a wide sweep of blue water, bordered by sloping banks, clothed with rich verdure; its surface dotted with islands, sparkling in the sunshine, like emeralds set in lapis lazuli." Furthermore, the area could be reached easily by boat and would be just far enough away to make a pleasant excursion from town. Here was a site waiting to be developed that would surely equal New Rochelle, Cape May in New Jersey, and Nahant outside Boston, all new resorts popular with New York City's middle class. And while the location offered no sandy beaches, seashells, or tides, there was "shade instead of sand, green sward instead of rock, and all manner of rural delights instead of Bowery boys and target shooters." The editors hoped that a private investor would see the opportunity waiting here and unlock its recreational potential by building a suitable boating destination on the island.[2] (Fig. 1.2)

Likewise, serious efforts were also under way to create a modern park within the city limits. In June 1851 the Committee on Wharves and Public Grounds recommended that a seven-and-a-half-acre site, which possessed "a beautiful growth of Forest trees," be acquired for the purpose.[3] The property, however, was located in the predominantly German Fourth Ward, where stiff opposition to the idea soon developed. On August 27, 1851, Dr. Frederick Dellenbaugh, acting as spokesman for over a thousand residents who had signed a petition against the creation of a park in their neighborhood, declared to the Common Council (the city's legislative body) that they refused to be taxed "for the proposed Park which they did not want, and which they considered useless."[4] Rather, Dellenbaugh said, they wanted to see the city invest tax dollars to improve the public market system, which would more directly benefit the people by reducing the cost of food. The anti-park forces gained the support of the city attorney, and soon the park proposal went down to defeat.[5]

In 1855, two years after the city expanded its borders to its present boundaries, park advocates tried again to

THE BEST PLANNED CITY IN THE WORLD

promote the cause of green space. In February of that year the Common Council received a "petition of sundry citizens" requesting that the city purchase a significant amount of land for parks in three separate parts of town. Once again the forces of progress were met with opposition from fellow citizens who feared the burden of higher taxes. Furthermore, the city attorney stated that the council had no power to buy land for parks and that bonds issued for that purpose would be declared void. Therefore, the council resolved to take no steps to purchase lands for parks unless the state legislature authorized it.

Money was less of an issue when, a few months later, two public-spirited citizens, the attorney Edward Bennett and the inventor Rollins Germain, offered the city land on the East Side for a public park. Despite

Fig. 1.2. Grand Island, between Buffalo and Niagara Falls on the Niagara River, was one of the locations that early park advocates proposed for a public park. *Harper's New Monthly Magazine* (July 1885).

some opposition to the stipulation that the city pay to erect a substantial iron fence around the property, the offer was accepted. Nonetheless, "Bennett Park" existed for only a short time, for the following year the council began discussions that eventually converted the land into a site for a new city market. "We have strength and spirits for work, but none for the serene enjoyment of quiet and homely pleasures," lamented an editorial in a local newspaper around this time. The editorial, however, also praised the same German community that had strenuously worked to kill the park for its ability to put aside labor and enjoy itself. While the Germans, said the writer, "were the most thrifty and prosperous of our population," nearly the entire community found time for "innocent pastimes, having for its only objects recreation and pleasure."[6]

Indeed, some park promoters pointed to the popularity of recreation among the German community as a reason to support the creation of places of amusement for the general citizenry. In 1856 "Civis" addressed a long letter to the *Commercial Advertiser* "concerning the deficiency of Buffalo in respect to public grounds" and informed native-born fellow citizens how they might gain access to a popular German private picnic grove known as Westphal's Garden. The writer admitted that he had only recently discovered this pleasant eight-acre site at the intersection of Delaware Street and Gulf Street (now Delavan Avenue). He gave the newspaper's readers a glowing description of this now long-vanished "forest of native trees," where the visitor "finds avenues and walks laid out among the hills and dells, all of them beautiful and many of them entirely impervious to the sun."[7] Seconding the writer's praise of this quaint place, which surely resembled many such places in American cities, another paper, the *Republic,* elaborated on the description of the grounds that Johann Westphal, a horticulturist, had created:

This Garden, although comparatively unknown to many of our citizens, is the loveliest spot within twenty miles around us. It contains many acres of ground and is profuse in vegetation, in flowers, trees and shade. The whole place is laid out in the most delightful rural walks, and groves, and arbors, and nooks. Winding pathways lead into shady dells and cool springs. The ground is undulating, and affords a delightful variety of locality. The walks are all graveled, the trees trimmed, and the borders as neat as a flower garden. A fine country villa occupies the center of these grounds, almost embowered in luxuriant foliage. . . . A finely-arranged hothouse of plants and flowers, the property of Mr. Westphal, is not the least among the attractions of this beautiful vicinity.[8]

Echoing a suggestion that Downing had made in 1849 for a way to fund a park, the garden's owner proposed that subscriptions be issued that would allow the purchasers to visit the grounds year round. All those families who signed up, affirmed the *Republic,* "can be in the city with all the delights of the country."[9] The *Commercial Advertiser,* however, took the opportunity to remind its readers of the larger need for a truly public park. Rather than have Westphal's Garden enjoyed only by those who were able to pay for the privilege, the paper's editors would "be glad to see any plan adopted by which so beautiful and capacious a park might be secured for the recreation of all inhabitants." They recommended that city authorities purchase Westphal's Garden and convert it to public use.[10] The call went unheeded. Nor would Olmsted be impressed with Westphal's Garden; its crisscrossing paths, showy flowerbeds, refreshment stands, and large greenhouse all crammed into a mere eight acres must have seemed antithetical to the spacious and tranquil natural landscape he thought suitable for an urban country park.

Midcentury attempts to add parkland to the city map were consistently thwarted by an alliance between representatives of the German ethnic population and American-born conservatives who wished to limit municipal spending to what they considered strictly essential public works. The struggle, however, David Gerber writes, "was the most intense civic confrontation of the period." Embittered by the city's failure to act, a local citizen complained to the press that "unfortunately, when land was cheap, and suitable locations for parks and public grounds of all kinds could have been had for a song, those whose business it was to look to such matters entirely neglected it."[11]

FOREST LAWN CEMETERY

While public park advocates were fighting a losing battle to emulate New York's Central Park, private efforts to create a large naturalistic landscape in Buffalo moved forward. Forest Lawn Cemetery was Buffalo's first extensive designed landscape. The new burial ground was the brainchild of Charles E. Clarke, a wealthy lawyer who at midcentury believed that city residents were ready for a more appropriate resting place for their deceased loved ones than was provided by the miscellany of small, unprepossessing graveyards scattered about the town. Clarke took inspiration from such well-known products of the rural cemetery movement as Hillhouse Cemetery in New Haven, Green-Wood Cemetery in Brooklyn, Laurel Hill Cemetery near Philadelphia, and Mount Auburn Cemetery in Boston. "The true secret of [their] attraction lies in the natural beauty of the sites, and in the tasteful and harmonious embellishment of these sites by art," affirmed Downing, whose writings Clarke surely knew. Downing also observed that these rural cemeteries "were rich portions of forest land, broken by hill and dale, and varied by copses and glades."[12] In 1849 Clarke purchased from the Granger family—who were among the area's first settlers—eighty acres of gently furrowed farmland situated three miles inland from Niagara Square, a site that embodied Downing's words.[13] Taking this "beautifully variegated" woodland in hand, Clarke, a self-taught gardener, undertook to lay out carriage drives himself, mark off plots, and generally improve the property for purposes of sepulture. "Even now in its infancy, it is the most attractive spot for a drive, a walk, or a lounge, to be found in the environs of the city, and, as such, has become a general resort," a local newspaper reported the year after the cemetery opened.[14]

Despite Clarke's high hopes, his picturesque enterprise floundered financially. Five years after the cemetery formally opened in August 1850, it was reorganized as the Forest Lawn Association, with Clarke as president. Prominent clergy gave their blessing to the venture, including John C. Lord, who the following year would come to the nation's notice for his sermon on the "higher law" and the Fugitive Slave Act. But distance from town seems to have discouraged burials. In 1865, with the city now rapidly advancing, the cemetery was restructured as a nonprofit corporation under the name of the Buffalo City Cemetery Association, although locals continued to refer to it as Forest Lawn. The new trustees, who included Joseph Warren, added to the original Forest Lawn boundaries land from surrounding farmsteads to raise the total holdings to 234 acres. The expanded cemetery was dedicated on September 28, 1866. (Fig. 1.3)

To assist in the task of enlarging the cemetery and placing its management on a modern footing, the trustees hired Adolph Strauch (1822–1883). Strauch was born in Germany, where he studied landscape gardening and was briefly associated with the renowned horticulturist and gardener Prince Hermann von Pückler-Muskau. Emigrating to the United States in 1851, Strauch settled in Cincinnati, a city about twice the size of Buffalo at the time. Together with Olmsted and Vaux, Strauch is revered as a pioneer of the profession of landscape architecture in America; Olmsted especially held him in high regard. In 1854 Strauch took over the management of Cincinnati's Spring Grove Cemetery, a fledgling rural cemetery that had fallen on hard times. With Germanic efficiency and determination, Strauch wasted no time in revising both the administration and the design of Spring Grove. His efforts attracted national attention. Olmsted thought Spring Grove "the best example in the world, probably, of landscape gardening applied to a burial place."[15]

Fig. 1.3. Forest Lawn Cemetery. Photograph by Andy Olenick.

One of Forest Lawn's trustees who was especially familiar with the Cincinnati cemetery was Lewis F. Allen (1800–1890), a correspondent of Downing and a man well known for his writings on farming, horticulture, and rural architecture. At the dedication in September 1866, Allen extolled the virtues of Spring Grove as the "one taking precedence as a model." What the citizens of Cincinnati enjoyed now lay within the grasp of Protestant Buffalonians, for Strauch had visited Forest Lawn and furnished the trustees with a plan for the new portions of the property. For Allen, the stage was set for the creation of an uplifting mortuary environment equal to that of Spring Grove. Allen foresaw that this new landscape, fashioned in partnership with nature, would "become the admiration of all who love to look on natural beauty or artistic effort."[16]

For Forest Lawn, Strauch prepared a naturalistic plan that Olmsted and Vaux would have found to their liking. (Fig. 1.4) As they would do in their park next door, Strauch capitalized on the potential of Scajaquada Creek, a "striking feature which distinguishes Forest Lawn from almost every other cemetery." (Fig. 1.5) The stream's "naturally stone-walled banks; steep, wooded sides; graceful curves; rocky bottom, and varied cascades, alternated with smoothly flowing waters—all variously shaded, with lofty trees, render it an object of peculiar interest and beauty," Allen remarked. Strauch further proposed to create an artificial lake of about two acres by damming the creek where it crossed Delaware Street. This now vanished body of water, which Olmsted would have seen, came to be known as Swan Lake. Along the crest of the high wooded western bank of the stream, Strauch proposed to lay out the Ramble (a name he surely borrowed from Olmsted and Vaux's Central Park), a "natural wilderness" where original forest trees and native shrubbery would be preserved.[17]

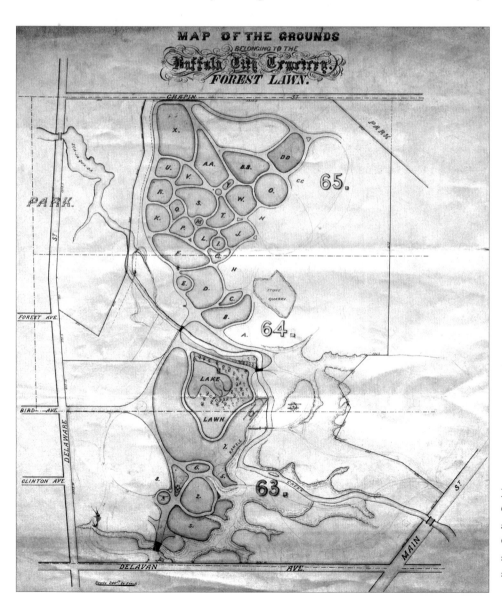

Fig. 1.4. This plan of Forest Lawn Cemetery c. 1870 shows the additions and revisions by Adolph Strauch. Olmsted probably stood in the area of section "X" when he viewed the future site of the Park. Courtesy Forest Lawn Cemetery.

THE BEST PLANNED CITY IN THE WORLD

Fig. 1.5. Adolph Strauch developed the Scajaquada Creek as one of the most attractive features in Forest Lawn Cemetery. Courtesy Forest Lawn Cemetery.

Even before Olmsted came to Buffalo, Forest Lawn had earned the love of the general public as a place for outdoor recreation. "The beautiful and secluded cemetery grounds," noted an observer in 1856, had regularly been so thronged with day-trippers that "the Trustees have been compelled, in defense of private rights, to admit visitors by tickets, in order to prevent the resting place of the dead from becoming a public pleasure ground."[18] Awareness of Forest Lawn's attractions could only have helped alert Olmsted to the possibilities presented by the adjacent land as a location for a large park. And for some local park promoters, the land next to the cemetery was already their top choice for a park site.

THE POST–CIVIL WAR PARK MOVEMENT

The national financial collapse brought on in 1857 by runaway inflation, rampant speculation in land and railroads, and fear that the federal government would default on its credit obligations had a deep and lasting effect on the local economy and stanched all further talk of park construction for several years. The downturn caused severe cutbacks among local businesses and curtailed the progress of Buffalo's nascent industries. The outbreak of war in 1861, however, proved to be a forceful stimulus. Buffalo experienced the rejuvenating effects of an expanding economy, which lasted until depression returned in 1873. Indeed, by reason of its strategic position well away from the theater of war on the major east–west transportation corridor, Buffalo grew and prospered during the conflict. By 1865 numerous railroads had reinforced the bonds of commerce that linked Buffalo to other regions of the country. In fact, railways had eclipsed the Erie Canal as the main route between the Great Lakes and the eastern seaboard. Year-round service also brought about a dramatic change in the work habits of people living in the city. When the canal was king, laborers and merchants alike had experienced a hectic concentration of activity during the warm-weather months, when the canal was in operation. Men toiled long hours every day to meet the demand for their services, and home life suffered. With economic activity spread more evenly throughout the year, the population could generally enjoy regular hours of work and leisure.

By the time the Civil War ended, Buffalo was rich. One of the nation's foremost cities, it was eager to take up the task of remaking itself in order to match its newfound status. "Progress is written on every street corner," the public-spirited city comptroller William F. Rogers proclaimed.[19] It was indeed a time of optimism, a period of city building whose effects would last into the mid-twentieth century. The city of expectations has long since receded into history. But when the International Industrial Exhibition opened in Buffalo in October 1869, the future looked bright indeed. The "success of the enterprise is beyond all question," the *New York Times* reported. "The city, its geographical position and facilities for railway and water communication, are acknowledged to be superior to all other points."[20]

Seizing the rising spirit, Buffalo's leaders implemented many progressive improvements: streets were paved before those in most other cities; the capacity of the waterworks was greatly increased; miles of new sewers were laid; a railroad bridge across the Niagara River was constructed to facilitate trade with Canada (it opened to traffic in 1873); a new city hall was erected, along with other public buildings, markets, schools, firehouses, and police stations; and a normal school was established. Nor were the finer things of life neglected. Already in 1862 the Buffalo Fine Arts Academy (ancestor to the present Albright-Knox Art Gallery) had been founded, a sure sign, stated William Dorsheimer, one of its trustees, that "a widespread interest in art—an interest in it, not merely as an ornament to life, but as a serious matter, worthy of the attention of serious men," had taken root in the young and active city.[21] The Buffalo Historical Society, with Millard Fillmore as its first president, was formed in the same year, and

the Grosvenor Library, which eventually amassed one of the finest collections in the country, opened in 1871. "The resources of the city are equal to a much larger expenditure," declared the forward-looking Comptroller Rogers in 1867, "and by the proper manifestation of an enlarged spirit of public enterprise can be increased to an almost indefinite extent."[22]

In January 1867 Rogers urged the city council to establish a large municipal park, stating that "public attention has been directed for several years past to the propriety of securing a tract of land, within the present limits of the city, for a Public Park, and I take the liberty of inviting your attention to this subject, while the city has the opportunity of securing what will, eventually, be considered a great public necessity." The comptroller's advice that day may not have stirred council members, but he did inspire prominent private citizens to take up the cause with him. His address might be taken as the prelude to the process that would lead two years later, during Rogers's mayoralty, to the adoption of the historic park and parkway system that Frederick Law Olmsted and Calvert Vaux designed for Buffalo.

Fig. 1.6. William F. Rogers (1820–1899). From Dwight H. Bruce, ed., *The Empire State in Three Centuries* (1898).

THE BEST PLANNED CITY IN THE WORLD

Newspaperman, military hero, politician, and unceasing promoter of the fortunes of his adopted city, William F. Rogers (1820–1899) had moved to Buffalo in 1846 from Philadelphia, where he had been associated with the *Enquirer,* to take over the management of the *Republic,* a local organ of the Barnburner wing of the Democratic Party. (Fig. 1.6) During the 1850s he became one of the city's leading citizens. When war broke out, Rogers, despite his Quaker background, eagerly took charge of a local regiment of the state militia. "Rogers's Rangers" saw action at Second Bull Run, South Mountain, and Antietam. Back in Buffalo after the conflict, Rogers—now known as Colonel—entered public life, first as auditor, then as comptroller, and finally, in 1868, as mayor. In this post Rogers vigorously pursued civic improvements. The ability to pay for these things, he believed, was well within the means of his fellow citizens. The "resources of the city are equal to a much larger expenditure, and by the proper manifestation of an enlarged spirit of public enterprise can be increased to an almost indefinite extent," he proclaimed.

In 1867 a group of citizens petitioned the Common Council to set aside a site on the waterfront for a park. This land, which commanded views over the lake and river, was adjacent to Fort Porter, the federal installation that since the early nineteenth century had guarded the entrance to the Niagara River from Lake Erie. In fact it enjoyed the informal status of parkland. The setting and past use seemed to make it a natural choice. Rogers, however, favored another location. In his January 1867 address as comptroller, he proposed the large undeveloped territory in North Buffalo between Main Street on the east and Niagara Street on the west, "beyond Forest Lawn," for a new city park. This area was traversed by two creeks (one of which was Scajaquada Creek, which flowed through the cemetery) that could be dammed to create artificial lakes.[23] Rogers predicted that this farmland could be easily improved to make it as attractive "as the far-famed Central Park of New York City." Also citing the example of Central Park, he affirmed that the increase in the value of residential property surrounding the new park would more than pay for the city's initial investment in its construction. Future generations, he declared, would always remember "those whose farsighted policy had snatched the most desirable location from the encroachments of brick and mortar."

SENDING FOR OLMSTED

Chief among those who shared Rogers's desire for a municipal park was the lawyer, politician, and man of culture William Dorsheimer. He became the postwar park movement's primary spokesman and most energetic advocate. In the winter of 1868 Dorsheimer suggested to a group of park promoters (possibly including Rogers) that if they were truly serious about creating a park in Buffalo, they should seek the advice of Frederick Law Olmsted.[24] (Fig. 1.7) Dorsheimer did not know Olmsted personally, but he was familiar with Central Park and could vouch for the reputation of its co-designer. Olmsted possessed "the widest experience in such matters [of] any man in the country," Dorsheimer assured his colleagues. "Send for him!" chorused his eager associates, and they

Fig. 1.7. Frederick Law Olmsted, c. 1868. Courtesy National Park Service, Frederick Law Olmsted National Historic Site.

backed up their command with a pledge of $750 (a handsome sum in those days) to foot the bill for his trip. On August 12, 1868, Dorsheimer wrote to Olmsted inviting him to Buffalo. Olmsted, who had been in the city briefly in 1863 on United States Sanitary Commission business, agreed to stop a few days later on his way to Chicago, where he was to discuss with the Riverside Improvement Company a plan to create a residential suburb on prairie land some twenty miles west of that city.[25]

On Sunday, August 16, Olmsted and John Bogart, the engineer assisting Olmsted and Vaux on the work at Prospect Park, arrived in Buffalo. Dorsheimer guided them around, showing Olmsted sites that had already been proposed for parkland. From the station, Dorsheimer drove his carriage to the center of town, Niagara Square. (Fig. 1.8) Here he no doubt pointed out the spot on the north side of the square where former president Millard Fillmore, the "Sage of Buffalo," resided in a picturesque Gothic Revival mansion. The dwellings of other prominent citizens also overlooked the tranquil open space, which must have reminded Olmsted of town commons in his native Connecticut, for Niagara Square had yet to feel the pressure of urbanization. This would have been an opportunity, too, for Dorsheimer to point out Delaware Street, which proceeded north from the square and was beginning to assume the status of Buffalo's grand residential avenue.

From the square, Dorsheimer took Olmsted along Niagara Street, another important residential thoroughfare, to the place where Fort Porter overlooked the Niagara River and the lake. (Fig. 1.9) Long before the military claimed the site, generations of Seneca hunters had visited the breezy crest to fashion arrowheads from the abundance of good flint to be

found there. The open land next to the fort had been spoken of for a park. It was also used by Buffalo's baseball players, who had adopted it as a playing field when the game became popular locally in the 1850s. Although Olmsted was of the opinion that creating a sizable park at this location would prove to be prohibitively expensive, he also saw more here than late-summer drought-parched grounds where the Rochester Alerts might slug it out with the Buffalo Eries. He strongly advised his guide that "the beautiful view of the lake and river from that point were extremely desirable to secure."

Turning away from the waterfront, Dorsheimer

Fig. 1.8. This woodcut by J. R. Chapin shows Niagara Square as it would have appeared to Olmsted in 1868. Millard Fillmore's Gothic Revival residence is shown at the upper center, where Delaware Street leaves the northern border of the square. The horse cars ran along Niagara Street. *Frank Leslie's Illustrated Newspaper* (September 20, 1873).

Fig. 1.9. Fort Porter. The beginning of the Niagara River and the Canadian shore are in the distance at the right. *Harper's Weekly* (September 28, 1861).

THE BEST PLANNED CITY IN THE WORLD

Fig. 1.10. "Here is your park, almost ready made." Photograph by Andy Olenick.

and Olmsted next proceeded inland over York Street and Rogers Street (now Richmond Avenue) and then out Delaware Street to Scajaquada Creek, some two and a half miles north of the center city. Here Olmsted would have seen for the first time the grounds of Forest Lawn Cemetery. The two men would also have inspected the area south of the cemetery, where lay the wooded grounds of Westphal's Garden, the private picnic grove that had been proposed as the site of a public park before the war. Dorsheimer then drove west along Clinton Street (now Potomac Avenue) to inspect land west of the cemetery, in the area that Rogers had recommended for a large park. Unimpressed with what he saw, Olmsted expressed to his host the desire to return to Scajaquada Creek so they might explore the terrain

north of the cemetery, gently ignoring Dorsheimer's assertion that there was nothing there to see. As they were going out Chapin Street (a street that no longer exists but once skirted the northern border of the cemetery), Olmsted asked Dorsheimer to stop "on an elevation about one third of the way to Main street." After a moment's reflection, Olmsted declared to his companion, "Here is your park, almost ready made." In his mind's eye he saw in the sunny, tree-studded meadows bordered by deep woods, a fine and extensive park landscape. (Fig. 1.10) The citizens of Buffalo, he said, "could consider themselves fortunate in having so good a ground, so near the city." "A very trifling expense would impart to it a park-like character," he believed.

From this historic vantage point, Olmsted and Dorsheimer traveled to the junction of Ferry and Jefferson streets, an elevated location on the east side of town that overlooked the city. This spot was also near the German community, a fact that Dorsheimer might have hoped would gain support for the park movement from that quarter. Olmsted told Dorsheimer, however, that he "did not consider this as good a ground for a large park as that about Chapin street." Nonetheless, the idea occurred to Olmsted that a small pleasure ground could be located here and be "connected with the main park by a boulevard."

During this whirlwind visit, it seems apparent that Olmsted formed in his mind the outlines of a three-part scheme that included one large and two smaller, widely separated parks that would be joined by broad tree-lined roadways. The origin of the Buffalo park and parkway system can surely be traced to that Sunday drive in early August 1868.[26]

Olmsted also found Joseph Ellicott's city much to his liking. He admired the way the system of broad radial thoroughfares was synchronized with a grid of smaller streets and how the entire plan conformed to the natural conditions. He also warmly approved of the prevalence of freestanding dwellings set back ten feet from the street line and "surrounded by a clear space of private grounds, more or less tastefully embellished." Compared to New York, Buffalo possessed an agreeable suburban character, with only one-tenth the population density of the old-fashioned tenement districts of New York. Overall, Olmsted thought, "no equal number of people was to be found in any American town so healthfully housed, and having the use of so convenient arrangements of intercommunication."[27] He looked forward to augmenting Ellicott's excellent plan in accordance with ideas of his own.

OLMSTED'S RETURN VISIT TO BUFFALO

After his initial visit, Olmsted had ample time to mull over what he had seen while on the train from Buffalo to Chicago, a city that, like Buffalo, was experiencing rapid growth. It was also a place that Buffalonians admired for its go-getter spirit, while at the same time they looked to New York to set an example in the arts and culture. In Chicago, Olmsted would continue talks that he and Vaux had begun concerning plans for establishing the suburban residential community of Riverside. Investors had recently acquired 1,600 acres of prairie land along the Des Plaines River and wished to transform it into a landscape of curving roadways, ample lots, and communal green space. Yet the trip would be unpleasant for Olmsted. By the time his train had traversed southern Ontario's "dreary forest country, nearly all perfectly flat," and arrived at Detroit, where he connected to a Chicago-bound train, summer had turned to winter.[28] Olmsted blamed the drafty Canadian carriage, which he compared to an icebox, for a severe cold that deprived him of his voice. Chilly temperatures and a blustery wind in Chicago only made things worse, and after spending a day on the open prairie inspecting the Riverside site he was forced to remain an entire day in bed. The delay left his last day so crammed with meetings that he and Bogart barely made their train late on Saturday evening, August 22.

They had promised Dorsheimer that on their way back east they would spend two days in Buffalo to make a more thorough investigation of the land for the proposed park than their cursory visit the week before had allowed. Having slept poorly on the train, Olmsted arrived late and tired on Sunday. To his dismay, he soon learned that his stay in Buffalo would involve more than the working mission and brief testimony before a citizens' committee which he had planned for. Park promoters informed him that on Tuesday evening he was to be the featured speaker at a public meeting chaired by ex-president Fillmore. (Fig. 1.11) The audience expected "to hear an address on the matter of a public park from the distinguished architect of the New York Central Park, Frederick Olmsted, Esq."[29] Still suffering from a bad cold and with little time to formulate his ideas, Olmsted felt unwilling and unready to make a public presentation on his embryonic park plan. As he must have recognized, however, he had little choice but to comply with his hosts' wishes if he hoped to advance the likelihood of the project.

The next day, Monday, August 24, he and Bogart rode around the city surveying possible park sites. With the help of a locally furnished assistant, they dug a number of pits to test the soil conditions. Things went much more slowly, though, than Olmsted had thought they would. He and Bogart were able to finish only half their work before darkness overtook them and they had to go off to dinner with a small group of "editors and lawyers," presumably to discuss plans for the next evening's meeting.[30] During the day on Tuesday, the two visitors continued their assessment, making an entire circuit of the city on horseback. From these investigations Olmsted became fully acquainted with the terrain in the undeveloped part of town. "Mr. Olmsted's knowledge of the suburbs of Buffalo," Dorsheimer declared, "and their relation to the main portion of the city, and the avenues of approach to them, was not equaled by that of any resident, as he had made them an especial study."[31]

The meeting on the evening of August 25 marked the culmination of efforts by park advocates over the years to define a plan. At that time Olmsted made his ideas known to a gathering of some sixty or seventy people who came to the Delaware Street mansion of Sherman S. Jewett, one of the businessmen who had paid for Olmsted's trip. A lengthy account of the evening's proceedings appeared the next day in the *Courier,* undoubtedly prepared by David Gray, the paper's editor, in consultation with Joseph Warren, its owner and the man who served as secretary at the meeting.[32] After the clink and rattle of glasses died down, chairman Fillmore asked Dorsheimer to give a brief history of the local park movement and to introduce Olmsted to the audience. His voice still hoarse from the lingering cold, Olmsted opened his remarks by saying that he "should not have consented to address such an assemblage" because he had had too little time to develop his ideas fully. Nonetheless, he proceeded to talk at length

Fig. 1.11. Millard Fillmore (1800–1874). Lithograph by F. D'Avignon, c. 1850. Library of Congress, Prints and Photographs Division.

about the plans that he had been turning over in his mind. Olmsted began by explaining that a park was "a work of art" that would take at least forty years to be realized and then went on to instruct his hearers in the true purpose and nature of urban pleasure grounds. "The object of a park, adjacent to a city," he said, "is to provide contrast, change, recreation and relief from the turmoil of the city." In order to realize this goal, "great breadth and openness of land are required to get rid of the sense of contraction produced by brick walls and paved streets." Moreover, the successful park must comprise a "variety of scenery, undulations of surface, freedom of motion, and a harmony of design." His words must have come as a revelation to those in the audience who thought of a park in terms of boisterous private picnic groves such as Westphal's Garden.

Olmsted then went on to unveil his novel idea, that the best course to pursue in Buffalo would be to create three parks rather than a single one, as New York and Brooklyn had done. The locales he enumerated were those that he had marked out on his day-long tour with Dorsheimer the previous week. They were the ground

Fig. 1.12. *View South from Fort Porter,* 1850s. Artist unknown. The painting shows the rear of James MacKaye's "castle" at the left and, in the middle distance, the open waterfront land that in August 1868 Olmsted and Dorsheimer considered as a possible park site. It would later become the Front. Courtesy Buffalo and Erie County Historical Society.

in the vicinity of Fort Porter, an area on High Street near the junction of Jefferson and Ferry streets, and the pastures north of the cemetery between Delaware and Main streets. Warming to his subject, he launched into a discussion of the merits of each of these sites. The first location he reviewed was the property on High Street astride a ridge some three miles back from the waterfront on the east side of town. This site, Olmsted said, afforded a first-rate view of the bustling city, with "a pleasant back ground of hills" in the distance. In fact, the panorama was so fine from there that he believed it was the ideal place to take a stranger "to show him the extent and the prosperity of Buffalo." Knowing that this area was being considered for the site of a new reservoir,

Olmsted suggested that the waterworks could be located within the thirty- or forty-acre park he envisioned here. In this case, he thought, the standpipe might be enclosed in an observation tower, which would be a capital location from which to survey the city.[33]

The second place that Olmsted talked about that night was the one near Fort Porter. It, too, afforded a fine prospect. Here one might look out over the broad waters of Lake Erie. There "can be no finer back ground than the horizon of the lake," Olmsted remarked, and the view of the Canadian shoreline he thought "not uninviting." (Fig. 1.12) Also from this spot one could witness the dramatic rush and tumble of the lake waters funneling into the narrow channel of the Niagara River. This

THE BEST PLANNED CITY IN THE WORLD

Fig. 1.13. Bird's-eye view of Delaware Street looking toward the lake and downtown from North Street. Steel engraving, 1875. Courtesy Buffalo and Erie County Historical Society.

thirty or forty acres, which already belonged to the city, could relatively cheaply be "turned into a magnificent marine parade and promenade."

The largest of the three locations that Olmsted discussed was the area north of Forest Lawn Cemetery. Here it would be possible to achieve the "great breadth and openness of land" that he had spoken of at the start of his address. This farmland already possessed "variety of scenery" in its natural pastoral state, as well as "some of the finest forest trees" he had ever seen. They were "particularly perfect park trees," he observed, the equals of which "could not be produced in fifty years." Moreover, the soil seemed "particularly adapted to the growth of the finest trees," and the creek could be dammed to create a new lake, which would be a "charming feature" of the landscape. All in all, he believed that on a tract of three to four hundred acres "a good deal of planting is to be done; but the land only requires improvement."

After reviewing his program for the three green spaces, Olmsted addressed his audience on the subject of street access to the main park. From the center of town, Delaware Street was "a stately avenue requiring very little change to adapt it to a central approach to the park." (Fig. 1.13) To connect the park on the East Side to the large park, he suggested that the embryonic Jefferson Street (now Jefferson Avenue) be widened to form a suitable link, while from the baseball grounds at Fort Porter to the main park he proposed that a "broad avenue" be constructed running eastward to Rogers Street, then northward "to the woods east of Clinton Forest [another private picnic grove] and the creek [Scajaquada Creek], and thence along the creek to Delaware street." The report in the *Courier* did not use the term "parkway" to describe these avenues that Olmsted spoke of, although surely Olmsted had used the term that night, for, we are told, he "explained in detail how these roads should be built." Defining these streets in terms of the parkways he and Vaux had proposed a few years earlier for Brooklyn, Olmsted said they were to be from "180 to 200 feet wide, with a pleasure drive in the centre, flanked with trees and walks, and a traffic road on the side." And surely Olmsted must have mentioned the fact that the Chicago proprietors were acquiring land for a parkway (to include a trolley line) linking Riverside to Chicago. Perhaps for an instant that evening he and his listeners foresaw a future summer day in Buffalo when carriages, pedestrians, and horseback riders would share sun-dappled, tree-shaded avenues on their way to enjoy a carefree afternoon in a verdant landscape of meadow, stream, and lake.

Olmsted concluded his remarks by discussing the matter-of-fact issue of cost. Overall, he was of the opinion that in order to create the system he had outlined, the city would need to acquire approximately five hundred acres of land. But because the land in question had few buildings on it at present, it could be bought relatively cheaply—he threw out the figure of less than $100 per acre. And he assured his hearers that the "expense of grading will be very moderate, and the roads can be constructed for one-third of the cost of those in New York and Brooklyn." A further cost benefit was the fact that the park grounds contained good sources of stone. "All needed material is at hand," he declared. And Olmsted affirmed his belief that the rise that inevitably occurred in the value of land around parks would result in higher property tax receipts from which the city could recoup all construction costs. He pointed in particular to the example of New York, where increased assessments had produced enough revenue to cover the interest on the bonds issued to construct the parks, and also gave other examples of how "parks pay a city even in a pecuniary way."[34]

PARK ADVOCATES AND OLMSTED'S PLAN

Olmsted himself was pleased with the way the meeting went. He wrote to his wife, Mary, that "the solid men of Buffalo" had given him a warm reception and that he had "talked for an hour with tolerable smoothness and I should think with gratifying results." All in all, he told her, "I think it will go." To his partner, Calvert Vaux, who was away in Europe, he likewise sent a positive account of the events in Buffalo. "I did a deal of talking, privately and publically, was cross-examined, etc., and got through very well," he said.[35] Indeed, Olmsted had spoken so persuasively that his words signaled the beginning of an era of park building. "The clear state-

ments of Mr. Olmsted persuaded everyone present that a park was not only practicable, but that it was the duty of Buffalonians to take immediate steps to secure the co-operation of the common council and the legislature in establishing one," proclaimed the *Courier.* To pursue this end, Fillmore appointed a committee composed of Dorsheimer, Warren, Sherman S. Jewett, Pascal Paoli Pratt, and Richard Flach. The newly constituted group asked Olmsted to submit a written report of his remarks and promised that they would petition the legislature in Albany to establish an official park commission. Olmsted forwarded his report to Buffalo at the beginning of October.

All of the men on the ad hoc committee had earlier advocated publicly for a park. Now armed with a definite plan, they looked with renewed enthusiasm toward finally achieving the outcome they had long desired. The generous host for the evening when Olmsted made his presentation, Sherman Skinner Jewett (1818–1897), had ties to many prosperous business enterprises. His principal source of income was his iron foundry, which manufactured kitchen stoves. He also served on the board of directors of several railroads. As a progressive member of the Republican Party, Jewett frequently opened his home to meetings of civic-minded citizens seeking the advancement of the city in some regard or other.[36] He was, however, especially devoted to the cause of parks and was later remembered as "always alive to anything which was intended to make the public breathing spots more attractive or more accessible to the common man."[37] During his long tenure—he was board president from 1879 until his death in 1897—he was a steadfast supporter of Olmsted's ideals. Pascal Paoli Pratt (1819–1905), like Jewett, was descended from early émigrés from New England. Richard Flach (1832–1884), like Dorsheimer, had ties to both the American and the German communities in the city. A native of Saxony, he had been trained as a baker before coming to America and settling in Buffalo in the late 1840s. Flach maintained a successful grocery business and was an active member of the Saengerbund choral society, the largest of several German glee clubs. A Democrat, as were many German citizens, Flach at various times held office as both a state assemblyman and a city council member.[38]

Joseph Warren had come to Buffalo from his native Vermont in 1853 after a stint as assistant editor of the *Country Gentleman* in Albany. By 1858 he had risen to the editorship of the *Courier* at a time when newspapers were both advocates of political parties and vital sources of information. Eventually Warren became the publisher of the morning *Courier* and the evening *Courier & Republic,* both of which were considered the official paper of the city. Always active in politics, Warren assumed the postwar leadership of the local Democratic Party, whose views the *Courier* consistently represented. Like the other men on the ad hoc committee, Warren lent his efforts to many civic endeavors, including the establishment of the state normal school, the Buffalo Fine Arts Academy, the Young Men's Association, and the medical school at the University of Buffalo. Dorsheimer would eulogize him as "a promoter of all generous enterprises which promised to add to the prosperity of the city."[39] His papers took the lead among the press in advocating for the park project. "If his [Olmsted's] scheme, or something like it, shall be carried out," the *Courier* informed its readers while the city waited to receive Olmsted's written report, "the crowds of citizens with their families who throng Main street on summer Sunday afternoons, will not need to wheel their perambulators on the stone pavement, and let their children play in the shade of brick walls, neither will Delaware street be the extent of the city's driving ground."[40]

This editorial, like most that appeared in the *Courier* at this time, undoubtedly came from the pen of the paper's editor, David Gray (1836–1888), Buffalo's most accomplished journalist. Born in Edinburgh, Gray spent his teenage years in rural Wisconsin, where his family had immigrated. In 1856 he came to Buffalo at the invitation of a relative who secured for him the position of librarian at the Young Men's Christian Union.

Toward the end of 1859 Gray came to the attention of Joseph Warren, who made him associate editor of the *Courier.* In effect, the two men ran the paper. In April 1865 Gray accepted an offer from the Buffalo businessman William G. Fargo, whose partnership with Henry Wells had produced the Pony Express, to chaperone his son during an extended period of study and travel in Europe. Gray returned to his post at the *Courier* in April 1868, just in time for Olmsted's first trip to Buffalo.

Gray came back to Buffalo considerably matured by his experience and eager to resume his full-time career in journalism. Because Warren was now often away or busy with political affairs, he left the editorship of the paper to Gray. But Gray also had time to cultivate his avocation as a poet and to become a bright light in the cultural life of the town. "His acquaintance at home and abroad had become large," noted his biographer, especially among men and women of letters and of art, and no one in Buffalo, during these years, entertained more visitors of distinction than he."[41] Gray enjoyed gathering local literati at his home on Saturday evenings, a cozy oasis of high-minded thinking in the generally arid intellectual environment of a boom city. Like his earnest friends, Gray was a strong supporter of the park movement. While in Europe he had enjoyed visiting attractive pleasure grounds in various cities. In 1866, writing back home from Geneva, he urged Buffalo's city fathers to "give us more parks and gardens and breathing-places." He maintained, as did Downing, Olmsted, and Dorsheimer, that such places exerted a refining influence on society, a stimulus that was sorely needed in the cities of the Scot's adopted country. "Perhaps, if the unwashed American had such places open to him, where he could lie, or sit, and drink beer, even," Gray asserted, "he would not stand, by day and night, at filthy bars, drinking in madness, damnation and death."[42] Surely it must have been gratifying for him to frame the *Courier*'s eloquent support of the park movement.[43]

The rival to Gray's *Courier,* the *Express,* was under the editorship of another well-rounded man of letters who would leave his mark on the city, Josephus Nelson

Fig. 1.14. David Gray (*right*) and Samuel Clemens. Detail of a photograph by Matthew Brady, 1871. Courtesy Buffalo and Erie County Historical Society.

Larned. Despite the fact that his paper was a Republican organ, Larned was a good friend of Gray's and an avid supporter of the local park movement. In the summer of 1869 Larned became the business partner of Samuel Langhorn Clemens, better known as Mark Twain, when the peripatetic writer moved to Buffalo to become part owner of the *Express*. Although Twain was in town at the very time when Olmsted, with whom he shared a love of natural scenery, was being engaged to lay out the new park system, he appears to have written nothing in the pages of the *Express* about this momentous local event.[44] This is all the more unexpected because Clemens was a close friend of Gray and a neighbor of Dorsheimer. (Fig. 1.14)

THE PRELIMINARY REPORT

In his report dated October 1, 1868, Olmsted outlined his philosophy of park planning and reviewed recent developments in urban park construction in London, Paris, and New York.[45] The first thing to bear in mind, he said, was that "the main object we set before us in planning a park is to establish conditions, which will exert the most healthful, recreative action upon the people who are expected to resort to it. With the great mass, such conditions will be of a character diverse from the ordinary conditions of their lives in the most radical degree which is consistent with ease of access." He went on to enumerate three classes of park users: those who were free to leave work and home for several hours or even an entire day; mothers, children, invalids, and others who were "not methodically occupied by any regular business"; and people who were able to leave their place of work for only a short time during the day. He had conceived his plan for Buffalo to accommodate the diverse needs of all these people.

One can easily imagine Dorsheimer and his colleagues skimming the opening didactic discourse and settling in for a closer reading of what Olmsted intended specifically for their city. First, Olmsted reasserted that he had put aside the idea of creating one large park. Instead, speaking for himself and his absent partner, he said "we would recommend that in your scheme a large park should not be the sole object in view but should be regarded simply as the more important member of a . . . comprehensive arrangement for securing refreshment, recreation and health to the people." As he had done when in town, Olmsted proposed the creation of three parks and elaborated on the merits of each. The site near Fort Porter on the west side of the city and the site on High Street on the east side would answer the needs of the people in his second and third categories. These spaces were much smaller than the main park, but they could serve neighborhood residents out "for a short stroll, airing and diversion, and where they can at once enjoy a decided change of scene from that which is associated with their regular occupations."

The main park would be much larger than the other two, and because it was far from town, most people would visit it when they had longer periods of time to enjoy its many recreational opportunities. Here,

THE BEST PLANNED CITY IN THE WORLD

Olmsted affirmed, among the pastoral scenery, the true goal of a rural park could be easily achieved: "to present nature in the most attractive manner which may be practicable." This park would be ample enough to evoke the sense of "contrast to the ordinary conditions of town life." It was to encompass both the wooded banks of Scajaquada Creek west of Forest Lawn Cemetery and the gently rolling meadows north of the burial grounds. And now Olmsted inserted a new element into the agreeable pastoral landscape. "By the construction of an embankment about a half a mile below the road, which is a prolongation of Delaware street," the report stated, "a body of living water might here be formed about twenty acres in extent with a very agreeable natural line of shore, the greater part of which would be shaded by beautiful groves of trees, already on the ground and most of which are now in their prime and of very desirable species." Furthermore, putting a large park at this location would "neither interfere with nor be interfered with by any existing or probable line of business communication, the character of the topography of the neighborhood not having encouraged the formation of roads from either side through it."

Access to and from the parks was a major element of Olmsted's report. Reiterating the remark he had made on August 25, Olmsted proposed that from the center of town to the main park, Delaware Street could easily be transformed into "an approach of stately proportions." In order to secure access to the main park from the west and east sides of town "without a journey long, fatiguing and discordant with the sentiment and purpose of recreation in view," he elaborated on his proposal to upgrade several existing streets to parkways. Travelers along these residential greenways would find them free of commerce, so that their journey to and from the main park could be made "in the midst of a scene of sylvan beauty and with the sounds and sights of the ordinary town business, if not wholly shut out, removed to some distance and placed in obscurity." Olmsted held out the promise that the "way itself would thus be more park-like than town-like." These lovely streets would themselves serve as small parks in the neighborhoods through which they passed. "Thus, at no great distance from any point of the town," Olmsted explained, "a pleasure ground will have been provided for, suitable for a short stroll, for a playground for children, and an airing ground for invalids." Concerned that traffic on these new arteries should always flow freely, he proposed that "at the crossing of important streets, the parkways might, for greater convenience in crossing and turning, be expanded in a circular or elliptical form." These circles, with their radiating streets, recalled the central feature of Ellicott's original plan for Niagara Square. Olmsted also suggested that these new features in the urban landscape might become striking focal points, "suitable positions for fountains, statues, trophies and public monuments." Such "artificial" adornments he and Vaux wished to keep out of their parks. Finally, he wanted people to be able to travel to and from the city to the park by boat. "It would be practicable at slight expense," he noted, "to make Scajaquada creek navigable for rowing craft and steam launches to the Park."[46]

Olmsted's report gave park advocates the document they needed in order to proceed with the legislative process required to establish new parkland. Henceforth his firm's report, which was published in full in Joseph Warren's newspaper, would be treated as a text proclaimed by prophets.[47] And surely the lengthy article that ran in the paper not long after on Chicago's plans to invest in parks—Olmsted and Vaux had been asked to plan South Park, which would provide recreational access to the Lake Michigan shore—was meant to remind Buffalo of the need to keep up with the city to which it often liked to compare itself. Likewise, it was reported in the local press, the Common Council in Albany had approved a park and parkway plan prepared by the partners that in some ways resembled the one for Buffalo.[48] Buffalo, however, was not found lagging. In mid-November the citizens' committee forwarded Olmsted's report to Mayor Rogers, who in turn formally presented it to the Common Council on November 23. The mayor recommended that a special committee of councilmen and citizens be formed to have legislation enacted in Albany authorizing the city to acquire the land needed for the parks and parkways.[49] On December 28, 1868, the council, having heard the idea warmly endorsed by civic groups such as the Board of Trade, agreed. "Thus, we may consider the long talked of proposition for a public park in Buffalo as at least fairly on the road to realization," stated the *Courier*.[50]

APPOINTING THE BOARD OF PARK COMMISSIONERS

Taking responsibility for securing approval to institute a park commission was a newly elected legislator, Asher P. Nichols (1815–1880). Though new to Albany, Nichols was not new to local politics. A native of Vermont who moved to Buffalo from central New York in 1836, he was one of the first lawyers to set up practice in Buffalo. And like the other men with whom he was associated in the park movement, Nichols was a highly cultivated gentleman. "Few men are more familiar than was he with the classics of our language," recalled a friend, who also noted that Nichols "had a keen sense of the beautiful in nature and art, and was a graceful interpreter of both."[51] One of his poems had even been read at the original dedication of Forest Lawn Cemetery in 1850. At the start of the new session in January 1869, Nichols introduced a bill to authorize the selection of grounds for Olmsted and Vaux's park scheme and to "provide for the sustenance and embellishment thereof."[52] The bill easily won the legislature's approval on April 14, 1869. A provision in the legislation, however, would alter the plan that Olmsted had outlined. Possibly to please the German community, the bill required that one hundred acres of park grounds (this could include parkways) be located east of Jefferson Street. This ruled out the reservoir site as the location for the East Side park Olmsted had proposed and removed Jefferson Street from consideration as a future parkway. During the same ses-

sion Nichols also introduced legislation authorizing the establishment of a large state psychiatric hospital in the city on lands that Olmsted had proposed be included in the western portion of the main park. This act was also approved by the legislature and would result in Olmsted and Vaux's modifying the West Side approach to the main park. With the success of both of these major items to his credit, Nichols returned to Buffalo in May at the end of the legislative session to a hero's welcome.

A major element of the new park legislation was the article establishing a board of park commissioners. These individuals, to be appointed by the mayor with the consent of the Common Council, would have the power to adopt a plan, authorize the purchase of property, and oversee the construction of the new park system. This process had worked well in New York and would allow the commissioners to pursue their work, funds in hand, largely independent of the Common Council. Five days after the legislative act establishing the parks was passed in Albany, the Common Council approved the slate of park commissioners that Mayor Rogers had submitted. They included Dorsheimer, Warren, and the others who made up the original citizens' committee that had invited Olmsted to Buffalo the year before, plus seven other members.[53] On May 3 the commissioners held their first meeting at Mayor Rogers's office. At that time, officers were elected, with Pascal P. Pratt named president. Other business included forming standing committees and ordering that twelve hundred copies of the law establishing the park commission be printed, five hundred of them in German. Before adjourning, Dorsheimer informed his colleagues that both Olmsted and Vaux would be in town the next day to meet with them.[54]

At that event Olmsted and Vaux were asked to elaborate on their park proposal of October 1, which Rogers affirmed had "given universal satisfaction." Earlier during the day, Olmsted revisited the Fort Porter site and the land north of the cemetery, presumably taking along Vaux, who was probably seeing the city for the first time. (Fig. 1.15) Vaux seconded Olmsted's initial

THE BEST PLANNED CITY IN THE WORLD

Fig. 1.15. Calvert Vaux, c. 1868. Courtesy National Park Service, Frederick Law Olmsted National Historic Site.

after more detailed proposals had been made. This led naturally to the board asking Olmsted and Vaux how much they would charge for making these plans. They replied that they would "furnish working plans at the rate of ten dollars an acre, or $5000 for five hundred acres." They would also provide a plan "from which the boundary lines could be fixed for the sum of $1000, this amount to be credited on the ten dollars an acre, if they were afterwards called upon to supply working drawings." Thus the board would be committed to pay $1,000 for an outline plan for purchasing land for the parks; if they chose to work further with Olmsted and Vaux, they would agree to pay $10 per acre for detailed plans, minus the $1,000 paid for the outline plan. After a brief discussion, the commissioners agreed to these terms.[55]

choice of three to four hundred acres of land north of the cemetery as the locale for the main park. To his practiced eye, the area possessed four advantages: "fine meadow-land, beautiful streams, luxuriant foliage, and a splendid avenue of approach ready-made." He also liked the Fort Porter site and, despite the greater expense it would take to create a park there, joined Olmsted in urging the commissioners to secure its fine view for future generations. A question arose, however, concerning the third park, on the east side of town. Since Olmsted had not inspected the ground east of Jefferson, he was not in a position to make a recommendation at that time as to the ultimate location of the third park. He still maintained, however, that it should be linked to the other two localities by a parkway. Concerning the next steps that the commissioners needed to take, Vaux advised them to follow the lead of their Prospect Park colleagues and prepare a report describing the land to be acquired "before the boundary lines were fixed." As had been the case in Brooklyn, the Buffalo park commissioners had a preliminary report as their guide for an outline; the precise park boundaries would come

"THE LONG CHERISHED PROJECT"

Olmsted and Vaux spent the next four months developing the plan for the Buffalo park system. In early August 1869 they came to town to present their final product to the commissioners. During this visit Olmsted spent two days at Niagara, where on August 7 he toured Goat Island with Dorsheimer and Henry Hobson Richardson, who was in town for discussions about the plans for the Buffalo State Hospital and the new house he was designing for Dorsheimer.[56] (It was after the arrival of Vaux on the eighth that Olmsted first broached his idea of creating a park to protect the great natural wonder that straddled the U.S.–Canadian border.)[57] In Buffalo on August 9 the landscape architects attended a meeting at Mayor Rogers's office where the commissioners, after some discussion, unanimously approved the partners' plans.

A few days later the *Courier* devoted a long article, supplemented by maps, describing Olmsted and Vaux's fully evolved park and parkway plan.[58] (Fig. 1.16) Subtitled "The Long Cherished Project Takes Form," this first thoughtful analysis of the diverse elements of the proposed park system surely came from the pen of David Gray, the best guide the citizens of Buffalo could have had for assessing the true worth of the momentous proposal. He began by explaining the initial difficulties that the plan's authors had to overcome. First among them was the necessity "that at least a part of the grounds should be close to the centers of population. But the only large tracts of land available at reasonable expense were found to lie outside a circle of at least three miles from the churches." This dilemma was ingeniously overcome by the planners, who "even turned it to good account" by extending "two widely diverging arms or *antennae*" from each side of the main park to two lesser satellite parks. "On the west," Gray observed, "the minor park commands the glorious river and lake view, but lies in the very midst of a rapidly populating portion of the city." A street railroad made it easily accessible from elsewhere. On the other side of town, Olmsted and Vaux had fixed a new location for the third park "at the threshold of the thickly inhabited German quarter of the city" a few blocks east of the site that Olmsted had originally proposed.[59] Gray believed that a new type of town landscape lay in the city's future. "Literally our park, when finished, will be an arc of health and beauty bent around a full half of suburban Buffalo," he wrote. Olmsted's biographer Justin Martin has likened the plan to a baseball diamond. With Niagara Square as home plate, he writes, "think of the parks as being placed in left field (the Front), center field (the Park), and right field (the Parade)."[60]

Gray proceeded to discuss the individual parks, which for the first time bear the specific names that Olmsted and Vaux suggested, and parkways (as yet unnamed).[61] The Front was Olmsted and Vaux's proposed name for the twenty-eight-acre park overlooking the lake and river, with Sixth Street (later Front Avenue, the present Busti Avenue), a street of large, attractive houses, forming

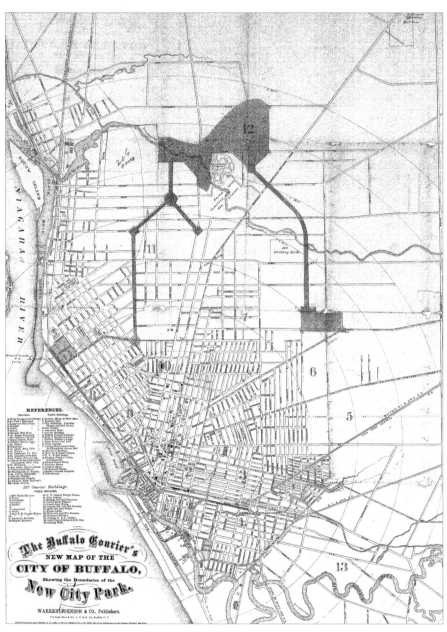

Fig. 1.16. Warren & Johnson & Co., "The Buffalo Courier's New Map of the City of Buffalo. New City Park." *Courier*, August 1869.

THE BEST PLANNED CITY IN THE WORLD

the park's eastern boundary.[62] Along the western border, toward the water, down below a step slope, scores of barges slowly plied their way along the malodorous Erie Canal, and smoke-belching locomotives chugged by on the busy mainline. "In laying out The Front," Gray explained, "the idea of Mr. Olmsted is to make of it a sort of *esplanade,* trees to be planted so as to conceal the unsightly features of the view and enhance those which nature has made beautiful." Gray also noted that efforts were already under way to get permission from the federal government to lay out walks and a drive within the grounds of adjacent Fort Porter to serve as a pleasant appendage to the park. In addition, Olmsted and Vaux's plans called for the creation of a traffic circle at the northeast entrance to Fort Porter, where Massachusetts and Niagara streets converged on Sixth Street. This high ground (later known as the Bank), Gray wrote, was "an invaluable spot for the magnificent river and Canadian view it commands." Eastward along the line of York and North streets toward Rogers Street, two blocks of venerable Prospect Place would be newly landscaped and integrated into "the grand scheme." At the juncture of Rogers Street, where one would turn ninety degrees northward toward the main park, the plan called for a six-acre landscaped circle. "This circle or *Rond Point,* as the Parisians call it," noted the well-traveled Gray, "will form an agreeable invitation to the further charms of the Park, of which, we daresay, the growing district lying in the angle north of North and west of Delaware streets will duly feel the attraction."

Traveling one-hundred-foot-wide Rogers Street, which Olmsted and Vaux proposed to rename The Avenue (known today as Richmond Avenue), one arrived at the juncture with Bouck Avenue (now Lafayette Avenue), a major crosstown thoroughfare. At this point Olmsted and Vaux's plan contained a dramatic element that had not figured in Olmsted's earlier proposals. Henceforth known as the West Side Park Approaches, it consists of an arrangement of three parkways two hundred feet wide and three spacious traffic circles that on the city plan resemble an inverted Y. (A fourth parkway, Humboldt

Parkway, joined the Park to the east side of town.) Circles linking converging streets to the approaches are located at the ends of the extended arms—Bidwell Place (now Colonial Circle; the original name commemorated Daniel Bidwell, a Civil War general from Buffalo) on The Avenue, Chapin Place (now Gates Circle; the original name commemorated William Payson Chapin, another Civil War hero from Buffalo) on Delaware Street (now Delaware Avenue), and Soldiers Place, the widest circle at the crux of the Y. From there, the "stem" (the present Lincoln Parkway) terminates at the main entrance to the Park. These approaches funnel traffic from Delaware Street on the east and The Avenue on the west to the main park entrance. (See Fig. 2.1)

The most easterly of these West Side circles, Chapin Place, marked the juncture of Bouck Avenue and Delaware Street and was "intended to provide a dignified and picturesque termination" for that existing thoroughfare as it came from the center of town. Beyond Chapin Place, Delaware became an ordinary thoroughfare of greatly diminished cachet. It was nevertheless an important traffic route to the north and would cross the park landscape near its center. At this spot, Olmsted and Vaux proposed sinking the road below grade, as they had done with crosstown roadways at Central Park. "The difficult problem—how to dispose of a thoroughfare too important to be blockaded, so that its passage shall not mar the solitude and beauty of the park, is, we think, very happily solved," Gray noted.

Still today, Olmsted and Vaux's Park Approaches introduce the drama of anticipation for those arriving at Delaware Park from downtown. Travelers along Richmond Avenue or Delaware Avenue see the scale of the streetscape change as they enter Colonial and Gates circles. These spacious foyers to the full-blown parkways proclaim the remaining stage of the parkward journey. From each of these roundabouts, two-hundred-foot-wide angled parkways converge on the grandest open area of all, Soldiers Place. After that one proceeds northward along Lincoln Parkway to the park. The cumulative effect of the approaches is still, as David

Gray said long ago, to "enhance the visitor's idea of the importance and dignity of that to which he is thus graciously invited."

The West Side Park Approaches, like Ellicott's earlier city plan, owed their origin to France. Gray recognized the similarity to Napoleon III's Paris, observing that something "remotely similar in effect was obtained by the Parisian architect who laid the approaches to the famous and beautiful Bois de Boulogne; for, to our Park, Soldiers' Circle will hold some such relation [as] . . . is held by the superb space in the centre of whose converging avenues towers the Arch of the Star." Paris was certainly the inspiration for this grouping of parkway approaches to the main park, and it may well be that Vaux had suggested them, for he had been in the French capital just prior to joining Olmsted in working out the Buffalo plan.

Having taken his readers to the main park, Gray proceeded to enumerate the attractions that they could expect to enjoy one day in its 305 acres. The first feature of the Park he discussed was the lake, which would be formed by damming Scajaquada Creek. "A patch of swamp land, with high and agreeably wooded banks, already marks out the forty or fifty acres which nature obviously meant to lend to art for this very purpose," he noted. Moreover, the valley of the Scajaquada was such that "islands, promontories, and an artistic line of shore" could easily be created there. Gray was proud to report that Olmsted had said that "nowhere in his parkmaking experience has he found facilities so ample and cheap for the artificial introduction of water into landscape."

From the lake, one would proceed north and east of the creek to the meadowland that Olmsted had praised as a park ready-made. "Its surface is undulating and, what is a supremely fortunate circumstance, it is already fairly supplied with woods of nature's planting," Gray remarked. "Such trees as the oaks, elms, beeches and maples, which now adorn the Park of Buffalo, New York [City] would gladly have purchased for her Central Park at a price greater than the land will cost us, trees and all." Buffalo would gain thirty years' progress toward real-

izing the fully matured park with these trees in place. Finally, Gray praised Olmsted and Vaux's idea to unite two existing stone quarries (which would be an inexpensive source of material for park construction) on the site into a sunken rock garden. He likened the proposed "quaint and effective" treatment of these "unsightly excavations" to the ancient stone quarries near Syracuse in Sicily, which he had visited during his travels.

From the Park to the East Side pleasure ground, Gray told his readers, Olmsted and Vaux now proposed laying out another parkway two hundred feet wide. Leaving the Park at its southeast corner, this parkway turned southward in a "noble curve" before straightening out and proceeding south parallel to Jefferson Street.[63] This mile-long boulevard was to become Humboldt Parkway, one of the most beautiful streets ever to grace an American city. The new parkway would terminate at the Parade, the sixty-two-acre park near the German quarter at Best Street and Genesee Street.[64] The name referred to a drill field that would be a feature of its design. This ground would also be open to "game players of various kinds, from the baseballists of America to the Turners of the Fatherland." In addition, the park would be planned as a place of "popular reunion." Parties of picnickers could gather here under the shade of a fine grove of trees while, said Gray (who spoke German), a large pavilion would provide diversions of the "popular and *gemuetlich* character."

Before completing his preview of the park system, Gray pointed out that all three locations would be easily accessible by means of public transportation. Street railways at the time ran along Niagara Street to the site of the Front, along Main Street to near the site of the Park, and along Genesee Street to the site of the Parade. Moreover, both the New York Central and the Erie railroads intended constructing suburban rail systems that would provide commuter service to the North Side parks and the neighborhoods that were sure to grow up around them. There already existed in the city "a strong tendency to suburban residence," Gray observed.[65] When the trains were up and running, he predicted, Buffalo

THE BEST PLANNED CITY IN THE WORLD

would have a "perfect railway system—a circumnavigation of the city's limits such as London enjoys in her Metropolitan railway, and like that which New York has so long log-rolled and hoped for." Thus the designers had ingeniously coordinated their 495-acre park system with the city's nascent urban transit network while at the same time, thanks to the new parkways, providing more affluent residents the pleasure of going to and from the parks by carriage or on horseback. Gray noted that "by this plan a much larger portion of the city's suburbs is beautified and improved, than would have been the case had the park been laid out in a single block." In particular, he foresaw the vast rectangle of mostly open land that lay between The Avenue and Delaware Street becoming desirable residential real estate along with the more exclusive addresses bordering the parkways. To Gray's educated eye, the multifaceted plan that Olmsted and Vaux had presented to the city, integrating passive and active recreation, natural scenery, and democratic socializing with improved urban conditions, was a stunning success. "One of Buffalo's vague and almost hopelessly cherished dreams," he informed his readers, had now been given concrete form.

THE ANTI-PARK MOVEMENT

By the time Gray's article appeared in September 1869, the commissioners were already at work appraising the lands the city would need to acquire to realize the Olmsted and Vaux plan. Yet even as they toiled, opposition to the grand project was building in certain quarters of the city. In early October a delegation of disgruntled citizens appeared before the Common Council to voice their objections to the proposed park system. Their spokesman, Dr. Edward Storck, an up-and-coming leader of the German community, labeled the plan a "scheme which did not originate in any great public necessity, or from any great public demand," and one that was "out of all proportion to the size, wealth and needs of the city, either present or prospective." The existing streets

and public squares were good enough for furnishing "pure air and exhilarating drives." Storck and the anti-park group, as they came to be known, also believed that the grand project called for "enormous expenditures of monies needed to be raised by assessment of real estate" that was already taxed enough. Finally, the *nein-sagers* were angry because they had "not been consulted or afforded an opportunity of being heard." For that reason, they called for a public referendum on the matter.[66] A few days later, Councilman George Orr from the Thirteenth Ward on the south side of the city continued the assault on the parks, adding to Dr. Storck's list of objections the city's recent decision to purchase Clinton Forest for $40,000 to donate it to the state for the new mental hospital.[67] To Orr, parks and boulevards were an extravagance that would serve the pleasure of a few and were no reason to increase taxes, which were already sufficiently burdensome. He endorsed the call for a referendum, but the majority of his colleagues on the council voted instead to deal with the issue as a committee of the whole at a future date.[68]

Park advocates were not deterred by these obstructionists. On November 8, 1869, Mayor Rogers submitted the commissioners' report inventorying lands selected for the parks and approaches.[69] Perhaps with the anti-park faction in mind, he reiterated that this major public works project would "stimulate many useful trades and occupations." In addition, the new parks' location beyond the established wards would "bring into use a large unoccupied region." This, too, would be a boon to the workingman, for Rogers foresaw that with the service of the Belt railway line, "mechanics will find cheap homes in the vicinity of the parks."[70]

THE DEBATE OVER
THE PARK SYSTEM PROPOSAL

A special session of the Common Council convened on the afternoon of November 25, 1869, to discuss the proposed park plans. The anti-park forces confronted the pro-park advocates in an attempt to relegate Olmsted and Vaux's plan to the dustbin once and for all.[71] Olmsted and possibly Vaux were in attendance, as well as Dorsheimer and the other park commissioners. When Olmsted was asked to speak, he again reassured the council that experience in other cites had shown that "increase in taxable valuation of property would more than pay the interest on the cost of the parks." He also mentioned that what distinguished the Buffalo park plan from those of other cities was that "the Buffalo plan had been adopted with deliberation and care." As a result, "the geography and interests of the entire city had been considered, and also its future growth and needs."

The council then subjected Olmsted to a round of questioning about the plan. One councilor asked him to justify the three locations and the parkways that linked them, since New York and Brooklyn each got along with one large park and no boulevard approaches. "It was desirable that the lines of approach should be agreeable," Olmsted replied, "in order that families could speedily reach park-like grounds, and as soon as possible experience the healthful change from city surroundings to sylvan sights and sounds. The small parks were desirable, because thousands could often go to them, who could not reach the main park." And though he could not say precisely, he believed that the added expense of the boulevards would be "quite insignificant" compared to that of laying out normal city streets.[72]

A more sinister line of questioning concerned how Olmsted came to choose the park sites. Councilman Orr was especially interested to know where Olmsted had been taken first when he came to town the previous year, and if it had not been "where the land speculators resided." He suggested that there was a "beautiful location" for a park at the Limestone Hill area in his own Thirteenth Ward in South Buffalo, which had been left out of the plans.[73] Olmsted denied any influence of land speculators on the park choices, adding that the first places he had been shown had not pleased him. At Olmsted's own suggestion, his host had driven in the direction where the park maker had "thought he saw

favorable indications" for the site of the main park. "The country about Buffalo was not generally favorable for a park; it was unattractive," he added, uttering an enduring truth and reinforcing the aesthetic correctness of his selection. Pressed further, Olmsted stated that when he had been escorted around town by Dorsheimer, he had been told that his host was acting on behalf of a "voluntary committee" of private citizens who wished to see a park created in their city. Olmsted had asked Dorsheimer specifically if "there were any property interests to be consulted" and was told there were none. Dorsheimer and his associates were concerned only that "the most eligible location" should be acquired.[74]

When Dr. Storck rose to speak as the secretary of the anti-park committee, he was conciliatory but firm in his opposition. He tipped his hat to Olmsted as an experienced professional in the design of parks and said that he did not believe that Olmsted had colluded with land speculators in any way. Neither did Storck think that the commissioners had been dishonest in their intentions or their dealings. What Storck, a resolute Republican who often gave speeches in German and English on behalf of the party's candidates, objected to was spending public funds on "a doubtful luxury" before other, more basic needs of the city were met. "If new city buildings were erected, if the gas monopoly were broken up, if the water-works were put in condition to properly supply the city, first," then the citizens he represented "would not object to anything done for the interests of the city." Addressing Storck, who had come to Buffalo in 1848 as a refugee from the failed liberal uprisings in Germany, Councilman George Newman from the Third Ward kindly observed that they were both young and "probably both anxious to get along in the world." He thought that what would help Buffalo would help them both. "The fact was," Newman lamented, "Buffalo was behind the age. She needed a little Chicago enterprise . . . and a cessation of the cry that we couldn't afford this or that." (Fig. 1.17)

The conciliatory tone was broken by Councilman John Sheehan from the predominantly Irish Eighth

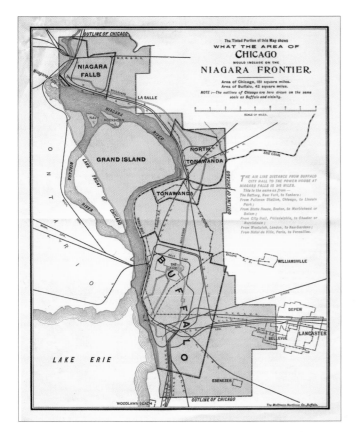

Fig. 1.17. Buffalo frequently compared itself to Chicago; on this nine-teenth-century map, the outline of Chicago is superimposed on the Buffalo–Niagara Falls area. *Buffalo and Niagara Power* (1894). Courtesy Buffalo and Erie County Historical Society.

Ward. His constituents favored the park proposal, and Sheehan let it be known that "he didn't wish a German faction to come into the Council and attempt to dictate what it should and should not do." The council, he asserted, would not be "bullied" by the Germans. Furthermore, he branded Storck a demagogue. Councilman Orr heatedly reminded Sheehan that the Germans paid more taxes than any other "nation" in Buffalo. Councilman John Gisel seconded this contention, claiming that German residents of the East Side accounted for 45 percent of the taxes in the city. Furthermore, he said that Sheehan had no right to speak of them as a nationality solidly opposed to the park. Differences of opinion existed among them on the subject. He himself was leaning toward approval. If the council

would delay the vote for a few days, he was willing to go to his constituents to discuss the matter. "Workmen would not oppose the park if they understood the lightness of the tax," he said, "and that it would bring labor to them."

A plausible reason for the opposition of some of the Germans may have been the fact that there already existed places, notably Westphal's Garden, Teutonia Park, and Spring Abbey, where German families went for recreation. These establishments featured eating, drinking, music, dancing, sports, games, and social-izing.[75] Olmsted himself had enjoyed such occasions when he had gone to see the thriving German immi-grant communities in western Texas during his trip through the South for the *New York Times* in 1854. Perhaps for many of Buffalo's Germans, Olmsted and Vaux's notion of visitors relaxing their stressed facul-ties amid scenes of pastoral beauty was an Anglophone concept that was too esoteric to attract widespread sup-port among them.

Debate continued among several councilmen, but the discussion became so "spicey" that the *Courier* was forced to omit a complete report of it. Finally, a vote was called by Elias Hawley, the quiet and erudite councilor from the Eleventh Ward (the location of the Front) on the motion that "the city declares its intention to take the land for the park." The measure carried by a tally of twelve to seven. Announcement of the victory "was hailed with great applause" from both supportive coun-cilmen and their allies who had come to watch the pro-ceedings. The *Courier*'s progressive-minded publisher, Joseph Warren, and its urbane editor, David Gray, must have been among those cheering triumphantly.[76]

Before Olmsted came to Buffalo in August 1868, he had little knowledge of the city. Yet, like the future Napoleon III planning in exile the modernization of Paris, a city he had never lived in, Olmsted brilliantly perceived the future needs of the place. In this he had the advantage over Napoleon III and Haussmann in that he did not have to confront the problem of destroy-ing existing urban fabric. Perceiving that the city should have more than a single municipal park, Olmsted took into account the original plan of Joseph Ellicott and extended it into unbuilt areas. And while Olmsted's choice of park sites incorporated some locations that others had already suggested, he considered all of them elements in a coherent and comprehensive urban scheme in which thoroughfares new and old were of equal importance with the new parks. To local citizens who had been seeking ways to advance the physical progress of their city, Olmsted and Vaux's fully evolved park and parkway system must have seemed both commonsensical and audacious.

INITIAL CONSTRUCTION OF THE PARKS

Once the city had committed itself to the historic decision to hire Olmsted and Vaux, it lost no time in implementing their plans for the citywide park system. Preliminary work began promptly in the spring of 1870, with actual construction commencing in September of that year. By the summer of 1874, a diligent corps of laborers (many of whom were veterans of the war) had completed Buffalo's parks and parkways in their basic form. Over the coming years, fledgling trees and shrubs would grow to maturity, additional plantings would impart lushness and variety of color and texture to the landscape, drives would be surfaced, and pretty structures and buildings would be erected.

In order to accomplish their intentions, the partners suggested that the city hire two professionals to direct the work on the ground. The first was George Kent Radford (1827–1918), a British civil engineer who had been in partnership with his architect brother, Edward, before both of them emigrated to Toronto in the early 1850s. There George became manager of the Toronto waterworks and, in 1854, won a competition to construct a new intake system. In 1858 George Radford decided to go back to England, where he stayed until Vaux met up with him during his 1868 trip abroad and offered him employ-

ment in New York. There Radford would be associated with Vaux and his partner, Frederick Clarke Withers, on architectural projects and with Olmsted and Vaux on landscape ventures. Olmsted would soon come to regard him as the best engineer in the country. Early in 1870 the Buffalo park commissioners followed the firm's recommendation and hired Radford to be the park system's chief engineer. Radford, who enjoyed socializing with others of British extraction in Buffalo, remained at his post for three years before returning to New York in the spring of 1873.[77] The time he spent in Buffalo was crucial to the later success of the new park system.

The second person the commissioners hired on Olmsted and Vaux's recommendation was William McMillan (1831–1899), a man who would have a profound and enduring influence on the Buffalo parks. (Fig. 1.18) Over the many years of his tenure, McMillan's devotion to the welfare of the park system was truly heroic. A native of Inverness, Scotland, McMillan came from a family that embraced generations of gardeners. After obtaining a degree in engineering in his native land, he came to New York in 1852 to study horticulture with his uncle

Fig. 1.18. William McMillan (1833–1899). Courtesy Donald McCarthy.

James McMillan, who maintained a nursery business in Flushing, Long Island. William later was employed as a gardener with his brother George at Prospect Park in Brooklyn, where he got to know Olmsted and Vaux. When the work in Buffalo began in earnest, Olmsted recommended that the commissioners hire George for the post of superintendent of planting. But when George died unexpectedly, Olmsted vouched for William to take his place. In September 1870, at the age of thirty-nine, William McMillan took up his duties as superintendent of planting; he would remain to oversee the management of the parks until 1897. During this time he guided the planting and maintenance of the landscape and scrupulously guarded the Olmsted and Vaux design philosophy. Described as reserved to the point where "very few men ever got sufficiently close to him to get a glimpse of his personal inner self through his rough and unbending exterior," McMillan possessed a true love of nature and expert horticultural knowledge. One who knew him condensed his contribution to a simple sentence: "Mr. McMillan was to fill in and round out the bare lines that Mr. Olmsted had drawn."[78]

McMillan's devotion to duty included resisting "political influence when it came to making appointments" within the parks department, a traditional haven for patronage. Instead, McMillan ran the department "irrespective of the wishes of individual members of the Park Board and sometimes irrespective of the wishes of the board itself." One of his longtime colleagues called him "a man of unimpeachable integrity and inflexible will," who insisted that everyone who worked for him "should do his duty." And although he "never overlooked a fault or a failure," he never spoke a harsh word. "The time will come," remarked his associate, "when the people of Buffalo will recognize the greatness of his work."[79] Modern scholarship has confirmed this judgment. Only at Prospect Park in Brooklyn did Olmsted and Vaux have the opportunity of seeing their plans so faithfully translated into physical form as they were in Buffalo under the firm hand of William McMillan.[80] After working with McMillan for many years,

Fig. 1.19. Pascal Paoli Pratt (1819–1905). From *Memorial and Family History of Erie County*, vol. 1 (1906).

Olmsted and his sons praised their colleague as a man of "unusual zeal, industry and competency" whose effectiveness was "such as is rarely practicable on our public works."[81] Truly, it would be more appropriate to confer on this extraordinary man than on anyone else the moniker "the Father of the Buffalo park system."

Responsibility for overseeing general progress on the parks rested with the first commission president, Pascal Paoli Pratt. (Fig. 1.19) A "man of futurity," Pratt, whose uncle, the second mayor of Buffalo, had given the city Prospect Place, had been a park supporter from the very beginning. He would guide the commission during its crucial first decade. By the time he was elected president of the park commission by his fellow commissioners in 1869, Pratt had achieved wealth and fame. His various business ventures included a nationally known hardware business and the founding of the Manufacturers and Traders Bank (the present M&T Bank). As the owner of an iron manufactory that employed eight hundred workers, Pratt was well versed in the art of directing men and apportioning money and resources. Moreover, like many of the businessmen with whom Olmsted associated, Pratt appreciated the fine arts and natural beauty. His Gothic Revival mansion on Main Street held a large collection of paintings, and together with Dorsheimer and others he had founded the Buffalo Fine Arts Academy. Pratt kept a special place in his generous heart for the new parks that Olmsted and Vaux had laid out on paper, and the presidency of the park commission was the only public office he ever consented to assume.[82] The organization of operations that Pratt put in place for the Buffalo parks, in the words of one biographer, "is probably unsurpassed in any of the cities of the United States."[83]

A "PROPHECY OF FUTURE ATTRACTIONS"

For an undertaking of such magnitude, the construction of the new park system went relatively quickly.[84] By the end of 1873 the commissioners felt proud enough

of their efforts to issue in their *Fourth Annual Report* a series of lithographs illustrating some of the main features of the parks. (Fig. 1.20) In May 1874 Olmsted visited to check on the progress of the work and certainly must have been pleased by what he saw. Several weeks later he returned to take part in a much-publicized tour of the park system organized by the commissioners to show Common Council members and other city officials what had been accomplished.

Olmsted may well have felt both professional satisfaction and some personal jubilation on this excursion. Together with the commissioners of Brooklyn's Prospect Park, the Buffalo park board had been the most hospitable group he had worked with. One of its members, William Dorsheimer, had become a close friend, and William McMillan had proved a most excellent park superintendent. The early summer trip to Buffalo also came at a time when Olmsted had recently emerged from a dark period in his private life. In January 1873 his beloved father had died. "The value of any success in the future is gone for me," Olmsted wrote dejectedly to a friend.[85] Not long after, his stepmother turned against

Fig. 1.20. South bank of the lake, view from the north bank. Lithograph, 1872. *Annual Report of the Buffalo Park Commissioners* (1873).

THE BEST PLANNED CITY IN THE WORLD

him and initiated legal proceedings contesting her husband's will, which had promised Olmsted a considerable inheritance. At fifty-one, with five children to care for and a new business just getting under way, he could ill afford to lose the bequest or engage in prolonged legal wrangling. Worries over money were exacerbated by uncertainty over the wisdom of splitting with Vaux, whose architectural practice was in the ascendant, and by the onset of the Long Depression, which followed in the wake of the collapse of the investment bank of Jay Cooke & Company in September 1873. He also missed his friend Richardson, who had left New York for Boston after winning the competition to design Trinity Episcopal Church. Olmsted had also suffered a bout of temporary blindness. But by the time he met his friends and appreciative colleagues in Buffalo in June 1874, his health and outlook had brightened considerably. A big boost had come that spring, when Congress engaged him to design the grounds around the Capitol in Washington. This was a job that Olmsted regarded as one of the most important of his career. Unfortunately he had no chance in Buffalo to discuss his good fortune with Millard Fillmore, the man who, nearly twenty-five years earlier, had been responsible for engaging the illustrious Downing to beautify Washington. The ex-president had died the previous March.

The outing, which took place on the afternoon of June 24, 1874, can truly be said to have marked the end of the initial phase of the park system's history.[86] With McMillan and Rogers, now secretary of the park commission, in the lead wagon, a large procession, including the four-horse "turn-out wagon" of the American Express Company, toured the entire park and parkway system.[87] Afterward the group retired to the picnic grounds on the south bank of the lake in the Park for a modest lunch and a round of speeches. Following the salads and sandwiches, all present offered a toast to Olmsted, the honored guest, who then rose to speak. As reported in the local press, he congratulated the citizens of Buffalo for having accomplished so much at a relatively small cost and promised his listeners that the real worth of their investment "would be found to be beyond value." As to the party's immediate surroundings, the Park, he said, possessed "the best grove, the most beautiful lake and the most perfect meadow of any park in the country. Its natural beauty, only waiting to be developed, excelled that of any pleasure ground." All this would be fully revealed in time, for at present the landscape held "only a prophecy of its future attractions." Dorsheimer also spoke, recounting the history of the park movement. His closing remark—"the Park would always be a place of resort for those who, weary of labor, came here, away from the society of men, and into the sacred presence of Nature and Nature's God"— received a hearty round of applause. For Olmsted, Dorsheimer, and others present who had been supporters of the parks from the beginning, the highlight of the day must have been the remarks of Edward Storck. In a "short and pithy" speech, the one-time champion of the anti-park movement conceded that the park system should "go on and that it would prove to be for the interest and pleasure of the citizens of Buffalo."[88]

TWO

The Making of the Park

The Park, a ground designated to be resorted to solely for quiet rural enjoyment. —Frederick Law Olmsted, "Late Additions to the Plan of Buffalo," 1876

During the first year of the Buffalo park system's existence, the greatest evidence of progress occurred within the Park, where George Radford had accomplished a considerable amount of work by the end of 1870.[1] As conceived by Olmsted and Vaux, the Park was divided into two distinct sections: the Water Park, a roughly rectangular area west of Delaware Street mainly occupied by boot-shaped Gala Water (the original name of the lake now known as Hoyt Lake), and the Meadow Park, a larger trumpet-shaped parcel of greensward located east of Delaware Street and consisting of 229 acres, 122 of which made up the meadow inside the Circuit Drive.[2] (Fig. 2.1) Within these two contrasting landscapes, the city's residents could enjoy a medley of pleasant amusements.

THE CREATION OF GALA WATER

The largest project begun that first year was the excavation of the forty-six-acre park lake, known as Gala Water. Creation of this water feature, Olmsted insisted, "should be forwarded rapidly because it requires much shifting of material over other ground, and the delay would cause embarrassment and hindrance to other operations."[3] This was indeed a major undertaking. Not only did the lakebed need to be dug out, but also Delaware Street, which bisected the lake site, had to be removed. The new line of Delaware would skirt the eastern edge of the lake and exit the northern border through a small ravine. (This is the present route of Delaware Avenue.) By the end of 1870, much of the thirty-six-acre area to the west of Delaware Street had been excavated.

At the beginning of the second construction season in early June 1871, a writer from the *Courier* visited Radford at his makeshift office in a former slaughterhouse to the west of the marshy banks of the creek. From there, Radford took his guest on a tour of the park grounds. The article that appeared in the next day's edition relates the earliest eyewitness account we have of the Park's emerging landscape.[4] After circumnavigating the park, Radford concluded the tour near the western end of the future lake, where the artificial body of water narrowed to about one hundred feet. Here the reporter found heavy timbers lying about waiting to be used in the construction of the attractive Lincoln Parkway bridge (also known as Gala Water bridge), which Calvert Vaux had designed. (Fig. 2.2) From here he also could survey one of the largest construction projects Buffalo had yet undertaken. A big crew of men was at work transforming a primeval landscape known to generations of Native Americans as a fertile summer wetland into a captivating locale for urban amusement.

Although boating on the western portion of the embryonic lake began as early as the summer of 1871, watering of the entire basin took longer than anticipated.[5] One reason was that diggers encountered unusual soil conditions which created unforeseen difficulties in the excavation process. The holdup was caused by the need to keep Delaware Street open until its new route along the edge of the cemetery could be constructed. In Octo-

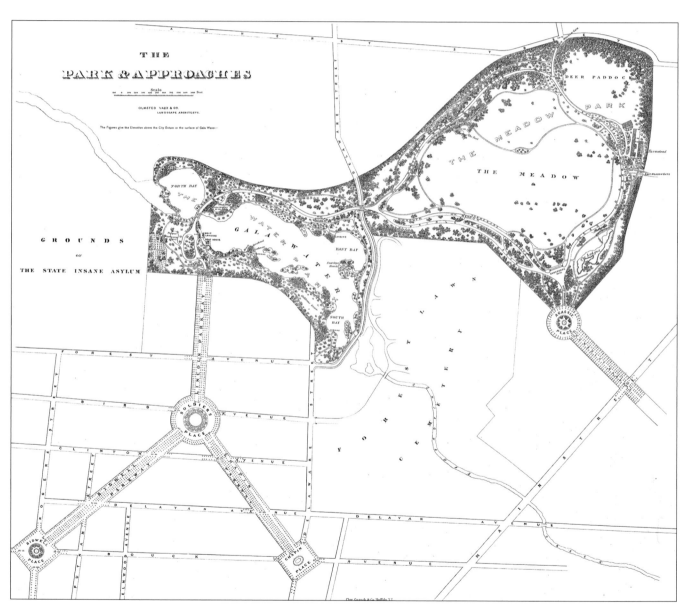

Fig. 2.1. Olmsted, Vaux & Company, plan for the Park and the four 200-foot-wide parkway approaches to it, c. 1870. Courtesy Frederick Law Olmsted National Historic Site.

THE BEST PLANNED CITY IN THE WORLD

Fig. 2.2. Lincoln Parkway bridge. Color lithograph, 1872. *Annual Report of the Buffalo Park Commissioners* (1873).

Fig. 2.3. The eastern end of Gala Water in 1876. The East Cape is visible in the center of the lake. The numerous evergreens were meant to provide temporary protection for other young growth. *Annual Report of the Buffalo Park Commissioners* (1877).

placid surface. In the early summer of 1874, William McMillan could proudly report that the lake was finished. "Its form is finely diversified by deep sinuosities and projecting headlands, and by the varying slopes and heights of the encircling banks," he declared.[7] The few existing photographs from the lake's infancy confirm McMillan's description, but they also reveal how raw and unembellished was the new shoreline. (Fig. 2.3)

"They Do Not Understand Our Business"

As Olmsted had said during the commissioners' picnic on the southern shore of the lake in June 1874, what was now needed for the Park in general to achieve its full potential was the continued planting of trees and shrubs. In the minds of Olmsted and Vaux, the new lake was a sight to be enjoyed like a fine landscape painting. "Visitors must be induced to *rest* under favorable circumstance for contemplating [the] shore," Olmsted asserted, and he and Vaux incorporated several spots explicitly for viewing in their general plan. To compose the image they wished people to appreciate, Olmsted insisted that great care be taken to render the shoreline intricately variable and luxuriantly verdant. The quality of the plantings around the edge of the lake was of special significance to Olmsted, who wanted the north shore especially to have a dense growth of vegetation. "Crowd the leeward bank of the lake," he instructed McMillan, "and by any means that can be contrived force [to grow] a low thicket which the wind cannot prevent from becoming strong, overhanging, picturesque and varied in form, with light and playful spray and which shall give a fine, soft, natural, mysterious" appearance to the water's edge.[8] Perhaps he

ber 1872 workers began in earnest hollowing out the eleven-acre section east of Delaware Street. Happy with the progress of these operations, the commissioners in their *Third Annual Report,* which covered operations for the year 1872, anticipated the impending beauty of Gala Water with a series of attractive color lithographs. Completion of the road awaited the building of a bridge over Scajaquada Creek and application of final touches to the roadbed. By July 4, 1873, this work was done, and an iron bridge, which Radford had designed himself, was in place, so that the new section of Delaware Street could be opened to city traffic.[6] The former roadway soon became a memory submerged beneath the water's had this advice in mind when he later told another gardener to "mix shrubs with the trees; to use shrubs to break the edges of the plantation; and to see that there are no sharp lines between groups of this and groups of that."[9]

Nonetheless, the economy-minded commissioners at first failed to comprehend the subtle nuances that Olmsted envisaged for the lake border, nor could their businessmen's eyes see how important these were to the success of the Park landscape. To get his way, Olmsted had to exert considerable pressure, even admonishing McMillan that the matter called into question their professional reputations. "It is no disgrace to the Commissioners that they do not understand our business and mismanage it," a frustrated Olmsted wrote to McMillan. "It is a disgrace to us if we neglect or allow ourselves to be driven from it year after year, and nobody has a right to compel us to disgrace ourselves."[10] At issue was the fact that during earliest days of the Park's construction, fast-growing species such as native willows and imported tamarisks (a small tree with feathery branches now considered an invasive species) had been "hurriedly planted" on the north shore and the slope behind it. This was done "with more regard to immediate effect . . . than to their permanent fitness for the location," McMillan admitted.[11] The shortcut had infuriated Olmsted, who was horrified by "the bare, lumpy, bald, shorn, machine shaped character" of the area, which he considered a "prominent feature of all the park."[12] In 1876, seeing no action being taken to correct the earlier mistake, Olmsted allowed his temper to boil over. "Every time I have come to Buffalo it has made me sick to see the offensive objects becoming constantly more offensive," he confessed.[13] Olmsted must have been especially disturbed because at the time he was presenting the Buffalo parks at the Philadelphia Centennial Exhibition as a model for the world to imitate.

He strongly remonstrated with McMillan and with Dennis Bowen, Grover Cleveland's law partner and a sympathetic commissioner, to rectify past errors. To Bowen he wrote:

I have often explained to you that in the original shaping of the banks of the lake and in much of the planting there and elsewhere the desire to accomplish in the main a [quick] result led to a method of work, in which the general outlines of my instructions were followed, but in the crudest possible way. All the material was brought to the ground and put nearly in its place, but not only were details and refinements neglected but by chance precisely the thing to be guarded against was done; the ground was lifted where it should have been depressed, depressed where it should have been lifted, shrubs for the water's edge exchanged places with shrubs intended to be 10 feet back. I could not blame anyone—the fault was incident to your desire to do a great deal of work requiring the most intelligent close and detailed supervi-

Fig. 2.4. Gala Water from the west landing, with Spire Head in the distance. Photograph by A. W. Simon, 1885. Courtesy Janice and Dale Rossi.

THE BEST PLANNED CITY IN THE WORLD

sion at an expense for superintendence suitable for a job of canal or railroad building. However, the result was an awful disappointment and eye sore to me and I have every year since and twice a year done my best to get it remedied.[14]

Eventually, Olmsted's admonitions and pleadings had the desired effect. At the end of 1876 McMillan could report that "in the fall the shrubbery of the water park was rearranged to a considerable extent, in order to bring into better relief the plants designed to form the permanent landscape composition." Work was yet to be done on fully embellishing the water's edge, he admitted; there he sought to establish "a supply of such plants as reeds, rushes, flags, sedges, and pond lilies."[15] (Fig. 2.4)

The North Bank of Gala Water

While the south bank of Gala Water was the province of strollers and picnickers, the north bank attracted those on horseback and in carriages, as well as visitors on foot. From the main park entrance at the head of Lincoln Parkway, riders could travel along a curving drive that took them to the north shore across Vaux's Lincoln Parkway bridge, which crossed the narrow strait separating the north bay from the main part of the lake. There the drive continued in two broad curves toward the viaduct at Delaware Street. Beyond that it continued on to the Meadow Park. Along the way, carriage riders and equestrians might pause at one of three concourses to take pleasure in fine views of the picturesque lake below. (Fig. 2.5) The first of these, known as North Cape Concourse (or Prospect Concourse), was just to the north of the park entrance in the area now occupied by the Albright-Knox Art Gallery. The second was the West Bluff

Concourse (completed in 1874 and also known as the Lower Concourse), which riders reached after passing the Lincoln Parkway bridge. The West Bluff Concourse was highest spot in the park and, Olmsted noted, the best vantage point from which visitors in carriages and on horseback might regard the picturesque waterway. "The concourse and the bay of the walk just under it," he said, "have been planned with this purpose in view and anything within sight for a quarter of a mile each way has been considered with reference to such an arrangement."[16] To improve the pleasing vista, Olmsted was even willing to remove existing trees in the line of sight. A third viewing concourse was located near the eastern end of the north shore and was known as East Bluff Outlook (or Upper Concourse). From here one could look back toward the sunset end of the lake as well as across to the south bank.

Walkers were also welcome to enjoy the beauties of the north bank of Gala Water. Here, as throughout the park landscape, pedestrians ambled on pathways that were distinct from the carriage drives.[17] (Fig. 2.6) From time to time, however, Olmsted and Vaux directed footpaths alongside carriage drives so that strollers could observe the passengers and even engage in companionable conversation with them. In the Water Park, the

Fig. 2.5. The carriage drive on the north side of Gala Water near the North Bay, 1890s.
Courtesy James Mendola.

Fig. 2.6. Pedestrian path in the picnic grounds on the south side of Gala Water. Photograph by A. W. Simon, 1885. Courtesy Janice and Dale Rossi.

Fig. 2.7. North Bay viewed from the Lincoln Parkway bridge. Photograph by Ulrich & Kingsley, c. 1875. Courtesy Janice and Dale Rossi.

two systems converged at the Lincoln Parkway bridge and at the Delaware Street viaduct. Both of these structures had sidewalks flanking the roadway. Vaux also designed the two bridge structures to aid the visitor's immersion in the park landscape. The Lincoln Parkway bridge had small balconies projected from either

Fig. 2.8. Calvert Vaux's Delaware Street viaduct around 1890. By this time the street had been renamed Delaware Avenue. Courtesy James Mendola.

side where strollers might sit to contemplate the lake scenery. (Fig. 2.7) The forty-five-foot-wide rusticated stone arch crossing Delaware Street (completed in 1874) shielded riders and walkers from non-park traffic passing on the highway below them, for the structure had eight-foot-wide borders of soil in which thick beds of shrubbery grew to screen the public street from view. (Fig. 2.8) Thus, throughout the park's restful landscape, visitors, whether on foot, on horseback, or in carriages, could move unhindered along three miles of drives and almost four miles of walks, virtually unaware of the outside world.[18]

*A Walk around the Lake
or a Voyage on Gala Water*

Those entering the park on foot from the main entrance on Lincoln Parkway might choose to turn westward to

THE BEST PLANNED CITY IN THE WORLD

Fig. 2.9. Spire Head House and the Beech Banks on the south shore of Gala Water. Watercolor, anonymous artist, 1876. Courtesy Buffalo and Erie County Historical Society.

walk around the smaller portion of the lake known as the north bay or turn to the right to stroll the south bank, an area of the park that afforded a variety of features.[19] Along the gently undulating south bank footpath, a sequence of pleasant attractions awaited visitors on foot. These included the boathouse, a small beach, a shady grove known as the Beech Banks (a popular picnic area), a promontory called Spire Head that jutted into the lake just east of the grove, a boat landing which Olmsted recommended be sheltered beneath "overarching birches," and a secluded tree-girded lawn reserved as the Children's Grove.[20] (Fig. 2.9)

From the Children's Grove, visitors could continue on their way to go around the lake. To reach the north shore one would have followed another path bordering the south bay (the "toe" of the boot-shaped lake) and then taken the path that ran along the eastern shore of the lake. (The original eastern bank disappeared in the 1930s, when Delaware Avenue was widened.) Midway along the east bank, a short side path digressed to East

Fig. 2.10. View of Gala Water from East Bluff outlook. Color lithograph, 1872. *Annual Report of the Buffalo Park Commissioners* (1873).

Cape, a diminutive headland that jutted into the lake (and corresponded to the "arch" of the boot), where another small beach and a boat landing were located. From here a vista of the length of Gala Water looking toward the Lincoln Parkway bridge in the distance might be had. Beyond East Cape lay the east bay (the "heel" of the boot), where one would have met the north shore paths. (Fig. 2.10)

Nineteenth-century walkers along the north shore of the lake likewise might enjoy additional highlights of the lake's scenery, especially a fine view from the East

Fig. 2.11. Delaware Park lake, looking back toward the western shore, c. 1905. Courtesy James Mendola.

Fig. 2.13. One of the two covered settees designed in 1874 by Calvert Vaux for the boat landing, c. 1880. Courtesy Janice and Dale Rossi.

Fig. 2.12. Gala Water with boaters. *Harper's New Monthly Magazine* (July 1885).

riage concourse and crossed the Lincoln Parkway bridge to return to the Lincoln Parkway entrance.

By 1875 there was ample provision within the Park for those who wished to abandon the land altogether and take to the water. Some chose to rent a boat and row around the lake; others preferred the comfort of larger vessels with colorful awnings, which embarked from the boat landing at the foot of the lake.[21] (Fig. 2.12) Passengers waiting at the main boat landing to board one of these delightful craft might nurse their anticipation under one of the two "ornamental settees," long wooden benches that Vaux designed with generous roofs to shade them from the summer sun. (Fig. 2.13) A voyage on Gala Water would feature waterside glimpses of the picturesque shoreline and close-up inspection of two islets near the south bank. These small islands were off-limits to humans. People could, however, go ashore for a walk along a shady path at any of

Bluff Outlook. (Fig. 2.11) After that, footpaths led to an area known as the Braeside, a quaint old term used to describe a shaded hillside. It featured Copse Brae (also known as Coppice Bank). For the final leg of the journey around the lake, one would have followed the path along the arcing shoreline beneath the west bluff car-

THE BEST PLANNED CITY IN THE WORLD

Fig. 2.14. One of the smaller boat landings on Gala Water, c. 1900. Author's collection.

several small wooden platform landings located around the perimeter of the lake. These humble embarcaderos became informal roosts where carefree summertime visitors might idle away an afternoon. (Fig. 2.14)

Olmsted, who had a love for water craft, modeled the park vessels on the canopied wooden sampans he had seen on his trip to China. He even furnished the commissioners with color schemes for them: one was to have an exterior of burnt umber "as dark as new black walnut" with an interior of light gray, another was to be painted chocolate on the outside and straw on the inside. Each was to have a different-colored ribbon painted on its side, and to carry a pretty banner bearing a name such as Iris or Lily.[22] As Olmsted would later explain to Daniel Burnham when designing the grounds for the World's Columbian Exposition, such boats were an important animating feature of the designed landscape and should be made to contribute to, not detract from, the overall scenic effect and happy mood.

The Boathouse and Spire Head House

The popularity of the south bank increased considerably when the city constructed an ample boathouse near the Lincoln Parkway entrance. In the fall of 1873 McMillan visited Olmsted at his office in New York, where they

discussed the need for visitor accommodations near the main entrance to the grounds. Olmsted sought to dissuade the commissioners from their idea of erecting several temporary buildings for these purposes. Instead, he told McMillan, the boathouse for which Vaux had prepared plans would "fully meet all wants."[23]

In early July 1875 Vaux's charming wooden boathouse (which no longer exists) opened to the public. (Fig. 2.15) It was designed and situated, as were all of Vaux's park structures, to take a secondary place in the landscape. McMillan especially appreciated the nature-sensitive aspect of the building, nestled in the wooded elbow of the shoreline. The boathouse, "though a structure of considerable size, and of quite original design, and though located near the most constricted portion of the Park, is not especially conspicuous to the eye from any point, nor does it obstruct any important view," McMillan observed. He also appreciated that "its ornate architecture and exterior decoration are by the unobtrusive location kept, entirely subordinate to the surrounding rural associations of our Park."[24]

In addition to providing rowboats that might be rented in summer (and stored in winter), the boathouse made available restrooms, cloakrooms, and a large second-floor restaurant. From here visitors had access to the structure's most original feature, the sixty-by-forty-foot sloping deck on the roof over the dock, where in warm weather patrons might enjoy light refreshments. Its chief purpose, however, according to the commissioners, was "to afford a commanding outlook over

Fig. 2.15. Calvert Vaux's boathouse (1875). *Annual Report of the Buffalo Park Commissioners* (1877).

Fig. 2.16. View from the boathouse terrace. Photograph by A. W. Simon, c. 1880. Courtesy Janice and Dale Rossi.

seen and heard gliding across the ice. (Fig. 2.17) One of the more romantic pleasures of a Buffalo winter was to take to the ice on a frosty night. "Skating is on!" declared a local newspaper shortly before Christmas in 1906, trumpeting a nocturnal activity that drew many to the park throughout the winter.[29] For the comfort of skaters, the lower floor of the boathouse remained open as a refuge from the cold.

The most fanciful architectural addition to the land-

Fig. 2.17. Skating on the park lake, c. 1905. Courtesy James Mendola.

the water."[25] McMillan was especially pleased that it quickly became a favorite spot for visitors.[26] (Fig. 2.16) To the sophisticated observer, such an amenity would have had a distinctly Continental air, as surely Vaux intended it should. Like park structures he would have seen in Europe, the building that Vaux and his associate Thomas Wisedell (who was responsible for the building's decorative details) designed evoked a festive atmosphere. Framing elements produced an attractive surface pattern (after French practice, or what in America came to be called the Stick style), carved ornament abounded to delight the eye, and a bright but subtle color scheme encourage a mood of gaiety. Accenting the cheery ensemble, a bright banner fluttered from a rooftop flagpole. "Very quaint and pretty" and endowed with "very happy effects" said a contemporary of this now long-vanished gem of park architecture.[27]

In summer visitors to the boathouse terrace might enjoy music from nearby public concerts; in winter the solitude frequently gave way to the happy clatter and chatter of skaters skimming over the frozen surface of the lake.[28] At times, several thousand skaters could be

Fig. 2.18. Spire Head House. Photograph by Webster & Albee, 1897. Courtesy Janice and Dale Rossi.

THE BEST PLANNED CITY IN THE WORLD

scape stood tucked away among the trees and bushes on Spire Head, an elevated spur of land extending out into the lake from the south shore. Spire Head House, which was constructed to Vaux's plans during the building season of 1874, was an exotic-looking octagonal wooden gazebo forty-two feet tall.[30] (Fig. 2.18) Beneath the shelter of the Spire Head House's distinctive conical roof, the interior, twelve feet in diameter, was encircled with built-in benches where visitors might rest while taking in the superb park scenery. Entering this space through the single doorway on the land side, one would have seen, framed in Moorish horseshoe arches, either the shining surface of Gala Water or the shady slopes of Beech Banks. The disappearance of this enchanting belvedere, which must surely have been a favored trysting place for many Gilded Age couples, should be

counted as one of the more lamentable losses the park has suffered.[31]

THE MEADOW PARK

Together with Gala Water, the other main division within the Park was the 122-acre meadow east of Delaware Street. (Fig. 2.19) Early visitors knew this area as the Meadow Park. It certainly typified the kind of pastoral setting Olmsted had in mind when he wrote, "There is no more beautiful picture, and none can be more pleasing, incidentally to the gregarious purpose, than that of beautiful meadows, over which clusters of level-armed sheltering trees cast broad shadows, and upon which are scattered dainty cows and flocks of black-faced sheep,

Fig. 2.19. Delaware Park Meadow. Photograph by Andy Olenick.

while men, women, and children are seen sitting here and there forming groups in the shade, or moving in and out among the woody points and bay."[32] Olmsted, who regarded the meadow in the Park as one of the finest he had come across, called it "the centre of admiration." It is no surprise that when, in 1887, a number of prominent citizens petitioned the commissioners to build a sixty-foot-wide drive across the meadow "where the rate of speed for driving is not limited by the park regulations," Olmsted strongly opposed it.[33] The meadow was open to both horseback riders and polo players, but when it was wet both activities were forbidden, to keep the turf from being torn up. The rule was difficult to enforce, but McMillan was firm in his insistence that in order "to enjoy permanently the privilege of galloping at full speed with perfect safety over the Park Meadow it is necessary that it should not be damaged by use when the ground is soft." Today, golfers stroll at leisure where frolicsome steeds once galloped.[34]

Olmsted and Vaux's original plan for the meadow area encircled the lush greensward with drives that followed the lay of the land. After crossing the viaduct over Delaware Street, those arriving by carriage or on horseback might choose to take either North Meadow Drive or South Meadow Drive.[35] "On week days may be seen elegant carriages and turnouts with their wealthy occupants wend[ing] their way around the smooth park roads," a park admirer wrote a few years after the work had been completed.[36] North Meadow Drive was especially inviting because it rambled through pleasant woodland (now much diminished). (Fig. 2.20) Through the trees, one would have had fleeting glimpses of the meadow. While a forest is apt "to be gloomy and to produce an oppressive sense of confinement," Olmsted observed, "the mystery of this confinement, so different from that of the walls of a town, makes it interesting and recreative." In addition, "vistas through which the light may stream in visible beams, touching the walls of foliage at the side with an infinite number of lustrous flecks, produces a most agreeable impression."[37]

Visitors on foot could equally take pleasure in the

Fig. 2.20. North Meadow Drive. Photograph by A. W. Simon, c. 1885. Courtesy Janice and Dale Rossi.

meadow and its scenery. Coming over from the Water Park by way of the Delaware Street viaduct, pedestrians were free to walk around the open greensward on several footpaths. Most frequented was a roughly heart-shaped system of paths inside the line of the circuit drive. At one point near the Deer Paddock, walkers might choose to proceed across the meadow to a clump of trees near its center and then continue on to rejoin the main trail near the Pool, a little natural pond that Olmsted and Vaux preserved on the northern edge of the meadow. Other paths proceeded from the Ledges Gate along the eastern border of the park to the East Meadow entrance at Jewett Parkway. A third of these now missing pathways ran from near the Deer Paddock through the north woods to a point near where the Delaware Street bridge merged with the main meadow path.

Animals played a supporting role in enhancing the rural nature of the Park. At various times the park commissioners purchased sparrows—Olmsted claimed they would help control insects that threatened trees—as well

THE BEST PLANNED CITY IN THE WORLD

Fig. 2.21. Sheep pastured on the meadow in Delaware Park, 1890s. Author's collection.

as squirrels and swans. The two most important kinds of creatures, however, were those most closely identified with English country parks: deer and sheep. Deer, which were kept fenced in the paddock so they would not damage trees and shrubs, were the quintessential emblem of the chase. As for the sheep, a herd of 125 of these useful and picturesque animals were introduced on the meadow in 1874.[38] (Fig. 2.21) McMillan explained that they would help maintain the turf by reducing the need to mow (since each mowing drained the soil of its fertility), and their droppings would act as a natural fertilizer. Moreover, the annual clip of wool would pay for their upkeep. At the same time, a flock of sheep grazing on the broad lawn would, McMillan suggested, "add much to the pastoral aspect, and natural, rural character of this important section of the Park."[39] In 1892 the sheep were joined by a pair of buffalo, which were allowed to graze on the meadow. These great native quadrupeds were already facing extinction. "For this reason and more especially because our city is named after the buffalo," the commissioners noted, "it is peculiarly fitting that an effort to perpetuate the species should be made by Buffalonians."[40]

THE FARMSTEAD

During his tour of the park system with the commissioners in June 1874, Olmsted spoke in favor of building sev-

eral structures that might aid in the proper management of the park: simple wooden stables for horses, sheds for tools and implements, and a barn for sheep.[41] Heeding Olmsted's practical and aesthetic advice, the commissioners created a picturesque assembly of structures that came to be called the Farmstead. These buildings, according to a newspaper report, were "intended to accommodate all the substantial business of the Park, to furnish shelter from the weather, and safe storage for all machines, wagons, implements and tools; to provide barn room for hay, feed and litter, and stabling and courts for all horses, cows, sheep, deer and fowls that may be kept on the Park."[42] Vaux was engaged to design this group of rural-appearing structures (which no longer exist) for a site just north of the East Meadow entrance. The most important was the square two-story house for the superintendent of the city's park system. (Fig. 2.22) The sturdy half-timber and masonry dwelling (the stone came from the park quarry) fully corresponded to the country mood that Olmsted and Vaux sought to maintain throughout

Fig. 2.22. The superintendent's house at the Farmstead, designed by Calvert Vaux (1874). Photograph by A. W. Simon, 1880. Courtesy Janice and Dale Rossi.

Fig. 2.23. William McMillan and his family in front of the Farmstead, c. 1890. Courtesy Donald McCarthy.

the Park.[43] Visitors coming to see the superintendent on business went directly to the office, which occupied a separate wing at the side of the house with its own porch.[44] The arrangement resembled that of Highland Garden, Downing's home and workplace at Newburgh, where Vaux had spent his early days in America.

The lovely house in the park that Vaux created served as the McMillan family home (William and his wife, Jane, also a native of Scotland, had two daughters) from the winter of 1876 until the superintendent departed Buffalo in the late 1890s. "His home life was like himself—unique, inspiring, and appreciative," recalled a close friend. "He loved his home, it was the sublimation of contentment and unalloyed happiness."[45] (Fig. 2.23) In 1883 Olmsted assumed Downing's and McMillan's way of life when he took up residence at Fairsted, his home and office at 99 Warren Street in Brookline, Massachusetts.

"THE PEOPLE HAVE CHEAP AND EASY ACCESS TO ITS BEAUTIES"

By the mid-1870s, earlier predictions that passenger rail service would one day surround the city and open up the northern suburbs to development had become a real-

ity. In their annual report for 1875, the commissioners stated that the new Belt Line railroad had established three passenger stations about a half mile distant from the park's eastern and northern boundaries. As a result, they asked Olmsted to plan new approaches to the Park from these locations. From the station on Main Street, Olmsted laid out a wide new street through the grounds of Willowlawn, the beautiful Jewett property. Known as Jewett Avenue (now Jewett Parkway), the roadway, as McMillan described it, was "constructed in a substantial manner with stone substructure and gravel surface on the general plan of the drives in the Park."[46] The thoroughfare terminated at the new East Meadow entrance, still the only entrance to the park on the eastern border.

Most of those who came to the Park in those earliest years of its existence, however, arrived by private carriage. Workingmen and their families were generally unable to make the journey from town, for inexpensive public transportation had yet to be extended to the site. For this reason, McMillan observed in 1876, the number of pedestrians in the Park was relatively small.[47] Until low-priced public transport arrived, he admitted, the amenities of the Park would be "inaccessible to the bulk of the population, and sectional and class jealousies regarding it will be more or less prevalent and annoying." The commissioners likewise conceded this when they wrote in their *Seventh Annual Report* that the "major portion of the community is thus, in effect, shut out from the main Park."[48]

By the end of the first decade of the Park's existence the situation improved, and public transportation services got better over ensuing years. In 1879 a streetcar line on Forest Avenue reached the grounds, bringing many new visitors to the park. "The experience of the [first] few weeks the line was opened showed that it was of great benefit to the general public," McMillan stated. On several days during the initial year of service, "it carried each way nearly one thousand people, the cars being run at intervals of only 7½ minutes."[49] The *Courier* noted especially how the streetcar had democratized the Park, observing:

THE BEST PLANNED CITY IN THE WORLD

Fig. 2.24. The boathouse around 1885, with 1883 addition by E. L. Holmes. Courtesy James Mendola.

One of the pleasantest sights the city affords, these summer afternoons, is the exodus of women and children by the branch street railroad to the park. One after another the loaded cars bowl along, each depositing its precious freight at the park entrances, till the wooded shores of the beautiful Gala Water fairly swarm with happy pleasure-seekers. So long as our noble but expensive park system simply afforded splendid drives for the equipages of the rich, it could not be said to be a success; but now that the people have cheap and easy access to its beauties, and freely avail themselves thereof, the wisdom of the city's investment begins to be vindicated.[50]

In the early 1880s the commissioners responded to the increase in park users by taking steps to improve accommodations. Since the refectory near the meadow that Olmsted and Vaux had originally proposed had never been erected, the boathouse had assumed this function. Now it had become inadequate to the number of people who showed up year round. In 1882 the commissioners decided to enlarge it. This work was taken up by a local architect, E. L. Holmes, who planned a double-story hipped-roof addition to the land side of Vaux's original building. (Fig. 2.24) On each floor large "public rooms" opened onto broad recessed porches overlooking the lake. On New Year's Day, 1884, many of the several thousand people who came to skate enjoyed its expanded hospitality.[51] The picnic grove and the south bank of the lake saw a marked increase in popularity. "The small grove is the chief summer resort of all visitors to the Park, except those in vehicles who are out chiefly for a pleasure drive," McMillan remarked. Indeed, the fact that people failed to picnic in other parts of the Park disappointed the superintendent.[52] Nonetheless, the south side of Gala Water remained the location of choice for most picnickers. The concentration of people there put increased pressure on the commissioners to augment visitor accommodations in this area and to add more land to the park on the southern border, a desideratum that Olmsted had argued for from the beginning.

When the legislature had approved the park bill in 1869, it had done so with a cost-cutting amendment that reduced the size of the Park by ten acres. Olmsted had warned that this penny-wise action would prove to be a mistake. "Its immediate effect was to compel a few acres of ground to be thrown out, which had before been included in the scheme. Had this not been done," he lamented, "the plan afterwards adopted for laying out the park might have been bettered at nearly all points."[53] In particular, the land along the northern border of the lake had to be narrowed "as much as possible without abandoning the design" and the picnic grove on the south side of the lake needed to be reduced in size. This latter alteration handicapped one of the park's chief amenities, and Olmsted frequently urged that it be corrected. In 1874 he warned the commissioners that the grove of mature beeches and maples left outside the southern boundary was the only "ground in or near any of your parks or places which for twenty years to come will be equally well adapted for large picnic parties."[54]

In 1886 the commissioners finally acted on Olmsted's advice. In that year they purchased the twelve-acre strip of wooded land along the park's southern boundary which had been thrown out earlier. They then turned to Olmsted, who saw himself vindicated by their action—he did not fail to point out that the cost to the city for the new land was far higher in 1886 than it would have been in 1869—for plans to integrate the new property with the existing south bank area.[55] The following year, McMillan directed work on improving the "rough and irregular character" of the new grounds according to instructions that Olmsted sent from Brookline. The principal challenge was to transform the long, crooked ravine that bisected the new woodland into a pleasant "dell" with a wide footpath running through it. In 1890 an arch made of rusticated native flint and limestone (the latter drawn from the park quarry) went up to channel the ravine pathway beneath the footpath that led from the nearby streetcar entrance on Forest Avenue to the Children's Green. McMillan promised that the unadorned segmental arch would be planted with ivy and other vines so that it would eventually "be as unobtrusive as possible."[56] Called the Dell Span, it would be known to later park visitors as the Ivy Arch. (Fig. 2.25) It is now the oldest structure in the park. Moreover, in its vicinity one comes closest to sensing the pleasurable mood of remoteness that Olmsted and Vaux wished visitors to enjoy in the woodland areas of the Park.[57]

Around the same time that the Dell Span was being contemplated, the park commissioners realized that Vaux's wooden Lincoln Parkway bridge, known also as the Gala Water bridge, was in need of replacement. The balconied span was of considerable importance to the park as both a practical and an aesthetic feature of the landscape. Its site, noted the commissioners, was "the focus of many attractive points of view on either side." In a testament to the merit and popularity of Vaux's design, the commissioners called back George

Fig. 2.25. Dell Span (Ivy Arch), c. 1900. Library of Congress, Prints and Photographs Division, Detroit Publishing Company Collection.

Radford after seventeen years' absence to build a more durable iron replica, which was in place by May 1890.

CONFLICT AND EVOLUTION UNDER THE "PARK CZAR"

For William McMillan, the cultivation of the Park represented more a calling than a job. During most of the 1880s and 1890s, McMillan watched as the Park evolved from the plans that Olmsted and Vaux had outlined on paper in 1870 into the full-blown creation they had envisioned. There were times, however, when the vigilant superintendent had to deal with the depredations of vandals. In 1890, for example, he directed the planting of a thick screen of thorn bushes on a slope near the south bank picnic grounds to discourage the "frequent trespassing of unruly visitors." Likewise, McMillan, whom miscreants once assaulted on the park grounds, complained of people jumping over and breaking down boundary fences. The damage that ensued, he said, was "due to wanton behavior of many visitors, who think they should be permitted to go through the grounds anywhere and everywhere and do as they please, regard-

THE BEST PLANNED CITY IN THE WORLD

less of all notices or ordinances to the contrary." This problem, then as now, afflicted all of the city's parks.

Not all threats to the Park came from vandals and ruffians. From time to time McMillan had to fend off proposals for changes or additions to the Park that violated the integrity of the original plans. In 1889, for example, he felt compelled to preach the gospel of Olmsted and Vaux to those who called for more flowers in the Park:

> In a large country park where all the dominant features of the natural landscape are strictly rural and pastoral in expression, any stray bits of garden finery will seem as inconsistent and offensive to good taste as the most elaborate and fanciful designs. For this reason, exotic bedding plants, except in immediate proximity to the buildings, as heretofore, would be wholly out of place in the broad pastures or the bordering woodlands of the Meadow park, or in the open glades that border the shrubbery coppice on the steep slopes of the Water Park. There is nowhere any detached or secluded space where the lay of the land is suitable for artificial decoration of a wholly different type.[58]

While McMillan remained in charge, the Olmsted legacy was generally safe in Buffalo. Olmsted himself acknowledged this fact. "On none of the public grounds that I visit do I find a superintendent who performs his duties as industriously, economically and intelligently as Mr. McMillan," he asserted. Nevertheless, Olmsted also saw pressure mounting to make significant changes to the Park that would be inimical to its purpose as "a ground designated to be resorted to solely for quiet rural enjoyment." It was one of the reasons why he proposed the creation of another large

park offering a variety of activities on lakeside land in the south side of town. Nonetheless, by the end of Olmsted's extraordinary career Delaware Park had come to occupy a unique place in his own estimation of his work. "There is no one of the 90 public works in which I have been engaged which, as I visit it from time to time, gives me more satisfaction," he confided to a local newspaper the year of the celebrated World's Columbian Exposition, the grounds of which he had laid out at Chicago. He was pleased to see that others shared his high personal regard for Delaware Park's beauty as well. "I have been struck by the fact that it makes a similar impression upon some of the very intelligent visitors who have come this year from Europe to the Chicago Exposition," he said.[59]

Some new features were sympathetically introduced to the landscape of the Park during the latter years of McMillan's tenure.[60] In 1894 a sizable elevated bandstand, since demolished, was installed at the main boat landing (the hooded settees were moved nearby). (Fig. 2.26) That same year, three greenhouses were ordered from the well-known firm of Lord & Burnham and erected in the southwest corner of the park (the area of the former nursery), and in 1897 a house for the assistant superintendent went up in the northwest corner of the

Fig. 2.26. Sunday afternoon concerts at the new bandstand erected in 1894 (visible at left) were well attended. Postcard, c. 1899. Courtesy James Mendola.

Fig. 2.27. Delaware Park Zoo. From H. Perry Smith, *History of the City of Buffalo and Erie County* (1908).

Fig. 2.28. Early cyclist in Delaware Park, c. 1890. Courtesy Janice and Dale Rossi.

park. (It is now the Julia Boyer Reinstein Center of the Buffalo & Erie County Historical Society.)

After the Deer Paddock had been fenced off into sections in 1892 for elk, buffalo, and deer, new facilities were constructed in 1894 for housing and displaying various other animals. (Fig. 2.27) This work marked the genesis of the extensive zoo that is now within the park limits. Finally, an additional entrance was opened in the northwest corner of the park to connect park drives and walks with the 150-foot-wide Scajaquada Parkway, a thoroughfare created along the northern border of the Buffalo State Hospital grounds in 1894. At the same time, the city constructed a stone bridge over the creek to carry the northward extension of another major thoroughfare, Elmwood Avenue, through the park.

As bicycles became increasingly popular, accommodations for this new mode of locomotion were also introduced into the park. (Fig. 2.28) Riding these vehicles on existing park drives was often dangerous because of competition with rigs and horses. Furthermore, the gravely surface of the drives was frequently either muddy or dusty, creating unpleasant conditions for bikers. In 1896, the year the commissioners changed

the name of the Park to Delaware Park to undescore its relationship with prestigious Delaware Avenue, McMillan supervised the construction of a path dedicated solely to bicycling. Frederick Law Olmsted Jr. had made a trip to town for the purpose of advising the commissioners on its best location.[61] In conjunction with the opening of a new carriage entrance road on Delaware Avenue that led up the hill to the main drive (now transformed into an expressway on-ramp), McMillan reported that a path for bicycle riders was built generally following the route of a bridle path proposed in Olmsted and Vaux's original plan.

The most ambitious project begun during the latter years of McMillan's tenure focused on the quarry in the southeast corner of the park. Toward the end of 1897, Olmsted Brothers (Frederick Law Olmsted Sr. had withdrawn from practice two years earlier) began working on plans for converting the unused quarry into an ornamental feature of the park landscape. Their plan, which they were delayed in finishing by the press of completing plans for the Louisville park system, was an almost Oriental essay on the beauty of water and foliage. Shady Pool, Floral Pool (the two were to have been linked by a path and a stream carried through a tunnel),

THE BEST PLANNED CITY IN THE WORLD

Narrow Pool, and Long Pool were to have been fed by "a continuous, slight, dribbling flow" of water trickling down the face of the cliff, and trees were to overhang their herbaceous borders. Other features included a spiral tower, a stairway carved into the rock leading down to the pools, and two bridges, the larger of which would be in the form of an elliptical arch. (Fig. 2.29) They stipulated that all of these elements be in a "rustic style" of architecture.[62] Today this subterranean world lies buried under tons of earth; the railing of the elliptical bridge is the sole reminder of what once lay beneath the lawn. As for William McMillan, the Olmsted Brothers' communication of February 8, 1898, laying out their ideas for the quarry conversion may well have been the last piece of official correspondence he read.

The new bicycle path added to Delaware Park in 1896 turned out to be the beginning of McMillan's undoing. Already by this time some commissioners resented his dogged devotion to Olmsted's principles and his autocratic management style. Indicative of the general erosion of McMillan's reputation were references that began to appear in the local press identifying him by such pejoratives as "the park czar," "wee wully," and "clipped McMillan."[63] His chief enemy on the park board was David Day. A prominent lawyer, Day was a powerful commissioner who railed against McMillan both at board meetings and in public. Looking for an excuse to fire him, Day fixed on the unexpectedly high

cost of the bicycle path as evidence of the superintendent's mismanagement. Because McMillan had decided to make part of the path sturdy enough to support maintenance vehicles, the price had risen considerably. McMillan's staunchest supporter, Sherman S. Jewett, died in February 1897. In December 1897, largely as a result of Day's insistence, the board voted in closed session to discharge McMillan, effective at the end of the month.

Admirers of McMillan in Buffalo and elsewhere decried the decision. The superintendent, who had been a devoted public servant for twenty-six years, had been "summarily dismissed without even being informed of the nature of his offence," reported *Garden and Forest,* a national magazine devoted to landscape architecture which Olmsted had helped his friend Charles Sprague Sargent establish. The journal suggested that the true cause for his firing was "differences of opinion between individual members of the Buffalo Park Board and its superintendent as to the wisdom of permitting the erection in the parks of museums and other buildings not intended for park purposes." Of McMillan's integrity the magazine had no doubts. "To those who know the Buffalo parks, that city has always appeared particularly fortunate in its park superintendent, who has shown himself one of best park managers we have ever had in the United States, honest, intelligent, faithful and unbending to the improper demands of the spoilsmen," the editors declared.[64] His national reputation notwithstanding, on March 1, 1898, the fallen superintendent packed his bags and left Buffalo. With McMillan's departure, the Olmsted era of the Buffalo parks ended. It was at around this time that the park system's beauty and integrity reached its apogee; henceforth would begin a gradual but steady erosion of Olmsted's legacy in Buffalo. (Fig. 2.30)

As the century drew to a close, fewer and fewer people came to regard Delaware Park as a place for passive recreation in rural surroundings. McMillan himself could have seen the future firsthand when he attended the World's Columbian Exposition in Chicago in 1893

Fig. 2.29. Quarry garden and bridge, c. 1900. Courtesy James Mendola.

Fig. 2.30. John Ross Key, *Delaware Park Lake*. Oil on canvas, 1901. This painting depicts three new structures by Green & Wicks: the casino that replaced Vaux's boathouse (*left*), the Albright Art Gallery (*left center distance*), and the third Lincoln Parkway bridge (*center right*). Courtesy Buffalo and Erie County Historical Society.

to read a paper on public parks. His words were well received and nationally circulated, but his presentation was more a eulogy for the Romantic landscape tradition than a manual for the future.[65] By the early 1890s, men like Richard Morris Hunt, Charles McKim, and Stanford White had succeed in establishing the Classical Revival style of architecture and art as expressive of America's new status in the world. Neoclassical architecture and Baroque Rome were to be the models for the short-lived exposition at Chicago and the long-lasting City Beautiful movement that swept the country in its wake.

The effects of the White City (as the central part of the Chicago fair was called) were soon felt in Delaware Park. In 1897 state senator Henry W. Hill succeeded in getting the legislature to pass a law enabling the historical society, of which he was a benefactor, to erect a

new building in the park. The preferred site was the Prospect Concourse overlooking Gala Water. McMillan had taken a stand against the proposal and probably lost his job because of it. When John C. Olmsted, heir to his ailing stepfather's office in 1895, wrote a strongly worded letter objecting to the plan to use this prime spot for viewing the landscape for a building, the president of the park board, William Hengerer, dismissed his objection as "silly." Eventually the new white marble Neoclassical edifice, the creation of the French-trained local architect George Cary, went up on another nearby site overlooking North Bay. (Fig. 2.31) During the Pan-American Exposition, which took place in Buffalo in 1901 adjacent to the northern border of the park, Cary's building served as the New York State Pavilion.[66] (Fig. 2.32) In 1899 construction began on the Albright Art Gallery, another, even grander white marble temple,

THE BEST PLANNED CITY IN THE WORLD

Fig. 2.31. George Cary's Buffalo and Erie County Historical Society building (1900), c. 1905. Courtesy Buffalo and Erie County Historical Society.

Fig. 2.32. The Pan-American Exposition, 1901. The grounds of the fair were immediately to the north of Delaware Park. In this view, the park lake is visible at the bottom. Courtesy Buffalo and Erie County Historical Society.

on the site originally proposed for the historical society building. The architects were Green & Wicks of Buffalo.[67] (Fig. 2.33) As a park commissioner from 1897 to 1900, William S. Wicks had voted to fire McMillan, the staunch advocate of Olmsted's view that such buildings did not belong in parks. That same year Wicks's firm planned the replacement for Vaux's boathouse, designing a bulky masonry building reminiscent of Pompeian villas which was far more conspicuous in the landscape than its predecessor had been. (Fig. 2.34) Thus Olmsted and Vaux's design philosophy—rooted in the Romantic love of nature—that architecture in country parks should be subordinated to the landscape was turned on its head, as prime viewing locations in the park gave way to prominent edifices.

Epic sculpture also began to intrude on the pastoral landscape. In 1903 Andrew Langdon, a wealthy coal merchant, onetime park commissioner, and staunch promoter of the historical society building, donated to Delaware Park a life-sized bronze reproduction of Michelangelo's Carrara marble statue of David. (Six years before, Langdon had been instrumental in placing a jet spray in the eastern end of tranquil Gala Water, in order, he said, "to give a brightening effect to the dead surface" of the lake.)[68] At Langdon's suggestion, the former West Bluff Concourse became the site for the heroic nude. (Fig. 2.35) The location was

Fig. 2.33. The Albright Art Gallery, designed by Buffalo architects Green & Wicks and opened in 1905, occupies a former carriage concourse. Postcard, c. 1905. Courtesy Catherine Schweitzer.

Fig. 2.34. Green & Wicks' boathouse of 1900 replaced Vaux's earlier structure. Postcard, c. 1900. Courtesy James Mendola.

Fig. 2.35. A bronze reproduction of Michelangelo's *David* (1504) was installed on the former West Bluff Concourse in 1905. Postcard, c. 1905. Courtesy James Mendola.

voted with Day for McMillan's ouster) erected a cenotaph to his memory. (Fig. 2.36) Made of rough-hewn blocks of Scottish granite, it supports basins where birds, horses, and park visitors might quench their thirst. In 1856 Vaux and others had placed a marble vase on the grounds of the Smithsonian Institution in Washington to the memory of Andrew Jackson Downing; a half century later, William McMillan became the second American horticulturist honored with a public monument.

During subsequent decades the Olmsted heritage in Buffalo was pushed further and further aside. As aesthetic standards declined and the popularity of active recreation grew, Olmsted and Vaux's plan for Delaware Park underwent changes that altered it in significant ways and compromised the original intent. Surely friends of McMillan must have informed him that shortly after he left his post and moved away, golf, baseball, and football began to be played on the meadow. Permanent facilities for such active sports were subsequently introduced into the landscape, including

probably chosen because at that spot the huge Renaissance work of art would be the focal point of the view from the Doric portico of Cary's historical society building, which the statue faces, turning his back on Gala Water and the park landscape. The introduction of the twenty-five-foot figure into Delaware Park flagrantly violated Olmsted's admonition that sculptures should "not be placed profusely in a park, or at all in situations where they will be obtrusive."[69] Braving public opinion, the son of David Gray told his fellow citizens that the statue was out of place and suggested that the money spent on it would have been better employed protecting the sylvan landscape.[70]

Nearby, in a once quiet grove now humming with the sound of high-speed auto traffic, is another memorial to heroic action in the face of daunting odds. Here, in 1905, a group of William McMillan's admirers (including a repentant Andrew Langdon, who had

Fig. 2.36. The neglected granite fountain monument to William McMillan installed in Delaware Park in 1905. Photograph by the author.

THE BEST PLANNED CITY IN THE WORLD

baseball diamonds, basketball courts, tennis courts, and a bowling green. In 1914 the meadow that Olmsted had envisioned as an uninhibited open space was transformed into a golf course. Over the years, the zoo greatly expanded its borders beyond the area of the former Deer Paddock. Its grounds, now isolated from the rest of the park, encompass the land that was once McMillan's Farmstead, which is now a surface parking lot. There have been other changes to the designed landscape as well. The border fence, which once set the park apart as a discrete recreational space with specific entrances, no longer exists. Footpaths, bicycle paths, and bridle paths have also disappeared. The lake, its name changed from Gala Water to Hoyt Lake, lost its former picturesque shoreline when

Fig. 2.37. The third Lincoln Parkway bridge, designed in 1899 by Green & Wicks, became an expressway entrance ramp in the late 1960s. Photograph, c. 1900. Library of Congress, Prints and Photographs Division, Detroit Publishing Company Collection.

much of it was filled with earth in the early 1960s. The twin islands that once stood off the south bank disappeared, too, and the boot-shaped outline devolved into a simple kidney shape—"streamlined" was the euphemism used at the time. Finally, as maintenance budgets shrank, the nineteenth-century investment in the park's horticulture deteriorated. The densely planted understory of shrubbery visible in historic photographs and talked about in McMillan's reports and writings, as well as many trees and species of flora, failed to survive and were not replaced.

With the advent of the private automobile, pressure from traffic outside the park has worked to alter the park roadways and landscape. In the mid-1930s Delaware Avenue was widened from a city street with a single lane in each direction into a four-lane divided drive. The transformation, which considerably straightened the curving roadbed, spelled the end of Vaux's single-span viaduct. It gave way to a much

larger twin-arch stone bridge from which all greenery has been forever banished. In the late 1950s, highway engineers obtained a license to transform the North Meadow carriage drive into a crosstown expressway with a clover-leaf exit and entrance on parkland at Delaware Avenue. The Neoclassical Lincoln Parkway bridge, which replaced Radford's iron span in 1900 and which is known today as the Three Tribes Bridge, became part of an expressway on-ramp. (Fig. 2.37) In 1960, when the Albright-Knox Art Gallery implemented plans to enlarge its 1905 structure with an addition by Buffalo native Gordon Bunshaft, the city razed one of the park greenhouses for a one-hundred-car surface parking lot for gallery visitors. At the time when all of these projects were under way, a writer in David Gray's old newspaper boasted that once they were finished, "Delaware Park, long-regarded as Buffalo's number one beauty spot, will be returned to the elegance traditional for a stately lady."[71]

THREE

The Front and Prospect Place

A ground in which the use is secured forever to the public of a steep bluff, from 50 to 60 feet above the level of Lake Erie, which commands a broad prospect over the lake, and an interesting view of the Niagara River and the Canadian Frontier.

—Frederick Law Olmsted, "Late Additions to the Plan of Buffalo," 1876

Unlike the Park taking shape in the undeveloped northern reaches of the city or the Parade in the working-class cottage district of the East Side, the Front occupied a prime waterside site in a well-off residential neighborhood. Prospect Hill, as this area on Buffalo's West Side was generally known, had its origins in the former village of Black Rock, a community named for a boulder in the Niagara River about two miles downstream from Lake Erie. At this distance from the lake, the shoreline of the river provided a good harbor. History credits Peter Buell Porter, a lawyer who had come to western New York from Connecticut, with promoting the earliest fortunes of Black Rock. In the initial years of the nineteenth century, Porter purchased a large tract here from the Mile Strip, a mile-wide swath of state-owned land bordering the Niagara River from Lake

Erie to Lake Ontario. (Most of the rest of western New York, including Buffalo, was the property of the Holland Land Company, which employed Joseph Ellicott as their agent.) In 1803 Porter laid out Black Rock in a series of streets that ran parallel to the river. Starting at the water's edge, Porter numbered the streets consecutively. Eighth Street, however, he called Niagara Street. It incorporated an old Indian trail leading to Niagara Falls some fourteen miles away. (The east–west route of North Street and Porter Avenue was more or less the original boundary between the two communities.) Niagara Street opened through the area in 1809, but no significant settlement existed at Prospect Hill until later.

Foreseeing the eventual merging of Black Rock with Buffalo, Ellicott took pains to align the streets of the village of New Amsterdam with the grid of Black Rock. By 1853, when Black Rock was annexed to Buffalo, Prospect Hill had become a residential neighborhood that many compared to New York City's Union Square area. When a horsecar line opened along Niagara Street in the late 1860s, side streets gradually began to fill up with comfortable homes. David Gray observed that the area was "a rapidly populating portion of the city" that was easily accessible from other parts of town.[1]

Two local landmarks were here as well, the city reservoir and Fort Porter. The reservoir was constructed in 1853 on the highest ground in the district. A marvel of engineering, the great basin stood behind massive stone walls on the north side of Prospect Place, the residential square that was the heart of the Prospect Hill neighborhood. Fort Porter was a federal installation dominating the entrance to the Niagara River. It had originally been the property of Colonel James MacKaye, a law partner of Millard Fillmore. In 1837 MacKaye had built a Gothic Revival stone "castle" there. A few years later he sold the house and land to the government for the fort, where, in 1845, the army erected a masonry redoubt that was said to be the largest blockhouse in the world.

FROM THE FORT TO THE FRONT

Adjacent to the fort was the large field that Dorsheimer had shown Olmsted as a possible park site. Because of its dramatic waterfront location, in addition to hosting baseball games, it had been used from time to time for civic events. (Fig. 3.1) In 1857 it was home to the State Agricultural Fair, one of the biggest events that had been held in the city. By then citizens were erecting large homes along Sixth Street, where they enjoyed fine water views across the open ground. It was this scenic river and lake view that Olmsted wished to preserve, and why he and Vaux named the park they planned here "the Front." The earliest indication of the plan of the Front is a sketch in Vaux's hand that must date from 1869. (Fig. 3.2) Showing both the park site and the adjacent triangle of Fort Porter, it reveals how Olmsted and Vaux regarded the two sites in tandem. The main elements traced there would inform the eventual park plan: a semicircular terrace and concourse on the western border, a large parade ground, and a carriage drive curving diagonally across the landscape from the main entrance at the southeast corner of the grounds at York and Sixth streets to the terrace. A separate pathway for pedestrians followed the route of the drive with another

Fig. 3.1. The bare lakeside public grounds adjacent to Fort Porter, which Olmsted saw in 1868, were popular with early baseball teams. From Frank H. Severance, *Picture Book of Earlier Buffalo* (1912).

footpath entering the park from Sixth Street near its northeast corner. The parade ground would later be forgotten, and the road would one day be continued through the grounds of the fort to the Bank, a circle three hundred feet in diameter that Olmsted and Vaux planned as part of the parkway system at the juncture of Sixth Street and Massachusetts Street.[2]

Olmsted and Vaux sent their fully evolved plan for the Front to Radford in 1870. (Fig. 3.3) The final design replaced the rectangular parade ground with an oval playground ringed by a running track and fitted at the southern end with spectator seating. A music pavilion now appeared centered between the playground and the carriage concourse. At first Radford held off construction on the park while the commissioners negotiated with federal officials for permission to extend the drive through Fort Porter's grounds. In 1871, however, the engineer put eighty men to work on the park's main feature, the terrace. Already in June a newspaper was able to report that "the almost unrivaled view obtainable from there to the Canadian and American shores, the bay, the lake, the river and its islands, is given to the eye, while the discordant features of the railroad, canal and tow-path shanties below is overlooked."[3] The next year Radford laid out walks and drives, and McMillan planted thick shrubbery on the steep terrace embankment. Also in 1872 the secretary of war allowed the

THE BEST PLANNED CITY IN THE WORLD

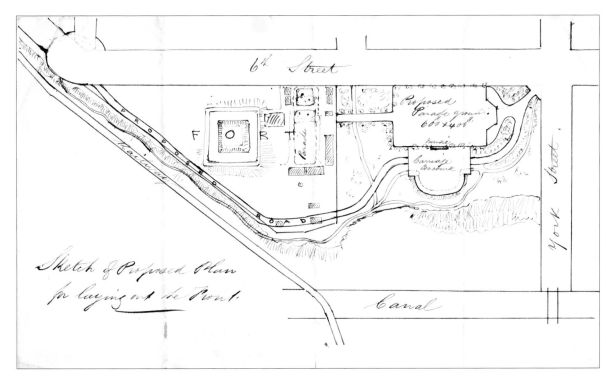

Fig. 3.2. Calvert Vaux's sketch of the Front, 1869. Courtesy National Park Service, Frederick Law Olmsted National Historic Site.

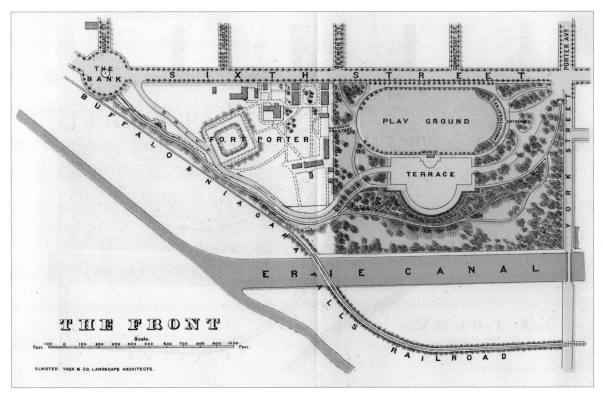

Fig. 3.3. Olmsted, Vaux & Company, plan for the Front, 1870. Courtesy Buffalo and Erie County Historical Society.

Fig. 3.4. The entrance to the Front in the 1890s, showing the drive leading to the terrace. Planted and transplanted trees had created a parklike setting on the formerly bare grounds. Courtesy James Mendola.

park commissioners to "improve" the grounds of Fort Porter as an extension of the Front. The federal government furthermore agreed to move some of the barracks in order to accommodate the proposed drive and to permit ivy to be planted on the blockhouse, which then stood in a state of picturesque ruin.[4]

This positive outcome to negotiations seems to have spurred the commissioners to finish the Front. They proposed to transplant large trees from the older Prospect Place and other nearby locations. Rather than wait decades, they intended to transform the land bordering the playing field into a shaded landscape in the course of a couple of years.[5] "Only strong language could do justice to its loveliness," reported the *Courier* in the spring of 1874. The writer went on to describe the park's charms in terms that render its present compromised condition even more distressing. "The drive through it is in excellent condition," he reported, "the trees that have been planted are flourishing, and the grass is as green and refreshing as one could wish."[6] (Fig. 3.4) In the summer of that year, with the drive through the grounds of Fort Porter as yet unbuilt and the music pavilion still a hypothesis, the city officially opened the park to the public. Buffalonians

liked their only waterfront pleasure ground, and many came especially to watch baseball on the new playground lawn. "Games have been frequent," McMillan reported, "and good order has uniformly prevailed."[7]

The View from the Terrace

For Olmsted and Vaux, the chief feature of the newly minted site known as the Front was the semicircular terrace that commanded a panoramic view of Lake Erie and the opening of the Niagara River. (Fig. 3.5) From behind a low wall, visitors could admire a view that Olmsted cherished as "a very fine one," especially at sunset. Here, too, he remarked, one could observe "a river effect such as can be seen, I believe, nowhere else—a certain quivering of the surface and a rare tone of color, the result of the crowding upward of the lake waters as they enter the deep portal of the Niagara."[8]

The specific location of scenery was less important to Olmsted than the aesthetic pleasure one could derive from looking at it. For Olmsted, the challenge facing modern cities was to protect such places as the Front so that their citizens might have their spirits raised and their mental balance restored by gazing at natural scenery. "What are we to think of the neglect that is apparent at many of our centers of civilization to preserve, develop, and make richly available their chief local resources of this form of wealth?" he asked. Why did Washington, D.C., spend great sums on monuments and formal gardens and leave the "charmingly wooded glen of Rock Creek in private hands"? How could an unnamed northern city be unmindful of "a passage of scenery in which, with some protection and aid to nature, and a little provision of convenience, there might be more of grandeur, picturesqueness, and poetic charm

THE BEST PLANNED CITY IN THE WORLD

Fig. 3.5. The terrace at the Front as depicted in a watercolor drawing commissioned by Olmsted for the 1876 Centennial Exhibition in Philadelphia. Courtesy Buffalo and Erie County Historical Society.

than it is possible that this city shall ever elsewhere be able to possess"? Why, in a famous seaport noted for its architecture, music, art galleries, and poets could a visitor "wishing to look down the harbor toward the sea . . . [not] find a foot of ground prepared for the purpose"?

Indeed, Olmsted thought, views out over water were especially to be valued: "No matter what is beyond, an expanse of water . . . cannot fail to have a refreshing counter interest to the inner part of a city; it supplies a tonic change at times even from the finest churches, libraries, picture galleries, conservatories, gardens, soldiers' monuments, parks and landward outskirts." Moreover, it is usually easy and inexpensive to provide such places of "grateful convenience" for enjoying such scenery. Yet waterfront towns that he had visited, notably Albany, Newburgh, New London, Louisville, St. Louis, Memphis, and Brooklyn, had ignored this treasure at their doorstep. To his great disappointment, San Francisco had rejected Olmsted's 1866 proposal to create there a plaza overlooking the sea. Before Buffalo, Olmsted could point to Quebec City, which he had visited as recently as 1866, as a prominent North American town that had capitalized on its waterfront view. (Fig. 3.6) In 1838 Quebec had constructed adjacent to Fort of St. Louis the fifty-meter-long Durham Terrace overlooking the St. Lawrence River. It may have been the inspira-

tion for the terrace at the Front, for it showed, said Olmsted, how a small urban space might "serve to present a choice refreshment to a city, provided the circumstances are favorable for an extended outlook upon natural elements of scenery."[9]

When Olmsted visited Buffalo in August 1886, he went to see the Front. "Years ago a traveler arriving in Buffalo asked in vain where he could go to look out on the lake," he recalled. "'The lake?' he would be answered in the spirit of the middle ages; 'nobody here wants to look at the lake; we hate the lake.'" The Front had suc-

Fig. 3.6. Durham Terrace in Quebec City (1838). *Harper's New Monthly Magazine* (January 1859).

ceeded in transforming negative opinion and opened people's eyes to the beauty that the physical situation of their city possessed. The Front, Olmsted was pleased to say, "is much resorted to, expressly for the enjoyment of the view."[10] It was surely after this visit that Olmsted penned the essay that appeared the following October in the *Century,* a popular national periodical, titled "A Healthy Change in the Tone of the Human Heart," a phrase he drew from the writings of the British art critic John Ruskin. By it he meant that modern people had come to appreciate the beauty of nature. "The civilization of our times, Mr. Ruskin thinks, finds greater pleasure," Olmsted wrote, "in rivers than in canals; it enjoys the sea, it enjoys the distinctive qualities of mountains, crags, rocks; it is pleasantly affected by all that in natural scenery is indefinite, blending, evasive. . . . It takes pleasure in breadth, sedateness, serenity of landscape. If modern art has any advantage over that of the middle ages, it is through the awakening of the value of these aspects of nature and its less respect for the more material wealth of man's manifest creation."[11] One can easily imagine Olmsted using similar words to coach the artist whom he commissioned to paint the view from the terrace at the Front for his display about Buffalo at the Centennial Exhibition.

The Front and Fort Porter

Almost from the beginning of the park system, the public regarded the grounds of Fort Porter as part of the Front. Though home to an army regiment, the fort had never seen combat. During peacetime it was a minor element of the American military establishment. In the early 1880s the federal government even recommended closing it. Local military officials, however, had a friend in Philip Henry Sheridan, the Civil War hero who took command of the U.S. Army in 1884. Sheridan decreed that the fort would remain open. And because the facility commander, Captain Charles Hay, enjoyed good relations with the park commissioners, the fort grounds remained available for public use.

The most important cooperative project between the park and the fort was the creation of the drive that Olmsted and Vaux had proposed should extend from the western edge of the park through the grounds to the Bank. In 1883, when the city renamed Sixth Street Front Avenue and paved all of it along the eastern border of the park to the Bank, McMillan saw it as an occasion to raise the issue of the fort drive. "Now that this portion of the avenue has been opened, the projected public drive should be constructed from The Bank to the Front along the top of the bluff, within the grounds of the Fort," he proclaimed. It was not merely a matter of pleasure driving, he added, for "a better and safer outlet for vehicles from the Front through these grounds is urgently needed."[12] The following summer, work began on the route, which was kept far enough back from the edge of the bluff to prevent noise from trains passing along the base of it from frightening horses. Soon thereafter the temporary roadbed, which required the demolition of some of the fort's earthworks and several unused gun emplacements, was opened to traffic. The scenic tree-shaded drive was named Sheridan Terrace in honor of Fort Porter's benefactor. (Fig. 3.7)

"As soon as the road was opened to the public, it became a popular drive, and the sidewalk border was at once an equally favorite promenade for pedestrians," McMillan was happy to report. The new entrance at the Bank solved the traffic issue, but most of all McMillan extolled the new possibilities for viewing water scenery from Sheridan Terrace. Because this land was actually one-third higher than the park terrace, the drive and walk commanded a "magnificent" vista that extended down the Niagara as far as Grand Island and, in the direction of Lake Erie, to the Cattaraugus Hills well south of town.[13] Sheridan Terrace became even more heavily frequented the following summer when Massachusetts Street (another element of the parkway system) was paved and became a popular shortcut to the park for people arriving from other parts of town. Before the decade was out, the fort administrators had demolished some sheds that had diverted a small section of the

Fig. 3.7. Sheridan Terrace at the Front, c. 1905. Courtesy James Mendola.

Fig. 3.8. Sheridan Terrace in the early twentieth century. Lake Erie is visible in the distance. Courtesy James Mendola.

years one of the most popular pleasure drives and walks in the city. (Fig. 3.8)

Additions to the Front

By 1880 McMillan could state that the Front was the most visited of all the three new parks. "On fine days in mid-summer about 5000 persons enter the Front, more than half of whom are on foot," he reported.[15] The most frequented areas of the park were those that offered the finest prospects: Sheridan Terrace, the terrace, and the slope in front of the terrace. The West Side location of the Front, near the most thickly inhabited portion of the city, and the good public transportation that served the site undoubtedly accounted for the large attendance. With all of this usage, the Front, said McMillan, stood in need of a shelter. In 1882 the demand was met when the Lake View House restaurant opened its doors. (Fig. 3.9) It went up on the site designated for the music pavilion on the original plan, and indeed a band often played from its second-floor gabled balcony. Instead of Vaux, however, the commissioners asked E. L. Holmes, the architect who enlarged Vaux's boathouse in the Park, to design the building. Holmes took inspiration for the smart wooden structure from Vaux's boathouse and the Parade House. The Lake View House featured an ornamental wraparound two-story veranda where visitors could look at the water or watch games on the playground.

The construction of the Lake View House reflected the sustained popularity of the Front, a fact that in 1884 led the commissioners to call for the expansion of the forty-eight-acre site. Attention focused on the lakeside land and beach below the bluff, where the Erie Canal

drive, removed the blockhouse remnants, laid out two new drill fields, and generally improved the grounds to make them more hospitable to the visiting public. McMillan had special praise for Captain Hay, who personally oversaw the transformation. "His work was planned," McMillan remarked, "with the special object of making the Fort grounds, as far as possible, an attractive addition to the Front."[14] Sheridan Terrace, depicted in numerous postcard views, would remain for many

Fig. 3.9. E. L. Holmes's Lake View House (1882). From Frank H. Severance, *Picture Book of Earlier Buffalo* (1912).

and railroad passed by the park. This area was occupied by a motley group of industrial properties, including a sizable icehouse, a sprawling stone yard, and a smelly asphalt paving works. This last business was particularly offensive, for, according to the commissioners, its operations frequently sent large amounts of smoke across the landscape of the Front. Before more businesses moved in, they urged the city to acquire the strip of land for public use. "This is now the only portion of the lake shore within the limits of the city to which our citizens can have convenient access. It is humiliating to think that so large a community, living on the very shore of this magnificent inland sea, should be in immediate danger of being shut off of the beach," they declared. In addition to denying access to the water, the industrial zone was doing serious damage to the Front's unique lake scenery. Sherman S. Jewett and his fellow commissioners complained, "It is aggravating to find that the public ground which was purchased by the city for the special purpose of affording an open outlook over the lake, should already be so shut in by offensive structures that from no point can any unobstructed view of it be obtained," and they gracefully observed that "this ocean-like body of water, forever changing in color and character in quick response to the ever-changing aspect of the sky and condition of the atmosphere, is at all times an attractive and impressive sight, so beautiful when quietly rippling in the sunshine, so grand when

fiercely raging in a storm."[16] (Fig. 3.10) As Olmsted was campaigning to have done at Niagara at this very time, the commissioners advocated for public acquisition of the lakeshore so that uses offensive to the senses could be removed and the land turned into parkland freely accessible to all. Some, at least, had absorbed the Gospel of Olmsted.

In the winter of 1886, the year after the state established the Niagara reservation, Buffalo acquired title to thirteen acres that straddled the railroad adjacent to the west end of the Front. Shortly afterward, the park commissioners sought Olmsted's advice on how to assimilate the new purchase to the existing park. When Olmsted visited the site in the summer of 1886, he observed that in addition to demolition of existing structures, a great deal of filling needed to be done before the extension could be turned into recreational space.[17] He was pleased, however, that the purchase secured for the Front an unimpeded view of the water. The December after Olmsted's visit, McMillan paid him a call at

Fig. 3.10. Sunset on Lake Erie. Photograph by C. L. Pond, 1869. Courtesy Janice and Dale Rossi.

THE BEST PLANNED CITY IN THE WORLD

Fairsted to discuss his ideas.[18] Conversion of the messy industrial acreage into park space, however, was stalled for several years by litigation that ensued over the title to the property. Eventually, at the end of 1891, F. L. Olmsted & Co. sent the "Plan for Additions to The Front" to Buffalo. (Fig. 3.11)

According to the Olmsteds' proposal, active recreation would predominate in the new area. From the bridge over the canal at Porter Avenue, a drive would wind its way around a Boys' Playground, cross the railroad on an underpass, and skirt a triangular lawn to end at a pier for small boats and a sheltered lakeside bathing beach. The gravel-surfaced Boys' Playground, which was encircled by a running track and had provisions for quoits, hammer throwing, and other sports, was paired with a smaller Girls' Playground, which featured a turf-covered running track. Between the two playgrounds (where there was to be a station on the Belt Line railroad), the planners slotted in a "sand court for infants" and a "women's gymnastic apparatus" court, which would be screened by a high fence from the eyes of drovers on the canal towpath. The neatly compact plan, which Olmsted surely conceived in collaboration with his stepson John, manifested the Progressive Era belief in the moral value of physical fitness in contrast to the Romantic faith in the restorative power of scenery which informed the original portion of the Front. Nonetheless, this adjunct to the Front never went much beyond the 1891 design on paper.[19] Eventually part of the land was leased to the Buffalo Yacht Club, which, in 1893, built a large Shingle style clubhouse that Henry L. Campbell designed to stand on a pier at the foot of Porter Avenue.[20]

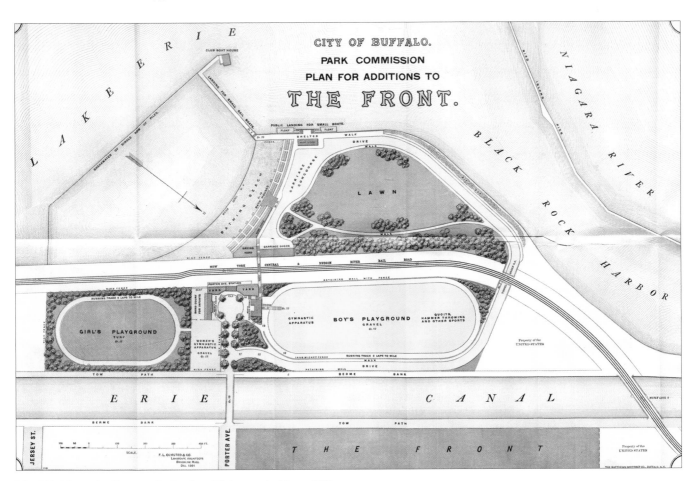

Fig. 3.11. Olmsted & Company's plan for additions to the Front, 1891. Author's collection.

In 1898, three years after Olmsted's retirement from practice, the park commissioners contacted the firm, now run by John C. Olmsted and Frederick Law Olmsted Jr. and known as Olmsted Brothers, for revised plans. The preliminary plans that arrived in Buffalo from Brookline in September 1898 called for "a large, ornamental pool, encircled by a driveway and promenade extending well out into the harbor," and a tunnel over the passing railroad. "If the plan now submitted . . . is eventually carried out," said the Olmsteds, "the City will possess one of the most unique and magnificent pleasure grounds, especially with regard to the views commanded from it, to be found in any city."[21] This ambitious scheme, which the landscape architects admitted would best be achieved in steps over a period of years, also came to nothing.

The new plan must have been shelved, because the following year the city proposed the Front as a site for the Pan-American Exposition, which was to take place in 1901. After the Centennial Exhibition at Philadelphia in 1876 and the World's Columbian Exposition at Chicago in 1893, the Pan-American Exposition was to celebrate the new century with another world's fair. In April 1899 the city hired a committee of three nationally prominent men to guide the site selection process. They were Daniel H. Burnham, the dynamic director of the Chicago fair; Warren H. Manning, the well-known Boston landscape architect who, as a member of the Olmsted firm, had been in charge of planting the grounds of the Chicago exposition; and John C. Olmsted. When the three men made their report in May 1899, they designated the Front and the land around it as their first choice. Like Frederick Law Olmsted Sr. before them, they were enthralled by the outlook on the lake and river. "The first, broadest, and grandest natural beauty of Buffalo is that of the lake," the three experts declared in their warm endorsement of the waterfront site. One can easily imagine Burnham, famous for his admonition "Make no little plans; they have no magic to stir men's blood," as the one who declared that the site "should be secured even at a considerable sacrifice of other advantages."[22]

Despite the experts' espousal of the Front location, as well as the existence of strong public sentiment in favor of it, the executive committee of businessmen rejected the recommendation. Specifically, they foresaw the necessity of building a breakwater to protect the shoreline as a daunting expense and feared that it would not be finished early enough to allow adequate time for the construction of fair buildings. The landscape historian Arleyn Levee also believes that street railroad interests may have influenced the decision, for the Front site, which was readily accessible, would have done nothing to encourage the expansion of the system.[23] Instead of the Front, the exposition organizers ruled in favor of a location farther inland, on empty land north of Delaware Park. Consequently, fair visitors were to be denied the opportunity to tell their children and their grandchildren about watching the purple Lake Erie twilight fade beyond the glittering display of illuminated buildings that would constitute the most extensive display of decorative electric lighting the world had yet seen.

Later History of the Front

The Front continued to be a popular place of resort well into the twentieth century. At the time of the centennial of the War of 1812, several Civil War–era canons took up fictive defensive positions facing the lake at the terrace.[24] (Fig. 3.12) Sculpture of a militaristic spirit also intruded into the peaceful landscape in the form of a monumental bronze image of Commander Oliver Hazard Perry, the hero of the battle of Lake Erie. From the center of the carriage concourse, Perry, with a strident gesture toward Presque Isle, forever relives in art his dashing exploit.[25] By the time the statue was put in place in 1916, the Lake View House had ceded its place to a round Neoclassical-style bandstand. (Fig. 3.13) The symbiotic relationship between park and fort would continue until 1926, when Fort Porter was absorbed into the site of the transnational Peace Bridge, the first automobile link across the Niagara. In later years, authorities permitted truck traffic to use the bridge. Sadly, the

Fig. 3.12. The Terrace at the Front with Civil War canons placed there in 1912. Postcard, c. 1912. Courtesy James Mendola.

Fig. 3.13. The bandstand that replaced the Lake View House in 1898. Postcard, c. 1900. Courtesy James Mendola.

disappearance of the fort and the arrival of the bridge signaled the beginning of the Front's slow decimation due to the ever-increasing demands of vehicles using the span.

Already in the 1950s, citizens were lamenting the whittling down of Front Park. "Successive partitions over the years have reduced its original acreage of 50 to about 20," stated an article in the *Buffalo Evening News* in 1957. Another twelve acres would soon be sacrificed to the New York State Thruway, which was about to be constructed on the former Erie Canal bed along the park's western border. This acreage was in addition to the land along the park's eastern border that the Peace Bridge had taken in 1926 for approach drives and the ten additional acres it acquired in 1951 to enlarge the original approaches. The park that "the distinguished landscape architect of that

day, Frederick Law Olmsted," had designed was, in the judgment of this midcentury observer, "now but a shell of the park it used to be."[26]

Today, Front Park (as it is now called) is held in the grip of New York State Thruway on-ramps and sprawling U.S. Customs facilities. Approach roads to the bridge blemish the park's now leaf-poor eastern border. The noise of traffic is pervasive, and the view of the lake from the terrace is compromised by an elevated concrete ramp that carries an international parade of Thruway-bound trucks from the bridge inspection stations. Along Busti Avenue (the former Sixth Street and Front Avenue), historic homes stand condemned, waiting to be replaced by expanded parking facilities for truck drivers and duty-free shoppers. Unlike the good Colonel Hay, the current occupiers of the former site of Fort Porter have no interest in the adjacent park or in accommodating themselves to a municipal environment. All the effort that went into creating a beautiful landscape and a popular urban amenity during Buffalo's golden age of enlightened urbanism has been lost. Few present-day residents of the city are even aware of Front Park's existence. Virtually no one comes to the terrace to watch the spectacle of a Lake Erie sunset.[27]

PROSPECT PLACE

The Prospect Hill area is home to one of the oldest public spaces in the city, an eight-acre residential square known for many years as Prospect Place (and today divided by Niagara Street into Prospect Park on the east and Columbus Park on the west).[28] (Fig. 3.14) The two-block parcel was donated for public use in 1836 by Hiram Pratt, the father of the first president of the park commission. (Fig. 3.15) The highest piece of ground in the area, Prospect Place once commanded a view of the lake across the sloping open land to the west that became the site of the Front. When Olmsted first visited Buffalo, it was a tree-shaded lawn bordered by residences in companionship with the reservoir on the north. He

Fig. 3.14. View of Prospect Place. The tower is the Connecticut Street Armory, which replaced the earlier reservoir. Photograph by Martin Wachadlo, 2012.

property between Prospect Place and the Front site was the reason why he told Dorsheimer and his colleagues that creating a large parkland in this area would be too expensive.

In 1870, however, at Olmsted and Vaux's suggestion (and perhaps with the distant hope that the venerable square would one day be united to the Front), the city incorporated Prospect Place into the new park system. In 1875 McMillan reported that all old fencing around the grounds had been taken down, so that, unlike in the main parks, persons on foot would enjoy unrestricted access to the landscape.[30] (Fig. 3.16) The following year Olmsted forwarded a plan for walks that would channel pedestrian movement diagonally through the square.

By the time Prospect Place became part of the park system—Porter Avenue, the longtime route to the lake that passed by the southern border, furnished the connection—it had assumed the aspect of a small urban forest. (Fig. 3.17) The property was home to so many fine shade trees that some of them could be spared to enhance the stark grounds of the Front. Even after that judicious thinning, McMillan reported in 1880 that

lamented that the city had not had the foresight to purchase the ground to the west of Pratt's donation in order to preserve the view of the water. Instead, he found that the "two large squares had been laid out, furnished and planted, leaving a block between them and the edge of a bluff to be so built as to shut off all view of the lake from the squares and toward sunset."[29] To him, this was a prime example of how Buffalonians had ignored their treasure of precious water scenery. Undoubtedly his calculation of the cost involved in purchasing the built-on

Fig. 3.15. The Hiram Pratt residence, built in 1835. Pratt donated the land for Prospect Place. From Frank H. Severance, *Picture Book of Earlier Buffalo* (1812).

Fig. 3.16. Prospect Place around 1910. After 1875 it was an unfenced public square. Courtesy James Mendola.

THE BEST PLANNED CITY IN THE WORLD

Fig. 3.17. The groundskeeper of Prospect Place feeding the squirrels, c. 1910. Courtesy Buffalo State College.

Fig. 3.18. Pierce's Palace Hotel for Invalids and Tourists, near Prospect Place. Photograph by L. E. Walker, 1880. Courtesy Janice and Dale Rossi.

"disorderly characters" took refuge there in the darkness of midsummer nights. It was important to remedy the situation, McMillan said, because the square was especially popular with women, young children, and invalids. This last group of visitors surely came mostly from Pierce's Palace Hotel, a hospital that went up across from the eastern side of Prospect Place in 1878. (Fig. 3.18) Dr. Ray Vaughn Pierce was famous around the world for his patent medicine cures, which were made in Buffalo. When Pierce decided to erect a hospital, he must have seen the placid park and the fresh breezes from the nearby lake as assets that would attract clients and help restore them to health. Surely he would have been eager to rid the grounds in front of his establishment of ruffians. Pierce must have been pleased when, in 1880, the commissioners agreed to McMillan's proposal to illuminate the area after dark and installed eleven gas lamps.[31]

Over the decades, significant changes occurred in the area around Prospect Place. In 1900 the Connecticut Street Armory, a mammoth Richardsonian Romanesque structure by the Buffalo architects Lansing & Beierl, replaced the waterworks and a block of houses on the north side of the square. On the eastern border, Pierce's hotel gave way to the campus of D'Youville College, a small liberal arts institution. The park grounds

themselves, however, have generally escaped drastic alteration. In the early twentieth century, a modest brick shelter house went up in the eastern portion, and in the 1960s a statue of Christopher Columbus was installed near the southwest section. The most unfortunate intrusion into the landscape occurred in 1957, when the library system received permission to erect a brick and plate-glass branch outlet and surface parking lot in the southeastern area of the park. By this time Olmsted and Vaux's injunction against putting otherwise worthwhile public buildings in parks had been repeatedly ignored in Buffalo and elsewhere. Nonetheless, bordered by an armory, a college, and numerous well-maintained homes, Prospect Place is still a restful urban oasis that lives up to McMillan's observation that "half of the enjoyment should be its neat and orderly condition."[32]

FOUR

The Parade

A smooth gently-sloping lawn designed for military drills, parades, attractive out-door sports and popular festivities.

—Frederick Law Olmsted, "Late Additions
to the Plan of Buffalo," 1876

Parade grounds where state militias might drill had been common in American cities from an early time. They had become features in public parks beginning with Central Park, when the commissioners included a parade ground in the competition requirements. One wonders if the decision to put Buffalo's new parade ground in an East Side location represented a wish on the part of city fathers to stage displays of American patriotism in the section of town most heavily occupied by foreigners. These urban military spaces remained important in the decades after the Civil War until, in the 1890s, newly constructed armories made the former parkland drill fields obsolete.

OLMSTED AND VAUX'S PARADE

The plan Olmsted and Vaux drew up for the Parade reached Buffalo in the summer of 1870. (Fig. 4.1) The fifty-six-acre L-shaped property was to include three major features: the Parade itself, a sweep of turf occupying the western two-thirds of the site; the Grove, a wooded area in the northeast section; and the Parade House, a large restaurant and dance hall in the southwest portion. More often than military drills, however, baseball and other sports took place on the green. In particular, the popularity among German youths of the Turnverein movement must have accounted for the "athletic and gymnastic practice and competitions" that McMillan tells us frequently occurred there.[1]

Construction proceeded more slowly at the Parade than at the Park. Radford gave little attention to the land in 1870 other than to erect a wooden fence around it. Until a street that crossed the site from north to south was removed, Olmsted and Vaux's plan could not be fully implemented. In 1871 the engineer tilled, graded, and seeded the parade ground and planted numerous trees along its border and elsewhere in the park. In June 1873 local National Guard troops began drilling there.[2] By the end of the following year, the intrusive public thoroughfare had been closed and the park's walks and drives finished. Likewise, a residential street on the northern border (the present North Parade) had

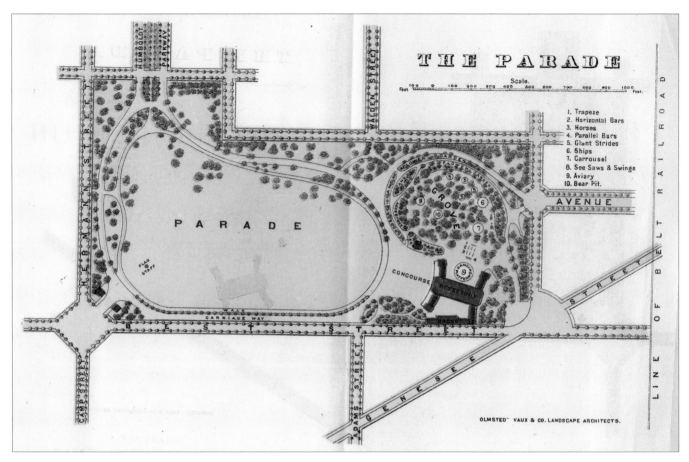

Fig. 4.1. Olmsted, Vaux & Company, plan of the Parade, 1870. The location of the Parade House refectory is indicated in red at the lower right.
Courtesy Buffalo and Erie County Historical Society.

been laid out, and new thoroughfares on the west (West Parade) and east (East Parade) had been opened. These streets allowed commercial and other traffic to move around the park without disturbing its users.

Olmsted and Vaux reserved the Grove for picnickers and youngsters and proposed to install a number of permanent children's amusements there. One gathers from reading McMillan's reports over the years, however, that the Grove failed to live up to its intended purpose; the continued popularity of nearby private picnic grounds may have stunted its attraction for the public. It also appears that children never had the opportunity to whirl on the carousel, swing on the trapeze, play on the seesaws and swings, ride the toy horses, climb the horizontal and parallel bars, or sail the marooned ships

that featured in Olmsted and Vaux's 1870 plan. Nor was the collection of "hardy animals" such as bears, foxes, opossums, raccoons, prairie dogs, and various birds that Olmsted and Vaux wished displayed there in movable cages ever installed in the Grove.[3]

THE PARADE HOUSE

Visitors coming from the Park, where such boisterous activities were excluded, reached the Parade via Humboldt Parkway, the grandest of all the new boulevards. Entering through the north entrance, carriages could proceed around either side of the roughly elliptical parade ground. Other carriage entrances were in the

THE BEST PLANNED CITY IN THE WORLD

Fig. 4.2. Calvert Vaux's design for the Parade House, 1871. Courtesy Buffalo and Erie County Historical Society.

southwest corner, the southeast corner, and near the midpoint of the eastern border. There was also a carriage entrance across from Adams Street (later Fillmore Avenue) along the southern boundary of the park, which paralleled Best Street, a major east–west artery. Whichever entrance a driver chose, he was directed by the roadway system to the big carriage concourse in front of the restaurant.

Designed by Calvert Vaux in 1871 and constructed between 1874 and 1876, this striking timber structure, which early accounts referred to as the refectory, soon came to be known as the Parade House, and it remained open year-round for music, dancing, theater, dining, and drinking. (Fig. 4.2) Such attractions, which would have been out of place in a "country park," made the Parade House a much-frequented place of amusement as soon as it opened in 1876.[4]

This double-storied, towered chalet summoned visitors to revelries simply by its wondrous appearance. The most striking feature was the great West Veranda, a two-level open-air gallery that stretched 250 feet across the front of the H-shaped building. In the center, a tall arched gable announced the entrance to a large public restaurant. (Fig. 4.3) Similar arches were repeated in

Fig. 4.3. The West Veranda of the Parade House. Photograph by George Barker, 1883. Courtesy Janice and Dale Rossi.

smaller form on end pavilions. Through its long extent, Vaux and his associate Thomas Wisedell elaborated the structure with a stunning display of incised, bracketed, and turned elements. (Fig. 4.4) These they made even more attractive by a fanciful color scheme. Framing elements were highlighted in olive, column shafts were painted a deep red, and carved scrollwork ornament was picked out in black.

The West Veranda was truly breathtaking. "But this does not comprise the whole of the delightful verandah," remarked a visitor to the building when it was new, for "it extends, also along the entire north side of the refectory, and at the eastern extremity of the building there is another extension running north, a counterpart of that at the front end."[5] Thus a person might walk around the 28,000-square-foot structure under the cover of porches that were wide enough, McMillan observed, "to allow more than a thousand persons to promenade freely without jostling."[6]

Sheltered from the elements, visitors could survey the park's varied surroundings. From the western porch, onlookers might watch events taking place on the parade ground. (Fig. 4.5) On the north side, which faced the Grove, the porches formed a U-shaped court (visible in Vaux's perspective drawing). "In the centre of this

partially enclosed plot," noted a reporter from the *Courier* shortly before the building opened, "is to be built a circular platform, for summer, out-of-door dancing." The orchestra played on a hooded balcony fitted with a

Fig. 4.4. Detail of the West Veranda. Photograph by Webster & Albee, 1897. Courtesy Janice and Dale Rossi.

Fig. 4.5. The Parade as depicted in a watercolor drawing commissioned by Olmsted for the 1876 Centennial Exhibition. The Parade House is visible in the distance. Courtesy Buffalo and Erie County Historical Society.

THE BEST PLANNED CITY IN THE WORLD

clock to remind party goers that "dancing may not be kept up too late." On the back or east flank of the building patrons might enjoy a light lunch gazing at "a beautiful parterre."[7] Here was also a tall annex that held an apartment for the concessionaire and spaces that could be rented for private theatricals. Those who climbed the stairs to the one-hundred-foot summit were rewarded with a panoramic view of the city. Only the south side of the building offered little of interest for visitors. In the area between the building and a long, narrow shed constructed along the border of the park, was a yard for stabling horses and parking carriages and wagons.

Several choices were on offer inside the Parade House. The ground floor welcomed all to a dining room measuring one hundred by fifty feet, in which rows of cast iron columns "in the French style" added to the festive atmosphere. At one side, a long bar dispensed refreshments to thirsty patrons. In warm weather the floor-to-ceiling windows along the outer wall opened so that people could move freely between the interior and the veranda. The open windows also allowed the rooms' occupants to glance beyond the porch filled with "gay seekers for pleasure and pastime, to the dancing platform," according to the *Courier*. At the rear of the dining hall a corridor led to several smaller rooms that clients could rent for private parties. The grandest space of all was the ballroom on the second floor. Reached by a wide staircase near the front entrance, the dancing accommodations filled the entire 250-foot length of the upper level. An early description tells us that it was "arched across with deep ribs every ten feet extending far up into the roof, forming a spacious apartment . . . thirty-five feet high which cannot but arouse the emotions of any tripper of the light fantastic." The dance hall, resplendent with "gaily painted walls," was, declared the *Courier,* "decidedly the best in the city, if not the States."[8]

Although the local press praised the Parade House when it opened as "an elaborate, complete and tasteful bit of architecture," many must have been unsure what to make of the lavish building. Taking their inspiration from both the wooden architecture of the Swiss Alps and the colorful veranda palaces of Mogul India, Vaux and Wisedell conjured up an edifice worthy of a glamorous potentate. As Englishmen, both architects would have been well aware of the plentiful heritage of buildings for pleasure in the British subcontinent, such as Tipu Sultan's eighteenth-century Summer Palace at Bangalore. The judgment of their compatriot, the architectural historian James Fergusson, that "nothing more elegant, or in Architecture more poetic," existed might well have been running through their minds as they conceived their fantastic pavilion.[9]

THE PEOPLE'S PARK

The Parade House opened to great fanfare on July 4, 1876, when the city chose it as the location to celebrate the centennial of the American Revolution. "If anything in our new Park will tend to popularize its particular locality," the *Courier* noted, "and draw our citizens from all parts of the city to it, it must certainly prove the Refectory."[10] Fifteen thousand people came to hear patriotic addresses, to listen to concerts by several German singing societies, and to watch a striking display of fireworks. "With the opening of the House," McMillan observed, "The Parade at once became a place of popular daily resort."[11] A local reporter was more descriptive: "Nightly congregates the young and tall and short and thick and thin," he wrote, "and a glance at the many faces gathered here opens to view the many sides of life. . . . The gathering there, was in fact, a congregation of all nations—a strange commingling of the plebeian and the aristocrat, the innocent and the depraved. . . . Those whose purses are not plethoric and who, therefore, cannot spend a portion of the summer in the 'country' find the refectory a good substitute and seem to enjoy the pleasures afforded by the place fully as much as if they were sojourning at the fashionable watering places where all is pomp and empty show."[12]

Attracting all classes of society was to Olmsted and

Vaux an important contribution that their public parks made to democratic civic life. Such places of free encounter as the Mall in Central Park and the Parade House in Buffalo, they believed, mitigated the ever-growing distance between the lives of working people and those of wealthy families. Olmsted, in particular, must have been pleased with the warm reception the German American community gave to the Parade House. Years earlier he had praised the moderately priced restaurants he had visited in German parks, observing, "Many families habitually resort to them for the evening meal, especially when, as was frequently the case, there is the additional attraction of excellent music."[13] Not only were such places pleasant to visit, but also their influence on society in general was, he thought, salubrious.

Regrettably, a year after Vaux's magical building opened, fire nearly destroyed it. Only the southern pavilion of the West Veranda survived the horrific blaze. In June 1878 McMillan informed Olmsted that the park board had hired Cyrus K. Porter, a Buffalo architect, to rebuild the structure. Yet despite a hefty insurance payment, the commissioners were in a parsimonious mood. Writing to Olmsted, McMillan informed him that Porter had been told to make plans "for a building not to cost more over $15,000," far less than half the price of the original. The board members declined to consult Vaux, whose drawings they surely still possessed, because they considered the job "a simple question of detail."[14] Conceding that Porter intended to reproduce the great West Veranda, McMillan felt that, nonetheless, "the whole matter should have been referred to Mr. Vaux." He hoped that Olmsted would intervene before final action was taken on the issue. Whether or not Olmsted spoke up on behalf of his former partner is not known, but in August 1878 reconstruction of the Parade House began under Porter's supervision. The reborn pavilion, which had a smaller restaurant and no tower or observatory, reassumed its role as the center of activity within the park the following spring.[15] (Fig. 4.6)

Throughout the 1880s and early 1890s, the Parade House enjoyed a reputation as a place of popular amusement. "During the summer months the Parade House is visited by thousands of people from all portions of the city," affirmed the *Courier* in 1890. "At the Parade House there was a crowd numbering something like 4000 or 5000 people," stated another reporter a year later. "It was," he observed, "the usual promiscuous pleasure-bent throng which finds its way there every pleasant day." Samuel Clemens's old paper, the *Express,* noted in 1892, "The Parade House, at East Buffalo, is our most popular hot-weather resort for people who like a lively social hour, music and beer." The music of two bands drew people "of all classes, who behave themselves and enjoy the cool evening, the light beverages, the conversation, possibly a little flirting, and the selections from first-class composers."[16] Local chronicler George Bailey listed the Parade House among places the city could view with pride. "Here, one may

Fig. 4.6. Dining hall in the Parade House, 1883. Courtesy James Mendola.

THE BEST PLANNED CITY IN THE WORLD

sit on Sunday, or on the secular days," he wrote, "in the refreshing open air of Buffalo's peculiar exhilarating climate, listening to the strains of sweet music furnished by both an orchestra of stringed instruments and the more martial sound of a brass band." Most of the patrons, Bailey observed, were German Americans, who came with their wives, sweethearts, children, and friends to enjoy the fresh air, good food, and refreshments. To Bailey's sympathetic eye, "the place wears a cosmopolitan aspect, is European in its flavor, and truly American in its gathering."[17]

Various events and spectacles also frequently attracted large crowds to the Parade House. In August 1880 the strains of "God Save the Queen" resonated through the grounds when the city fathers feted visiting dignitaries from Brantford, Ontario, with a "bountiful repast." The next summer, hundreds filled the porches of the West Veranda to watch Company D, a group composed entirely of Civil War veterans, march smartly on the green; in 1891 an amazed crowd of onlookers saw the inventor P. C. Campbell set off on a tour of the city in his proto-blimp "air ship." Two years later, a large audience that had gathered to see daredevil Billy Thomas leap from the roof of the Parade House watched in horror as the famous "aeronaut's" parachute failed to open and he fell to his death.[18]

The ambience that reigned at the Parade House was unmistakably less refined than it was at the boathouse in the Park. This was made abundantly clear from a fictional 1885 account of a visit by a West Side couple, Meg and Marcantonio. After an autumn drive through the Park, where "glimpses of shady paths and dim cool recesses enticed the sight" and "lingering birds were singing their sweetest, and the peace of God's first temples seemed everywhere," the friends came within sight of the Parade. "Suddenly there smote upon the ear a crash of brazen music," says the anonymous narrator who accompanied the pair.

There arose before us a huge building gay with flaunting flags. Many carriages stood before it and a constant stream of people was flowing in its doors.

"What is that?" Meg asked.

"That is the Parade House," Marcantonio answered, trying hard to look unconscious.

"Let us go in," suggested Meg.

After a long silence Marcantonio asked:

"Do you mean—that you—a lady—would like to go in there?"

Now, for some time, Meg, having heard and read so much of the Parade House, had secretly resolved to see that place with her own eyes and not another's. . . . Accordingly she answered stoutly:

"Yes; I want to see what it is like. Why should not I go in? I have been in great beer gardens in Germany and New-York, and as I believe in patronizing home talent and industry."

"Very well," interrupted Marcantonio with the calmness of despair. . . . "We will go in." We entered.

I wish, dear readers, you might have seen my friend Dorothea's face when I told her we had been to the Parade House. I wish you might have seen her aristocratic nose tip heavenward. And you should have heard the icy rigidity of her voice as she said, "I am now prepared anything of you. How could you go to such a horrid—such a common place." But—drawing her chair closer to mine and sinking her voice to a confidential whisper—"tell me, what is it like—*Is it so very dreadful?*"

To their friend, Meg describes her memories of the beer gardens that she, like Olmsted, remembers fondly from a visit to Germany. It was all so "picturesque and artistic," she thinks. But in the end, the Parade House fails to live up to Meg's expectation of encountering a replica of those jovial Continental watering holes. The Parade House Meg judges to be simply "a great barn of a building filled with Americanized Germans and Germanized Americans, with indifferent music, with no interesting accessory of costume or custom—and beyond all, with the peculiar restlessness of America instead of the *dolce far niente* of Germany."[19]

To many, the Parade and the Parade House were too strongly redolent of Old World morality. As this tale suggests, the place had a dubious reputation among Buffalo's Anglo-Saxon Protestant society. They identified the Parade

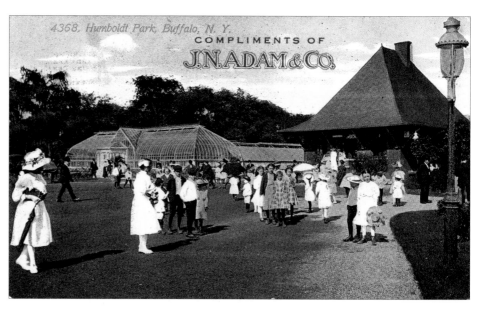

Fig. 4.7. Humboldt Park (formerly the Parade), c. 1920. The red brick shelter that replaced the Parade House is visible at right. Courtesy James Mendola.

House with gamblers, prostitutes, and other lowlifes. Not unexpectedly, when the original building burned, some citizens opposed rebuilding it. "But why give any sort of countenance to the pressure to reestablishing . . . a place of resort, which, popular at first, soon became a public scandal and an open disgrace to the City that owned it and was in fact the landlord?" demanded an editorial.[20] Most often the Parade House was the subject of controversy because beer and wine were served there, even on Sunday. "Don't you drink beer? Didn't you ever drink beer?" asked a German councilman of a colleague during a heated Common Council debate over the issue in 1879. "Yes, when I was a fool," was the curt reply.[21] The Citizens Reform Association often sent "spotters" to the site to report on goings-on there and, in the early 1890s, succeeded in having alcohol banned from the premises. Even so, the reputation of the park itself failed to improve among genteel society. At one point, when land values were rising as the city began to engulf the area, the Common Council contemplated selling the entire property of the park, which some called "a disgrace and a nuisance." The resolution went down to defeat thanks to the efforts of the local councilman, Henry Zipp, who later said that

he would always consider the park "a monument to his efforts as a so-called obstructionist."[22] The demise of the Parade House came in 1903, when the last remnant of this masterpiece of High Victorian architecture was demolished. The present small brick chalet was subsequently erected on the site to designs by a local architect, Robert Wallace. (Fig. 4.7) The Parade House and the high times and low life that it had witnessed faded from recollection.[23]

"A BARREN COMMON"

Treasured by many, disliked by others, the Parade always seemed cast in the role of the neglected errant sister of the Front and the Park. East Side civic leaders often complained that their park received less attention than the others within the system. Insult was compounded by injury in 1896 when the park commissioners promoted a resolution in the Common Council to convert the Parade House into a public bathhouse. To local residents, the commissioners' action suggested that they were more in need of personal hygiene than of

THE BEST PLANNED CITY IN THE WORLD

parks. Nor did McMillan's declaration that the park was in want of an iron fence to keep people of a certain class off the grass sit well.[24] Yet the superintendent's suggestion came in response to a serious problem of vandalism.

By the time the National Guard terminated its use of the parade ground in 1893, the Parade landscape by and large was in a sorry state. In 1894 McMillan bemoaned the fact that "the large green of nearly twenty acres prepared expressly for military maneuvers, is used only as a baseball ground for small amateur clubs mostly composed of boys," adding, "Its usual aspect is that of a barren common." Furthermore, the rest of the park was almost as dreary. "All the most attractive shrubbery was destroyed years ago," McMillan said, "and only the mutilated forms of the more sturdy sorts now remain."[25]

Seeking to reverse the deterioration of the Parade, the park commissioners solicited Olmsted's advice. He responded with a lengthy reply which addressed the nagging problem of vandalism that parks in many cities continually faced. He concurred with the commissioners' assessment that much of the damage to the Parade was due to "the habit which some people have of walking across the ground as suits their convenience, chiefly in taking short cuts, and in such a manner that the turf is trodden out in lines and patches." Unfortunately, he saw the tendency to "sacrifice public to private interests . . . stronger in the public grounds of Buffalo" than in any other city he knew. "If it continues," he warned, "as population in the vicinity of the parks increases, it is but a question of time when the beauty of all your public grounds will be destroyed because of the shabby character of what have been designed to be fields of living green." To halt the destruction, he suggested two remedies. The first was to erect physical barriers to block off short cuts. "Watch for places where a path is beginning to appear," he said, "and as soon as it is seen, [place] obstructions compelling people to avoid walking in these places."[26]

The other method for protecting lawns was to prohibit walking on them. "This is the plan generally adopted in the London Parks where turf has twice the life that it has in Buffalo," Olmsted observed. British authorities bordered walks with iron fences to prevent people from diverging from the footpaths onto the grass. "These detract greatly from the beauty of their scenery," Olmsted admitted, and to adopt this practice in Buffalo would be a last resort of "great misfortune." He firmly believed that it was "most desirable that people should be allowed to make use of the turf if they can be induced to do so only in such a manner as not to tread it to death in streaks and patches." It was especially important, he asserted, that children should be allowed to play on the grass. All it took was "a little skillful management" so that they might do so without injury to the landscape. "Nothing so much needs to be constantly impressed upon the public with respect to the use of pleasure grounds," he affirmed, "as the maxim that 'you cannot have your cake and eat it.'"[27]

REMAKING THE PARADE INTO HUMBOLDT PARK

In a moment of pique provoked by the sad state of the Parade, Olmsted went so far as to suggest that the city relinquish the park and lay out the land in streets and building lots. It was, however, another remark of Olmsted's that would influence the commissioners' future course of action at the Parade. "If you think it best to let a few people through the practice of thoughtlessness, selfishness or improvidence, destroy your turf," he told them, "you ought to have your parks redesigned and re-made in an entirely different fashion, with reference to ideals of beauty and means of refreshment for the people very different from those that have been contemplated in their original design."[28]

In 1895 the city called on Olmsted, Olmsted & Eliot, the name by which Olmsted's firm was known from 1893 to 1897 (the third partner was Olmsted's protégé Charles Eliot), to come up with a revised plan for the Parade. It seems clear from the design that the park commissioners wished to transform the Parade into a far more respectable place than it had been. The new designs, which arrived in Buffalo in January 1896, were greeted with special pleasure by East Side residents. (Fig. 4.8) "They felt that at last the Park Board, which they had considered an enemy to their section of the city and a friend only to the West Side, had taken notice of them, and was going to do something for them," reported the *Express*.[29]

The firm's plans called for the creation of outdoor and indoor flower displays and significant water features consisting of three shallow basins on the former parade ground. The largest of these was a reflecting pool five hundred feet in diameter and nearly five acres in extent, located at the eastern end of the green. (Fig. 4.9) Newfangled electric light standards would ring the basin with a nocturnal necklace of lights, and an opu-

lent candelabra fountain would spray and sparkle in the center. In summer, the shallow water welcomed wading children; in winter, the ice hosted skaters. Between the reflecting pool and a smaller circular basin, the firm placed a 275-foot-long rectangular basin for aquatic plants. (Fig. 4.10) A stone buffalo, carved by Buffalo's own budding young sculptor Charles Cary Rumsey, surveyed the lush lily pond from the center of the far wall. Jets of water animated the third basin (175 feet in diameter), which was apparently intended to be used as a bathing pool. (Fig. 4.11) Together with the construction of these revisions, many new shrubs, trees, and flowerbeds would be planted throughout the park. The Parade had been reinvented, and the strictly decorous character and arrangement of the water features, colorful flowers, and exotic plants signaled the taste for for-

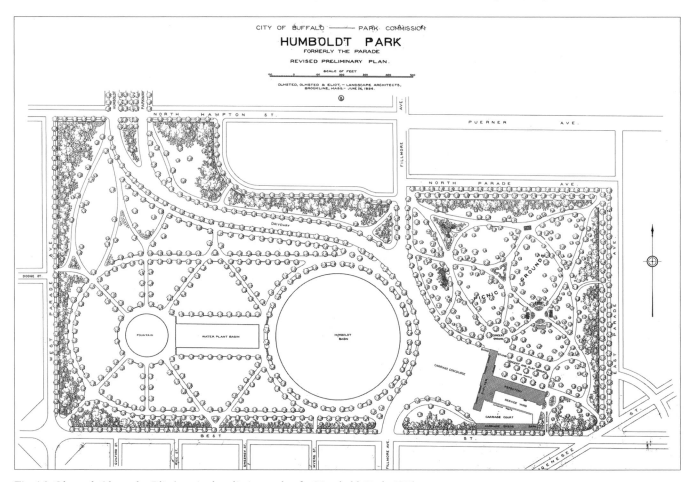

Fig. 4.8. Olmsted, Olmsted & Eliot's revised preliminary plan for Humboldt Park, 1895. Courtesy National Park Service, Frederick Law Olmsted National Historic Site.

THE BEST PLANNED CITY IN THE WORLD

Fig. 4.9. The large basin in Humboldt Park, c. 1900. Courtesy James Mendola.

mality that was fast gaining ground in American park and garden design. Following the Buffalo example, in the early twentieth century the Olmsted firm would install similar basins in other parks, notably Volunteer

Fig. 4.10. Aquatic garden in Humboldt Park, c. 1900. Courtesy James Mendola.

Park and Cal Anderson Park in Seattle and Riverside Park and Forest Park in Springfield, Massachusetts.

Inspiration for the park makeover seems to have come from the example of London's Metropolitan Public Gardens Association. Founded in 1882, the association promoted the creation of gardens and playgrounds in London's underprivileged East End. By 1892 the association had laid out sixty-five attractive gardens. It also lobbied for public gymnasiums and for outdoor public swimming pools. Under the leadership of the earl of Meath, the group and its allies came to exert considerable influence on the redesign of older public parks. Additions to Victoria Park, the major East End park, which had been created as a country park in the 1840s,

Fig. 4.11. Smaller basin with water jets, c. 1900. Courtesy James Mendola.

Humboldt Park, where tuneful concerts were a regular feature at the refurbished Grove, was to be the city's preeminent public garden for several decades to come, a popular attraction visited by the well dressed from all over town. It was enhanced before World War I with the addition of a propagating house and a conservatory designed by the local architectural firm Esenwein & Johnson in 1909. In these gentrified surroundings, flowerbeds, hothouse displays, and lily ponds replaced the greensward that once rang with the sounds of military drills, energetic sports, and crowd-pleasing spectacles. (Figs. 4.12 and 4.13) It is not surprising, then, that the Parade House, the last vestige of Buffalo's beer garden days, after being somewhat upgraded as part of the new work, was soon demolished. "How time goes!" reflected John C. Olmsted on learning of the grand pavilion's ultimate demise. "The boat house in Delaware Park was also designed by Vaux and built probably in 1871–72, or perhaps later," he recalled, "and that decayed and was torn down before the Pan-American [Exposition]. Of course, changes of fashion and other causes had something to do with it in both cases. They could have been kept in repair."[32]

represented the greatest success of their efforts. By the 1890s it had flowerbeds, a conservatory, and a concrete-bottom swimming lake. Surely Olmsted's sons and their associates were aware of the association's principles and its aim to provide the working classes with refined places in which to spend their leisure time. "These garden areas," notes H. L. Malchow, a historian who has written about the organization, "with their labor-intensive ornamental flower beds, were material images of an idealized social order."[30] The Olmsted firm and its clients may also have shared the British view that a pretty park might induce refined behavior and attract more affluent visitors to the neighborhood.

Pleased with the radically new look of the Parade, the proud commissioners took the occasion to change its name. "Instead of 'The Parade' it is now named 'Humboldt Park' to conform to the name of the parkway connecting it to Delaware park," they declared. "No doubt many will unwittingly cling to it for years to come," they grumbled; "therefore, there is more need that in all reference hereafter to this Park, by intelligent persons, the new name only should be used."[31] Apparently relieved that the landscape to which so many dubious associations adhered had been erased from the city's topography, they were eager as well to erase its name from the city's collective memory.

TWENTIETH-CENTURY TRANSITIONS

Major change came to Humboldt Park once again in the late 1920s, when the city chose the northwest corner as the location for a science museum. The large Neoclassical building designed by Esenwein & Johnson filled the park's foremost entrance at Humboldt Parkway.[33] Together with City Hall and the New York Central Terminal, the Buffalo Museum of Science was one of three major buildings in the city either begun or opened in the fateful year 1929. They soon became monuments

Fig. 4.12. Humboldt Park flower beds, c. 1900. Courtesy Catherine Schweitzer.

Fig. 4.13. Carpet bedding display, Humboldt Park, c. 1900. Courtesy James Mendola.

East Side. After World War II, upwardly mobile Poles abandoned the area for the suburbs. Their place was taken mainly by African Americans coming north in search of work during the Great Migration. In recognition of the changed neighborhood population, Humboldt Park was rededicated in 1976 as Martin Luther King Jr. Park, and the city erected a sculptural monument to the great civil rights leader near the south-central entrance.

The rest of the park, however, had suffered from a severe lack of attention. The beautiful flowers were gone (except inside the surviving greenhouse), few trees of any girth grew except in the southeastern section, the great basin was dry year round, and the lily pond had become a lawn forlornly presided over by Rumsey's eroding buffalo. Basketball courts with bleachers had obliterated the round bathing pond, and a stark brick casino erected in 1926 between the lily pond and wading basin had been closed and vandalized.

Despite the sad later history of the Parade, it has not lacked for advocates. In 1982, after the park was deemed to possess nearly 80 percent of the original elements of the two historic plans, it received listing in the National Register of Historic Places.[34] Nonetheless, eight years later, the city erected a large public school behind the museum and laid out a sizable parking lot along the western border. More recently, the Olmsted Parks Conservancy has developed a master plan to bring back many of the elements of the 1896 plan, including the great basin.

to a vanishing prosperity as heavy industry and transportation began to abandon the city.

By the Great Depression, German influence in the life of the East Side was a spent force. Kaisertown had come to be known as Polonia, as working-class Polish immigrants outnumbered German residents on the

FIVE

Parkways, Circles, and Squares

If an artist had *carte blanche* . . . [and] the good fortune to be able to plan a future city, I would recommend the study of the beautiful plan of the able American landscape architect Mr. F. Law Olmsted for the city of Buffalo. The diverse parts of town are bound together by a system of parks and shaded boulevards that is most grand and sensible. —Édouard André, *L'Art des jardins,* 1879

In the spring of 1876 Olmsted wrote to William F. Rogers, who was then secretary of the Buffalo park commission, explaining his plan to prepare a map and several characteristic views of the Buffalo park system for the Centennial Exhibition being held later that year in Philadelphia. In addition to showing the location of recreation grounds, the map would highlight the city's exceptional "convenience of street arrangements." The map and explanatory text would illustrate how Olmsted and Vaux's "late additions" of the parkways to Joseph Ellicott's original plan of wide radial "trunk thoroughfares" combined to make the city a model of urban engineering. "Whether used for pleasure travel, or for general traffic," Olmsted declared, "the fortunate location and liberal width of the trunk thoroughfares of the older portion of the city most happily exemplify the

wise forethought of Mr. Ellicott. The parkways provide equally liberal accommodation for travel through the newer sections, and simply supplement the original plan in fit accordance with the general design." This included the "advantages which the city will possess in respect to fire risks, the parkways having an important bearing in this regard."[1] Presumably he meant that, as with Haussmann's Paris boulevards, the exceptional width and geographical span of the parkways would speed the arrival of emergency vehicles to scenes of trouble. For the same reasons, they might also serve to limit the spread of building fires, one of the now forgotten menaces of earlier urban life. Together with the parks, the system of parkways, circles, squares, and avenues one hundred feet wide would serve as a example to other cities of how to promote the public well-being through thoughtful planning.

Buffalo was justifiably proud of being lauded by Olmsted as "the best planned city in the United States, if not the world." In September 1881 the *Express* published its own updated version of Olmsted's vision of the city.[2] The pamphlet included a color-coded map titled *Olmsted's Sketch Map of Buffalo,* which graphically depicted how the entire vast low-density residen-

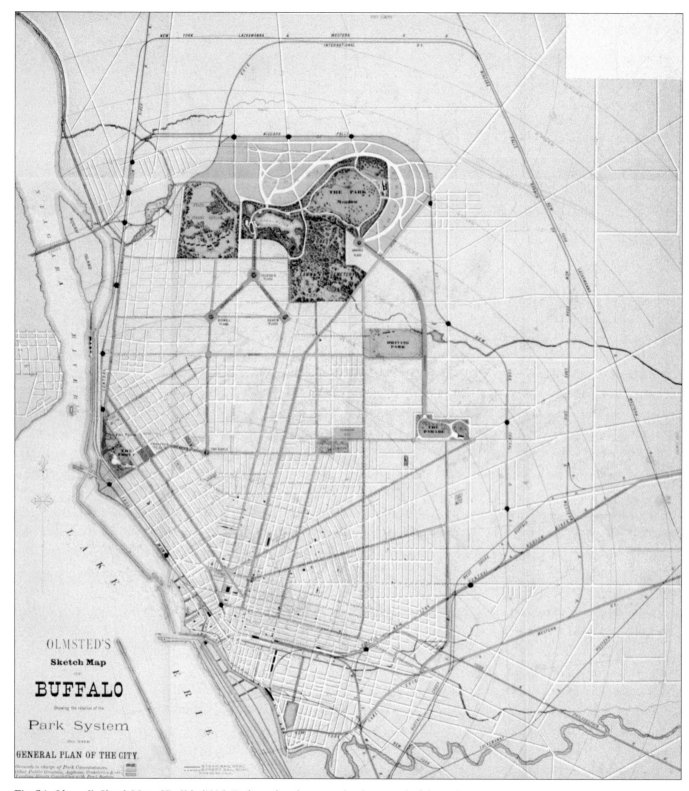

Fig. 5.1. *Olmsted's Sketch Map of Buffalo* (1881). Parks and parkways under the control of the park commissioners were indicated in green. Other public spaces and streets that coordinated with the parks and parkways were shown in purple. Author's collection.

THE BEST PLANNED CITY IN THE WORLD

tial quarter that was developing around the park and parkway system in the northern part of the city was integrated with the older lakefront city by means of extending preexisting streets. (Fig. 5.1) As if to emphasize how convenient it had become for people to work in one part of town and reside in another, the map highlighted streetcar and passenger rail lines. The text enumerated the significant efforts that the park commissioners had made in the past eleven years to realize Olmsted's far-reaching plans. During that time the city had spent $375,000 for land and $875,000 for improvements. This money had funded one of the most extensive construction projects in the country. Six hundred acres of parkland and twelve miles of parkways and avenues had been "worked over and graded," all soil in the parks had been "deepened and enriched" so that good turf could be established, surface and subdrainage systems—including a bypass which ensured that sewage from Scajaquada Creek would not enter Gala Water—had been installed throughout the park system, sewer and water lines laid, and "permanent macadam" surfaces had been constructed on all drives and paths.[3] Moreover, the commissioners had undertaken the greening of the new cityscape. Nearly 75,000 trees and shrubs, embracing four hundred different species, had been planted in their jurisdiction.[4] In addition to paved and well-lit streets, water lines, and sewers, Buffalo residents in the 1880s began to make use of natural gas (abundant in the area) for heating and lighting their homes. "During this marvelous decade," remarked a local witness, "it seemed as if nature, as well as man, was conspiring to do its best for the coming metropolis of Western New York."[5]

By the mid-1890s the city Olmsted had envisioned when he first began to plan its future had fulfilled his promise. Almost 20 percent of the city's area was given over to parkland, amid nineteen miles of parkways and boulevards. "These are magnificent wide avenues," reported a local magazine, "running around the outskirts of the city between almost continuous rows of majestic shade trees." (Fig. 5.2)

Fig. 5.2. Lincoln Parkway, c. 1900. Author's collection.

These thoroughfares were also a marvel of modern street engineering. In 1882 the city began to pave parkways and streets with Trinidad asphalt—gravel bound together with bitumen from a lake in Trinidad. It was considered, after granite block paving, the most durable road surface, and according its promoters it eradicated "the almost unbearable din" of wagon wheels and horseshoes, lessened wear and tear on vehicles, and improved street sanitation. Of special importance to the new parkway neighborhoods was that it also raised residential real estate values. A local writer observed that "an avenue of mansions is ugly if paved with antiquated stone blocks," whereas asphalt paving "marks the beginning of a real estate boom." By 1890 Buffalo was able to boast that it had more asphalt-surfaced roadways than any other city in the world. Visitors to the Pan-American Exposition of 1901 were told that they would never fully appreciate the city's many attractive features "until they have enjoyed a noiseless ride over its smooth asphalt pavements."[6] (Fig. 5.3)

Users of public transportation were just as well served as vehicle owners. The Belt Line railroad encircled the city, linking the parks and residential areas in the northern suburbs to the downtown commercial and lakefront industrial quarters. In 1896 electricity began

Fig. 5.3. Richmond Avenue, one of the many asphalt-surfaced road-ways in Buffalo, c. 1886. From H. Perry Smith, *History of the City of Buffalo and Erie County* (1908).

Fig. 5.4. The Chapin Parkway home of General John C. Graves (1885; demolished), who succeeded McMillan as park superintendent, was typical of the large dwellings that went up along the park approaches in the late nineteenth century. From Frank H. Severance, *Picture Book of Earlier Buffalo* (1912).

to be transmitted from new power plants at nearby Niagara Falls. (Nikola Tesla, the inventor of alternating current, predicted, "Niagara power will make Buffalo the greatest city in the world.")[7] The city soon developed an extensive electric trolley system; by 1897 there were over 150 miles of electric rail lines in the city, and another 50 miles were projected for the following year. Service was not only clean and reliable but also cheap. For a single fare of five cents, a passenger could circulate anywhere in town and at all hours of the day or night. Moreover, service extended beyond the city limits. "Buffalo is now the center of an electric road ganglion of extensive proportion," noted a well-informed contemporary. Nearly every town and village of any importance on the Niagara Frontier was accessible by these now vanished means.[8]

With this fine infrastructure in place, the city was filling out as Olmsted and the original park promoters had foreseen it would. "Workingmen no longer hesitated to mortgage their future to pay for suburban homes," observed a contemporary, "and the character of the growth of the vast districts north and northwest and east of Buffalo was defined to be the growth of a city of homes."[9] (Fig. 5.4) The area above North Street, between Main on the east and The Avenue on the west,

became the locale of many fine middle-class dwellings. This area, proclaimed businessman George Bailey, was the residential section "of which the city can with most reason be proud."[10] What had been largely open ground from North Street to the Park was by the mid-1890s known in real estate lingo as the Elmwood District. It drew its name from Elmwood Avenue, the broad thoroughfare that ran through the area, between and parallel with The Avenue and Delaware Avenue. "The rapidity with which this [area] has filled up with splendid homes is one of the most striking evidences of Buffalo's recent stride towards a city of gigantic size," a local observer boasted. Another declared that it was "doubtful whether any section of any city in the world has ever filled up with new homes so quickly."[11] These were all "big, solid houses, each standing on its own lawn and having flowers about it in the summer," recalled Mabel Dodge Luhan, who knew the newly minted neighborhoods as a youngster in the 1880s and 1890s, long before she became the spirited patron of modern artists.[12]

Although the equestrians and trolleys are gone and the stately elms have disappeared from Elmwood Avenue, this part of town still preserves much of its original character and is now looked upon as a historic neighborhood. "There is a strong tendency in our civilization to

THE BEST PLANNED CITY IN THE WORLD

build parts of towns with reference . . . strictly to business," Olmsted reflected at the end of the 1880s, "and to build other parts of the same towns with reference . . . to the enjoyment of life apart from business and in such a manner that more and more ground shall be appropriated to a given number of houses. . . . The effect of the tendency on the whole will be to spread out the domestic parts of a town and to include in the idea of a town a much larger proportion than at present of decidedly *rus-urban* elements."[13]

Moreover, as Olmsted and Vaux had predicted, the park and parkway system brought a rise in property values. Indeed, the late 1870s and 1880s became a period of rapid and dramatic price increases for land, especially in the new West Side residential districts beyond North Street. A contemporary testified that numerous land speculators "rose from poverty to wealth in the five years from 1876 to 1881, and have been getting richer ever since."[14] Another observer agreed, noting, "All Buffalo land was good buying, and the good buyers were not long in coming." This flow of assets raised many boats, large and small, for the opportunities to make money extended beyond the rich. "Those of small resources," remarked the same author, "banded themselves into land companies and, uniting their wealth, acquired as corporations the purchasing power of wealthy men, and so got equal chances to profit by the wonderful advances in prices."[15] Of course, the city was pleased with these developments, for they swelled the coffers of the treasury with increased tax revenues.

Construction of the new parkways was initiated in tandem with the construction of the parks. In 1873 Chapin Place, Chapin Parkway, Soldiers Place, and Lincoln Parkway were in a condition to be officially opened, and the following year, Agassiz Place, Humboldt Parkway, Bidwell Place, and Bidwell Parkway started to accept limited traffic. By 1876 the commissioners had laid out twelve miles of the parkways and connecting avenues that Olmsted and Vaux had drawn on the map of their city. (This included East Side Boulevard, now Fillmore Avenue, which the commissioners had added to Olmsted and Vaux's original scheme by 1872.) Though functioning by the centennial year, the parkway system was far from finished at that time; like the trees along parkway borders, the system would take many years to reach maturity.[16] When Olmsted saw the parkways in their infancy, secured from their undeveloped surroundings by ranks of sentinel saplings, he remarked that "in due time, when these trees shall be more fully grown, their stately aspect and pleasing shade will be prominent features of the Park scheme."[17] Locals quipped that travelers on the new boulevards might accumulate real estate in the form of dust.

THE PARK APPROACHES

The most important of the new parkways were the four boulevards, each two hundred feet wide, that funneled traffic from downtown, the West Side, and the East Side to the Park. In the aggregate they covered three miles. These park approaches McMillan described as "suitably embellished with wide strips of green turf and several rows of shade trees, each tree uniform in age, in species, and in distance apart, with other trees in the same row."[18] The nexus of three of the West Side park approaches was Soldiers Place, a circle seven hundred feet in diameter that was the proposed location of a military monument.[19] Beginning at Bidwell Place (now Colonial Circle), Bidwell Parkway connected Soldiers Place with The Avenue (now Richmond Avenue).[20] Starting at Chapin Place (now Gates Circle), Chapin Parkway linked Delaware Avenue, the main route to the Park from the center city, to Soldiers Place, from where Lincoln Parkway proceeded northward to the main entrance to the Park south of Gala Water.[21] The nearly two-mile-long Humboldt Parkway conducted traffic through the East Side from the Parade to the entrance to the Park at Agassiz Place in the southeast corner of the meadow. In coming decades, the park approaches, on which heavy wagon traffic was prohibited, would develop into the finest residential addresses.

Humboldt Parkway, which opened to limited use in 1873, came to be regarded as one the most beautiful streets in America. (Fig. 5.5) Six rows of trees shaded this linear park, which Olmsted and Vaux chose to plant with linden and tulip trees rather than with the elms that lined the other parkways. Nineteenth-century horticulturists found that these two trees shared a similar style of foliage. The linden (the American variety is called basswood), which develops a dense round head above a bare trunk, did well in cities. The tulip or whitewood tree, according to McMillan "a magnificent native tree of tall, pyramidal habit," also develops a bare trunk for some distance above the ground; it has glossy green leaves and bears a profusion of pretty white flowers in spring.[22]

When, in 1876, the renowned French landscape architect Édouard André, who had worked closely with Alphand and Haussmann in the rebuilding of Paris, took Olmsted's advice and visited Buffalo, he was greatly impressed by the nascent boulevard. Olmsted and Vaux were surely pleased to read his glowing account of their work in André's monumental volume *L'Art des jardins: traité general de la composition des parcs et jardins,* which was published in Paris three years later.[23] Humboldt Parkway was one of the *avenues-parterre,* André's word for parkway, which, he said, surpassed anything in Europe. Such streets, which he had seen in Chicago, Boston, and Buffalo, were "less like avenues and more like promenades." André applauded Olmsted and Vaux for their wise insistence that their parkways be lined with a single species of tree. These monoculture urban vistas, which are out of favor with modern-day landscape architects, provided a unity and grandness of effect that mixed plantings could never achieve, André maintained. By contrast, in Philadelphia he had been displeased to see streets where the city had allowed the inhabitants to plant whatever trees they wished in front of their houses. "The result," he said, "is the most grotesque *mélange,* and the boulevards thus embellished have a most disgraceful appearance."[24]

Humboldt Parkway impressed André most of all. He praised it for its spaciousness and grandeur and gave his readers a detailed description of it, with diagrams. As instructive as André's diagrams were, no plan on a page could convey the splendor of the urban forest that Humboldt Parkway would become. Historic photographs confirm the assertion that it was once indeed one of the nation's most fine-looking avenues. "I walked under the shadow roof of the beautiful trees in Humboldt parkway, enjoying the pulsating life of the city revealed in the uninterrupted flow of traffic," wrote the German-born city planner Walter Curt Behrendt in 1937. "Many a European city would envy Buffalo for her wide, spacious avenues bordered by such beautiful trees."[25] (Fig. 5.6)

A middle-class neighborhood of comfortable houses and handsome churches, the Humboldt Parkway address, however, never achieved the aura of wealth that Lincoln Parkway and the West Side approaches did. Perhaps for this reason, in the 1960s city lead-

Fig. 5.5. Humboldt Parkway, c. 1910. Author's collection.

THE BEST PLANNED CITY IN THE WORLD

Fig. 5.6. Humboldt Parkway, c. 1910. Courtesy Buffalo and Erie County Historical Society.

ers decided, as many feel today about the Front Park area, that the distinguished boulevard and its surrounding neighborhood were expendable. As in many other places, a sense of history and an appreciation for urban life were absent from the city's political circles. Transportation, one of the major forces that built the city, would now begin to destroy it. In the early 1960s Humboldt Parkway and its magnificent stand of mature trees were sacrificed to a highway system linking the suburbs to downtown. Photographs showing ranks of decapitated tree trunks awaiting removal record (to borrow a phrase from André) a most disgraceful appearance. The demise of Humboldt Parkway was the most egregious of many insults that the park and parkway system was to suffer in the latter half of the twentieth century.

The West Side Approaches

In 1875 McMillan reported that the one thousand elms that had been planted on most of the parkways and The Avenue had "shown vigorous growth."[26] The "waving elm" had been a favorite tree of Olmsted's since his New England childhood. McMillan thought that "for shade and purposes of nobleness of stature there is no tree in the north which equals or excels the American elm. Its

great height and spreading, drooping branches place it above all rivals."[27] André, whom McMillan had shown around Buffalo in 1876, had also praised the elm as a street tree. "When the elms attain their full development," he wrote, "they are the most noble and beautiful tree."[28] Yet most of the elms that had been planted along Paris streets since the time of Jean-Baptiste Colbert, the French minister of finance under Louis XIV, who had also championed this species, had by André's day been killed by insects. Although a similar fate would begin to claim the urban American elm as early as the 1890s, the great stands that turned Buffalo's parkways into impressive cathedrals of green endured well into the twentieth century. (Fig. 5.7) Sadly, by the 1970s most of them had succumbed to the devastation wrought by Dutch elm disease. (Leaking gas mains and poor paving practices also caused the death of many trees.)

The longest of the West Side approaches was The Avenue (now Richmond Avenue). (Fig. 5.8) One hundred feet wide, the street runs for a little more than a mile from the Circle (now Symphony Circle) at its southern end to Bidwell Place (now Colonial Circle), where it joins the two-hundred-foot-wide parkway approaches to the Park. Yet although it opened in 1873 and by the following year two rows of young elms had been planted on either side of the carriageway and sidewalks, it would be a while into the future before The Avenue attracted homeowners. In 1880, by which time the thoroughfare

Fig. 5.7. Mature elms along Delaware Avenue, 1939. Courtesy Buffalo State College.

Fig. 5.8. Richmond Avenue (formerly The Avenue), c. 1890. Author's collection.

had been renamed Richmond Avenue (apparently in honor of Buffalo's Dean Richmond, one of the founders of the New York Central Railroad), the roadway was still dirt and was nearly impassable in wet weather.[29] Finally, in 1885, the municipal foot-dragging ended. "The most important work of the year," proclaimed McMillan in his annual report, "has been the paving of Richmond Avenue . . . with 'Barber's Trinidad Asphalt.' "[30]

During the 1890s and into the early twentieth century, Richmond Avenue became home to upper-middle-class families who built the large Queen Anne and Neoclassical style dwellings, many of which still line its borders. Because lots were only thirty feet wide, however, it never evolved into a street of mansions to rival Delaware Avenue, where properties were much bigger. Nonetheless, during Buffalo's snowy winters the long, straight avenue often became an informal racecourse favored by the city's equestrian class. The spectacle, one resident remembered, included "beautiful, well-bred

high-strung race horses complete with fine special equipment." (Fig. 5.9) The street turned into a "gorgeous festival of sleighs, bells and furs." Between events, lightweight open sleighs for one or two people, called cutters, "went along the raceway or on the side streets, their occupants swathed in sealskin caps, mittens, boots with black lynx and buffalo robes."[31] In better weather early bicyclists adopted the street as their own, until the automobile took over and effectively banished all earlier forms of transportation. Providentially for Buffalo, which has lost many former middle-class residents to suburbia, in recent years this gracious street has begun to make a comeback as a desirable in-town address. (Fig. 5.10) Sadly, the elms that McMillan planted and that once overarched Richmond Avenue, turning it into an emerald summertime passageway, have disappeared.

The preeminent address in the new city was Delaware Avenue (before 1879 called Delaware Street), the radial boulevard that Ellicott named in honor of one of the native American tribes that had inhabited the area.

Fig. 5.9. In winter, Richmond Avenue was a favorite location for sleigh races. Photograph, 1895. Courtesy Buffalo and Erie County Historical Society.

THE BEST PLANNED CITY IN THE WORLD

Fig. 5.11. Delaware Avenue in the 1880s. *Harper's New Monthly Magazine* (July 1885).

Fig. 5.10. View down Richmond Avenue at Ferry Circle. Photograph by Andy Olenick.

(Fig. 5.11) In Olmsted and Vaux's scheme the thoroughfare assumed the role of the principal and most direct link to the Park from the center of town. By the centennial year Olmsted could report that it was "lined throughout its entire length by villas and gardens and shaded by trees already voluntarily planted by their owners."[32] Millard Fillmore, William Dorsheimer, and Samuel Clemens had made their homes here, as had many other locally prominent men and women. By the end of the nineteenth century, the stretch from Niagara Square to Chapin Place (now Gates Circle) became known as one of America's grandest avenues. "The Delaware Avenue of my early days was the champion street of the United States," recalled A. Conger Goodyear (1877–1964), who in later life founded the Museum of Modern Art. "Further west in Cleveland," Goodyear said, "Euclid Avenue had some pretensions, but we did not admit a great rivalry." When Goodyear's parents moved to the avenue in 1879, the "great elm arched street" was increasingly attracting citizens of wealth who wished to affirm their success in life by erecting an imposing dwelling.[33] The high-class street, with wide carriageway, sidewalks shaded by double rows of elms, and spacious lawns fronting all properties, was the perfect setting for such self-assured architecture, which ran the gamut of popular styles. Some of the homes were designed by well-known out-of-town firms, while many others were built by talented designers whose names stood out in local annals, such as Green & Wicks, Bley & Lyman, and Edward A. Kent.

The decade of the 1890s, especially, was a golden age for the city, and the avenue embodied completely its dream of attainment. Among the neighbors whom Goodyear grew up knowing were Cicero J. Hamlin, a nationally prominent racehorse owner; John G. Milburn, a lawyer who would bring the Pan-American Exposition to Buffalo, and in whose home President William McKinley would die after being shot while attending the exposition; William J. Connors, owner of the *Courier;* Wilson S. Bissell, postmaster general under Grover Cleveland; Eldridge Gerry Spaulding, the congressman who became known as the "Father of the Greenback"; George

Cary, the first Buffalo architect to study at the École des Beaux-Arts in Paris, and his aunt Maria Love, who corresponded frequently with Olmsted; the Rumsey family, who together with the Carys were considered the social arbiters of the time; Dr. Roswell Park, an internationally known surgeon who founded the nation's first cancer treatment center; Seymour H. Knox, founding partner with his cousin of the Woolworth stores and a patron of

the arts; S. V. R. Watson, builder of many of Buffalo's now vanished trolley lines and patron of the artist John LaFarge; Jacob F. Schoelkopf, father of hydroelectric power generation at Niagara Falls; George L. Williams, a successful banker who asked McKim, Mead & White to design the grandest of four houses the firm built in town; and William Gratwick, a steamboat magnate who commissioned the last residence that H. H. Richardson was to design. (Figs. 5.12 and 5.13)

Second only to Delaware Avenue as an address of consequence, Lincoln Parkway required all houses to be set back fifty feet from the street line; thus one's front door was three hundred feet from the neighbor's entrance across the way. (Fig. 5.14) Lined with six rows of elms, this majestic drive to the Park featured a central carriageway flanked by a bridle path and a bicycle path. At the outer margins of the boulevard, narrow service roadways provided access to residences; all-weather footpaths allowed pedestrians the same unimpeded movement that the "separation of ways" offered them within Olmsted and Vaux's parks.[34] Rules were also in place to ensure that future development along this and all the parkways would be consistent with the existing

Fig. 5.12. North Street at Delaware Avenue. The house designed for George L. Williams by McKim, Mead & White (1894) is at the right. Library of Congress, Prints and Photographs Division, Detroit Publishing Company Collection.

Fig. 5.13. The Delaware Avenue residence that Richardson designed for William Gratwick in 1885–86 (demolished), shown here in a photograph taken around 1900, was the architect's last major commission. Author's collection.

Fig. 5.14. This view of Lincoln Parkway around 1910 shows how Olmsted and Vaux's parkways separated various types of traffic: vehicles in the central carriageway, horseback riders on the adjacent bridle paths, and pedestrians on outer sidewalks. Between the bridle paths and pedestrian walks, a service road gave access to houses bordering the parkway. Author's collection.

THE BEST PLANNED CITY IN THE WORLD

high standards. "Restrictions as to the minimum cost, the purposes for which buildings are to be used and their location at a uniform distance from the street line," reported the *Courier,* "are imposed as a protection to all against the reception of unsightly buildings."[35]

Fillmore Avenue

From the very beginning of the park system, Olmsted had urged the city to create a parkway running south from the Parade through the largely German East Side of town. In 1872 the state legislature passed a law transforming the former Adams Street into a parkway under the control of the park commissioners. The new thoroughfare would make it much more convenient for the less well-to-do residents of the East Side to reach the Parade and from there the Park. The Common Council, however, was slow to fund the undertaking. To those who complained that the new street would cost the city too much, the *Courier,* now firmly converted to Olmsted's way of thinking, noted that even in the low-income Cottage District of the city, the new boulevard would "give direction to the improvement of real estate and add very largely to the assessed value of the land." The East Side German community, which was contributing tax dollars to support a park system that was largely inaccessible to it, strongly favored the enterprise. Stiff opposition to creating the new street, however, came from more well-heeled West Side voters. Championing the former group, the *Courier* characterized the project as "a plan of improvement which is demanded by a large and influential class of citizens, and which we believe is for the interests of the tax-payers of the whole city, as well as a matter of geographical justice in connection with the Park system."[36]

The city's better angels eventually carried the day. In 1874 the new boulevard, which was named Fillmore Avenue in honor of the former president, who had died in March of that year, opened for a mile and a quarter between the Parade and William Street, where a railroad passenger station and new residential neighborhood were about to be constructed.[37] Like The Avenue on the West Side, the new tree-lined street, which was sometimes referred to as the East Side Boulevard, was one hundred feet wide with a fifty-foot roadway and four-foot-wide plank pedestrian walks.[38]

Surrounded by controversy at its birth, Fillmore Avenue endured a troubled history. One doubts that it ever saw "the gay and international procession of coaches, landaus, dog-carts, and English phaetons" that *Harper's* reported thronging the other parkways in town.[39] Indeed Olmsted, who had nothing to do with its design or layout, rejected it as a true element of the parkway system. In 1887, when he was considering the proposition to create a new waterside park in the southern part of town, Olmsted disparagingly referred to the avenue, which crossed two busy rail lines at grade, as having been created as an extension of the original park system by order of the Common Council. "Such a road is certainly not adopted to pleasure travel," he insisted. To his mind, Fillmore Avenue differed "in no respect from other ordinary tree-bordered avenues of the city."[40]

To be sure, heavy commercial traffic regularly clogged the roadway at the southern end (below William Street), and the entire thoroughfare was subject to noisome usage. "Cattle, horses, goats or pigs are continually roaming at large on some portions of the avenue," McMillan complained in 1882, "and in addition large droves of animals from the stock-yards are almost daily driven through it." Furthermore, stray horses and goats, as well as horses illegally hitched to trees, gnawed the bark off trunks, destroying ten to twenty trees every year. Animals also damaged the grass plots along the margins, and drivers ran their teams on the sidewalks at will. "And, worst of all," lamented McMillan, "I have seen very little evidence, among the residents or property owners on the avenue, of any public spirit, private taste, or personal regard for these improvements, sufficient to afford me any aid in preventing the continuance of such careless mishaps and wanton destruction."[41] Finally, businesses and saloons vied with houses for addresses on the prominent new avenue. Eventually, by the early twentieth century, commercial development along the northern portion of the street and industrial and railroad development south of William Street made it impossible for the park commissioners to maintain Fillmore Avenue as a parkway.

Scajaquada Parkway

It is remarkable to see how attached Buffalo became to the parkway-and-circles concept that Olmsted and Vaux first introduced to the city in 1870. Every new large park that was proposed after that date had a parkway approach included in the scheme. And in the case of South Side parks, parkways were considered as important as, if not more important than, the parks themselves for the future growth and development of the surrounding areas. This "parkway mania" had partly to do with the fact that the public treasury would absorb half of the construction costs, as well as the awareness of private investors that they were a means to obtain higher profits from the sale of lots and homes. They had learned their lesson well from Olmsted's instruction. There also seems to have been a genuine sense of civic pride that favored the creation of these new and gracious thoroughfares. In the 1890s and early 1900s, books and articles began to appear both locally and nationally calling attention to the beauty of the city's residential areas. (Fig. 5.15)

In the late 1890s the park commissioners undertook the construction of a new parkway that was planned without the presence of houses along its borders. It hugged the south bank of Scajaquada Creek from the western edge of Delaware Park to Grant Street. The city intended that the road would eventually be extended to link the older park with the new Riverside Park, which the Olmsted firm was designing along the

Fig. 5.15. Lincoln Parkway with its canopy of American elms, c. 1945. Author's collection.

Niagara River in the Black Rock section of town. The commissioners, however, seem not to have consulted the Olmsteds on the design of the new thoroughfare, which they called the Scajaquada Parkway. Nonetheless, the wide pleasure drive echoed the pattern that Olmsted and Vaux had established in their 1870 plans for original parkways and park approaches. (Fig. 5.16) Following a gently curving course, it wound its way across the northern edge of the grounds of the Buffalo State

Fig. 5.16. Scajaquada Parkway, c. 1905. Courtesy James Mendola.

THE BEST PLANNED CITY IN THE WORLD

Hospital (the state had donated land from the institution's farm for the road) and provided separate ways for vehicles, horseback riders, and pedestrians. Specifically, McMillan noted, "the plan . . . provides for a footpath 10 feet wide near the water margin, a ride 20 feet wide next to the state land border, and a central drive 40 feet wide, each to be bordered and separated by planting spaces of about equal width."[42] To this program the commissioners soon added a bicycle path.

Grading and filling for the new road began in 1894. In the late winter of that year, during the depths of another economic depression that had gripped the country, McMillan reported that the park board and a local charitable organization had pooled their resources in order to employ a large labor force for two weeks on building the new roadway. At the time, McMillan still cherished the hope that the creek could be turned into a navigable channel and be used, as Olmsted and Vaux had intended, by "water craft carrying passengers to and from the Park and the whole water front of the city." But, he warned, if precautions were not taken both in planning the area where the parkway joined the park and in designing a new bridge to carry Elmwood Avenue over the parkway near that point, serious damage could be done to the little bay beyond the dam holding back the waters of the park lake.[43] This unobtrusive body of water Olmsted and Vaux had envisioned as the landing area for boats arriving from and departing for town. Sadly, boats never ferried passengers between downtown and Delaware Park.[44]

RESIDENTIAL SQUARES AND CIRCLES

Another significant feature of the system borrowed from French urban planning were the numerous cir-

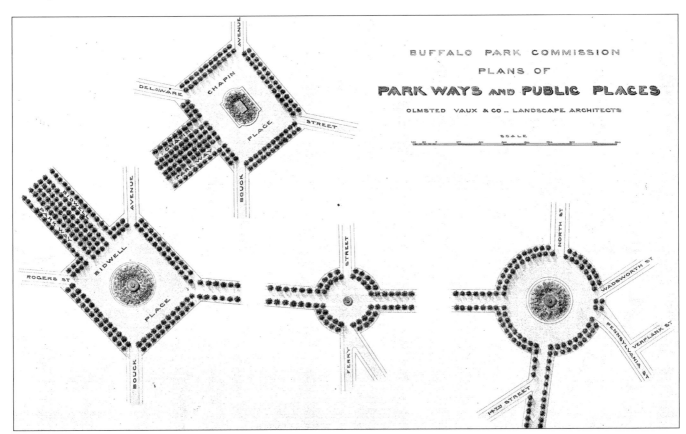

Fig. 5.17. Olmsted, Vaux & Company, plans for squares and places, c. 1870. Courtesy National Park Service, Frederick Law Olmsted National Historic Site.

cles and squares that Olmsted and Vaux introduced at major junctions throughout the system. (Fig. 5.17) The designers gave these urban residential squares a more formal character than they thought appropriate to the parks. Each of the new squares would be surrounded by large freestanding homes—*maisons particuliers,* the French would have called them—facing toward the center of the space, which would be ornamented with a basin or a fountain.

Soldiers Place, Bidwell Place, and Chapin Place

The hub of the tripartite group of parkway approaches to the Park was Soldiers Place, which Olmsted and Vaux first referred to as the Central Circle. (Fig. 5.18) Inspired by the example of the Place d'Étoile in Paris, with its celebrated arch commemorating Napoleon's military victories, Soldiers Place was, as its name implies, intended as a monument to local members of the armed forces killed in the Civil War and earlier conflicts. Even before Olmsted and Vaux prepared their plans for Buffalo, city, county, and private donors had contributed $20,000 toward the memorial. "With that sum," observed a local journalist, "it would not be difficult to command at the hands of the greatest living sculptors, a group in marble or bronze, which would at once express the sentiment of patriotic gratitude, and stand to the future ages as a memorial of the city's taste and liberality."[45] The future monument was also envisioned as having "a massive stone shaft of considerable height."[46] The challenge for the landscape architects would be to create an appropriate setting for such an object.

The fact that Soldiers Place sits at the juncture of the three broad parkways determined its exceptional spaciousness. As the intention was to locate a monument in the center of

the 700-foot site, Olmsted and Vaux originally laid out a circular grass plot some 320 feet in diameter, ringed with a carriage drive 100 feet wide. The arrangement would have allowed for any monument to be "viewed to best advantage at a considerable distance off," noted the park commissioners. Furthermore, the width of the encircling drive afforded "ample room for vehicles to stop or move leisurely from point to point, while the occupants examined the monument without interrupting or being interrupted by the general stream of travel."[47]

By 1874, however, the city had decided to erect the war memorial in Niagara Square. Consequently, the commissioners asked Olmsted for advice on what should be done with the original Soldiers Place. "Upon mature consideration," he replied, "I am decidedly of the opinion that each of the changes which have been suggested in it, including those I have myself advanced, would greatly injure its value in your park system." He was, however, certain that "a few narrow ribbons or diminutive beds of flowers will seem paltry in a large place." Instead, he thought the best thing to do for the present would be simply to "enlarge the great grass circular centerpiece so as to reduce the width of the roadway to 50 feet" and leave the question of an appropriate

Fig. 5.18. Soldiers Place with the entrance to Lincoln Parkway in the distance, c. 1910. Courtesy James Mendola.

THE BEST PLANNED CITY IN THE WORLD

Fig. 5.19. Lafayette Square with George Keller's Soldiers and Sailors Monument (1882) in the center. The Olmsted firm provided the landscape plan. Photograph, c. 1905. Library of Congress, Prints and Photographs Division, Detroit Publishing Company Collection.

centerpiece for a later date. (The drawing he included to show how grading and finishing might be done is now lost.) "Any other inexpensive arrangement that I can devise while it would be satisfactory in itself would, I fear, seem to preclude a satisfactory arrangement for the future and would thus bear the stamp of blundering," he concluded.[48]

In 1882 the notion of a war memorial in Niagara Square was scrapped, and the present Soldiers and Sailors column went up in Lafayette Square. (Fig. 5.19) The desire to honor the martial life in Soldiers Place,

however, endured into the twentieth century. In 1908 several large cannons took up position beneath the elegant lampposts that lit the central grass pad; but once automobiles became common, peace-loving drivers regarded the cannons as a hazard to passage, and the city removed them. This action also put an end to the sport that young hooligans enjoyed of rolling down Lincoln Parkway the lead balls that stood by in readiness.[49]

Bidwell Place (now Colonial Circle) is only slightly less grand than Soldiers Place, but because it is somewhat smaller in diameter, it conveys a more compact

Parkways, Circles, and Squares

Fig. 5.20. Colonial Circle (formerly Bidwell Place). Photograph by Andy Olenick.

sense of space. (Fig. 5.20) Over the years, Bidwell Place has been sympathetically looked after and still retains the feel of earlier times. Fine early-twentieth-century dwellings now look out onto a central circle of green, where a ring of mature trees shelters a bronze equestrian statue of General Daniel Bidwell.

Chapin Place (now Gates Circle), at the juncture with Delaware Avenue, was significantly enhanced in 1902 when the circle received the city's most elaborate public fountain. The gift of Mrs. Charles Pardee (née Gates), the circular granite complex was designed by Green & Wicks, Buffalo's lead-

Fig. 5.21. Pardee Fountain in Gates Circle (formerly Chapin Place). Photograph by Andy Olenick.

122   THE BEST PLANNED CITY IN THE WORLD

ing architectural firm at the turn of the twentieth century. "It was Mrs. Pardee's desire," reported one of the partners, "to make the spot a delightful and beautiful resting place which will attract the public generally to enter and sit down and enjoy its quiet and tranquility."[50] Because in 1874 Olmsted proposed a fountain basin with spraying water for the center of Niagara Square, one can assume that he would have approved of Mrs. Pardee's gift. Unfortunately, few people these days venture to cross this busy roundabout to sit on the granite benches that ring the fountain basin, and children no longer wade in its refreshing waters during summer months. Moreover, the once elegant circular park has experienced several changes for the worse. A large hospital building, some small commercial buildings, and an empty lot compromise its former charm. Nonetheless, the Pardee fountain is an admirable statement of City Beautiful movement urbanity, a public amenity that was surely inspired by the desire to prolong the memory of the glorious 1901 Pan-American Exposition that took place nearby. (Fig. 5.21)

Fig. 5.22. The Circle (now Symphony Circle) looking toward Porter Avenue, c. 1905. Courtesy James Mendola.

The Circle

The Circle (now Symphony Circle), at the southern end of The Avenue, had become by the close of the nineteenth century another prestigious address. In addition to The Avenue, several other major streets met here. East from Delaware Avenue came venerable North Street. West of the Circle, Porter Avenue, a former city thoroughfare widened and planted to became part of the parkway system, led three-quarters of a mile to the Front. (Fig. 5.22) On the south side of the Circle, two smaller streets entered from the adjacent Allentown neighborhood.

Before any work could commence at the Circle, the city had to relocate a small cemetery that stood on the spot. Once this was done, in the summer of 1873, the commissioners asked Olmsted to furnish a design for the eight-acre space. Although he and Vaux had sketched a plan for the Circle in 1870, Olmsted, now working on his own, presented a more complex scheme. (Fig. 5.23) The plan he submitted in 1874 artfully transformed the junction into a parklike space that both welcomed pedestrians and accommodated the smooth flow of vehicular traffic. Olmsted, who referred to the spot as North Street Circle, coordinated crossing travelers in five different directions by guiding the tree-lined streets into the heart of the Circle. A handsome gasolier (recently re-created) ornamented the central turning point, and handsome *lampadaires* lit the way of pedestrians within the circle. (Fig. 5.24) This urban oasis was further embellished with four fountains (Olmsted recommended that they be cast in concrete, all from the same mold), flowerbeds, lawns, and three concentric footpaths. With an eye to economy in a time of depression, Olmsted assured his clients that his plan provided "for no more than the absolutely necessary."[51] He also conceded that the fountains and the ornamental central lamp could be added at a later date. By the end of the year, McMillan was able to report that the ground had been graded, footpaths completed, and lines laid for

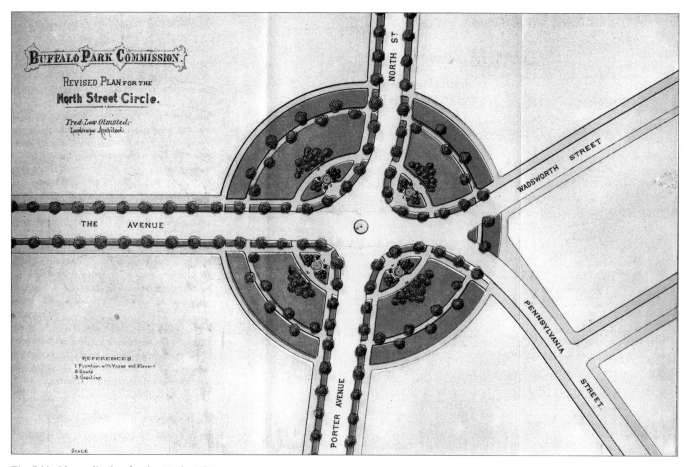

Fig. 5.23. Olmsted's plan for the Circle, 1874. Courtesy Buffalo State College.

Fig. 5.24. Symphony Circle today (formerly the Circle). Photograph by Andy Olenick.

fountains and gas lamps, and sixty trees, all at least twenty-five feet in height, had been transplanted to the site by two tree-moving machines.

During the last quarter of the nineteenth century, the Circle became another desirable parkway address. (Fig. 5.25) In 1885 Jane Mead Welch informed the readers of *Harper's* that it was one of those places in town where men of wealth were prepared to "erect a palace of medina sandstone, or a cypress-shingled villa rivaling those of Newport or the famous Jerusalem Road."[52] Two prominent residents of the Circle were George K. Birge, pro-

THE BEST PLANNED CITY IN THE WORLD

Fig. 5.25. Nineteenth-century houses on Symphony Circle. Photograph by Andy Olenick.

prietor of a nationally known wallpaper firm, who in 1896 erected a Georgian Revival house to the designs of Boston architects Little & Brown, and Truman G. Avery, local businessman and philanthropist, whose imposing Neoclassical mansion was the largest dwelling on the circle. In 1939 the Avery residence was torn down to make way for Eliel and Eero Saarinen's Kleinhans Music Hall. (In 1958 the Circle was rechristened Symphony Circle in deference to this national historic landmark.) The scale, proportion, and setback of the great concert hall did little to disturb the architectural character of the Olmstedian space.

NIAGARA SQUARE

Together with fashioning pleasant residential squares for the new parkway system, Olmsted was asked in 1874 to redesign the central element of Joseph Ellicott's city plan, Niagara Square. (Fig. 5.26) At this time Niagara Square retained much of the residential character it had had since the early days of the nineteenth century, but this sleepy transplanted New England common was being transformed by the press of prosperity into a busy urban crossroads. By the 1930s, all the houses had given way to large public buildings. From this downtown nexus eight major thoroughfares radiated, most of them away from the waterfront. Olmsted and Vaux had designated several of them as direct links between the center city and their new parks: Sixth Street led westward to the Front, Genesee Street led eastward to the Parade, and Delaware Street led northward to the Park. The challenge for Olmsted was how to improve the historic square to better reflect its central importance in the city.

Niagara Square, wrote Olmsted in December 1874, when he had finished his plan for its renewal, "is first of all a place of thoroughfare . . . and nothing should be done which will seriously injure its character in this respect." He actively resisted suggestions that this downtown junction, like the Circle in the new residential quarter of town, should be treated as a "public garden." Instead, he proposed that the main part of the space be left open to facilitate the free movement of traffic, which included a trolley line. Such a large open area, he acknowledged, would need "some effective decoration" in the center, but it should neither interrupt the view nor hinder traffic. Olmsted proposed placing there a low fountain basin, one hundred feet in diameter, from which several water jets would rise. He had in mind stocking the water with luxuriant aquatic plants like those that he and Vaux had installed recently in a similar basin in New York's Union Square. In the angles between the various streets, Olmsted proposed to create small triangular plats of grass and trees. At the head of each of these shaded triangles, seats, "the backs of which connected by railings will protect the turf and trees from injury," would invite pedestrians to sit and watch activity in the square.[53]

The most important feature of the remade square,

Study of Plan
for Improvement of
NIAGARA SQUARE.

New York October 1874
FRED LAW OLMSTED.
Landscape Architect.

Diagram showing proposed grouping at the termination of walks.

SECTION.

STREET

NIAGARA

COURT

STREET

GENESEE

DELAWARE

STREET

Scale

Fig. 5.26. Olmsted's plan for remodeling Ellicott's Niagara Square, 1874. Courtesy Buffalo State College.

however, was to be an arch erected to the memory of soldiers and sailors who had died in America's three major conflicts, the Revolutionary War, the War of 1812, and the recent Civil War. Originally, the military tribute had been planned for Soldiers Place, but, as Olmsted acknowledged, there was "a certain advantage to be gained by placing a memorial object in the midst of the city rather than in its suburbs." (Perhaps he had learned of Ellicott's intention to erect a triumphal arch like the one in Paris in Niagara Square.) Already by the summer of 1874, the Ladies Union Monument

Association, formed under the leadership of local philanthropist Maria Love, had raised money for a memorial arch, which H. H. Richardson was engaged to design. (Fig. 5.27) A striking perspective drawing of it, attributed to Stanford White, who was working in Richardson's office at the time, demonstrated how truly fine it would look. "I think the design a very original and noble one," remarked Olmsted.[54] (Fig. 5.28)

In June 1876 the members of the association approved the final plan of the memorial. A few days later, on July 4, Maria Love and Caroline Fillmore, widow of the former president, led groundbreaking ceremonies. By that time the association had raised over half of the estimated cost of $15,000. It must have pleased Olmsted to see the lead on this challenging project taken by women, for his days with the Sanitary Commission had taught him to respect their managerial capabilities. "I think that hardly another man has as high an estimate of the possible capacities of women compared with men in respect to organization," he once told a close female friend.[55] Undoubtedly sharing in this opinion, Dorsheimer, who was now the Democratic lieutenant governor, held honorary membership in the association. He had had a hand in bringing together the patriotic Love and the cosmopolitan Richardson, a southerner who had sat out the Civil War in Paris.

Richardson's arch, which combined classical and Romanesque elements, was to have gone on the north side of the square, where it would span the thirty-six-foot-wide roadway of Delaware Street. The materials, according to a local newspaper, were to have been

Fig. 5.27. Augustus Saint-Gaudens, *Maria Love.* Plaster relief, 1879. Courtesy National Park Service, Saint-Gaudens National Historic Site.

"white Medina stone, the best quality of Ohio stone, and Pictou or Caen stone."[56] A sculpted frieze around the upper level would depict figures emblematic of the three wars. It is likely that Richardson had the French sculptor Frédéric Auguste Bartholdi (who at the time was busy creating the Statue of Liberty) in mind to carve the frieze, for he had already worked with him on another project for a Boston church. Staircases in the arch piers climbed to the rooftop viewing platform, where, seventy feet above the ground, visitors might watch the comings and goings in the square. Looking northward, they could contemplate lower Delaware Street with its stately homes, including the nearby Francophile house that Richardson had designed for Dorsheimer.

Many people at the time recognized the general resemblance between the Buffalo arch and the Arc de Triomphe, commissioned by Napoleon I for the center of the Place d'Étoile in Paris. For several reasons, however, Olmsted thought that Richardson's arch would be

best located at the edge of Niagara Square rather than in the middle. For one thing, in this position it would receive the best light, making the inscriptions and reliefs readily discernible. And at the same time it would be seen to greatest advantage from all parts of the square. "Placed in the center," he reasoned, "its principal front would be seen satisfactorily from only about a third part of the Square." Tangentially, he was implying a criticism of the Parisian arch, which he had seen a number of times. Underlining this contention, he added that "the two spaces on which the largest number of visitors can stand on the Square, without disturbance by carriages, will be opposite to it, and the best distance for viewing it comprehensively." But the most important reason for putting the arch where he suggested was that it would frame Delaware Street and thus serve as the grand gateway to this principal route to the main park, some three miles distant. "It is to be presumed," Olmsted told the park commissioners, "that the private rights now held in the borders of Delaware street will at some time be extinguished, the trees and walks in them be arranged on an uniform system, and that it will in all respects be treated and used as a public promenade and approach road from the center of the city to the Main Park, as was intended and expected when the park system was designed. To such an approach and promenade the arch, placed as proposed, would form a fitting and noble entrance."[57] To demonstrate its gateway function, Olmsted had the artist he commissioned to paint a hypothetical view of the arch for the 1876 Centennial Exhibition emphasize its setting, something almost entirely lacking in Stanford White's beautiful rendering. In this watercolor, the arch is viewed straight on so that we can see tree-lined Delaware Street projected into the hazy distance beyond it. (Fig. 5.29)

Alas, no soldiers were ever to parade through the arch nor tourists climb to its parapeted viewing platform. Despite promising beginnings, the association failed to raise the funds needed to complete the ambitious memorial. Olmsted would, however, have the opportunity after Richardson's death to see a near facsimile

Fig. 5.28. Drawing of Richardson's arch attributed to Stanford White, 1874–76. Courtesy Houghton Library, Harvard University. MS TYP 1096 (ARC F1).

Fig. 5.29. For the Centennial Exhibition in Philadelphia, Olmsted commissioned this watercolor showing how Richardson's arch would look framing Delaware Street leading to the Park. Courtesy Buffalo and Erie County Historical Society.

of the Buffalo arch built as part of his 1889 quadrangle scheme for the new campus of Stanford University in Palo Alto, California. When Charles Coolidge, architect of the university buildings and a former assistant in Richardson's office, was pressed to come up with a design for a dedicatory entrance to the Inner Quad, he hurriedly cribbed Richardson's unrealized Buffalo project. Regrettably, this West Coast version of the Niagara Square monument proved ephemeral, falling victim to the great earthquake of 1906. A more enduring offspring is the memorial arch that Stanford White designed for New York's Washington Square. Erected first in wood in 1889 and then in stone six years later, the Greenwich Village landmark, which commemorates the centennial of George Washington's inauguration as president, is more academically classical in design than the one White would have remembered his mentor putting forward for Buffalo. Yet the location of the arch near the northern side of Washington Square at the foot

of Fifth Avenue mimics the location that Olmsted had proposed for the Soldiers and Sailors arch in Niagara Square.

Olmsted's 1874 plan for Niagara Square fared no better than did Richardson's arch design, for the city failed to implement his concept. Eleven years later the *Express* laid the blame for inaction at the feet of the Common Council, which had never turned jurisdiction of the square over to the park commissioners. "The Common Council have controlled it," stated the editorial, "and have made it a comparative desert, as they have all other open spaces whose care has been entrusted to them."[58] Even when, the following year, the council did cede the square and other public open spaces to the park commissioners, nothing was done to improve the look of the city's focal point. In 1895 the park commissioners once again asked the Olmsted firm for advice on beautifying the centerpiece of Ellicott's plan. The revised scheme dispensed with the benches and arch of

THE BEST PLANNED CITY IN THE WORLD

the 1874 design but retained the small triangles of trees and shrubs between entering streets. In the middle of the busy traffic intersection, the Olmsteds proposed installing a pedestrian safe haven adorned with either a fountain or a piece of sculpture. This second plan is closer to what exists today, minus the triangles of green. Since 1907, Carrère & Hastings' obelisk commemorating President William McKinley, who was assassinated in Buffalo while attending the Pan-American Exposition, has occupied the center of the square.

CITY AND COUNTY HALL

In 1875, the year after Olmsted prepared his plan for Niagara Square, the park commissioners asked him to help them with a suitable design for the grounds around the new city hall. The three-story granite building, a clumsy variant of High Victorian Gothic architecture, had been designed in 1871 by Andrew Jackson Warner, the politically connected architect who was supervising construction of Richardson's Buffalo State Hospital. (Olmsted doubtless thought Warner's building no match for the works of his New York associates Frederick Withers, Thomas Wisedell, and Jacob Wrey Mould, all masters of the Ruskinian style.) When Olmsted was contacted by Dennis Bowen, a devoted park commissioner and a member of the commission that had guided the construction of the new municipal facility, the building was nearing completion.[59] It would open in July 1876. (Fig. 5.30)

The challenge for Olmsted was to come up with a suitable landscape design for the massive towered edifice, which took up much of the sloping site of the former Franklin Square. The task

was not an easy one. For one thing, the commissioners stood in need of instruction themselves, for they had little idea of what they wanted. "The problem was long under discussion and in the process of discussion there was occasion not simply for plans but for many tentative sketches, diagrams, actions and trial studies," Olmsted recalled.[60] One the first steps he took was to caution the commissioners against following the failed example of most public buildings in American cities that had small parks placed around or in front of them. These spaces, he observed, seldom fared well. Walks soon become ugly from overuse and neglect, and "the trees, shrubs and turf" were more often than not "sadly abused" by the public who constantly visited the place. In a long letter to Bowen, Olmsted outlined his ideas. He sternly warned his clients against introducing elaborate plantings around their building, whatever the public might have come to expect in the way of ornamental flowerbeds and other floral displays as emblems of good government. It would be necessary, he maintained, to avoid any kind of "decoration . . . that will not bear rough usage or which, after the tramping on or about it of a turbulent crowd, cannot be made as good as new with

City Hall, Buffalo, N. Y.

Fig. 5.30. A. J. Warner's City and County Hall (1876), for which Olmsted designed the landscape plan in 1875. Courtesy www.CardCow.com.

water and a scrubbing brush."[61] Olmsted advised a simple planting scheme and cautioned that citizens should be dissuaded from using the grounds as a resting place.

Aesthetically, Olmsted expressed the notion that the landscape plan should work in concert with the building to enhance its appearance. This contrasted with the position that he and Vaux had maintained concerning architecture in country parks, where structures were to be subordinated to the landscape. Olmsted had somewhat earlier put forward his theory concerning landscapes around public buildings when he received the commission to devise a plan for the eighty-acre grounds around the U.S. Capitol. In the spring of 1874 Congress had hired him to undertake this nationally important project, and Olmsted submitted his design in January 1875, shortly before he was contacted by the Buffalo park commissioners.

In designing the grounds around Buffalo's City Hall, the plans for which were finished by April 1876, Olmsted undoubtedly drew on his experience in Washington. One can assume from critical remarks Olmsted made about the recently enlarged Capitol, which also sat on a sloping site, that he found Warner's symmetrical H-shaped building ungainly in its proportions and its pale gray monochromatic stone walls unpleasantly brilliant. His job in both instances would be to make the monumental buildings more appealing to the eye by taming their overbearing presence and chilling appearance. Olmsted told his Buffalo clients, "It is not desirable that the building should seem to have been thrust abruptly through a flat bed of turf." Rather, he advised, "the ground should be so arranged as to obviously be one in design with it and to support it." And because Warner's building was "so tall and straight

and independent of other buildings," it required a "verdant drapery to set if off" and "solid outworks that will have the effect of a pedestal in connecting it with the ground."[62]

Olmsted's final plan, which the commissioners accepted, called for surrounding City Hall with lawns that sloped away from the structure down to the bordering sidewalks. By this means Olmsted provided the edifice with the visual pedestal he had spoken of. The grassy earthwork, which would be planted with only a few strategically placed trees and shrubs, mitigated the ungainly height of the building by hiding the basement. The entire site would be surrounded by a low stone wall to discourage entry.[63] (This was in keeping with his advice that areas surrounding public buildings should not be treated as parks.) For practical reasons, Olmsted cut a small court into the sloping lawn at the southwest corner of the building so that deliveries (as well as prisoners being brought for arraignment) could be taken directly to the basement from the street. For

Fig. 5.31. At the back of City and County Hall Olmsted created ramps approaching the entrance. On the south side he added a small courtyard to give direct access to the basement from the street. Postcard, c. 1900. Courtesy Catherine Schweitzer.

THE BEST PLANNED CITY IN THE WORLD

the more steeply pitched ground at the rear of the building, he designed a terrace. (Fig. 5.31) (This layout of lawns, stairs, and ramps disappeared in the 1960s when the city added a multistory annex to the building on the site.) When the grounds of Buffalo's City Hall were finished in 1877, the site provided the country a modest preview of how its national Capitol might look once a delaying Congress furnished the appropriations necessary to complete Olmsted's plans for it.

Olmsted felt that he had devoted more of his attention to the City Hall landscape project than his normal fee reflected, and this led him to seek additional compensation. The commissioners, however, rejected his claim. Apparently they believed—perhaps because Olmsted's solution was so simple—that he had merely adapted the design from other work (presumably the U.S. Capitol). They also questioned whether Warner, whose office had enlarged some of Olmsted's drawings, had not had a hand in the design. The misunderstanding struck at the heart of Olmsted's concept of his profession and at his reputation. "I have raised my calling from the rank of a trade, even of a handicraft, to that of a liberal profession—an Art, an Art of Design. I have been resolute in insisting that I am not to be dealt with as an agent of my clients but as a counselor—a trustee, on honor," he later would write.[64]

Such thinking prompted Olmsted to seek legal advice. In a long letter to a Buffalo law firm, he laid out his case. "It must be recognized," he argued, "that the design is novel in conception, that it is suggested by and adapted to the special local circumstances, that it is in all its details thoroughly original." Furthermore, the paper documents were not to be viewed as the only service he had rendered; they were merely the result of a creative process informed by his expert knowledge of landscape architecture. What was customarily paid for, Olmsted insisted, was the "value of the aid which they [the commissioners] had in deliberating what to do with the ground about the City Hall and of the conception, discussion and elaboration into practical working form of its design which they have caused to be carried out." As to Warner's association with the project, Olmsted explained that the architect's office had merely made some copies of plans that Olmsted had sent to Buffalo. If the commissioners thought Warner had "added anything of value I should be interested to know in which particular he did so," wrote Olmsted testily. "I do not believe that he would claim that he gave so much as a penny's worth of planning—that he did anything but direct a boy to make enlarged drawings from mine," he said. In the end, Olmsted asked his attorneys to approach the commissioners informally about the matter rather than initiate a court case. He was confident that if the commissioners, who were all business and professional men, were "to take the trouble to ask what is the usual and reasonable compensation for such services in any civilized community, they will find it impossible to regard my bill as excessive" (though we don't know whether he was right).[65] Olmsted's experience was one skirmish among many that he and others, including Vaux, fought in their time to achieve recognition of landscape architecture as a bona fide profession.

SIX

Parkside, Buffalo State Hospital, and Smaller Parks

The city had thus been so built as to secure within itself much of the sanitary advantages of a suburb.

—Frederick Law Olmsted, "Late Additions to the Plan of Buffalo," 1876

Almost as soon as their work on Buffalo's park system began, the park commissioners realized that the project they were directing would have a profound effect on the lands beyond the parks' borders. In their *Third Annual Report* of 1873, they stressed to the Common Council the importance of commissioning a survey of the northern and eastern portions of the city, "with the view of having the streets so laid out to harmonize with a general system, with the Parks and their approaches as the objective points." It was as if the specter of Joseph Ellicott had pointed the way to them. Furthermore, these practical-minded men of business asserted that "the adoption of some general plan as here indicated would enhance the value of the land and bring it speedily into the market, soon to be occupied by suburban homes."[1]

Homes were certainly much on the minds of Olmsted and Vaux when they first came to Buffalo to design the park system. Vaux had written a book on domestic

architecture in which he had stated, for example, "It is not for ourselves alone, but for the sake of our children, that we should love to build our homes, . . . [for] the young people are mostly at home; it is their storehouse for amusement, their opportunity for relaxation, their main resource; and thus they are exposed to its influence for good or evil unceasingly."[2]

For his part, Olmsted was in the process of preparing a volume of his own on the subject. He was paying special attention to the evolution of suburban residential neighborhoods set apart from business and industry, something that he felt distinguished the modern city from its historic predecessors. Ten years earlier he and Vaux had proposed to lay out the residential neighborhood of Washington Heights in streets that respected the natural topography in stark contrast to the rest of Manhattan's gridiron plan, which Olmsted considered both inefficient and monotonous. In Buffalo, Olmsted hoped to have the chance that he and Vaux had missed in New York to plot a new section of town where residents might enjoy home life as he had depicted it in 1860, as affording the benefit of tranquility and opportunities for recreation. Olmsted later elaborated on this idea to his Buffalo clients:

My observation convinces me that there is a radical change taking place in the style of city building. People are hereafter going to do business in one quarter of a town and live in another. Cars, telephone, and other modern conveniences for rapid transit and still more rapid communication have made this a more desirable way of living. Let the citizen build up his stores and his warehouses as high and as close together as he pleases, but he doesn't want to live among them and there is no longer any need of his doing so. He can live in much better style and cheaper in a part of the city entirely given up to dwellings.[3]

In February 1870 Olmsted addressed the subject of the modern city and its improvement in a notable lecture at Boston's Lowell Institute. Olmsted approved of the shift from agrarian to urban society that was transforming America. It was only in well-designed cities and their suburbs, he believed, "that many of the graces of civilization could be enjoyed: effective and effortless sanitary arrangements, goods and physical comforts, obtainable in the country only by hard work; services to match every need; and leisure, society, recreation, and intellectual pleasures," as Olmsted's primary biographer, Laura Roper, observes.[4] His ideal of middle-class life envisioned families living in comfortable homes with spacious grounds and front lawns. He did not, however, wish people to live so far apart that they felt isolated from one another. "Probably the advantages of civilization can be found illustrated and demonstrated under no other circumstances so completely," he remarked, "as in some suburban neighborhoods where each family abode stands fifty or a hundred feet or more apart from all others, and at some distance from the public road."[5] Together with ease of travel to the center city and other parts of town, such a physical arrangement ensured that residents could enjoy the benefits of both a sense of community—"communitiveness" was the term Olmsted favored—and what he had called "the metropolitan condition of society."[6] It seems clear that the social theorems and design principles that Olmsted expressed that evening in Lowell shaped his vision for the new lands in North Buffalo.

PARKSIDE AND VILLA PARK

After Olmsted parted from Vaux in 1872, he became involved with private investors in Buffalo who wanted to create their own version of Chicago's suburban residential community of Riverside adjacent to the Park. This proposed new city neighborhood, the plan of which Olmsted harmonized with the new public parkland, assumed the name of Parkside. Riverside, which was far from town, had included a generous amount of community green space, a factor that increased its cost and contributed to the project's eventual bankruptcy during the depression of 1873.[7] With Parkside, all of the land could be devoted to residential development, for the homeowners would enjoy easy access to the beautiful adjacent park, where they might participate in the "congregated human life" that Olmsted had told his Lowell Institute audience was necessary to the health of modern society.[8]

The story of Parkside falls into two periods: the first dates from 1874 to 1876, when Olmsted prepared his initial plan for the Parkside Land Improvement Company; the second phase begins in 1885, when a new group of investors asked the Olmsted firm to revise the earlier proposal. Initially Parkside was described as a three-mile-square "detached suburb" wrapping around the eastern and northern sides of the Park, within the projected route of the New York Central Belt Line railroad. (Fig. 6.1) Among the private investors backing the project was the ever optimistic William Dorsheimer. He was so confident about the success of the venture that he assured Olmsted, "[This] scheme of ours will lead to your employment to lay out *all* the unoccupied lands within the city limits."[9] Other partners in the Parkside Land Improvement Company were also park advocates, notably Bronson C. Rumsey and Elam Jewett.

THE BEST PLANNED CITY IN THE WORLD

By the summer of 1874 Olmsted was hard at work on diagramming streets for both the newly annexed Twenty-third and Twenty-fourth wards in the Bronx and for Parkside. In both instances he would scrupulously avoid the usual grid plan that he disliked so intensely. "Even where the circumstances of the site are favorable for this formal and repetitive arrangement," he had declared a few years earlier, "it presents a dull and inartistic appearance."[10] Assisting on the Buffalo subdivision was the highly competent George K. Radford. After leaving Buffalo in 1873, Radford had gone west to assist Olmsted with his plan for the future site

of Tacoma, Washington. Olmsted's scheme, which was ultimately rejected by the Northern Pacific Railroad directors who had hired him to lay out the new city, called for major thoroughfares that smoothed the way for carriages to negotiate the steep landscape.[11] The roadways in Parkside would also follow easy curves. There would be no hard angles of intersection. An article of faith that Olmsted shared with Vaux was that "gracefully curved lines" and "generous spaces" implied "leisure, contemplativeness, and happy tranquility."[12] Parkside, as Olmsted envisioned it, would apply this type of suburban planning to a new neigh-

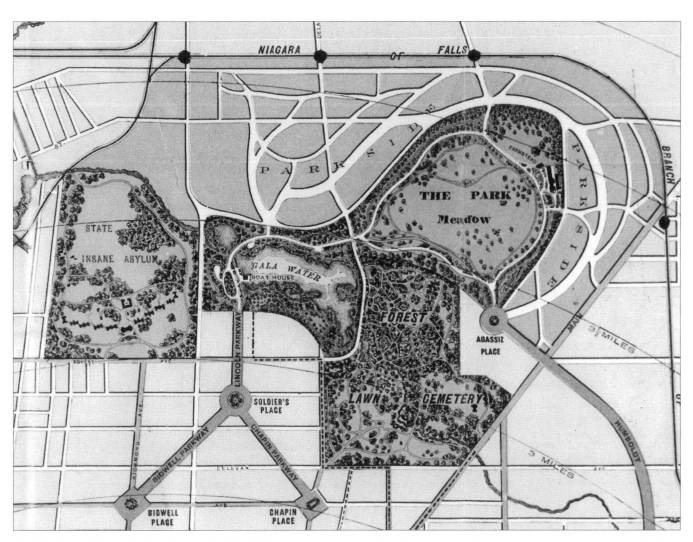

Fig. 6.1. Detail of *Olmsted's Sketch Map of Buffalo* (1881) showing the relationship of Parkside to the Park, the major parkways, and the Belt Line railroad. Author's collection.

Parkside, Buffalo State Hospital, and Smaller Parks

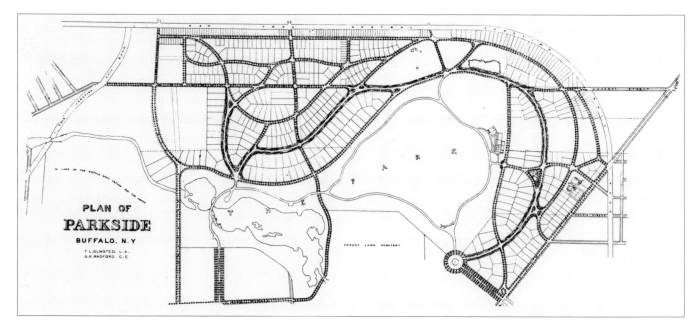

Fig. 6.2. Olmsted and George K. Radford's original plan for Parkside, c. 1875. Courtesy National Park Service, Frederick Law Olmsted National Historic Site.

borhood that would be distinct from the rest of town because of it.

Probably the earliest plan for Parkside is a map bearing the names of Olmsted and Radford that surely dates from late 1874 or early 1875.[13] (Fig. 6.2) It shows a network of widely spaced streets winding in an unhurried way through the landscape like variations on the ebb and flow outline of the Park and the ninety-degree turn of the Belt Line railroad around the east and north sides of the Park.[14] (This railway line would be an important adjunct to the plan.) In addition, sidewalks provided safety and convenience for pedestrians, diminutive green spaces embellished principal points of intersection, and trees took up regular positions along all the roadways.

Trees figured prominently in Olmsted's thinking about the modern street. "Foliage acts mechanically to purify the air by screening it," he declared. In Parkside, he would avoid the haphazard planting of street trees that often took place in American cities. Here he would see them planted as he believed they should be, in strips of ground reserved for them so that they might grow "naturally and gracefully" and never interfere with the sidewalks or carriageways.[15]

The overall plan for Parkside falls more or less naturally into northern and eastern portions of the site. Throughout both sections, Olmsted drew lines for generously sized building lots, with some smaller properties confined to the less desirable border along Main Street. The area north of the park was bisected from east to west by the straight line of Amherst Street, a major crosstown route from which new streets branched off. In this regard, the general pattern resembled the plan Olmsted had made in 1865 for Mountain View Cemetery in Oakland, California.[16] On the east side of the park (the area known today as Parkside East), Olmsted's plan featured a principal thoroughfare arcing its way from Agassiz Circle to Amherst Street near the northeast corner of the park. Jewett Parkway, the single transverse road, followed an undulating course from Main Street (where a commuter station was planned) to the park entrance on the east side of the meadow. The seventy-foot-wide roadway with tree-shaded sidewalks had been privately constructed in 1875 by Elam Jewett through his estate, Willowlawn. In 1883 Jewett deeded the thoroughfare to the city with the proviso that it be maintained as a parkway. In addition, three other curved streets traversed this

THE BEST PLANNED CITY IN THE WORLD

eastern area of Parkside from north to south. The map of the Buffalo park system that Olmsted displayed at the Centennial International Exhibition in Philadelphia in 1876 and again in Paris at the Exposition Universelle in 1878 included his and Radford's street plan for Parkside. The Parkside that visitors to the fairs saw, however, was to exist only on paper, for before the opening of the Belt Line railroad, investors found the property too far from the center of town to justify the expense of constructing Olmsted's first-rate plan.

When the Belt Line finally did begin service in 1883, a group made up of former and new investors revived interest in the Parkside project. Under the leadership of Bronson C. Rumsey, who had extensive land holdings in North Buffalo, it seemed as if Dorsheimer's prediction might come true. "To Mr. B. C. Rumsey is due the idea of laying out . . . the land of the Hyde Park Land Association, the Parkside Land Association, and the Villa Park Land Company according to one consistent and harmonious scheme," the *Express* reported. "Mr. Frederick Law Olmsted, the celebrated landscape architect who laid out the Buffalo City Park, is engaged to make the plans." In January 1885 Rumsey, an officer in the new Villa Park Land Company, wrote to Olmsted to ask how much he would charge to map out 350 acres. He was now collaborating more and more with his thirty-three-year-old stepson, John Charles Olmsted, a man who would come to play an important role in the firm's Buffalo projects. By the spring of 1885, as the *Express* noted, the Olmsteds had completed "a grand and practicable plan" that embraced more land than the former Parkside.[17]

Construction began on the revised plan for the eastern section of Parkside, the area between the Park and Main Street. (Fig. 6.3) It featured more streets, smaller lot sizes, and less sinuous roadways than the Olmsted and Radford plan had displayed. The seventy-five acres that lay north of Jewett Parkway were owned by the Parkside Land Improvement Company; the area between Jewett and Humboldt Parkway was the property of the Main and Humboldt Parkway Association. On November 22, 1885, a local paper reported that "six curving streets have been laid out north and south" in this eastern section of Parkside. Moreover, "streets corresponding to those laid out in the above district" now ran through the tract south of Jewett Parkway owned by the Main and Humboldt Parkway Association. Today

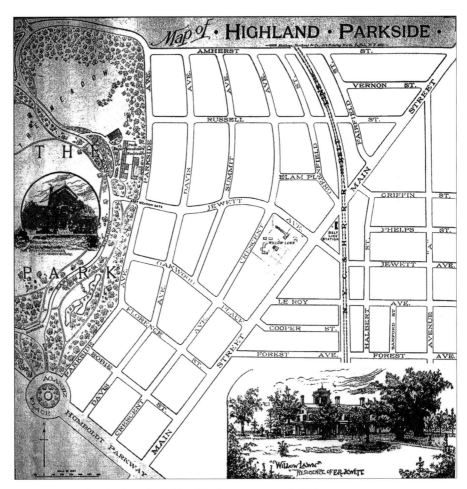

Fig. 6.3. Map of Parkside and Highland Park as constructed, 1886. Courtesy Buffalo State College.

this entire eastern area of Parkside generally conforms to the pattern of streets laid down at this time and has been named the Parkside East National Register Historic District.[18]

Upwardly mobile Buffalonians began to erect houses along the new streets of Parkside East in the mid-1880s almost as soon as sewer, water, and gas lines were in place. In 1889 the *Express* observed that the promising suburb was making "rapid strides" and predicted that within a few years its curving carriageways would be pleasantly shaded by the recently planted trees. Most of the houses then being built in this privileged setting, according to the *Express,* were of "a higher grade than are usually found in the new sections." The grandest street was Jewett Parkway. Here, where the lots were bigger (at least ninety feet of frontage) than elsewhere in Parkside, the area came to be known as Highland Park. Considered "the flower of the entire Parkside region," it appealed to well-to-do buyers.[19] In the late nineteenth and early twentieth centuries, many costly houses were erected along Jewett Parkway in the Highland Park sec-

tion. In 1890 the impressive half-timber residence of the local architect William S. Wicks, a future park commissioner, went up at the corner of Summit Avenue. The most remarkable home, however, began to go up in 1903 across the street from Wicks. It was for Darwin D. Martin (the director of John D. Larkin's flourishing national enterprise, the Larkin Soap Company), who commissioned Frank Lloyd Wright to plan for him a residential compound that represents a full-throated expression of Wright's concept of Prairie style living.[20] (Fig. 6.4)

At the same time that the eastern section of Parkside was being revised, the dream of a wealthy suburb adjacent to the park on the north took on renewed life. Villa Park was the undertaking of John D. Larkin, Bronson C. Rumsey, and other investors who had formed several land companies. In January 1885 Rumsey wrote to Olmsted expressing interest in developing the land north of the Belt Line railroad and Amherst Street, south of Hertel Avenue, and east of Delaware Avenue.[21] In the late summer of 1886, the Olmsted firm forwarded their draft for the area showing "a handsome arrangement of streets and playgrounds."[22] The *Express* reported, however, that objections arose to the plan because the investors wished to run a boulevard to Niagara Falls through the center of the property north from the Colvin entrance to the Park. Ignorant of this, Olmsted had drawn Colvin "too much curved for that purpose."[23] He went back to the drawing board. At the end of the year the directors of the Villa Park Land Company informed Olmsted that they were "very much pleased" with the revised plans the firm had made. Moreover, in addition to disliking the curved route of Colvin Street, the investors had

Fig. 6.4. The house designed by Frank Lloyd Wright for Darwin Martin (1904) occupies an important site in Parkside. Photograph by Jack Boucher, 1965. Courtesy Library of Congress, HABS NY, 15-BUF, 5-5.

THE BEST PLANNED CITY IN THE WORLD

found the first study generally too original; the new plans, said the directors, harmonized "more with our own ideas of what they should be in the interest of the general policy of the company." In short, "leisure, contemplativeness, and happy tranquility" were all well and good, but they took second place to profit.[24]

The investors nevertheless remained committed to the unconventional undertaking and told Olmsted that they looked forward to receiving the firm's completed design. In May 1887 a local real estate journal reported that these plans envisaged a "handsomely-designed system of parkways, to be lined with foliage trees, extending from Delaware Avenue on the west to Main street on the east."[25] In the winter of 1888, John C. Olmsted wrote to Larkin on behalf of himself and his father that "the plan can be lithographed in order to supply every one interested with copies and to advertise the fact of there being villa sites for sale."[26] Advertisements for Villa Park lots began to appear in the city's newspapers that year. A local paving company published a map that showed the area laid out with many curvaceous streets bearing names of famous writers, supplied by Olmsted. (Fig. 6.5) "It would be best to leave the placing of the names in your hands," the investors had told him, "as it is a matter which requires good judgment and your experience certainly would enable you to display that."[27] It is safe to assume that the names cataloged Olmsted family favorites. But in fact no one would ever read *The Stones of Venice* on Ruskin Street or relive "The Charge of the Light Brigade" on Tennyson Street. Villa Park had yet to be realized and never would be.[28]

In 1889 James Tillinghast, an executive with the

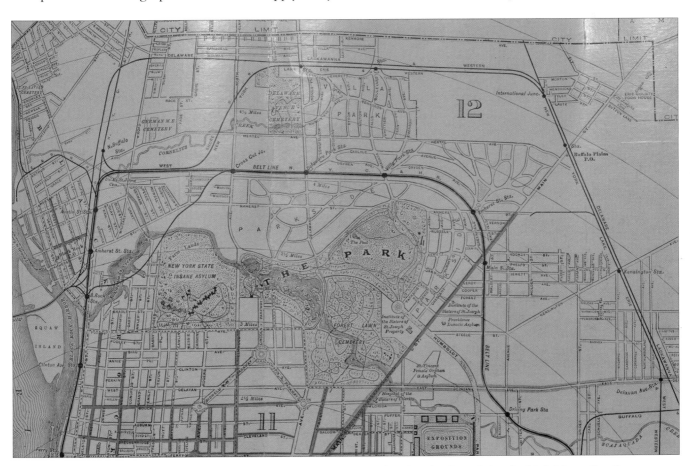

Fig. 6.5. Map of North Buffalo, 1888, showing Parkside (south of Belt Line railroad) and Villa Park (north of Belt Line railroad). Courtesy Martin Wachadlo.

New York Central Railroad, announced that he and another investor had acquired the section of land northeast of the park, part of the area included in the 1876 plan for Parkside. These sixty acres, where the new owners planned to create another residential suburb, were bounded by Amherst and Colvin streets and the Belt Line. Tillinghast was aware of the existing Olmsted plans but thought they were "much more elaborate than those usually adopted in laying out a suburban residence park."[29] If Olmsted ever read these words, he may have recalled what his friend Charles Eliot Norton had written to him a few years earlier: "You are preaching truth above the comprehension of our generation."[30] By the mid-1890s, the land that Tillinghast owned was laid out with long streets that roughly paralleled the railroad and joined streets in the eastern Parkside district from Amherst Street to Colvin Street.[31]

West of Colvin, the greater part of the land immediately north of the Park that had been envisioned as part of the 1875 plan for Parkside still lay vacant and would remain so until the 1920s. In 1899, referring to this large empty space that extended west to Elmwood Avenue, the real estate journal *Greater Buffalo* confirmed that "there has been little residential development in these sections and there will be but little for many years to come." One reason it gave was the prospect of the Pan-American Exposition occupying part of the land; additionally, "the policy of the owners of the rest is to await high prices."[32] Consequently, Dorsheimer's buoyant prediction that his friend Olmsted would be the one to transform the farmland of North Buffalo into sylvan suburbia failed to materialize.

BUFFALO STATE HOSPITAL FOR THE INSANE

Local lobbying for the establishment of a state mental facility in Buffalo began in 1865, immediately after the state authorized the creation of several public mental institutions.[33] When, in July 1869, Joseph Warren was appointed to a commission formed to determine a hospital location in western New York, he took the lead in advocating for his city. In October, Buffalo's Common Council, eager to have such a worthy institution erected within the city, agreed to pay $50,000 for land that would be donated for the site of the hospital. The property being eyed was the Clinton Forest picnic grove along the southern border of Scajaquada Creek. This was part of the area that Olmsted had earlier suggested be included in the main park; in fact, it was where he initially proposed to locate the entrance to the park from The Avenue. The open land lay immediately to the west of the Park, and this surely had influenced the hospital's supporters in their choice of the site for the new five-hundred-patient facility.[34] For their part, Olmsted and Vaux certainly knew of the city's intentions for these two hundred acres as they were developing the park's final plan in August 1869. By the time the Common Council deliberated on whether to approve the park proposal, the state commissioners had agreed to locate the mental hospital there (see Fig. 6.1).[35] The future presence of the hospital on that site required Olmsted and Vaux to modify the park approach from the West Side and may also have contributed to their invention of the Y-shaped group of parkways that forms the monumental approach to the Park.

In May 1870 the governor appointed ten members to the hospital's board of managers.[36] The group included park promoters Asher B. Nichols and Joseph Warren, who assumed the role of chair of the executive committee. One of their first decisions was to engage Dr. John P. Gray, the well-known director of the Utica Asylum, to consult on the plan for the new building. Gray dictated that the building follow the Kirkbride system of asylum design, in which separate pavilions extended to either side of a central administration building. This arrangement, which originated in the 1840s with new mental institutions planned by Dr. Thomas Kirkbride, facilitated the classification of patients by their type of affliction. It also made the mammoth institution seem less monolithic, and it promoted fire safety because in

Fig. 6.6. H. H. Richardson's Buffalo State Hospital (now the Buffalo Psychiatric Center), 1870. Courtesy Buffalo and Erie County Historical Society.

case of emergency, individual wards could be isolated from one another.

In May 1871 H. H. Richardson was formally appointed architect of the project.[37] One can only speculate on how the youthful designer got this important commission. Did Dorsheimer and Olmsted speak up for him? Or did Nichols, for whom Richardson had planned a house in 1869, perhaps influence the choice? In any event, because Richardson's office was in New York City (he was a partner there with Robert Gambrill at the time), the board named Andrew Jackson Warner of Rochester to act as supervising architect.

It took Richardson until 1872 to settle on the final design of the formidable structure, the first big step toward his fully evolved Richardsonian Romanesque style of architecture. (Fig. 6.6) The rambling plan consisted of five wards on either side of a central administration building that Richardson dramatized with two enormous stone towers. These remarkable features, which drew inspiration from William Burgess's unrealized 1866 design for the London law courts, had no apparent function but added dignity and meaning to this refuge from the troubling world. Sadly for the architect, whose close association with the project seems to have ended in 1876, the entire hospital, which was the largest building of his career, did not reach completion until 1890, four years after his untimely death.

Olmsted and Vaux became officially involved with the project in January 1871, when managers consulted them on plans for the hospital grounds. (Fig. 6.7) The board of managers surely turned to Olmsted and Vaux knowing that they had had considerable experience landscaping mental hospitals. Both men were friends of Dr. D. Tilden Brown of New York's Bloomingdale Asylum, and in 1860 they furnished plans for the grounds of that well-regarded institution.[38] In the same year they were engaged by Dr. John S. Butler to create a "therapeutic Arcadia" around the buildings of the Hartford Retreat for the Insane (now the Institute for Living) in Olmsted's hometown of Hartford, Connecticut. For the Retreat, where Olmsted's father served as a director, they prescribed a quiet pastoral setting. In front of the existing building they laid out a large meadow dotted with trees standing singly and in groups. Dense vegetation bordered this calm and tranquil environment, sheltering it from the world outside. The Retreat was one of several asylums that members of the Buffalo institution's committee on plans visited during the planning stage.[39] Certainly the committee was also familiar with the Sheppard Asylum, a progressive private mental hospital near Baltimore. While Olmsted was away in Washington and California during the war years, Vaux, in consultation with Dr. Brown, had designed its buildings. Once they resumed their partnership after the war, the two men were asked in 1867 to landscape the extensive grounds around Frederick C. Withers's Hudson River State Hospital at Poughkeepsie, a High Victorian Gothic masterwork based on the Kirkbride system and one that influenced Richardson's Buffalo project.

Taking up the challenge of the Buffalo asylum, Olmsted and Vaux made numerous practical suggestions. In their report, which was ready in July 1871, they recommended that the strung-out echelon of wards—which has been compared to a flight of birds—be sited along the top of a small ravine near the southern end of the property so that the ground at the rear of the buildings would be lower than that at the front. The sloping site would allow for a lower-level courtyard to be introduced at the rear of the administration building. This feature, they explained, "would form a centre, under the eye of the Superintendent, for the exterior communication of the institution . . . [so that] incoming patients, after having been received and entered at the Superintendent's office, would be sent to the proper ward by way of the administrative court and a system of rear approaches." They also advised that below-grade passageways be created on either side of the main building to allow people and vehicles to move between the front and back of the complex without having to circumnavigate the wards, "the distance to be saved being over half a mile."[40] The notion recalled the sunken transverse roads that had been a novel feature of their plan for Central Park. And although this is not mentioned in the report, by align-

ing the entire complex toward the southeast, Olmsted and Vaux ensured that the interiors of the wards would receive the maximum hours of daylight during the winter months.

For the grounds around the buildings, the landscape architects introduced elements that psychiatrists like Gray believed to contribute to patients' mental and physical health. The area in front of the asylum they treated "in a very simple park like way with groups of trees and large open spaces of turf." (Fig. 6.8) These

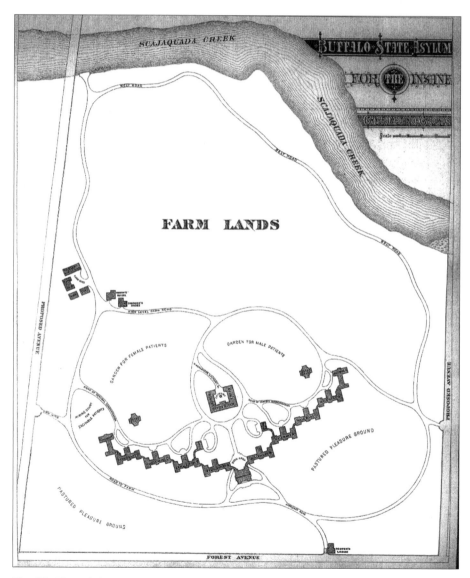

Fig. 6.7. Olmsted, Vaux & Company, plan for the grounds of the Buffalo State Hospital, 1871. Author's collection.

THE BEST PLANNED CITY IN THE WORLD

"pastured pleasure grounds," as they were labeled on the plan, deliberately avoided confronting troubled minds with the subtle complexities that distinguished the partners' park landscapes. The land immediately to the rear of the wards was divided into gardens for male and female patients. Beyond that, the greater part of the acreage was given over to farmland and hayfields. Here, able-bodied patients might work for the benefit of the community and themselves, for Gray believed in the power of manual labor to restore mental balance. (Fig. 6.9) Finally, a dirt road bordered the entire site to facilitate movement around the grounds. It was also to serve as a pleasure drive for that class of patients "whom it might not be desirable to take out on the public streets." Viewed as a whole, the institution's outdoor surroundings mirrored those of a large country house. Downing's Highland Garden and Frederic Church's Olana followed the same pattern of lawn fronting the main house, kitchen garden at the rear, and farmland out back.

Construction of Richardson's buildings proceeded slowly. Several years would pass before the institution was ready to give attention to the landscape. In 1877, with the administration building and the two wards to the east nearly finished, the twenty-five-foot-wide carriage entrance drive was constructed.[41] The year before, the board of managers had asked Olmsted, who was now working on his own, for planting plans for the grounds. One of his drawings shows how, as at the Hartford Retreat, he intended the space in front of these buildings to be an expanse of turf embellished with a variety of trees and shrubs. (Fig. 6.10) Many must have found tranquility in this amiable environment, where, from time to time, patients also played team sports. As Olmsted had done at the U.S. Capitol, here he also employed

Fig. 6.8. Meadow in front of Buffalo State Hospital administration building, c. 1900. Library of Congress, Prints and Photographs Division, Detroit Publishing Company Collection.

Fig. 6.9. Reapers harvesting hay from the fields behind the hospital buildings, 1890s. Courtesy Buffalo Psychiatric Center.

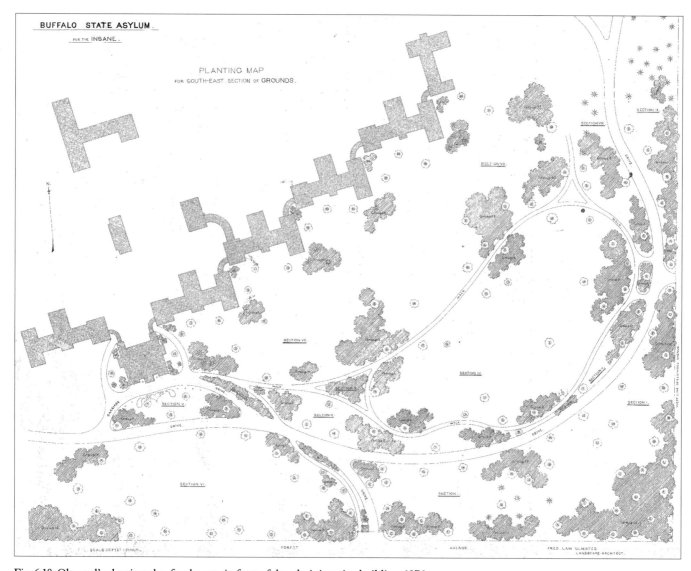

Fig. 6.10. Olmsted's planting plan for the area in front of the administration building, 1876. Courtesy National Park Service, Frederick Law Olmsted National Historic Site.

plantings to heighten one's appreciation of the architecture. Along both sides of the approach road, which he laid out so that those arriving at the main entrance would see the building from an angle rather than straight on, an abundance of trees and shrubs focused and framed the view of the soaring towers. (Fig. 6.11) Moreover, on the street fronting the fenced property (Forest Avenue), Olmsted partially drew aside the curtain of green, allowing the passerby to glimpse the fine architectural perspective of the impressive administration building.[42]

Time has proved unkind to both the Victorian philosophy of the "moral" treatment of mental illness and the well-being of Richardson's early masterwork, as well as the Olmsted and Vaux landscape in which it stands. Three pavilions on the east side of the complex were torn down in the 1960s, and those that remain have been empty of patients for decades. Construction of many additional buildings, service roadways, and parking lots has left little to remind us of the landscape that historic photographs record. These evocative images reveal that

Fig. 6.11. Drive to the main entrance in the administration building, with Olmsted's mature plantings, c. 1900. Author's collection.

at one time the physical appearance of the hospital and its grounds was as life-enhancing as the park and parkway system that lay just beyond its borders. Finding an adaptive reuse for this national historic landmark constitutes a major preservation problem for the city. The task is now being tackled by the nonprofit Richardson Complex Corporation, which is overseeing an impressive master plan.[43]

To visitors who saw his exhibit about Buffalo at the Philadelphia and Paris expositions of 1876 and 1878, Olmsted was pleased to point out that, taken together, the Park, Parkside, Forest Lawn Cemetery, and the Buffalo State Hospital grounds created a "district nearly three square miles in area, extensively planted and guarded against any approach to dense building."[44]

These landscapes of recreation, residence, memory, and healing today constitute an exceptional urban green space (see Fig. 6.1).

SMALL PARKS AND PUBLIC SPACES

In July 1886 the Common Council, acting on legislation recently approved in Albany, turned over to the park commissioners control of all of the smaller parks and public squares in the city. Immediately the commissioners contacted Olmsted to ask his advice on what should be done with a number of these diminutive but important civic spaces. On August 21 Olmsted stopped in town to survey these grounds while on his way to San Francisco to work on his plan for Stanford University. He was accompanied by his sixteen-year-old son, Frederick Law Olmsted Jr., who he hoped would one day follow in his footsteps and assume leadership of his business, and Henry Sargent Codman, a recent graduate of the Massachusetts Institute of Technology who was apprenticing with Olmsted and fast becoming his right-hand man. In the company of McMillan, Olmsted and his associates toured the various sites and offered suggestions for their improvement and maintenance. The circuit included stops at the Terrace, a strip of land in downtown overlooking Lake Erie that since the earliest days of the city had been dedicated to public use; Johnson Park, a small residential square dating from the pre–Civil War years; Day's Park, another antebellum residential square; the Potter's Field, the former paupers' cemetery that was now to be converted to recreational use; and Lafayette Square, the busy downtown public square where, in place of Richardson's arch, the city had erected George Keller's columnar Soldiers and Sailors Monument in 1882. Olmsted would also be asked to make a plan for Bennett Park, the land for which had been donated to the city in 1854.

Always one to think in citywide terms, Olmsted told McMillan, "It is desirable that each small park should have a plan and serve a purpose as distinct as possible from all the others."[45] Consequently, for each of these locales Olmsted formulated different ideas that he, Codman, and his stepson John worked up into formal plans back in Brookline. The undertaking would be added to the happy burden of work at the Olmsted office, which was so busy with clients that operations were spilling over into the dining room of the house. The Buffalo plans, which bore the name of the firm at the time, F. L. & J. C. Olmsted, Landscape Architects, were in Buffalo by April 1887, and construction was under way by the summer.

The Terrace, Day's Park, and Johnson Park

The Terrace, which consisted of two strips of ground, was an especially honored feature of the city. Before Joseph Ellicott's day, it had been a gathering place for Seneca tribesmen, who enjoyed looking out over Lake

Erie from the elevated ground. Ellicott himself, according to local memoirist Samuel Welch, had intended "to lay out, grade and beautify it in a picturesque manner, making of it sort of Champs Elysées" that would serve as "the resort of the people in their leisure hours." Ellicott had planned to terminate the promenade at Niagara Square, where a triumphal arch like the one recently dedicated in Paris would be erected.[46] During the War of 1812, the Terrace had been occupied by an army hospital, and when Olmsted visited, it was fairly dilapidated. Olmsted wished to renew the historic site as a community amenity that would, on a more modest scale, recall what Ellicott had envisioned. In Olmsted's view, the space was too small to be dealt with other than as an area of sidewalk-bordered turf shaded by several parallel rows of elm trees. Once the trees had grown to maturity, Olmsted predicted that the Terrace, which now exists only as a name on a signpost beneath an ele-

Fig. 6.12. Day's Park, c. 1900. Courtesy James Mendola.

THE BEST PLANNED CITY IN THE WORLD

Fig. 6.13. Johnson Park, c. 1912. Courtesy James Mendola.

vated highway, would prove an attractive promenade for area residents.

Day's Park, a slightly larger rectangular space that is now part of the Allentown Historic District, already had some fairly mature trees when Olmsted redesigned it. (Fig. 6.12) "This finely shaded Place," McMillan reported, "is much used as an airing ground for invalids and children during the summer months."[47] Residents, however, were dismayed by the way children from the grammar school on the western border of the park ruined the lawn by playing games there. Olmsted's blueprint for solving this vexing problem was to establish a graveled play area across from the schoolhouse to tempt the frolicsome youngsters away from the turf.

Johnson Park was a larger oblong residential green that had a reputation as a dignified address. It was surrounded by the homes belonging to some of Buffalo's most venerable families. The stone cottage of Dr. Ebenezer Johnson, the city's first mayor, was chief among

them, although by the 1880s it had been converted into a private school. With a few judicious alterations, Olmsted believed that the square could be made an even more pleasant in-town place in which to live. Primarily, seeing no need to retain the existing footpaths that marred the lawn of this urban oasis, he called for their removal so that the residents could enjoy an outlook on unbroken verdant lawn. In the spring of 1887, five hundred loads of good soil were brought in to obliterate the unsightly walks. In addition, Olmsted advised that the basin of the central fountain (no longer extant) might be enlarged a bit, missing trees be replaced, and a sturdy curb be installed at the street line.[48] (Fig. 6.13)

Bennett Place

Bennett Place, in the southern part of the city, had been a substantial private property before 1854, when the family had donated it to the city for a public park. The

Fig. 6.14. The Philander Bennett house, dating from the 1830s, was donated by the family for Bennett Place. From Frank H. Severance, *Picture Book of Earlier Buffalo* (1912).

The two-story pavilion between the lawn and the playground performed an important role in the organization of the grounds. In addition to restrooms, it contained a passageway that provided the sole access to the enclosed play area, and the deep front porch facing the lawn afforded welcome shelter from rain or sun. The handsome building was conceived by the local architect Henry L. Campbell in the Shingle style, the mode of design that Richardson and McKim, Mead & White had done so much to make synonymous with the architecture of the American upper-class summer home. Campbell had brought a bit of Newport to an out-of-the-way Buffalo neighborhood, most of whose hard-

plan that the Olmsted firm prepared for the two-and-a-half-acre rectangular site called for the removal of the stone Bennett mansion and the creation of a pleasant breathing space and playground for the residents of a thickly settled neighborhood.[49] (Fig. 6.14) The design shared a certain affinity with the projects for small parks that Calvert Vaux and Samuel Parsons Jr. were devising around this time for tenement districts on the Lower East Side of Manhattan. Its dominant feature was a lawn bordered on three sides by trees and flowering shrubbery that screened the pretty space from the adjacent streets. A fenced-in children's playground was located on the north side of the park, facing busy Clinton Street.[50] But since the entire park was surrounded by a five-foot-tall iron fence, there was no fear for the youngsters' safety. Between these two spaces stood a large shelter house. Ornamental gates at each corner made it easy for visitors to enter and leave the little park from any direction, and a simple internal system of ten-foot-wide flagstone paths permitted them to move about the grounds easily. (Fig. 6.15)

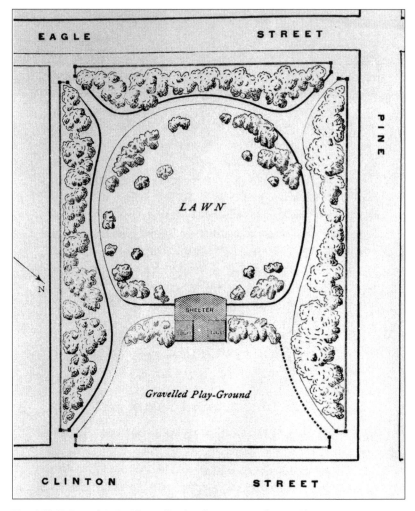

Fig. 6.15. F. L. and J. C. Olmsted's plan for Bennett Place, 1887. *Annual Report of the Buffalo Park Commissioners* (1888).

THE BEST PLANNED CITY IN THE WORLD

Fig. 6.16. The Bennett Place lawn area, c. 1910. Courtesy James Mendola.

working residents never had the opportunity to take a seaside vacation. Here, at least for a while, adults could enjoy quiet leisure time in a beautiful setting while children might romp and race in the protected play space. (Fig. 6.16)

As soon as Bennett Place opened in the summer of 1889, it became popular. "The rules for the orderly behavior of visitors have been duly respected, and the ornamental features of the place fully appreciated," McMillan reported.[51] Unfortunately, Bennett Place proved to be an ephemeral neighborhood amenity. In the 1920s Campbell's lovely shelter house was torn down, the playground was removed, and the lawn was used for various sports. By the end of the twentieth century, Bennett Place had disappeared beneath asphalt tennis courts.

Masten Place

Masten Place was similar in size to Bennett Place but located near the spot where in 1868 Olmsted had recommended the city build its East Side park. The area was fast becoming a "cottage" neighborhood, inhabited primarily by German immigrant families. Since 1832 the land for the new park had been the Potter's Field,

a city-owned burying ground that by the mid-1880s was no longer used for interments. The high, thinly wooded site, with its splendid view over the city and lake, was now available to accommodate the living. Olmsted urged the city to act so that the "fine outlook could be permanently maintained," and when asked, he provided a plan.[52] The city quickly approved Olmsted's design for the property which now bore the name Masten Place (or Masten Park) to honor the memory of Joseph G. Masten, an early mayor. (Fig. 6.17) According to Olmsted's scheme, entrances at the four corners opened onto ten-foot-wide paths that defined a heart-shaped lawn in the high central area. A diminutive brick shelter building (built in 1888) provided restrooms at the crossing point of the footpaths. Because of the steepness of the site it was not feasible to have a playground. Therefore the commissioners decided to allow "certain quiet games" and "general play at special hours" to take place on the lawn once the turf had had time to establish itself.[53]

Construction of Masten Place required a considerable amount of effort. In addition to two thousand cubic yards of sandy loam and one thousand cubic yards of sand that needed to be removed, fifteen coffins that were exhumed had to be relocated. After that, in order to create a healthy lawn, a large quantity of good soil was brought to the site. Infilling raised the cost of construction. This may have been the reason why the board ignored Olmsted's suggestion to McMillan that the city combine Masten Place with the adjacent site of a new reservoir to create an arboretum of woody New York State plants.

In the summer of 1888, when Masten Place was finished, the commissioners opened negotiations with the bishop of the Roman Catholic diocese to obtain an additional strip of land eighty-eight feet wide on the western side of the site which held a small cemetery. Two years later the city acquired the land in exchange for acreage elsewhere in town. The mayor, however, then proposed that the acquisition be used for a new school rather than for parkland. This would, he argued, save the city the cost of buying additional property in the neighborhood. The park commissioners strongly objected to this idea, and their opposition

eventually carried the day. The deconsecrated land became part of Masten Place.[54]

A few years later, in 1894, with economic depression stalking the country and reducing the city's coffers, the superintendent of education again brought the issue of building a school on Masten Place before the Common Council. In response, the Olmsteds telegraphed Sherman Jewett, then president of the park board, condemning the notion. It would, they said, destroy the park's value to the neighborhood for "general recreation," adding that "there should be more rather than fewer public recreation grounds in that part of Buffalo."[55] Nonetheless, this time the council overruled the commissioners and called for a large high school in the center of the small park. The council agreed, however, to allow the remaining area to stay under the control of the park commissioners for use by the general public. "We protest most earnestly against any scheme to take possession of this or any other park property for any purpose," the commissioners declared, and they argued that parkland in the heart of the city was particularly important to retain: "If the present generation is indifferent, the next will feel keenly the evil results when the vicinity population will be much denser than now." In support of their claim, they pointed to Boston, New York, Brooklyn, and Philadelphia, cities that were now forced to provide "at enormous cost numerous small parks like Bennett and Masten places" in the built-up parts of town. Moreover, the commissioners condemned the notion

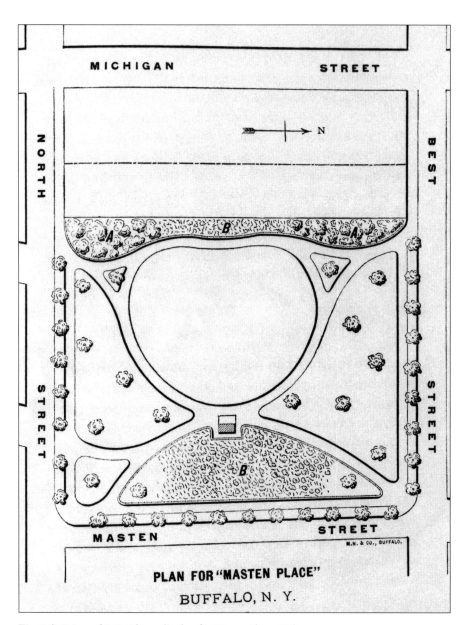

Fig. 6.17. F. L. and J. C. Olmsted's plan for Masten Place, 1887. *Annual Report of the Buffalo Park Commissioners* (1888).

Fig. 6.18. Masten Park High School (1897) usurped the site of Olmsted's Masten Park. Courtesy James Mendola.

that a school could coexist with the park. "The two objects are wholly incompatible," they noted. "The proximity of the school with all the adjacent space necessary for the travel and business traffic daily resorting to it would destroy all quiet enjoyment of the park section."[56] Despite their earnest objections, the school was built.[57] (Fig. 6.18) As the commissioners foresaw, the park eventually disappeared.

SEVEN

The Emancipation of Niagara

The lesson of which Niagara Falls may be said to have been a pioneer teacher, is the State's right of eminent domain over objects of great scientific interest and natural beauty—the inherent right of the people to the free enjoyment of the wonders of nature.

—Andrew Haswell Green, "The Last Public Address by the Late Hon. Andrew H. Green, Concerning the State Reservation at Niagara," 1903

Already before the opening of the Erie Canal in 1825, Niagara Falls, some seventeen miles downriver from Buffalo, was an important tourist destination. (Fig. 7.1) The opening of the canal brought more visitors, both American and foreign, and the development of rail lines to the town in the 1840s significantly boosted their numbers. Among those making the pilgrimage to this great natural wonder was the young Olmsted. In 1828 his scenery-loving father took him there after a stay with his uncle Owen Pitkin Olmsted in Geneseo, in upstate New York. In later life Olmsted remembered how in those early days of tourism "a visit to the Falls was a series of expeditions, and in each expedition, hours were occupied in wandering slowly among the trees, going from place to place, with many intervals of

rest. . . . People, then, were loath to leave the place; many lingered on from day to day after they had prepared to go, revisiting ground they had gone over before, turning and returning; and when they went away it was with grateful hearts and grateful words."[1]

In 1868 Olmsted returned to the falls while on one of his early trips to Buffalo. What he found there was deeply dismaying to him, for the desire for amusement clearly dominated the way tourists were encouraged to spend their time at the site. Sightseers paid handsomely to ride the *Maid of the Mist* boats that dared the torrents at the base of the falls, to climb a tower perched precipitously on the brink of Horseshoe Falls, to become drenched while walking on rickety boardwalks along the base of the American Falls to see the Cave of the Winds, and to negotiate slippery stairways, steep walks, and crowded outlooks to view the spectacle from all angles, near and far. Additionally, a privately owned place of amusement called Prospect Park (opened in 1872) included Prospect Point, where, proclaimed the proprietor, "shielded by a stone parapet wall built upon the edge of the high bank," visitors might enjoy the best view of both the American and Canadian falls available on the American side. It was

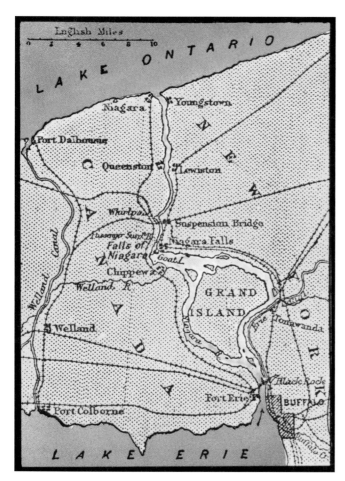

Fig. 7.1. Niagara Falls is located on the Niagara River about halfway between Lake Erie and Lake Ontario. Courtesy New York State Archives.

Fig. 7.2. The unobstructed edge of Prospect Point was the spot where early visitors stood to view the entire cataract. Photograph by George Baker, 1860s. Courtesy Janice and Dale Rossi.

here that in earlier days painters and photographers, unimpeded by a wall, had often stood to take the best view of the cataract. (Fig. 7.2)

The eleven-acre wooded grounds of Prospect Park offered many other attractions. For those willing to pay the forty-cent entrance fee, the owner touted a large pavilion for "dancing, recitations, singing, etc.," and an art gallery with "several hundred representations of the most notable scenes of European and Oriental" historical and natural sites, "all enlarged microscopically, and so arranged that one hundred persons may at the same time be pleasantly occupied in their examination." There were also small "refreshment rooms" throughout the grounds, which had the reputation as a rendezvous

of men and women of easy virtue. If tourists wished, they might descend on the inclined railway, built in 1844, to the river's edge, "where a sublime view of the American Fall can be had from its base." On clement nights, electric lights powered by "Brush's Dynamo-Electric Machines" afforded visitors the opportunity of beholding the "sublime and novel effect of the reflected light and the Electric Bow painted upon the spray-clouds of the American falls and its surroundings."[2] To Olmsted's sensitive eye, the blatant aim of the tourist businesses at the falls was "to make money by the showman's methods."[3] He knew that Niagara had so much more to offer.

Standing in pristine wilderness near Prospect Point in 1678, Father Louis Hennepin, the Belgian Franciscan missionary who is reputed to have been the first European to publish a written and visual account of Niagara Falls, reported how "two great sheets of water, which are on the two sides of the sloping island that is in the middle, fall down without noise and without violence, and glide in this manner without din." He was describing the parting of the broad and seemingly placid waters of the Niagara River on either side of Goat Island, a sixty-acre piece of land that divides what are now called the American Falls from the larger Canadian or Horseshoe Falls. (Fig. 7.3) And no one has penned a more evocative description of these two 180-foot-high cascades than Father Hennepin. "When this great mass of water reaches the bottom," he wrote, "then there is a noise and a roaring greater than thunder. Moreover the spray of the water is so great that it forms clouds above this abyss, and these are seen even at the time when the sun is shining brightest at midday. . . . [A]ll these waters fall with an impetuosity that can be imagined in so high a fall, so prodigious, for its horrible mass of water. There are formed those thunders, those roarings, those fearful bounds and seethings, with that perpetual cloud rising above the cedars and spruces."[4]

After the French and Indian War, Niagara Falls passed from French to British hands. Two decades later, following the American Revolution, the Niagara River became the boundary between the United States and Canada. Since the international border follows the middle of the river, the falls are divided between the two nations. The eastern shore (called the mainland above the falls) and Goat Island are part of New York State; the western shore belongs to the Province of Ontario. Impressive rapids enliven the waters on either side of Goat Island immediately before the river plunges over the falls. These are known as the American Rapids or the Upper Rapids on the New York State side of the

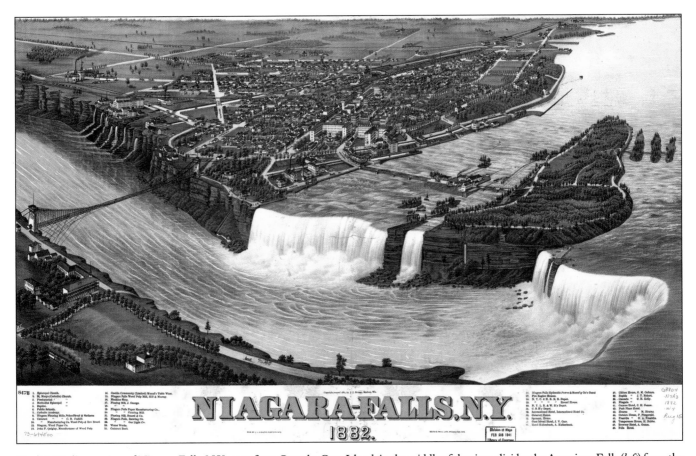

Fig. 7.3. Bird's-eye view of Niagara Falls, N.Y., seen from Canada. Goat Island, in the middle of the river, divides the American Falls (*left*) from the Horseshoe or Canadian Falls (*right*). In the Canadian Rapids are the Three Sisters islands. The village of Niagara Falls is on the mainland shore.

Lithograph by H. Wellge, 1882. Library of Congress, Prints and Photographs Division.

The Emancipation of Niagara

Fig. 7.4. William H. Bartlett, *The American Rapids above the Falls*. Steel engraving. From N. P. Willis, *American Scenery* (1840).

falls the thrill of what the eighteenth-century philosopher Edmund Burke had defined as the "sublime"—something that inspires in the observer a sense of awe tinged with fear. "This was a scene which I was unprepared to expect," wrote the poet Timothy Dwight, one of America's first tourists, on his visit to Niagara Falls in 1804, "and an exhibition of the force of water I had never before imagined. The emotions excited by the view of this stupendous scene are unutterable."[6] To the more educated class of visitors, like Dwight, the sublime promised spiritual experience and moral improvement.

river and, on the other side of the island, as the Canadian Rapids. (Fig. 7.4) The international division continues down the river beyond the falls to where, some thirteen miles distant, the Niagara empties into Lake Ontario at Youngstown, New York, and Niagara-on-the-Lake, Ontario. After the falls, the Niagara—in reality a strait between the two easternmost Great Lakes—passes through the narrow seven-mile-long Niagara Gorge, where the confined waters churn over spectacular rapids and, making an abrupt turn, swirl through a dizzying whirlpool. Beyond the whirlpool, the river widens again and flows calmly the last six miles to its mouth.

Awed by the beauty and majesty of the falls, many of those who came to Niagara spoke of the experience in religious and philosophical terms. "The power and presence of the Almighty seem fearfully manifest. You gaze, and tremble as you gaze," stated a guidebook published in Buffalo in 1842. In his essay "My Visit to Niagara," Nathaniel Hawthorne compared his trip to a spiritual journey. The Scottish statesman and poet John Douglas Sutherland Campbell, marquis of Lorne, found the rushing waters evocative of the biblical Flood: "So poured the avenging streams upon the world/When swung the ark upon the deluge wave," he wrote in his poem "Niagara."[5]

There was also to be had in the presence of the

HARNESSING NIAGARA FALLS FOR MANUFACTURING

When established in 1805, the village of Niagara Falls optimistically bore the name of Manchester. Clearly the founders had in mind the material enrichment to be derived from the falls, not the spiritual nourishment they might provide. The history of harnessing the flow of the river for manufacturing started when the area was still part of New France. In the 1750s Daniel Joncaire, the keeper of the portage route around the falls, began to divert river water above the Upper Rapids into a short millrace to turn the wheel of a primitive sawmill. The advent of this ancient form of driving power initiated the transformation of the area around the falls from untouched wilderness to what would become in the twentieth century one of the world's most extensive industrial landscapes.

During the opening years of the nineteenth century, the State of New York began selling the land around the falls to private enterprise. Lovely Goat Island, which early locals called Iris Island because of the flower that grew wild in abundance there, was acquired by Augustus Porter, brother of Peter Buell Porter, the developer of Black Rock next to Buffalo. By the time the village of Niagara Falls incorporated in 1848, it was home to a number of small and mid-sized businesses that utilized the swift-moving river water to produce mechanical energy freely and abundantly. Moreover, Suspension Bridge, a separate small community a little north of the village, was the site of an international railroad bridge, constructed by John A. Roebling in 1855, connecting the American side of the gorge with Niagara Falls (then known as Clifton), Ontario. Facilitating trade between the two countries, the bridge further bolstered the area's commercial and industrial fortunes.

By the late 1860s, spurred by demand during the Civil War, an assortment of mills turning out various products had grown up along the American shore above the falls. (Fig. 7.5) A canal had been dug here parallel to the river from the beginning of the Upper Rapids to near Prospect Point. It was bordered by a number of enterprises, including a laundry, a furniture factory, a paper mill, planing mills, and a foundry. All of these buildings received power from shafts or rope drives propelled by the age-old system of waterwheels. On Bath Island (the present Green Island), which lies between the mainland and Goat Island in the American Rapids, there operated a paper mill and a tannery that was said to be among the largest in the country. (Fig. 7.6)

Well before the war, another, more ambitious attempt had been made to use the river's power. In 1853 engineers constructed the 4,500-foot-long Hydraulic Canal. It began a mile above the falls and crossed the village diagonally to a spot about one thousand feet north (downriver) of the American Falls. This area on top of the gorge came to be called the High Bank. Augustus Porter, the primary

investor in the project, soon augmented the canal by creating a large holding basin at the edge of the cliff. The plan was to generate power by having water descend from the basin to turn wheels mounted in a one-hundred-foot vertical channel carved in the face of the cliff. In 1857 a flour mill was built on the High Bank, inaugurating the disfigurement of the scenic gorge cliff.

Other businesses were slow to come, however, and by 1877 the Hydraulic Canal was sold at auction. The

Fig. 7.5. *Village Shore just above American Falls.* The view was taken from Bath Island. Photograph by George Barker, 1879. Courtesy Local History Department, Niagara Falls, N.Y., Public Library.

Fig. 7.6. *Bath Island in the American Rapids.* The Whipple bridge across the American Rapids is in the foreground. Photograph by George Barker, 1879. Courtesy Local History Department, Niagara Falls, N.Y., Public Library.

buyer, Buffalo businessman Jacob Schoelkopf, would be responsible for a great leap forward in producing energy from the river. In 1881 one of Schoelkopf's tenants on the Hydraulic Canal built an electric generator that ran by mechanical power supplied by the canal water. Current from the generator, which was one of the first of its kind in the world, ran arc lamps in the village. The inauguration of the streetlights was celebrated with a public parade, and visitors from other parts of the country began to come to Niagara Falls to see them. Realizing the potential of electricity, Schoelkopf in 1882 erected a small powerhouse at the end of the Hydraulic Canal. Here water power was converted to electricity by means of a dynamo, a type of generator invented in England in the 1830s. A smart businessman, Schoelkopf quickly undertook to convert his Hydraulic Canal to the production of electricity. The process added large, ugly metal penstocks to the cliff face to carry water from the basin to the power station at the river's edge. By 1896 Schoelkopf's Hydraulic Power and Manufacturing Company had four riverside turbines supplying 35,000 horsepower of direct current

to a number of large mills lined along the brink of the High Bank. (Fig. 7.7) The picturesque wilderness that had once existed here was by then a memory.

OLMSTED'S 1869 VISIT TO THE FALLS

Distressed by what he saw at the falls in the 1860s, Olmsted vowed to undertake a campaign to rescue the great eastern natural wonder from the grasp of hucksters who were degrading appreciation of its true loveliness and manufacturers who were erecting ugly factory buildings on the shoreline and the islands. "I had shortly before been engaged in establishing the State reservation of California for the preservation and free Public use of the natural scenery of the Yosemite Valley and the Mariposa Grove and the question had been on my mind whether something should not be done with a similar purpose at Niagara," he later explained.[7] In 1869 Olmsted began his efforts to have the area around Niagara Falls on the American side acquired by the State of New York. It was anticipated that the Canadians would do likewise.

In early August 1869, while he and Vaux were in Buffalo to present their plan for the Buffalo park system to the Common Council, they spent a couple of days at Niagara Falls, where they stayed at the Cataract House hotel overlooking the American Rapids. Also along were William Dorsheimer and his architect, the young H. H. Richardson. "While rambling on Goat Island with Mr. Dorsheimer and Mr. Richardson," Olmsted recalled, "I brought the subject before them and, as there were, at the time, two or three other gentlemen at Niagara with whom we had been associated

Fig. 7.7. By the late nineteenth century, much of the Niagara gorge in the city of Niagara Falls had become home to industrial facilities. Shown here is the area known as the High Bank. From H. Perry Smith, *History of the City of Buffalo and Erie County* (1908).

in the project of the Buffalo Park and the Buffalo State Lunatic Hospital ground, they were asked to meet in the evening at Mr. Dorsheimer's room to consider the matter." The next day, at Olmsted's suggestion, the group, which included Buffalonians Dennis Bowen, Joseph Warren, and Henry Richmond, drove down the river to the end of the gorge at Lewiston. (Fig. 7.8) Olmsted hoped that land might be taken "for a public road to be so laid out from the Falls to Lewiston that from it a good free view could be secured to the public of the Falls, the whirlpool and the entire gorge of the river." One assumes that they also drove their carriage across the new Falls View Suspension Bridge, which had opened in January close by the American Falls, to enjoy the panoramic view of the entire cataract that only the Canadian side offered.[8] A few days later the same men met at the Buffalo Club in Buffalo. At that meeting, the group considered creating a parkway linking the Park at Buffalo with the scenic gorge route that Olmsted had proposed.

"THE DISTINCTIVE CHARMS OF NIAGARA SCENERY"

In Olmsted and Vaux's view, a visit to Niagara Falls should be leisurely and thoughtful, a pilgrimage providing a variety of uplifting encounters with nature beyond the celebrated spectacle of the great cataract itself. Indeed, Olmsted's persistent use of the name "Niagara" rather than "Niagara Falls" to describe the area signified this larger reference to the other natural attractions present there. Goat Island, the rapids, and especially the Three Sisters Islands (triple islets in the Canadian Rapids accessible from Goat Island), possessed, he believed, "infinitely varied beauties of water and spray and of water-worn rock," as well as "the great variety of indigenous perennials and annuals, the rare beauty of the old woods, and the exceeding loveliness of the rock foliage," and the charm of hanging foliage and foliage-framed views of the water.[9] Olmsted wished that the public's eyes might be opened to such things instead

Fig. 7.8. The gorge below the city of Niagara Falls remained in its natural condition. From H. Perry Smith, *History of the City of Buffalo and Erie County* (1908).

of being so narrowly focused on the sublime pageant of the falls. Even without the falls, Olmsted believed, Niagara "would be a place of singular fascination."[10]

To Olmsted's mind, Goat Island was the jewel of Niagara. Vaux also regarded it as "a beautiful example of natural landscape design."[11] Because of its position in the middle of the falls, the island supported abundant flora of many types. (Fig. 7.9) In fact, botanists proclaimed that this thirty-acre, roughly triangular landmass supported a greater variety of vegetation than any other spot of similar size in all of the eastern United States or even Europe. David Day, the Buffalo park commissioner who cataloged the flora on the island in the 1880s, marveled at Goat Island's "vernal beauty," which he believed was "attributable, not merely to its variety of plants, conspicuous in flower, but also to the extraordinary abundance in which they are produced."[12] After many years of travel in search of the picturesque, Olmsted confessed that he had not encountered "the same quality of forest beauty . . . which is still to be observed in those parts of Goat Island where the original growth of trees and shrubs has not been disturbed."[13] He would undoubtedly have seconded the opinion of his contemporary, the journalist Charles Dudley Warner, that "the walk about Goat Island at Niagara Falls is probably unsurpassed in the world for wonder and beauty."[14]

Since the early 1850s, Goat Island had been accessible from the mainland by a bridge that traversed Bath Island. Both islands were owned by the Porter family. While they had sought aggressively to develop commerce and industry in the village, they had scrupulously guarded Goat Island and the appended Three Sisters Islands from modern encroachments. Responsible stewards, the Porters maintained Goat Island in its

Fig. 7.9. *View in the Primeval Woods on Goat Island.* Wood engraving after a sketch by Thomas Moran, c. 1879. Author's collection.

THE BEST PLANNED CITY IN THE WORLD

primeval condition as a private park, allowing tourists to visit for a fifty-cent fee. A carriage drive "laid out with sufficiently fair taste through the natural forest," wrote a traveler in 1865, ringed the island. A footpath more or less paralleled the carriageway on the land side, and other trails led through the woods to Terrapin Point and the Three Sisters Islands. At intervals seats invited visitors to pause and take longer pleasure in the surroundings.[15] Wooden bridges conducted them in safety to the Three Sisters Islands and Luna Island (a small piece of land on the brink of the American Falls that diverts a portion of the water over the lesser Bridal Veil Falls). It was through this lovely setting, much of which was out of view of the falls themselves, that in August 1869 Olmsted rambled with Dorsheimer and Richardson, discussing his dream of securing eternal protection for all of Niagara's forest and water scenery.

THE CAMPAIGN TO SAVE NIAGARA

Throughout the 1870s and early 1880s, Olmsted would orchestrate a national and international campaign to "save" the Niagara landscape. In this effort he had the constant political assistance of his friend Dorsheimer. Others who would lend support include Vaux, the landscape painter Frederic Church, the noted art historian Charles Eliot Norton, and Thomas V. Welch, a Niagara Falls legislator. Numerous Buffalo citizens, including Grover Cleveland, would also lend valuable support. It would take more than fifteen years before a portion of Olmsted's vision became a reality with the establishment by the New York Reservation at Niagara.

During the years immediately after the Cataract House meeting, Olmsted made little progress on his proposal for public acquisition. Apparently the men of affairs who had met with him at the Buffalo Club advised him that the postwar boom years in the Empire State were not right for such an anti-development enterprise. Olmsted, however, must surely have renewed discussion of his vision for Niagara on his many visits to Buffalo.

Others also broached the topic of Niagara's peril. Articles in newspapers and journals attested to the growing public perception that the falls faced the danger of being completely overwhelmed by greedy industry and commerce. Henry James, an acquaintance of Olmsted's, writing in the *Nation,* the journal of political opinion that Olmsted had helped E. L Godkin found in 1865, noted in 1871 that although the Porters had been good stewards of Goat Island and had refused many times to sell their property, "they are human, and the offer may be made once too often." It was surely with knowledge of Olmsted's plan that he suggested, "Before this fatal day dawns, why should not the State buy up the precious acres, as California has done the Yo-Semite?"[16] In 1875 William Morris, the father of the Arts and Crafts movement in England and an early advocate of the preservation of historic buildings, after visiting the falls complained in print of the legion of ill-informed guides, vendors of vulgar souvenirs, aggressive carriage drivers, and unscrupulous restaurateurs he had encountered. "It would seem that the very pick of touts and rascals of the world had assembled there," he remarked.[17]

A turning point came in the summer of 1878, when Olmsted's distant cousin, the painter Frederic Church, took up the cause of preserving Niagara Falls. In 1857 Church had depicted the falls in a painting that was regarded as the definitive representation of the great cataract. In the summer of 1878, without Olmsted's knowledge, Church met with the cultivated outgoing governor-general of Canada, Lord Dufferin, to suggest that the falls be placed under the joint protection of the Dominion of Canada and the State of New York. Shortly thereafter Lord Dufferin spoke personally to New York governor Lucius Robinson about the proposal. As Queen Victoria's representative in Canada, Dufferin believed that his overture on behalf of the park would be another in a series of measures he had taken to cement friendly relations with the United States. In September 1878, in his farewell address to Canada before taking up his new post as British ambassador to Russia, Dufferin told the Toronto Society of

Artists about his idea. This first public airing of the novel concept met with favorable if cautious response in the American press. "Lord Dufferin's untiring efforts to cultivate pleasant relations between Canada and the United States were beautifully illustrated in his speech yesterday before the Society of Artists," reported James Gordon Bennett's *New York Herald*. "He mentioned his meeting a few weeks hence, meeting with the Governor of New York[,] when he had proposed to establish an international park around the Falls of Niagara," an idea the paper applauded because it would "create a pleasant bond of sympathy between American and Canadian visitors" while preserving the great natural wonder for future generations.[18]

While in firm agreement with Lord Dufferin's intentions, Calvert Vaux took strong exception to the Englishman's remark that "the proposed international park must not be desecrated, or in any way sophisticated by the puny efforts of the art of the landscape gardener." In defense of his young profession, Vaux affirmed that if the natural landscape of Goat Island were to be entirely destroyed by fire, "a similar effect (if a record had been kept) could be reproduced with comparative rapidity, if the resources of the art of the landscape gardener were consecrated to the work." To substantiate his contention, he pointed to the naturalistic landscape he and Olmsted had so convincingly fashioned from wasteland at Central Park, where a famous visitor had unwittingly declared, "They've left it alone better than I thought they would." Pleased by the deception, Vaux explained that "the object in view all the time was, of course, the permanent retention of the interesting features of the landscape, and the preservation and emphasis of every natural characteristic of the site." He assured Lord Dufferin that this same philosophy could be applied successfully at Niagara.[19]

Governor Robinson reacted favorably to Lord Dufferin's scheme. His enthusiasm for the idea was unexpected, for Robinson, a reform Democrat, "held very strongly that view of the limited function of government which forbids all taxation except for necessary expenses of government, strictly construed."[20] Robinson had even avoided the ceremonies celebrating the opening of the new capitol, which Richardson and Olmsted had designed along with Leopold Eidlitz, because he considered the building a reckless extravagance. Nonetheless, in his annual address to the state legislature at the opening of its session in February 1879, he proposed that an international "reservation" be created to preserve the natural scenery at Niagara Falls. The falls, he said, were "the property of the whole world," not just the United States and Canada, and attracted visitors from around the globe; therefore "it would seem incumbent on both governments to protect such travelers from improper annoyance on either side."[21]

Robinson's speech brought the issue of state action before the legislature and the people of New York. In fact, there were already a number of strong "reservationists," as those backing state acquisition of the falls came to be known, including former governor Samuel Tilden and his associate Andrew H. Green. Dorsheimer, who was now lieutenant governor, however, thought that the idea of an international park was too impractical for immediate implementation. Seeing no possibility of the measure's passing, on the last day of the legislative session he shepherded a compromise drafted by Olmsted through both the Assembly and the Senate. It authorized the Commissioners of the State Survey (the body responsible for mapping the state) to undertake an investigation of the land around the falls with a view to its future purchase by the state. James T. Gardner, the highly competent director of the survey, was to carry out the work with Olmsted's participation.

Gardner and Olmsted presented their report to the legislature in March 1880. In it they called attention in words and images (taken by Niagara Falls photographer George Barker) to the commercial and industrial abuses that disfigured the mainland shore and Bath Island. (Figs. 7.5, 7.6, 7.10) They also noted the high fees that visitors had to pay in order to view the falls properly. Moreover, Goat Island was now under threat of development. As Henry James had foreseen, the Porter fam-

THE BEST PLANNED CITY IN THE WORLD

ily was close to selling the island to commercial interests. "I made careful inquiry concerning the nature of the proposals for purchase," wrote Gardner in the report. "By some it has been proposed to cut the woods off the Island and make a race-course of it; others think it a favorable site for a great summer hotel; others wish to make a rifle range upon it, while another and more practical party suggests cutting a canal down the center of the Island and building a row of factories along its front between the American and Canadian Falls." Not surprisingly, the authors of the report recommended that the state buy Goat Island. They also identified for purchase Bath Island, Prospect Park, and the mainland shore. These built-on lands were to be restored to their natural appearance. To demonstrate their mental picture of the future, they included an "ideal view" of the river bank with its Edenic appearance reconstituted.[22] (Fig. 7.11) They looked forward to the day when the state would invite visitors to enjoy all of Niagara's wonders free of charge.

Support for the report's conclusion was widespread. Locally, Sherman F. Jewett and his fellow Buffalo park commissioners were aware of the recommendations. Backing Olmsted and Gardner, they expressed hope "that the great state of New-York will not hesitate to embrace the opportunity now presented, to become the preserver of Niagara, and throw it open for the free enjoyment of the people of all climes who seek and enjoy the grand and sublime in Nature." Moreover, noting the proximity of Buffalo to the falls, the com-

missioners saw the opportunity to augment their own city's exceptional park system by linking it to the new grounds at Niagara. "May we not realize at no distant day the opening of a boulevard connecting our park system with that of the International Park, and thus bring our city within two hours' [travel] of a resort attract-

Fig. 7.10. *Village Shore of Upper American Rapids.* Photograph by George Barker, 1879. Courtesy Local History Department, Niagara Falls, N.Y., Public Library.

Fig. 7.11. Francis Lathrop, *Ideal View of the American Rapids after the Village Shore and Bath Island Are Restored.* Drawing reproduced in James T. Gardner, *Special Report on the Preservation of the Scenery at Niagara Falls . . . for the year 1879.* Courtesy Local History Department, Niagara Falls, N.Y., Public Library.

ing tourists from all parts of the civilized world?" they asked.[23] Elsewhere, Charles Eliot Norton undertook to obtain signatures on an international petition. The list of seven hundred names that he presented to the governor of New York and the governor-general of Canada included leaders from all walks of life in the United States, Canada, and England. Proud to be among them were such notables as John Ruskin, William Dean Howells, minister Phillips Brooks, Thomas Carlyle (one of Olmsted's heroes), Ralph Waldo Emerson, Charles Darwin, and Henry Wadsworth Longfellow. With one voice, they called upon the two friendly governments to act on behalf of the "civilized world" to preserve one of the "most valuable gifts which providence has bestowed upon our race."[24] Neither the new Republican governor, Alonzo B. Cornell, nor a majority of the legislature, however, was impressed by Gardner and Olmsted's report or by the petition. Cornell remarked that the falls were a spectacle that the public should expect to pay to see. Likewise, two bills introduced into the legislature to carry out the recommendations of the survey failed to receive the votes needed for passage.

ESTABLISHMENT OF
THE NIAGARA RESERVATION

Reservationists realized that in order to achieve their goal, they would have to mount both a vigorous political campaign and a sustained effort of public education. For the next several years Olmsted worked particularly with Jonathan B. Harrison, a well-known Unitarian clergyman who was a close friend of Norton's, to build a broad base of support for preserving Niagara Falls. Harrison had been an avid abolitionist; after the war he wrote extensively about life in the new South and championed Indian rights, conservation, and other reform causes. On behalf of the "free Niagara" movement, Harrison published forceful letters in the New York and Boston press decrying the terrible conditions at the falls. Late in 1882 Olmsted, together with Harrison, organized

a strategy meeting at the home of Howard Potter, the Episcopal bishop of New York City and a generous supporter of the Niagara preservation effort. Leading participants included Dorsheimer (who in 1880 had moved to the city to become editor of the New York Star), Gardner, Norton, Vaux, and a number of influential New Yorkers. The group agreed to form the Niagara Falls Association, an organization dedicated to directing the political campaign to rescue the falls. Over the next several months, the association published tracts and sent Harrison on lecture engagements throughout the state. His ardent speeches did much to arouse public awareness of "the danger of the obliteration of the distinctive charms of Niagara scenery."[25]

The association, which had given up on the notion of a joint American–Canadian park in favor of a scenic reservation only on the New York State side, received a significant boost in 1883 when Grover Cleveland, former mayor of Buffalo and a political ally of Dorsheimer's, became governor. After a dinner with Cleveland and Dorsheimer, Richardson wrote to Olmsted to inform him that the new governor was "strongly in favor of Niagara."[26] (It must have been quite a dinner, considering the corpulence of the three men.) Later that year the association drafted a bill that called for the acquisition of land by the state around the falls and the creation of a five-member commission to administer the new reservation. In mid-April 1883 the bill passed both houses of the legislature, and on April 30 Cleveland signed it into law.

Cleveland wasted no time in appointing five unpaid members to the new Niagara Reservation Commission. Dorsheimer was the natural choice for the commission's president. From western New York were Sherman S. Rogers, a successful Buffalo attorney who was an ally of Cleveland's in the civil service reform movement and a generous patron of the arts in his hometown, and Martin B. Anderson, the highly respected president of the University of Rochester. Two men from New York City were also appointed: J. Hampden Robb, a successful businessman, civic leader, and parks commissioner

Fig. 7.12. Andrew Haswell Green (1820–1903). From John Foord, *The Life and Public Services of Andrew Haswell Green* (1912).

who would serve as secretary, and Andrew H. Green, a militant advocate for good government and, like Dorsheimer, a close associate of Samuel Tilden. Green, who had been New York City comptroller in the late 1850s and early 1860s, had been Olmsted's nemesis at Central Park. (Fig. 7.12) "Not a dollar, not a cent, is got from under his paw that is not wet with his blood and sweat," Olmsted had remarked of the difficulty of obtaining Green's authorization for park expenditures.[27] Indeed, Green's appointment to the Niagara commission so grieved Olmsted that for a time he privately threatened to have nothing further to do with the reservation.

The commissioners met for the first time in May 1885 and immediately decided to visit the falls as soon as possible to determine which lands to recommend for purchase. They also agreed to ask Olmsted, Vaux, and Gardner to join them as informal advisers. On June 9 the historic rendezvous took place.[28] Surely Olmsted's thoughts must have drifted back to that earlier meeting in 1869 when he and Dorsheimer and Vaux had first toured the area with a view to its preservation. Now,

after going over the ground armed with authority to acquire it, he and most of the commissioners were in favor of adopting Gardner's 1879 survey as the catalog of future reservation lands. Vaux and Green, however, were of a different opinion. When the commission met on July 6 to consider the matter formally, Green proposed to expand the boundaries. In support of this view, he read a letter from Vaux, who, in addition to Central Park, had worked with Green on a number of other projects in New York, including the recent establishment of the Metropolitan Museum of Art. Vaux held the position—perhaps formed as long ago as during the drive he had taken along the gorge to Lewiston with Olmsted in 1869—that the reservation should include the wild and picturesque gorge beyond the falls. "It is evident," Vaux maintained, "that the natural landscape boundaries of your projected reservation include the Niagara river, the rapids of the Horseshoe falls, the American falls, the Whirlpool rapids and the Whirlpool." In particular, he could not "help considering the whirlpool as the logical turning point in any general plan for preserving the scenery of the falls." (Fig. 7.13) Beyond that turbulent feature, he saw no remarkable scenery. Vaux also proposed that a carriage drive and footpath with frequent viewing places be constructed as far as the whirlpool, beyond which a bridge could be built to the Canadian side so that visitors might return to the falls along a road to be constructed there. Thus people would be able to make a circuit that would take them along both sides of the scenic waterway. Green hoped that the commissioners would agree to add a survey of the river down to the whirlpool to the map of the area immediately around the falls. In this way, he said, they would be able to determine "intelligently whether the work would be complete without the addition proposed by Mr. Vaux." Green was decidedly of the opinion that without it, their job would be only partially done.[29]

Dorsheimer, however, was skeptical of the entire proposal. Although he might have shared Vaux's and Green's love of the gorge and the whirlpool, he feared that to enlarge the scope of the commission's charge would be a

Fig. 7.13. Whirlpool Rapids below Niagara Falls, c. 1890. Courtesy New York State Archives.

serious political mistake. The obstacles in the way of adding more river land to the reservation were formidable. Not only were the railroad bridge, the Hydraulic Canal, and High Bank to be contended with, but so were "the private interests that had grown up since the scheme for the preservation of the scenery originated." First among them would have been Schoelkopf's nascent electrical generation plant and the industries that would want to use its cheap power. Moreover, Dorsheimer revealed, "another railroad bridge three hundred feet above the present one was projected." All of these impediments, he contended, would surely bring the cost of the additional improvements that Vaux was proposing to "more than the islands and the lands immediately at the Falls." To pursue Vaux's admirable suggestion would, Dorsheimer argued, endanger the entire project.[30] Harrison agreed.

THE BEST PLANNED CITY IN THE WORLD

In a letter to the *New York Sun,* he warned that the "the scenery there is not threatened as it is near the Falls. . . . [T]his enormous enlargement of the proposed reservation, and of its cost, . . . would, I think, insure the defeat of the original enterprise."[31]

Dorsheimer's realistic view of the matter carried the day, and the commissioners voted to lay claim only to the area immediately around the falls. This encompassed all of Prospect Park, a strip of land varying from 50 to 150 feet in width along the mainland from Prospect Point to the head of the American Rapids. Bath Island, Goat Island, the Three Sisters Islands, and other islets between the Canadian border and the American shore were also included. Indeed, Dorsheimer may have realized that with the advent of electrical generation at Niagara, the old water-powered industries along the mainland shore and on Bath Island would soon be obsolete. The cost of their acquisition therefore would be reasonable, and opposition to their demolition weak. To go after land that would figure in the future industrialization of Niagara Falls would, however, be a far more difficult matter, as Thomas Evershed, the state engineer who would draw the map of the lands and islands that the commissioners wished to acquire, might well have told them.[32] The controversy raised by Green, who, according to Olmsted, remained "ugly to the last," would not be the only one that Dorsheimer would be called upon to smooth over.[33]

In 1885, with the assessment log compiled, the association spearheaded a final effort championing the creation of the reservation. When the bill came before the legislature to appropriate funds to buy the land cataloged by the commissioners, Jonathan Harrison was once again sent around the state to lecture in favor of the measure. Thomas V. Welch, the Niagara Falls assemblyman, also worked indefatigably on behalf of the bill in Albany. In 1883 he had spoken eloquently in favor of the bill permitting the state to identify land to be taken for a future reservation, and two years later he advocated just as forcefully for authorizing funds for its acquisition. Addressing his colleagues, Welch insisted on using the term "reservation" rather than "park" to describe the legislation's intent. "The word 'park' as used in connection with this project is clearly a misnomer," he argued. "Nothing like a park in the ordinary acceptance of the word is contemplated or desired at Niagara. Nature there presents a spectacle of more beauty and grandeur than all of the artificial parks of the world combined, and any attempt to improve it by ornament should be regarded as sacrilege."[34]

On April 30, 1885, the new governor, David B. Hill, prodded by a personal message from Cleveland, who now occupied the White House, and Samuel Tilden, who had nearly done so, signed the necessary bond issue.[35] It was a great victory for all those around the state and, indeed, around the world who had lent their efforts to the "emancipation" of Niagara, as Harrison, the former abolitionist, had christened the movement. "Success was obtained by the cooperation of multitudes," he was later to say, "but the indispensible factor was Mr. Frederick Law Olmsted's thought. He was the real source, as he was the true director, of the movement, and but for him, there would be no State reservation at Niagara today."[36]

The following July 15 the Niagara Reservation was formally opened to the public with stirring ceremonies attended by visitors from the United States and Canada. (Fig. 7.14) Thousands crossed the Falls View Suspension Bridge between the two countries. Those present that day realized that the falls and surrounding scenery were no longer in danger of being overrun by the unchecked forces of commerce, manufacturing, and hucksterism. Meeting in the parlor of the nearby Cataract House hotel (which would remain standing until 1945), where Olmsted had first proposed the idea of preserving the falls, Dorsheimer and his fellow commissioners approved regulations that would ensure the public's comfort and safety. Henceforth hackney drivers were forbidden to solicit for passengers, liquor was prohibited anywhere on the grounds, and carriages were restricted to a speed limit of six miles an hour.[37]

Soon after the dedication of the reservation, work

Fig. 7.14. *Guide of the New York State Reservation at Niagara* (c. 1888). Issued by the commissioners, this map represented the grounds of the reservation under Andrew Green's tenure. Courtesy John Weiksner.

began on dismantling existing buildings on the mainland and on Bath Island. In August 1887 Edward B. Perry informed the readers of the *Century,* the popular national magazine, that "many eye-sores and encumbrances in the shape of mills and fences and vulgar places of amusement have been already removed."[38] Overseeing this prodigious task was Thomas Welch, whom the commissioners had chosen to be the first superintendent of the reservation, a post he would hold until his death in 1903. "Great crowds came and went as quietly and orderly as if the reservation had been established for years," he was proud to report during his first year on duty.[39] Under his able direction, the task of removing structures was nearly finished by the end of 1887.

The creation of the reservation gave renewed impetus to the project to construct a pleasure drive between Buffalo and Niagara Falls. In June 1885 the *Express* and the *Niagara Falls Gazette* devoted long articles to the subject. Sherman Rogers, one of the reservation commissioners, spoke in favor of the idea. The most popular proposition appears to have been to lay out a boulevard along the banks of the Niagara River to the falls. Olmsted himself favored the Park as the starting point for a parkway to the reservation, where it might link up with the drive he hoped would be laid out along the gorge as far as Lewiston. In 1888, possibly with his participation, the state legislature approved the creation of a riverside boulevard twenty-two miles long and two hundred

feet wide from Buffalo to Niagara Falls. It failed to receive Governor Hill's signature that year or the next year, however, when it passed both houses of the legislature. (The proposal met opposition from residents of Niagara Falls who thought it too costly.) After that, the momentum seems to have been lost, and the project was allowed to die until early automobilists campaigned for the creation of Niagara Falls Boulevard.[40]

OLMSTED AND VAUX'S GENERAL PLAN FOR THE NIAGARA RESERVATION

The commissioners were quick to name a superintendent but slow to see the need for professional advice on how to restore the damaged landscape and to arrange the reservation for large numbers of visitors. At first, it seems, they thought they could handle the job themselves; "they saw nothing to be done that the common sense of the Commissioners could not easily determine," Olmsted scoffed.[41] Dorsheimer and Green, who had had experience with public park undertakings in Buffalo and New York, knew better, but the two men disagreed on who should be hired. In May 1886 Green moved that Vaux alone be asked to prepare a plan for the reservation; Dorsheimer proposed Olmsted and Vaux as a team. Green, who disliked Olmsted, stood his ground and in a letter to Dorsheimer implied that Vaux had been the chief

THE BEST PLANNED CITY IN THE WORLD

designer of both Central Park and Prospect Park.[42] The matter dragged on well into 1886. In October, on his visit to Buffalo to discuss park matters there, Olmsted solicited Sherman Rogers's support. He also wrote to the governor defending, as Vaux had had to do many times before, his equal status with his partner in the planning of Central Park and Prospect Park. It would certainly have struck his friend as ironic to know that Olmsted now felt the need to pen the words "Our responsibility for the design of both parks is precisely equal."[43] In the end, Dorsheimer settled the dispute by introducing a motion to hire both Vaux and Olmsted to plan the reservation. At the commissioners' meeting on November 3, 1886, Green's was the only dissenting vote. "The commissioners seem to think," remarked the *New York Times,* "that the restoration of the river banks and the islands will never be complete till these have felt the magic touch of those famous landscape architects, Messrs. Olmsted and Vaux."[44] The commissioners' wise action brought together America's two greatest landscape architects one last time to prepare a plan for one of the world's natural treasures.

The brilliant plan they prepared for the reservation in 1887 sought to restore what had already been lost to commerce and manufacturing and to make accessible to all the diverse beauty of Niagara. (Fig. 7.15) Both Olmsted and Vaux found the task daunting. According to Olmsted, it was "the most difficult problem in landscape architecture to do justice to, it is the most serious—the furthest above shop work—that the world has yet had." During the fall of 1886, the two men worked diligently together, with Vaux making frequent trips to Fairsted to confer with Olmsted. Sketches by both men preserved in the Olmsted Papers in the Library of Congress offer graphic evidence of their evolving thinking. By December they seem to have fixed the major outlines of their scheme. In the new year, as the deadline approached for presentation to the commission in time to win its approval and go to the Senate for funding, Vaux and Olmsted were still exchanging ideas for revisions to the written document, the editing of which seems to have been mostly Olmsted's responsibility. It must have been like the old days for them. "He helped me and I helped

Fig. 7.15. Olmsted and Vaux, *General Plan for the Improvement of the State Reservation at Niagara,* 1887. Courtesy National Park Service, Frederick Law Olmsted National Historic Site.

him and at some points each of us crowded the other out a little," said Olmsted.[45] Their report was submitted by the end of January 1887. When the commissioners postponed a meeting set to discuss the document, Olmsted seemed more disappointed at the delay than relieved to have more time to mull over his remarks. "Being all primed and cocked" for the presentation to the board, he was "rather 'cut up'" by the date change, his stepson John told Vaux. "Then, too, he had been working every night and getting but little sleep. . . . He can't take writing easily. He must worry over it till the moment when it is delivered and he can alter no more."[46]

Olmsted and Vaux's report, which incorporated ideas that Welch had previously put forward, easily won the commissioners' approval. In transmitting the report to the legislature, Dorsheimer and his fellow commissioners noted that while "modifications may be desirable in details," they were in full agreement with its "main principles and features." The fundamental precept was "to restore and conserve the natural surroundings of the Falls of Niagara, rather than attempt to add anything thereto." As Welch had done earlier, the commissioners affirmed that "not park, nor pleasure ground, but 'Reservation'" was the name by which the "property now happily recovered to the people" would be known. It was, they declared, a place "*reserved* and sacred to what Divine power has already placed there rather than a proper field for the display of human ingenuity." With the approval by the commissioners of Olmsted and Vaux's report, the final element of the campaign to save Niagara was in place. The *Boston Herald* and other papers praised the state's commitment to preserving the natural features of Niagara, equating the decision with the foresight shown by Governor DeWitt Clinton in creating the Erie Canal.[47]

Olmsted and Vaux's *General Plan for the Improvement of the Niagara Reservation* is a masterly blueprint for achieving the commissioners' three main goals: preserving the scenery that still existed, restoring what had been destroyed by man, and making all of the prime sites safely accessible to visitors in ways that would preserve the landscape from deterioration due to the passage of thousands through it. Olmsted and Vaux cast their report in two parts: a long introduction, in which they expounded on the philosophy behind their plan, and a detailed analysis of what they proposed should be done in each of the major sections of the reservation. "The plan aims at nothing else, anywhere upon the reservation, but to make a suitable provision of roads and walks, of platforms and seats, at the more important points of view, and of other accommodations, such as experience has shown to be necessary to decency and good order when large numbers of people come together," they announced at the beginning.[48]

To their minds, what was "mainly important" was "that the one purpose for which the State invites the reservation to be visited—namely, the enjoyment of certain passages of natural scenery of a distinctive character—shall plainly control all the arrangements it makes." By this they ruled out elaborate floral and plant displays and sculptures or other works of art. "Some such would, in our opinion," they wrote, "be as undesirable as the ornaments of stained glass, cut stone, plaster, paint and fountains" that the commissioners had been hard at work removing from the reservation grounds. Underscoring their point, they insisted that even if "a costly object of art" like Bartholdi's Statue of Liberty, a gift of the French people which had been dedicated in New York Harbor during the period when Olmsted and Vaux were preparing their report, "should be tendered to the State on the condition that it should be set up on Goat Island, the precept to which our argument has tended would be obliged a declension of the gift as surely as it would the refusal of an offer to stock the Island with poison ivy or with wolves or bears." Likewise, restaurants, theaters, and souvenir stands would be out of place; only buildings that were absolutely necessary for the comfort and safety of visitors would be constructed. Walks, roads, bridges, stairways, seats, and other "furniture of convenience" would be kept "smaller and less showy" so as not to intrude upon the eye and compete with the predominance of the natural scenery.

The early commissioners would heed these admonitions and were especially adamant in stating that "no monuments, memorials, or gifts of any character, whether ornamental or of practical utility, shall be accepted or placed upon the lands of the Reservation."[49]

Prospect Point

After the rather longwinded preliminaries, Olmsted and Vaux got down to specifics, taking the commissioners step-by-step through the reservation as these two geniuses of art and planning would create it. The main entrance would be at Prospect Point, where offending buildings that already stood in the partially wooded grounds would be removed. A polygonal concourse at the end of the trolley line from the Falls Street railroad passenger stations would welcome visitors and give them their first glimpse of the river. From this "vestibule" to the reservation, tourists would enter Propsect Point, which in Olmsted and Vaux's new plan would be divided into two sections, the Upper Grove, closest to the village and out of sight of the falls, and the Lower Grove, which bordered the river and offered views of the cataract. "The point in the Reservation that will be first reached by visitors coming directly towards the Falls from the railroad stations is in the Upper Grove," Olmsted and Vaux observed. For the comfort of these travelers, they proposed to erect a large single-story stone reception house "in which there shall be an office of advice and guidance, a check-room, and large lavatory, toilet and other conveniences, of the general character of those to be found in a few of our best railway stations." There would also be nearby a building for the administration of the reservation. In addition, ample picnic accommodations would be provided so that visitors might eat before setting out. After "having been refreshed and brought to a state of body and mind more favorable to their enjoyment of the scenery and to the exercise of good nature in pursuit of that enjoyment," noted the authors, tourists would then leave the Upper Grove singly or in small parties, on foot or in carriages, to see various parts of the reservation. Some would also go to the northern edge of the Upper Grove and cross over to Canada on the Falls View Suspension Bridge, which was a de facto element of the reservation. By encouraging people to pause and disperse in this way, Olmsted and Vaux sought to alleviate the crowding that resulted when waves of rail voyagers arrived and proceeded immediately to the falls.[50]

The finest views of the falls from the American side were to be had from the Lower Grove. After the removal of remaining "structures for ornament or amusement" from the former Prospect Park days, Olmsted and Vaux proposed redesigning the area so that people could safely and comfortably enjoy the view. At Prospect Point, the plan included a thirty-foot-wide esplanade running along the edge of the cliff back to Hennepin's Point. (Fig. 7.16) From this open area, visi-

Fig. 7.16. The esplanade Olmsted and Vaux planned to overlook the cataract. Photograph, c. 1890.
Library of Congress, Prints and Photographs Division, Detroit Publishing Company Collection.

Fig. 7.17. Prospect Point with the wall that had been erected in the 1870s. Photograph by George Barker, c. 1880. Courtesy Janice and Dale Rossi.

Fig. 7.18. Olmsted and Vaux called for the replacement of the barrier wall at Prospect Point with a thin iron railing designed by Vaux. Photograph by W. H. Jackson, c. 1898. Library of Congress, Prints and Photographs Division.

tors could appreciate the classic view that encompassed the American Falls, the rapids above the falls, the Canadian Falls, and the cataract below. They planned to have this area slope down slightly toward the river to permit visitors to see over the heads of those nearer the edge. And to replace the existing stone wall which marred the view of the brink, Olmsted and Vaux proposed a railing that would provide equal security "without holding the eye." (Fig. 7.17) They affirmed that the aim of the plan for improving this critical point of the reservation was to provide "much larger and simpler accommodations for visitors, to restore, as nearly as it is now practicable, the original aspect of the brink of the Falls and the verge of the Chasm." (Fig. 7.18)

At two other viewing spots along the brink of the gorge, they proposed constructing balconies projecting on brackets over the edge of the cliff. One was above the long shed covering the inclined railway, which took people down to the base of the American Falls and the dock for the *Maid of the Mist* steamboat, which was

heavily frequented. (They also suggested that windows be pierced in the side walls so passengers could view the falls while going up and down.)[51] The other was at Hennepin's View, the spot where it was thought that the priest stood when he saw the falls in the late seventeenth century. A precarious wooden balcony—which, according to Olmsted and Vaux, "commands the best general view of the Falls to be had from the Reservation"—they proposed replacing with a more secure and less conspicuous one of cast iron.[52]

The Mainland Shore

Olmsted and Vaux had determined that the area of the reservation in the greatest need of remediation was the mainland shore. "For half a mile above the Fall the present shore is in part a substantial stone wall, in

THE BEST PLANNED CITY IN THE WORLD

part a crib-work construction of stone and logs, and is everywhere built out from ten to thirty feet beyond the old natural shore," they reported. There was virtually nothing left of the original bank that had been "strewn with boulders and overgrown with bushes and grass." They laid out an ambitious plan to regain much of its primitive appearance. "Causeway, embankments, ridges and mounds" would be reduced, "canals and other excavations" filled in, and all the waterside cribwork and walls removed so that the land could be graded with "flowing lines of varying inclination toward the river." Much reforestation would also need to be done in this section. Ultimately, they foresaw the area covered with tall, healthy forest trees, some of which would be transplanted from Goat Island. "Individual tree beauty is to be little regarded," they specified, "but all consideration given to beauty and effectiveness of groups, passages and masses of foliage." They expected fully three-fourths of the original trees planted to be thinned out, explaining, perhaps with Superintendent Welch, who had no experience in such matters, as their intended audience, that "the less promising will have constantly been selected for removal with little regard to evenness of spacing." Through the survival of the fittest, only those "of the most vigorous constitution, those with the greatest capabilities of growth, and those with the greatest power of resistance to attacks of storms, ice, disease and vermin" would remain.

Through this new manmade forest would wind a drive called the Riverway, and between it and the water's edge a path for pedestrians. The Riverway would begin at the entrance to the reservation at Prospect Point, where carriages could be hired, and terminate in an oval concourse at Old French Landing above the American Rapids.[53] And those who followed the Riverway by carriage would be sure to enjoy views of the water as they went, for Olmsted and Vaux stipulated that "the trees are to be placed with the intention, while avoiding formality, to leave frequent clear spaces between their trunks, the center lines of which spaces will be diagonal to the shore line, in the direction that

will leave the Rapids open to view from the drive." Here was yet another example of how the desire to draw attention to the natural scenery informed every aspect their plan. Pedestrians who wished to walk the mainland shore could also start at the entrance concourse and follow the riverside footpath to Old French Landing. At this point visitors might rest and from a summerhouse the partners proposed be built there take in the scene of the placid, lakelike river above Goat Island. Along the way, walkers could pause at many spots to observe water scenery. Olmsted and Vaux indicated numerous smaller walks branching off from the main path to secluded locations at Niagara's edge, which would be replanted with naturally growing thickets of "native underwood." Here, stone seats, some of which would have "simple trellises over them upon which canopies of vines and creepers" might climb, would invite people to tarry and contemplate "interesting points in the Rapids."[54] These benches, like the forest, to this day have never materialized.

Goat Island

The centerpiece of the reservation was beautiful, verdant Goat Island. Crossing from the mainland to the island was itself a surpassing experience. In place since 1856, the sturdy iron-truss bridge, based on a design by Squire Whipple, allowed people to traverse the raging rapids perilously close to the brink of the American Falls.[55] (Actually, the crossing was in two stages: a longer span joined the mainland to Bath Island, and a shorter span linked Bath Island to Goat Island. In 1901 the present stone arched bridge took the place of this older metal structure.) Olmsted and Vaux saw no necessity to replace the existing bridge with a new one, but at some future date, they suggested, it might be widened with the addition of "outriggers" or balconies where visitors might stop to contemplate the magnificent rapids. Indeed, Olmsted and Vaux valued the bridge to Goat Island as a perch for viewing the scenery. The view upstream of the American Rapids from the middle of the bridge between the mainland and Bath Island, they believed, had "nothing to compare with it in the entire world." (Fig. 7.19) To those who had suggested that the present bridge be replaced with one farther upriver, they responded that "no possible form of bridge" could be placed there "that would not greatly injure" the breathtaking view of rapids and sky from the existing bridge. (Apparently oblivious to Olmsted's injunction, in the 1960s engineers situated at this point the steel span bridge that now carries automobiles to and from Goat Island.) On Bath Island itself, they hoped visitors would pause to observe the rapids from two stone benches they proposed to place facing upstream. Their sketch for these viewing spots indicates that they wanted them screened by bushes from each other and the footpath and carriage drive so that those contemplating the rushing waters would be undisturbed by passersby. As for the proposal to link some of the wild islets in the American Rapids with footbridges, Olmsted and Vaux, once again maintaining the primacy of the scenery in their thinking, believed that nothing would be gained in doing so or compensate for "the injury which the bridges and the people who would be seen upon them and upon the islands would bring to the scenery."

Fig. 7.19. The American Rapids upstream from the nineteenth-century bridge to Goat Island. Photograph, c. 1900. Library of Congress, Prints and Photographs Division, Detroit Publishing Company Collection.

THE BEST PLANNED CITY IN THE WORLD

The partners and the first commissioners shared the view that the best way to enjoy Goat Island, and indeed all of Niagara, was on foot. "Carriages may often be seen," Olmsted and Vaux observed, "driving past the most charming passages of the scenery, their occupants not having their attention called to them. . . . Had they been on foot and following the circuit walk of the plan such a loss would have been impossible to them." It would be a simple matter to inform people, even as they left the trains, of the system of walks they were proposing. Correcting what had previously existed on the island, Olmsted and Vaux would place the footpath that ringed the island on the outside of the carriage drive, thus giving pedestrians priority in access to water views over those in vehicles.[56]

In addition to this circuit walk, they outlined a network of trials through Goat Island's woods, which Welch had portrayed as "a majestic primeval forest . . .

Fig. 7.21. A path led walkers through the woods to the brink of the falls at Terrapin Point. Photograph, 1890s. Author's collection.

Fig. 7.20. Olmsted and many others treasured the lush flora of Goat Island as one of the gems of American nature. Photographer George Barker had his family pose for this commercial image, one of three he titled *Niagara, Listening to the Birds,* and *Heart of Goat Island* (1890). Courtesy Janice and Dale Rossi.

[with] grand old trees that looked down upon Father Hennepin." They also called attention to the underbrush, which they said was "a charming characteristic of the place" that nature lovers would rejoice to see preserved. Olmsted and Vaux took special care that the walking public might enjoy this unique aspect of the island's scenery. (Fig. 7.20) In their plan, they wished to remove a popular path that crossed directly from the mainland bridge through the woods to the southwest corner of the island, where Terrapin Point afforded the best view of Horseshoe Falls. (Fig. 7.21) In its place they proposed a rambling network of sinuous trails that induced less hurried movement through this extraordinary habitat, where the songs of many species of birds mingled with the distant murmur of rushing waters. And to further encourage a sense of "forest seclusion," Olmsted and Vaux planned the walks to be little more than "trodden foot-paths." (Fig. 7.22)

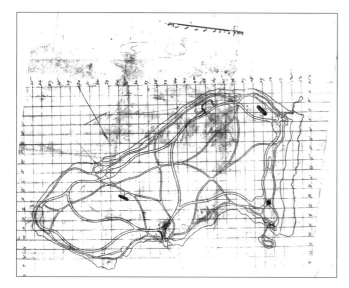

Fig. 7.22. Olmsted and Vaux's study for a system of walks and drives on Goat Island. Pen and ink sketch, 1886. Pedestrians and vehicles found their way to the major vista points by a circuitous network of drives and paths that responded to the shape of the island. Carriage drives are distinguished from footpaths by their slightly wider dimension. Library of Congress, Manuscript Division, Olmsted Papers.

Three Sisters Islands

A walk on Goat Island, where two modest woodland shelters would provide strollers refuge from a sudden shower, had also to include a side trip to the Three Sisters Islands. (Fig. 7.23) The Porters had joined these three islets in the Canadian Rapids to Goat Island by wooden footbridges. Then as now, the brief island-hop out into the middle of the river brought one face-to-face with a compelling sight. Here the Niagara, wrote Chateaubriand in 1815, "is less a river than an impetuous sea whose hundred thousand torrents rush toward the gaping mouth of a chasm."[57] Olmsted and others found the view upriver from the Three Sisters more inspiring and beautiful than the falls themselves. "The islands above the Falls enable one to stand in the midst of the Rapids, where they rush by lashed into passionate haste, now boiling over some hidden swellings in the rocky bed, or dashing over greater but yet hidden obstructions with such force that the crest of the uplifted mass is dashed about as freely as a white charger's mane," William

Robinson wrote on his visit there in 1870.[58] (Fig. 7.24) The Irish gardener's description was so apt that Olmsted was fond of quoting it.

Just as dear to Olmsted and even more evocative of what he must have felt while viewing the rapids from the Third Sister Island were the impressions of George Campbell, eighth duke of Argyll, a widely traveled man known throughout the English-speaking world as the

Fig. 7.23. Three Sisters Islands, c. 1890. Courtesy New York State Archives.

Fig. 7.24. Canadian Rapids, from the Third Sister Island, c. 1900. Courtesy New York State Archives.

THE BEST PLANNED CITY IN THE WORLD

Fig. 7.25. "It is as if the fountains of the great deep were being broken up, and that a new deluge were coming on the world." Canadian Rapids, from the Third Sister Island, c. 1900. Library of Congress, Prints and Photographs Division.

greatest orator in the House of Lords, who visited Niagara in the summer of 1879:

I am inclined to think . . . that the most impressive of all the scenes at Niagara is one of which comparatively little is said. The River Niagara, above the Falls, runs in a channel very broad, and very little depressed below the general level of the country. But there is a steep declivity in the bed of the stream for a considerable distance above the precipice, and this constitutes what are called the Rapids. The consequence is that when we stand at any point near the edge of the Falls, and look up the course of the stream, the foaming waters of the Rapids constitute the sky line. No indication of land is visible—nothing to express the fact that we are looking at the river. The crest of the breakers, the leaping and the rushing of the waters, are still seen against the clouds, as they are seen in the ocean, when the ship from which we look is in the trough of the sea. It is impossible to resist the effect on the imagination. It is as if the fountains of the great deep were being broken up, and that a new deluge were coming on the world. . . . An apparently shoreless sea tumbling toward one is a very grand and a very awful sight. Forgetting, then, what one knows, and giving oneself to what one only sees, I do not know that there is anything in nature more majestic than the view of the Rapids above the Falls of Niagara.[59] (Fig. 7.25)

THE NIAGARA RESERVATION AFTER 1887

Starting in 1888 the state began the gradual implementation of many of the suggestions in Olmsted and Vaux's *General Plan,* for which the authors were paid $2,320.[60] In March of that year, however, tragedy struck as far as Olmsted's association with Niagara was concerned. On a trip to the South, Dorsheimer contracted pneumonia and died unexpectedly. His death two years after that of Richardson must have hit Olmsted hard, for Dorsheimer had been a trusted friend and constant supporter. In his place, Green, at age seventy, assumed the presidency of the commission, a position he would occupy for the next fifteen years, until he was shot to death in a bizarre case of mistaken identity in 1903. "His grasp upon the affairs of the reservation was such that subsequent appointees for some time left the administration practically to him," recalled Charles Mason Dow, who followed Green as president of the commission. "His orders and directions to the Superintendent became equivalent to the action of the Board."[61] Given the long-standing animosity between Olmsted and Green, it is not surprising that Olmsted severed his association with the reservation after writing the report with Vaux. Not wishing to relive the difficult days of Central Park, he may have chosen to withdraw voluntarily, leaving all future consulting to Vaux. (He may also have been acting out of generosity toward his old friend, for Vaux in his later years saw his income dwindle.) Olmsted's disappearance from the scene did not spell the demise of the vision he and his friend had articulated for the reservation. Vaux could be counted on to carry the torch of their ideas.

Over the years that followed, Vaux, together with his son Downing and their associate Samuel Parsons Jr., advised Green and the commissioners.[62] Moreover, Green himself maintained unwavering devotion to the philosophy enshrined in the *General Plan*. During his tenure as president of the commission, the spirit of that remarkable document guided his decisions. In any event, the Goat Island carriage drive was constructed in 1892 much as Olmsted and Vaux had indicated, together with a footpath that ringed the shoreline. Vaux's iron railing, which cleverly reconciled safety with aesthetics, replaced the masonry wall at Prospect Point and for many years protected tourists there and at other places on the grounds. (Fig. 7.26) Yet the old diagonal path through the Goat Island forest to Terrapin Point was retained, and none of the other wood-

Fig. 7.26. Vaux's railing was installed at many places in the reservation. This view is from Goat Island looking toward Luna Island and the American Falls. Photograph, c. 1900. Library of Congress, Prints and Photographs Division.

THE BEST PLANNED CITY IN THE WORLD

land walks Olmsted and Vaux proposed seem to have been laid out.

The most significant remaining structure that Vaux planned is the stone arched bridge that carries pedestrians from Goat Island to the First Sister Island. (Fig. 7.27) Early on, Green decided that all new structures on the reservation would be built of stone, both for beauty and for durability. Designed in 1893 to replace an earlier wooden span, Vaux's rustic bridge, which resembles the Riftstone Arch in Central Park, was made of rough-cut stones taken from the face of the cliff below the whirlpool. If its material pays homage to place, its plan embodies the central aim of the *General Plan,* "the enjoyment of certain passages of natural scenery of a distinctive character." At either end of the graceful span, Vaux placed curved balconies where visitors might pause to watch the shallow current flowing over the tranquil Hermit's Cascade, a spot beneath the bridge that was described as "one of the prettiest nooks at Niagara." A third balcony on the other side of the bridge invited visitors to gaze through the screen of woodland foliage toward the distant torrent of the Canadian Rapids.[63] (Fig. 7.28)

Beginning in 1896, after Vaux's death and Olmsted's retirement from practice, Green and the commissioners would turn to John C. Olmsted and the Olmsted firm for plans and advice. During the ensuing years, the state frequently sought, in particular, Frederick Law Olmsted Jr.'s help on issues affecting the reservation. He was especially concerned, as Vaux and Green had been before him, that

the scenic beauty of the American side of the gorge be conserved. In the early twentieth century, both he and John C. Olmsted were also asked by Canadian officials to consult on the park on their side of the border. "In this way," observed Olmsted scholar Charles Beveridge at the time of the centennial of the *General Plan,* "Olmsted's concept of a comprehensive scheme for protecting the manifold scenic beauties of the Niagara region was

Fig. 7.27. Calvert Vaux's First Sister Island bridge (1894) with the Hermit's Cascade below, c. 1900. Courtesy Local History Department, Niagara Falls, N.Y., Public Library.

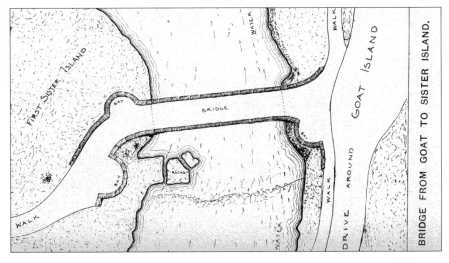

Fig. 7.28. Vaux's plan for the First Sister Island bridge, showing semicircular viewing balconies, 1894. Courtesy Local History Department, Niagara Falls, N.Y., Public Library.

carried well into the present century by the next generation of his family and firm."[64]

In 1903, looking back on his fifteen years of service, most especially the period from 1898 to 1903, Green proudly declared: "The Reservation speaks for itself. The improvements were begun at once and continued upon a single plan, to which we have consistently adhered, namely, to restore the environment of Niagara Falls as nearly as possible to its natural aspect, to remove every objectionable condition that in any way impaired the fullest aesthetic, educational and moral enjoyment and benefit of the spectacle, to facilitate public access in every way possible and to exclude everything of a commercial nature from the limits of the Reservation."[65] By the end of the year, Green, Olmsted, and Welch had all died, truly closing the first and most heroic chapter in the history of New York State's stewardship of Niagara. In recognition of Green's devoted service, the board had voted in 1895 to change the name of Bath Island to Green Island in his honor.

Even during his tenure a new battle for the lifeblood of the falls began. The Brush Company's experiment with dynamos and Schoelkopf's success inspired a bold scheme to use the Niagara River to drive electrical generators. In 1886, three years after he had drawn the preliminary map for the reservation, Thomas Evershed proposed digging a huge tunnel, beginning just upstream from the reservation boundary, to drain large amounts of water from the river to turn giant underground turbines. While Evershed and a number of international advisers were working out technical problems, Edward Dean Adams, president of the Cataract Construction Company, and William B. Rankine, a Niagara Falls attorney, assembled financing from American and European investors. Through their efforts the Niagara Falls Power Company was formed in 1889. The following year Evershed began directing an army of laborers in the construction of the 7,500-foot-long passageway. In 1895 the first two buildings of the power generation plant (which operated until the mid-1920s) were constructed to the

designs of McKim, Mead & White in the rugged version of Romanesque that Richardson had introduced in the early 1870s at the Buffalo State Hospital. In the summer of 1895 the company delivered electricity for the first time to local customers, including the reservation, which, by formal agreement, was to receive power free of charge. In November of the following year, thanks to the genius of Nikola Tesla, it transmitted electricity over lines to Buffalo some twenty miles away. The event was the first significant instance of the long-distance transmission of hydroelectric power in the world. "The hydroelectric development of Niagara Falls in the 1890s," notes the geographer Patrick McGreevy, "seemed to many as a sort of capstone on humanity's victory over nature."[66] As a result, the city of Niagara Falls soon became one of the world's foremost centers of electro-process industries.

Ironically, many of the early investors in electrical generation at the falls had supported the creation of the reservation in the form Olmsted had envisioned. Several, such as Adams, Rankine, and Welch, were members of the Niagara Falls Association. In the view of Ginger Strand, author of *Inventing Niagara,* the existence of the reservation may have facilitated the rise of industry at Niagara Falls. It created, she writes, a "division of purpose—over here is nature, over there, behind the hedge, is industry—that enabled the full industrial exploitation of the Falls to begin."[67] In 1907 the power company asked Olmsted Brothers to prepare a plan for a large industrial complex it proposed to lease to various manufacturers near the power station.[68]

The development of hydroelectric power generation at Niagara Falls provoked a second campaign to save the falls, for it was within the capability of engineers to divert the great river completely for electrical generation. By 1889 several private companies had been given charters to take as much water from above the falls as they wished, without paying any fees to New York State. It was conceivable that Niagara Falls could become completely dry, a relic of "humanity's victory over nature." (Fig. 7.29) The story of preserving the water flow over

THE BEST PLANNED CITY IN THE WORLD

Fig. 7.29. J. S. Pughe, *Save Niagara Falls—From This*. This cartoon shows water completely diverted from Niagara Falls to provide power for factories. *Puck* (April 1906). Library of Congress, Prints and Photographs Division.

dian treaties and legislation beginning in 1906, today water passes over the falls at a rate of at least 100,000 cubic feet per second during the daylight hours in the tourist season, from April through October.[69] The torrent can be reduced to 50,000 cubic feet per second at night during this period and throughout the rest of the year. The flow can be so much less than in Olmsted's day that the whirlpool reverses direction.

Green himself recognized that the Niagara Reservation represented a historic step forward in the American park movement. It set a precedent, he felt, that other places would follow in the future to preserve their own natural and historic sites. In 1895 he himself founded the American Scenic and Preservation Society and, late in his life, purchased picturesque Watkins Glen in central New York to save it from commercial exploitation. Shortly before his death in 1903, Green told a gathering in Buffalo of the members of the American Park and Outdoor Art Association, an organization whose officers included John C. Olmsted and Charles Mulford Robinson, that the "lesson of which Niagara Falls may be said to have been a pioneer teacher, is the State's right of eminent domain over objects of great scientific interest and natural beauty—the inherent right of the people to the free enjoyment of the wonders of nature. This principle, which during the past twenty years we have come to recognize as almost axiomatic, was, at the time of the passage of the law of 1883, a new one." Green, who was descended from Quaker stock, believed in "the almost universal influence" such places have on the imagination. In "the revelation which they give of the wonderful operations of the laws of the universe; the expansion of thought and elevation of spirit

the falls is outside the purview of this book, but suffice it to say that Andrew Green was one of the first to see a need to establish an international treaty by which a certain amount of water would always flow into the great cataract. As a result of a series of U.S. and Cana-

Fig. 7.30. A. H. Green at the Niagara Reservation, which he safeguarded from 1888 to 1903.

Photograph, 1890s. Courtesy Local History Department, Niagara Falls, N.Y., Public Library.

which they produce; and the irresistible power with which they draw the mind away from selfish and artificial to nobler and better things," he maintained, they "exert a highly educational and moral influence."[70] By the time he wrote these words, New York State had protected large areas of the Adirondack and Catskill mountains (Dorsheimer had been instrumental here), and the U.S. Congress, which had set aside Yosemite in 1864 and Yellowstone in 1872, had designated several other national park sites in the West. The era of the National Park

Fig. 7.31. Niagara Falls from the modern observation tower near Hennepin's View. Photograph by Andy Olenick.

THE BEST PLANNED CITY IN THE WORLD

Service, established by Woodrow Wilson in 1916, lay not far off in the future. (Fig. 7.30)

If Olmsted, Vaux, Dorsheimer, and Green were able to visit Niagara now, more than 125 years after the establishment of the Niagara Reservation, they would find many things they would not have expected to see. On Goat Island, much of the forest has been sacrificed to surface parking; a large restaurant overlooks Terrapin Point; and other structures house a police station, a souvenir shop, and fast-food concessions. There are virtually no footpaths through the meager remnants of the Goat Island forest, which itself has lost most of its ancient flora. On the mainland, surface parking and elaborate gardens occupy much of the ground of the Upper Grove. In the Lower Grove, a metal and glass tower gives elevator access to the base of the falls and supports a large platform cantilevered far out over the gorge, roughly where Olmsted and Vaux had proposed a modest balcony at Hennepin's View. (Fig. 7.31) Nor has the early commissioners' prohibition against works of art been respected. Visitors to Goat Island encounter a large bronze statue of Tesla together with an architectural fragment transported to the site from the demolished Adams power station, while on Green Island there is a monument to Jacob Schoelkopf. Paradoxically, these incongruous souvenirs to human ingenuity honor an industry that, like the water-powered manufactories of the pre-reservation era, valued the falls more for their utility than for the majesty and beauty of their natural scenery. Markers, literature, and uniformed tour guides barely refer to the contribution that Olmsted and his colleagues made to the preservation and restoration of the landscape around the falls. Guides, both public and private, mechanically recount astonishing details about water volume and speed, daredevils, suicides, and miraculous rescues; none take note of Olmsted's "enjoyment of certain passages of natural scenery of a distinctive character." (Fig. 7.32)

It is also likely that Olmsted would be dismayed that officials have chosen to abandon the name Niagara Res-

Fig. 7.32. Amos W. Sangster, *Path to Terrapin Point, Goat Island.* Etching, 1888. Courtesy Local History Department, Niagara Falls, N.Y., Public Library.

ervation; today it is known as Niagara Falls State Park. If he could contemplate the modern-day landscape, Olmsted might well repeat what E. B. Perry, editor of the *Century,* had written of his and Vaux's reservation plan in 1887: "The main thing to remember through all the coming years, is that the property must not only be made, but kept, what its wisely chosen name implies— *a piece of nature defended as strictly as possible against all intrusion of artificiality.*"[71]

EIGHT

South Park, Cazenovia Park, and Riverside Park

It is time that we began to use our noble lake front for pleasure purposes.   —*Express,* May 27, 1889

From the time of Olmsted's first visit to Buffalo in 1868, he had explored the possibility of creating a park in the flat, low-lying southern section of town near Lake Erie in the district known as the Thirteenth Ward. In February 1887 a group of citizens petitioned the Common Council to have a park built there, linked to those in the north by a system of new parkways. The council responded favorably to the request and instructed the park commissioners to take steps toward its realization. They, in turn, called upon Olmsted for advice. Fresh from the completion of the plan for the Niagara Reservation, Olmsted visited Buffalo on March 22–23, 1887, to discuss the matter. After making a tour of the area with a committee of the park commissioners' board, he attended a meeting of Thirteenth Ward citizens who came to air their views on the subject of new parks and parkways on the south side of town. Olmsted apparently said little at the time, but what he saw on the tour and heard at the meeting opened his eyes to a monumental challenge that few in the city seemed to comprehend.

About three weeks later he sent a long letter to the commissioners summarizing his impressions and outlining his recommendations. These were the product of Olmsted's fully evolved gift to perceive park making comprehensively.

Olmsted began by recalling conversations he had had with citizens of Buffalo nineteen years earlier. When Dorsheimer and others had first asked him to advise them on the location for a "rural park," he recalled having said that "it should, if possible, be on the shore of the lake."[1] He had two main reasons for this. One was that, in his view, nothing was "so refreshing and grateful to a man escaping temporarily from the confinement of ordinary life as an unlimited expanse of natural scenery such as would be provided without cost in any situation overlooking the lake. Every acre of park land, therefore, so situated, may be worth many acres elsewhere." (Fig. 8.1) The second reason was that "it is a great advantage to a city to have a park approachable by water." Boats were inexpensive and pleasant vehicles; just taking a ride in one was a relaxing and enjoyable experience. Being a very different mode of travel from that provided by street vehicles, a boat ride, Olmsted observed, was an "anti-urban" form of recreation in and of itself.

Fig. 8.1. *Lake Erie from Buffalo at Sunset.* Photograph by C. L. Pond, 1869. Courtesy Janice and Dale Rossi.

The Djurgården, a park situated on a long island in the Swedish city of Stockholm, was a leading instance of what he meant. It was reputed, wrote Olmsted, to be the most beautiful park in the world. When he had spoken of this in 1868, however, his audience failed to listen. To their minds, the lake suggested storms, shipwrecks, and masses of ice that prolonged winter unduly into spring. Nonetheless, in the face of this distaste for the lake, Olmsted had urged the acquisition of the Front and was now pleased that it had become so popular.

Now, he happily acknowledged, all Americans were becoming more appreciative of the recreational value of water. As an example, he might have mentioned the plans he had drawn up in 1884 for a thousand-acre park on Detroit's Belle Isle, an island in the Detroit River. (Fig. 8.2) Locally, Fort Erie, on the Canadian shore of Lake Erie, had become a popular destination for

boat trips, with steamboat service running during the summer months from Buffalo to a beach resort there. Buffalonians were right to want a place of their own, accessible by boat, where they could bathe and enjoy the lakeshore. It was now time to act on this desire. Echoing what he had told his listeners in 1868 about his choice of site for the Park, he urged the city to secure outlying land at cheap prices for future park purposes. "If the population of Buffalo should increase at a rate not greatly below the average rate of its increase during the last twenty years," Olmsted observed, "it will not be long before it is twice as large a city as it was when its present park was begun."

As to the location of this new park, Olmsted enumerated four specific principles that guided his thinking:

> First, . . . it should be in a direction from the city opposite that of the present park; second, . . . it should command a broad view over the lake; third, . . . it should be conveniently, safely, and pleasantly accessible from distant parts of the town by boats; fourth, it should be adapted to the production of natural features of rural scenery (other than in views over the lake) which will be pleasing and refreshing in a different way from those of the present Park, so that it cannot be said that one is better than the other; only each is excellent of its distinctive kind.

In fact, the citizens who had petitioned the Common Council had shown him an empty lakeside site in the Thirteenth Ward that met these criteria. Moreover, when "the breakwater shall have been extended, as I am told it is likely to be in a few years," he wrote, "there will be a still-water boating-way to it from the northern parts of the city."

But the question of precisely where to locate a new park and what it would look like could not be advanced, Olmsted noted, until more fundamental problems afflicting South Buffalo were addressed. The land there presented many serious obstacles to urban expansion. For

Fig. 8.2. Belle Isle Park, Detroit. Photograph, c. 1900. Library of Congress, Prints and Photographs Division, Detroit Publishing Company Collection.

one thing, it was so "low, flat, liable to be flooded, difficult of drainage, and so cut by a broad, deep, and exceedingly crooked water-way [Cazenovia Creek], that to extend a convenient street system through it under any circumstances would be a difficult undertaking." Moreover, these adversities were compounded by the fact that several railway companies had procured a great deal of the land adjoining the built-up part of the city, where they had laid down track and erected structures "with little regard to the interest of others." The result was a half-mile-wide strip of land containing a welter of crisscross-

ing rail lines. Anyone wishing to traverse this belt to reach the south side of town needed to negotiate many dangerous grade crossings. Accidents and fatalities were common, and the low embankments on which the rail lines rested impeded the already sluggish natural drainage of the low-lying land. In fact, during the very week when Olmsted was in town, storms had created severe flooding of the entire area. Olmsted concluded his jeremiad by observing that "the difficulties in the way of establishing a judicious system for such enlargement of the city to the southward . . . are every year increased by new construction planned without thought of the common and lasting interests of the city as a whole." For these reasons, South Buffalo had not seen the kind of residential development that the northern part of town had experienced. Park planning must wait on urban planning.

The solution to the drainage problem might be incorporated into the construction of the new park, Olmsted suggested, noting that the city's engineer had proposed diverting the course of Cazenovia Creek at a certain point so that it flowed more directly into the lake. If the city were to adopt this elegantly simple idea, he observed, "the new outlet of the creek will come not far from the situation had in view for the park, and may easily be made to coincide with it." By taking advantage of this water supplied by the creek and the great amount of earth that would have to be moved to achieve this plan, the city would have the opportunity "to establish the basis of a passage of natural scenery of an unusual type and of a park of unique character."

The problem of crossing the railroad tracks was also to be solved by engineering. During the meeting of citizens, Olmsted had been struck by the fact that most of the people who spoke were more interested in the establishment of parkways in the southern sections of the city than in the actual park itself. And each person had proposed a different route for the new parkway, "to the effect," he noted, "that each petitioner was of the opinion that the most suitable route for the parkway would be the one that would carry it nearer his front door." Olmsted was in sympathy with the desire to provide the new areas of the city with pleasure drives, but none of the speakers had offered a solution to the problem of getting from the center city to the South Side over the half-mile-wide belt of rail lines. Therefore, the South Side parkways would not be connected to the north parkway system. His solution was to supply this missing link before deciding where the new parkways in the south would be located. He proposed that the city negotiate with the rail companies to have some lines abandoned and others moved; in this way "the space of extreme difficulty will be narrowed."

Once this was done, the city could provide for safe and convenient passage between the older parts of town and the developing sections of the Thirteenth Ward and beyond. The first step toward a "rationally comprehensive system of improvement for the southern part of the city," Olmsted advised, would be to erect "a single viaduct" over all the rail lines. This skyway should be so wide that it could be divided "into several ways, one suitable to heavy and slow traffic, one for pleasure carriages and light traffic, one for street cars, and one or more for footmen." At its northern end, which would be near the center of town, streets would converge from all parts of the existing city. From the other end, "lines would be laid down for broad avenues in several directions, so that, eventually, without excessive indirectness, branches from them would really come to every man's door, and all the country beyond be made conveniently accessible." One route could lead to the new lakefront park.

Olmsted knew that his remarks were certainly not what the park commissioners had expected. He was hopeful, however, that the current generation of politicians would have the foresight of their predecessors and look to the future needs of their growing city. A decade earlier he had written that "the plan of no other city gave more evidence of shrewd forecasting study of the future interests of its citizens than that of Buffalo as originally devised, and as the limits of this plan were outgrown it was hoped that the same spirit might characterize the enlargement of it."[2] He would proceed with the preparation of a more detailed plan based on the preliminary notions contained in his letter, but he emphasized that at this point all park planning must be considered tentative, both for the reasons he outlined and because of the unknown cost of acquiring the land.

THE 1888 PLAN FOR SOUTH PARK

Having accepted Olmsted's preliminary appraisal, the park commission instructed him to proceed with the development of a full plan for a lakeside park. He wished to prepare a provisional plan in consultation with the city engineer, he told the commissioners. By November 1887 the city engineer had forwarded a survey of the area to Fairsted. The following July, Olmsted and his stepson John spent two days in town looking over land the commissioners had identified on the lakefront. After his visit, the *Express* reported that Olmsted was still struggling to overcome numerous challenges that the site posed if it was to become a worthwhile addition to the city's park system. "The matter is still under consideration," reported the paper, "and will not be settled for some time yet."[3] The process, as Olmsted remembered it, was nearly as challenging as the work on the Niagara reservation. "Investigation gradually brought to light facts showing that the information upon which the preliminary report had been based was far from accurate or complete," he recalled, "and that the problem of a plan was more complex and difficult than had been supposed." He abandoned so many ideas one after another that at one point he questioned whether a park on the lakeshore would be so expensive that the commissioners should look for another site. (Olmsted had taken upon himself the task of surveying other sites but found none as good as this one.) Redoubling his efforts, he recast and redrew the plan "for the fifth time."[4]

On October 1, 1888, Olmsted dispatched his scheme to the Buffalo park commissioners in the form of two illustrated reports. The date surely held special meaning for him, because it was exactly twenty years to the day after he had sent his letter to Dorsheimer outlining his plans for the Buffalo park system. Regrettably, neither his old friend nor David Gray was alive to read the brilliant sequel. In collaboration with his stepson, Olmsted explained his ideas for a large new park on the lakeside land that the commissioners had shown them in March of the previous year. (Fig. 8.3) Although one assumes that the elder Olmsted was the principal author of both documents, John certainly played a role in their creation. He may in fact have been the unacknowledged delineator responsible for the engaging pen and ink sketches that appear in both reports, for he was an accomplished artist. The first report concerned the design of the park, which the Olmsteds now referred to as South Park; the second discussed the parkway and waterway approaches to it.[5] Both documents, which Olmsted acknowledged were unusually elaborate, embodied extraordinary concepts.

In the opening paragraphs of his *Plan for a Public Park on the Flats South of Buffalo,* Olmsted was fully justified in cautioning his readers to take their time considering the ideas being presented to them, for they were so novel that they were "little to be judged by ordinary standards." He introduced his subject by recalling how Delaware Park, which for purposes of the report he called the North Park, had been created twenty years earlier. He warned his readers that just as it had been then, it was now time for the city to purchase outlying farm and vacant land before it became too expensive. "It is likely," he insisted, "that if the site of the North Park had not been secured about the time it was, it never would have been." If the city had waited, either Forest Lawn Cemetery would have expanded into the park area or the state mental hospital would have occupied the ground, and the Belt Line railroad might have been cut through rather than around it. If the city had hesitated and these things had happened, he was sure that Buffalo would have been forced to acquire an inferior site somewhere else for its main park. There was no question in his mind that the commissioners must start now to enlarge the city's park system "in a deliberate way, pursuing the same steady, methodical, frugal but efficient methods that have distinguished the proceedings of your Commission from its origin."

Turning to the design of the new South Park, Olmsted stated that it would be very different in character and purpose from the superb country park in the northern part of town. Observing that Delaware Park was to a rare degree "adapted to certain quiet forms of recreation, favoring a contemplative or musing turn of mind and restful refreshment," he predicted that it would gain in beauty every year and "take a more and more distinguished position among the parks of the world." But,

Fig. 8.3. F. L. and J. C. Olmsted, plan for South Park, 1888. From F. L. and J. C. Olmsted, *The Projected Park and Parkways on the South Side of Buffalo: Two Reports by the Landscape Architects* (1888). Courtesy National Park Service, Frederick Law Olmsted National Historic Site.

he acknowledged, not everyone desired "merely soothing, out-of-door refreshment," especially people who worked in "monotonous occupations and amid somber surroundings" in the industries that now employed so many working-class Americans. These men and women wanted forms of recreation that offered "gayety, liveliness, and a slight spirit of adventure." A mature urban park system should therefore provide its citizens with the opportunity to take pleasure in both passive and active recreation. If it did not, there would surely be pressure to add facilities to the existing country park that would compromise its integrity. The question he posed to his clients was: *"Twenty years hence shall Buffalo have one park, of a poor, confused character, or two,*

each of a good, distinct character?" His proposal for South Park answered that question by providing a 240-acre pleasure ground that would be distinctly different from Delaware Park. First, it would "annex itself to the grandeur of Lake Erie." The city had too long overlooked the treasure at its doorstep—the lake to which it owed its importance as a city. "It has in Lake Erie," Olmsted affirmed, "really great natural scenery." But having made no use of its "good fortune" in the creation of its first park, it ought now to exploit it in its second citywide park. In addition, South Park would be primarily a landscape to be enjoyed by people in boats rather than by visitors in carriages, on horseback, or on foot.

Even though Olmsted was not the one who chose

THE BEST PLANNED CITY IN THE WORLD

the site—it was chosen by the park commissioners—he saw many possibilities in it. It overlooked the lake, it was already accessible by rail from other parts of town, and because it was soggy bottomland subject to flooding it had little agricultural, commercial, or speculative value and so should be acquired cheaply. The landscape, however, posed formidable obstacles to the creation of a suitable public park. For one thing, the lake waters frequently rolled in from the north and west, and the nascent beach was often eroded away by action of the lake that washed out the "black muck" that underlay the sand. Five-foot levees would have to be built along both the northern and western borders of the park to secure the site from flooding in bad weather. Other major earth-moving projects would also be required within the park to realize Olmsted's plan.

Capitalizing on the site's advantages and working with its shortcomings, the Olmsteds, mentor and pupil, invented a design that was a stunning embodiment of the philosophy that had inspired Olmsted (and Vaux): always to preserve and advance the genius of place. "Growing largely out of the peculiar conditions of the locality and the distinctive requirements upon the designers," declared Olmsted, "the result would be a park of unique character." The plan encompassed three sections within the roughly triangular footprint. The thirty-acre westernmost area, which narrowed toward the lake at what was known as Stony Point, would be devoted to bathing and various active pastimes. It was to be centered on the Green, a twenty-acre meadow that could be used as a playing field and at times, Olmsted suggested, for "parades, exhibitions, balloon ascensions, and public ceremonies." This area, which was traversed from north to south by a public road along the shoreline known as the Hamburg Pike, was higher than the rest of the parkland and had been home to a vegetable farm. Olmsted proposed keeping the farmhouse and remodeling it for the convenience of those using the "Athletic Ground," an oval area surrounded by a bicycle path that would be constructed near where the road entered the park on the south. The Green itself would be encircled

by a tree-bordered carriage road and footpath. The drive expanded in the southwest corner of the Green into a concourse where visitors in carriages and on foot could enjoy a panoramic view of the water. From the shore itself, Olmsted proposed to build two parallel piers out into the lake to create a protected passage to a small boat harbor. Surprised at the relative lack of private pleasure vessels on Lake Erie, Olmsted, himself an able sailor, hoped to encourage this "wholesome form of recreation" by providing residents with a pleasant place to visit by boat. At the same time, he predicted that the piers would aid nature in the creation of a crescent-shaped sandy bathing beach along the narrow strip of park waterfront. A changing house would give access to either the beach and "surf bathing" or a pool at the rear for "still-water bathing." Intended for use by "delicate persons and children," this shallow triangular basin would be heated by the sun to a higher temperature than the open waters of Lake Erie. On the eastern side of the Green, a pullout from the drive afforded views of an extraordinary interior water feature Olmsted intended to maintain by bringing water from Cazenovia Creek to the site.

The central 180 acres of South Park Olmsted proposed to transform from inchoate swampland into a water park like none other. "What we proposed for this is that it shall, in the first place, be thrown into ridges and furrows, mounds and hollows, the material taken from the depressions forming the elevations, being heaped for the purpose upon the intervals of flat land left between them. The ridges being often discontinued, so that furrows will wind round the ends of them, and water being then let in to a suitable height, the result would be a body of water nearly a mile in length and a third in breadth, within which the elevations will form islands, savannas, capes and peninsulas." Water for filling this lagoon would come from either diverting Cazenovia Creek or laying a pipe from the creek to the site. The system would work on the principle that landscape architects today term "flow and dump." As Olmsted explained, "The water thus brought would flow first through the park, then into the still-water bathing pool, and thence between the piers into the Lake." This clever system would also solve the vexing problem of flooding that the creek frequently caused.

The complex lagoon formed from the barren flats would become a verdant paradise, for the rich peat piled up on the islands would build a fertile base in which abundant plant life could thrive. (Fig. 8.4) "The conditions will be favorable to types of vegetation, such as it is rare to see profusely displayed in nature . . . and which it is still rarer to see exhibited in a large and intricate way in works of gardening," Olmsted declared. In a passage that must be considered one of the most evocative in the literature of American landscape architecture, he went on to paint a vivid picture of an environment that surely had its origin in the exotic land that had so fascinated him on his trip across the Isthmus of Panama many years before:

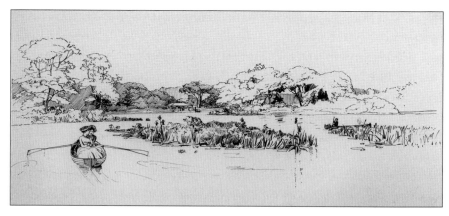

Fig. 8.4. Proposed South Park, 1888. Sketch showing the lagoon and islands. From F. L. and J. C. Olmsted, *The Projected Park and Parkways on the South Side of Buffalo* (1888). Courtesy National Park Service, Frederick Law Olmsted National Historic Site.

By varying the conditions, so that the water will at points be comparatively shallow and at others deep, and the land at points low and at others high, the shores here abrupt, there gently inclined, giving them, sometimes the form of beaches, at others of banks, and the banks being at some places shaded by trees, at some overgrown by bushes, at some dressed with turf, at some hidden by rushes, flags, irises and other waterside plants, an extended series of intricate passages of scenery will result. At intervals there will be long vistas over water under broad leafy canopies; there will be coves completely over-arched with foliage, forming verdant grottoes; some of the islands will be large enough to have within them spacious forest glades; some will be low and densely wooded, their shores so shallow that boats cannot land upon them, and their skirts so hedged with thickets as to be impenetrable. These will be nurseries for song birds, where their nestlings will have protection from natural enemies. The waters will everywhere abound with water-fowl, for the breeding of which other islands, unapproachable by visitors, will be set apart.

To increase the sense of distance from everyday life, Olmsted intended that visitors would gain access to this extraordinary place, a sort of watery version of the Ramble in Central Park, almost exclusively by boat. For those unable or unwilling to float through the tranquil waterscape in a solitary rowboat or canoe, there was to be "a special class of boats gaily painted, decorated by day with bright awnings and bunting, and at night with colored lights." A voyage around the lagoon on one of these delightful public conveyances would last approximately forty-five minutes. And to aid nighttime navigation, as well as to enhance the enchanting atmosphere, small electric lights would indicate the shorelines. Electricity for the illumination system, according to Olmsted, who did not hesitate to introduce the machine into the garden, was to be supplied "from storage batteries charged by dynamos to be run by windmills, for the use of which the locality has special advantages." Moreover, the movement of boats on the water would, in Olmsted's view, provide as much pleasure for those watching them on shore as they did for those riding aboard.

Although most of the islands were to be natural habitats, four of them would welcome human visitors. The largest was twenty acres in size and an easy walk from the northeastern entrance to the park. (Fig. 8.5) For those arriving by boat, a landing was provided. Five feet above the waterline, the island would support a healthy growth of lawn and scattered trees. A refectory would welcome diners, and swings, sandboxes, and other play items would entice children. The other three islands, which were only one to two acres in extent, could be rented for private parties. "They may be used," noted Olmsted, "as parts of the parks of Paris are much used, for wedding parties, or for anniversary festivals or all manner of associations." And to ensure privacy for the temporary castaways, the islet landings would have bars that tenants could put in place to keep out uninvited guests.

The third section of the park was a narrow strip of land that lay east of a railroad corridor that effectively isolated it from the lagoon and the Green. Here the Olmsteds proposed to establish a rifle range for the local militia. Fortunately, it was far enough away from the rest of the park to pose no danger or disturbance to visitors. In winter, when the soldiers would be gone, the area could take on a very different aspect. Then, Olmsted suggested, it could be flooded to create toboggan runs and coasting courses, thus bringing people to the park for yet another type of active recreation. Skating and sledding, however, would be prohibited on all the waters of the lagoon, because such activities could damage delicate shoreline vegetation.

Having described his plan for the new South Park, Olmsted anticipated the skepticism with which many readers would greet his proposal. "Looking upon the ground as it now appears," he wrote, "there may be a doubt whether what we had said does not represent a day-dream of impracticably romantic character." He answered potential skeptics with this reflection: "In truth, the process to be used for realizing the design which we are now trying to suggest, so far as the production of effects of natural scenery is concerned, will be simpler and surer, and, in this sense, of a more practical character, than those used to bring about the existing water-side scenery of the North Park." Continuing the comparison with the earlier park, Olmsted pointed out that people in Buffalo had forgotten that they had obtained the North Park at remarkably low cost. The reason for this was that fewer features needed to be created there than were necessary in many of Olmsted and Vaux's other parks and because the topography was so well suited to the purpose that little grading had been required. Moreover, in praise of the commissioners and their able superintendent, Olmsted remarked that the work at the Park had been done "under circumstances unusually favorable to economy, steadily, with freedom from political embarrassments." Finally, the site recom-

Fig. 8.5. Proposed South Park, 1888. Sketch showing the largest island in the lagoon, with Lake Erie forming the far background. From F. L. and J. C. Olmsted, *The Projected Park and Parkways on the South Side of Buffalo* (1888). Courtesy National Park Service, Frederick Law Olmsted National Historic Site.

mended for the South Park, which was one-third smaller than the North Park, should be obtainable at a modest price, for very little of it was fit for farming or housing, whereas the land taken for the Park had been prime agricultural terrain that would eventually have become valuable residential property.[6] After he had consulted with local experts, Olmsted estimated that the new park would cost $620,000 to build over a ten-year period.

Just how this unprepossessing landscape was to be converted into a place of beauty and an integral part of the larger city was the subject of the Olmsteds' second document, *Report on the South Parkway Question*. They foresaw the day when new parkways would structure the growth of residential neighborhoods in South Buffalo, the way they had decades earlier in North Buffalo. The key that would unlock the area's potential, they thought, would be the creation of a way for traffic to cross safely the network of railroad lines that formed a barrier between the northern and southern parts of town. The Olmsteds, who warmly acknowledged William McMillan's significant contribution to the report, felt compelled to urge the city that in order to avoid disaster, it should act soon to make improvements in South Buffalo. "On one of its margins Buffalo is beginning to be built out upon a flat region with no constant drainage outlets," they warned. Development of this flood-prone area was soon to be accelerated by grand plans of the Lehigh Valley Railroad to establish a complex of "foundries, factories, storehouses, coal docks, lumber yards, shipyards, and the like" there. Inevitably, this would sprout new neighborhoods. The great danger, as they saw it, was that "as long as such progress of building continues without the adoption of comprehensive, systematic, scientific measures for providing drainage and sewerage outlets; for determining the courses and grades of streets; and for the regulation of building upon and between them with reference to drainage and sewage, another great evil will be growing upon the city. . . . It will be brought

to an end . . . when the whole city is in mourning and its business suspended because of disease of which this region will have been the propagating ground."

Once again the Olmsteds stated that the best solution for crossing the belt of railroads that separated South Buffalo from the northern section would be a causeway. They specifically rejected the notion that some had put forth that the new South Park be linked to North Buffalo by way of a parkway connected to the southern end of Fillmore Avenue. This route, they said, was interrupted by many hazardous at-grade rail crossings. Furthermore, the East Side route was out of the way for most of the city's population. Much better would be a route that joined the Thirteenth Ward with the center of the city around Niagara Square, some three miles away. They were encouraged by the fact that the city and the railroads had entered into discussions and hoped that these would soon result in "a system of city streets passing over or under railroads."

Once provision had been made "for streets clear of railroad tracks," the Olmsteds suggested that an artery 90 to 120 feet wide, "for all ordinary traffic between the central parts of the city and the country to the southward," be designated as an approach to the new park. The route they favored passed through the center of the Thirteenth Ward and was deliberately roundabout in order to spur residential and commercial development.[7] Thus, once again, the Olmsteds had moved beyond the realm of park planners to take on the role of nascent urban planners.

In the visionary spirit of the South Park plan, the Olmsteds also suggested a more unusual link between the center city and the new South Park. Noting that the Lehigh Valley Railroad had begun developing the flats just north of the proposed park site, they pointed out that the company had already constructed a lakeside levee to protect its property from flooding. The Hamburg Pike, which connected Buffalo with the town of Hamburg some twelve miles to the south and which crossed the park site, followed the crest of this levee within the land owned by the railroad. The city engineer had proposed that a similar levee together with several pumping stations be built on the north and west sides of the park site to keep it well drained. Why not, suggested the Olmsteds, unite these dikes, widen them, and extend the system northward toward Buffalo's harbor?

Fig. 8.6. Sketch showing the canal proposed by the Olmsteds, leading to South Park. From F. L. and J. C. Olmsted, *The Projected Park and Parkways on the South Side of Buffalo* (1888). Courtesy National Park Service, Frederick Law Olmsted National Historic Site.

Fig. 8.7. Sketch showing the promenade the Olmsteds proposed for the top of the levee between the lake and the canal to South Park. From F. L. and J. C. Olmsted, *The Projected Park and Parkways on the South Side of Buffalo* (1888). Courtesy National Park Service, Frederick Law Olmsted National Historic Site.

To obtain a part of the material required, the least costly process would be that used by the Lehigh Valley Company, namely, to dredge a canal on the eastern side of the line of road, and form the levee of the material (stiff clay), that would be excavated. . . . Plantations having been grown on the borders of the canal, there would, by this process, have been prepared a pleasant water-avenue, proving a direct inside passage for boats between the park and the lower wharves of Buffalo Creek. The western slope of the levee would be everywhere washed by the waters of the lake, and in passing along the parkway upon it, the full expanse of the lake, clear to the horizon, would be open to view. It would thus form a superb promenade, and as it would be crossed by no streets, but be bordered by a belt of wood on one side and by the lake on the other, it would in effect bring the park a mile nearer the city; that is to say, within two miles of City Hall.)

To make their ideas clearer to their readers, the Olmsteds supplemented their written account with sketches in the style of those that illuminated their essay on the wished-for park. (Figs. 8.6 and 8.7)

THE DEBATE OVER THE SOUTH PARK PROPOSAL

The daring plan that Olmsted had laid before the Buffalo public quickly became a topic of lively debate. The commissioners ordered copies of it printed and distributed around town as a pamphlet. Newspapers that had long supported the park system lavished much praise on the proposals. "It is a splendid project," announced the *Express*. "It would be pre-eminently a water park, but so are some of the most beautiful parks in the world." The paper gave special praise to the proposed boating route. It also recognized that the park would ensure "the health and sanitary welfare of rapidly growing districts which will one day be thickly populated."[8] An editorial in the national magazine *Garden and Forest* praised the plan as "a novel project for a public park" and gave its readers a detailed account of its features. It recognized that the authors of the design had gone far beyond what people had come to expect in a municipal park; this would be "not merely a pleasant resort, but a great and varied public playground." The magazine, which was edited by Olmsted's friend Charles Sprague Sargent, recognized the South Park plan as a true work of genius. "The extraordinarily skillful way in which, in other works, Mr. F. L. Olmsted has united usefulness and beauty, is one of his highest and most peculiar titles to respect as a landscape-architect," the editorial declared, "but his talent in that direction has never been more clearly displayed than in the present scheme."[9]

Unfortunately, six days before the readers of *Garden and Forest* learned about Olmsted's remarkable South Park plan in the magazine's November 21 issue, the Buffalo park commissioners voted against it. Many in town voiced dismay at commissioners' decision and worked to have them reconsider the matter. At a large public meeting in mid-December a number of prominent citizens spoke in favor of the Olmsted scheme.[10] In the end, however, nothing persuaded the commissioners to change their minds. "While fully realizing the merits of this magnificent design, and acknowledging the full force of the arguments by which it was supported," wrote Sherman S. Jewett and his fellow board members in a letter dated January 1, 1889, to the Common Council justifying their action, "we were constrained to reject the scheme for various reasons, which still seem to us conclusive." Chief among these was the cost of construction, followed by the risk of frequent damage from lake storms, the distance of the location from the built-up area of the Thirteenth Ward,

and the limited number of good building sites adjacent to the park from which revenue could eventually be derived. These men, who had worked with Olmsted over the years and seen the park system take form and assume world renown, rejected his finest plan with deep regret. "The many attractive features of the plan touch our imagination strongly," they acknowledged, "especially the sail to and from the Park, either by Lake Erie or the proposed Parkway Canal, the smooth bathing beach, the broad outlook upon the Lake, the distinctive character of the Water Park scenery, and the convenience of the proposed methods of navigation through its winding channels." Nonetheless, they told the council, "the realization of these is impossible except at a cost to the City which we cannot recommend your Honorable Body to incur."[11]

Their statement became the epitaph for one of Olmsted's greatest works and for the dreams of those who had championed a large municipal park on the city's lakeshore. Olmsted's masterpiece was to exist only in the words and images of its creators. Olmsted confided to a disappointed McMillan that printing a thousand copies of his report had done little good for the cause. "It is remarkable, as is usual," he remarked bitterly, "with how little considerative reading of them, the debate has been carried on, on both sides."[12] Olmsted was also upset by false allegations that ill-informed critics of the plan were making: that he, rather than local people, had identified the site, which lay partially outside the city limits; that his cost estimates, which had been carefully prepared with local input, were not to be trusted; and that he had exceeded the instructions given to him by the board and would demand an exorbitant fee for his efforts.[13] His final words on the subject proved prophetic: "Judging from the general drift of public opinion with reference to such matters, as I have had occasion to follow in other cities, the project of a lake shore park will be from time to time revived until, from regard to the interest of the city as a whole, it is adopted."[14] The *Express* echoed his sentiments. "It should never be lost sight of," declared

THE BEST PLANNED CITY IN THE WORLD

Mark Twain's old paper. "It is time we began to use our noble lake-front for pleasure purposes."[15]

THE SECOND SOUTH PARK

After the rejection of the Olmsteds' South Park proposal, the commissioners instructed McMillan to make a survey of other possible sites for a park or parks in the southern part of the city. These sites were to be inland, away from the lake. By early December 1888, McMillan had reported on three such locations, one of which was a private picnic ground known as Red Jacket Park. The local press, however, did not give up hope that the commissioners would reconsider and seek a big lakefront site. "Give us a seascape—a lacustrine park," urged the *Express,* "something unique here, but which every other town with a waterfront has, and that Buffalo has longed for these many years."[16]

Apparently Olmsted had been kept abreast of developments in the search for new sites and had even been asked at one point to begin preparing plans for a parcel of land that the commissioners seemed sure to acquire. This he declined to do, and his reply offered a glimpse of his well-ordered thinking processes. "It is always my practice," he wrote, "to avoid getting my mind fixed on parts of a plan until I had made a thorough comprehensive study of the capabilities of all parts." He would then proceed from the "more comprehensive to the less comprehensive considerations; from leading to subordinate motives, from large features to small, from general affairs to local details." But arriving at a suitable plan, he said, was never an easy matter; "it cannot be had by any forced mental process." Instead, like a work by one of his many artist friends, "it must be reached by a natural and fluent, deliberately contemplative action of the imagination" and "by the weighing of many possibilities, one against another." But unlike a painting or sculpture, a designed landscape required the creator to look "to what may be attained after many years of growth." And as his late friend H. H. Richardson must have told him

about his own creative process, Olmsted remarked, "We have never succeeded in satisfying ourselves with the first draught of a park plan." It always took at least four months from the time he got the topographical maps of the site to arrive at a design that satisfied him, and in some cases a year was required.[17]

Throughout 1889 the commissioners struggled unsuccessfully to settle on a spot for a park. "We are still unable to report any final decision of the whole matter," they stated in their report for that year. Coming close to apologizing for the widespread lingering disappointment over the demise of Olmsted's grand scheme, they acknowledged that "much regret is felt by most of our citizens that no park site has been selected on the lake shore." Yet they staunchly defended their judgment, reiterating that "the Olmsted scheme to transform a large area of the adjacent low flats into an attractive water park, would require too large an expenditure for construction, as was fully explained in our last report."[18]

Finally, in 1890 the commissioners acted. Rejecting the dilapidated Red Jacket Park site, they purchased other land for two new inland parks. (Fig. 8.8) The larger of these, which became known as South Park, was a 156-acre tract (fifteen acres of which were a cemetery) located about a mile inland from the former lakeshore site, on the east side of the railroad tracks that had traversed the eastern edge of the original South Park plan. While it had many advantages, including ease of access by rail and by road (the present South Park Avenue formed its eastern border), any park that would go there was sure, according to McMillan, to be much poorer than the one Olmsted had portrayed. Lacking lake frontage and having no "distinctive character of its own," the landscape would be "a weak imitation of the North Park, so inferior to it in many respects as to provoke odious comparisons," said the faithful superintendent and loyal advocate for all of Olmsted's ideas. The other site was a seventy-six-acre treeless field that straddled Cazenovia Creek near a new residential neighborhood. When Olmsted saw the sites for himself, he was unenthusiastic. After spending a day looking over the parcels with McMillan, he wrote to his stepson John that "they are all most uninteresting, flat, low and more or less gullied or swampy. Too large for local grounds, too narrow and cut up for parks."[19] Furthermore, the noise

and smoke from locomotives that frequently passed by on the western edge of the South Park site (referred to at the time as White's Corners) would detract from the peace and quiet and foul the air. And because this part of the site was a swamp, it would be nearly impossible to establish a growth of trees that would screen the railroad from the eyes and ears of those within the grounds.

Despite his misgivings about the new park sites, Olmsted participated in the preparation of plans for both of them. In April 1892, with Olmsted on his way to Europe for several months, the firm, now F. L. Olmsted & Co., forwarded preliminary designs for both locations, which they thought of in tandem with each other. The principal features of the 156-acre South Park, which somewhat resembled the firm's plan of the year before for Cadwalader Park in Trenton, New Jersey, were "a broad pastoral valley, with occasional groups of trees," a "fine large grove of trees, affording a grateful shade and seclusion in Summer," and "high level land suitable for playgrounds and gardens, and for raising ornamental trees, shrubs, and flowers."[20] Clearly they were trying to fit a lot into a small space.

The scenic landscape was a valley or dale that would be skirted by a curvilinear circuit drive. Footpaths ran alongside the roadway and wound through the sylvan picnic grove along the northern border. Proceeding along the central drive and walks, people would enjoy "charming, pastoral views." Once the widespreading trees, planted "singly or in

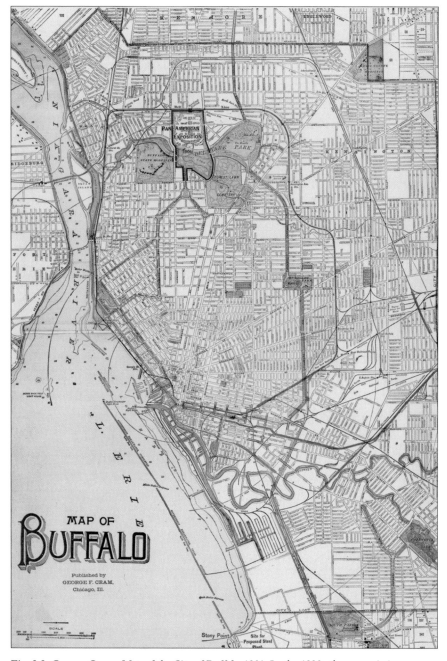

Fig. 8.8. George Cram, *Map of the City of Buffalo,* 1901. In the 1890s the commissioners purchased the present sites of South Park and Cazenovia Park, which appear in the lower right corner of the map, instead of implementing the Olmsteds' 1888 plan for a lakeside park at Stony Point. Courtesy Barry Lawrence Ruderman, Antique Maps, www.RareMaps.com.

THE BEST PLANNED CITY IN THE WORLD

groups," had matured, this park, the Olmsteds declared, would recall "the world-renowned beauty of the English deer parks." The swamp was to be excavated to form two small ponds that would be kept filled with water supplied by a pipeline from nearby Cazenovia Creek. These picture-perfect ponds of less than five acres were deliberately kept small, according to the designers, to be in proportion to the small meadowland. They feared that anything bigger would "destroy the distinctive character of the true English park," for which the landscape was best suited. Still, these diminutive water features would give "life and contrast to the landscape, by [their] ripples and color and by reflecting the sky, the moving clouds and nodding trees." For those who wanted a lake large enough for boating, this would be provided in the sister park, where the creek could be easily dammed for that purpose. (Fig. 8.9) "It is not wise or prudent," the firm advised, "to make each of a series of parks contain exactly the same attractions and features so that when a person has seen one, he has seen all."

In addition to the pastoral experience, South Park would also offer visitors an opportunity to pursue active recreation and to admire a formal garden. On land adjacent to the picnic grove, the Olmsteds proposed to locate an "athletic ground." This would resemble the one they had laid out in Boston's Charlesbank and would contain a variety of athletic equipment. Next to the gymnastic paraphernalia would be a baseball diamond, beyond which was to be located an ornamental garden with "choice trees, shrubs, perennial flowers and fine clipped lawns."

The firm would comply with numerous requests from the commissioners for changes to this first draft before the park became a reality. In late April 1892

Fig. 8.9. Early view of the lake in South Park. From Otis H. Williams, *Buffalo Old and New* (1901). Courtesy Buffalo State College.

Henry Codman, Olmsted's trusted assistant, who was supervising the ongoing construction of Olmsted's plan for the grounds of the World's Columbian Exposition in Chicago, represented the office at a meeting of the Buffalo park commissioners. "I have had a pretty tough time of it," he wrote back to Brookline after the session. The commissioners had especially questioned the small size and location of the ponds in South Park and demanded that they be enlarged to form a lake suitable for boating. "I didn't agree with the desirability of this but again was overruled," Codman reported. "I have agreed to have these plans corrected and before them *on a week from next Tuesday*," he informed his colleagues. "It's mighty short time I know but I was forced to take them up and stop their disagreeable talk."[21]

With the elder Olmsted away, the firm obediently returned to the drawing board and quickly revised the scheme to include a twenty-two-acre boot-shaped lake (Fig. 8.10). This altered plan, which was in Buffalo by early May, was adopted by the board and became the basis for the park that exists today. (Fig. 8.11) It made the lake the dominant feature in the landscape. Yet John

Fig. 8.10. The lake in South Park with wild island in the distance. Photograph by the author, 1991.

Olmsted confided to McMillan his deep misgivings about the alteration, writing, "It does not seem sensible to dig a large pond and bring water a long distance to it by an aqueduct when the enjoyment of everyone can be more conveniently provided for in Cazenovia Park." Echoing the sentiments of his absent father, he later told McMillan, "We distinctly do not believe in making a series of parks in a city as much alike as possible in their general features and provisions for enjoyment, especially in the case of two parks so near each other as Cazenovia and South Parks are." And as to enlarging the lake in Cazenovia Park, which the commissioners had also demanded, he could not see why they would be willing to sacrifice "nice meadow well adapted for playgrounds" when they could easily purchase additional land nearby

that was "ill adapted to any other purpose than making a pond." In this case he advised McMillan do nothing "until Mr. FLO's return" from Europe.[22]

Clearly, the notion of public park design had changed in the 1890s from what it had been when Olmsted and Vaux first came to Buffalo. Including a variety of compatible experiences within the boundaries of a park had always been part of the Olmsted and Vaux philosophy; in South Park, however, the Olmsted firm sought to integrate eight major features in a space that Olmsted and Vaux would surely have thought too small to contain them comfortably. In the Park and in Olmsted's 1888 plan for South Park, for example, the water feature and the meadowland had been separate areas; in the new South Park, which was less than half the

THE BEST PLANNED CITY IN THE WORLD

size of the Park, they were together. Moreover, in their original park scheme Olmsted and Vaux had carefully apportioned incompatible activities among their three parks. In South Park, active and passive recreation were to share the single landscape.

In August 1892 McMillan began supervising a large workforce at the site. By the end of the year they had excavated a portion of the lakebed and used the earth to build up the irregular shoreline. Two years later the lake,

which had been planned with three wild islands, was linked to Cazenovia Creek by a pipeline that ensured a constant supply of water to it and to two ponds near the park's eastern border. For many years the lovely South Park lake has preserved more of its picturesque "Olmstedian" character than many similar bodies of water in other Olmsted parks—including Gala Water in Delaware Park.

Even as construction was under way, the park's

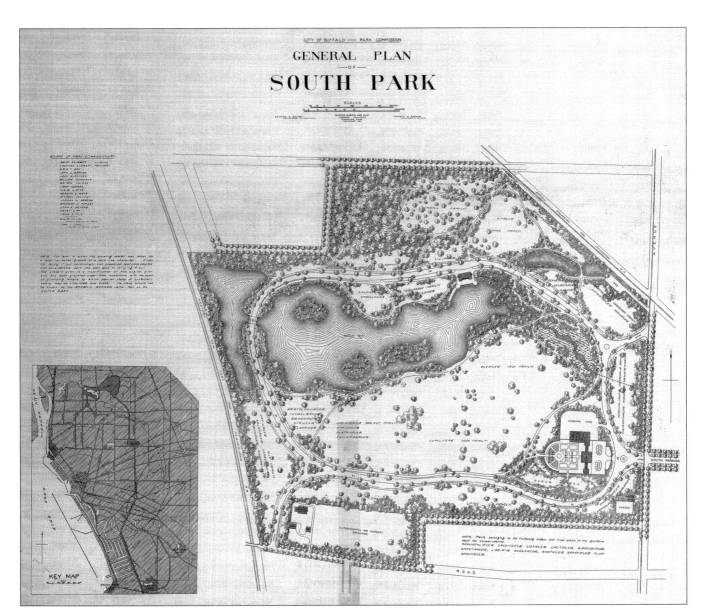

Fig. 8.11. Plan of South Park, 1894. Courtesy National Park Service, Frederick Law Olmsted National Historic Site.

design continued to evolve. "We believe that a botanic garden would be an interesting and instructive feature of our park system," the commissioners declared in their report for 1892. Noting that South Park "offers some advantages as a site for such a garden on a modest and inexpensive scale," they informally asked the Olmsted firm to determine how it could be "incorporated harmoniously with the general features of the plan."[23] In May 1894 John F. Cowell, a well-known botanist from Buffalo, was named director of the new Botanic Garden, as the South Park grounds also came to be commonly known. In the coming years Cowell would be responsible for establishing and managing the garden, the broad purpose of which was "to show the wealth of the world's hardy and tropical flowers and a complete collection of all the native hardy trees, shrubs, and herbaceous plants of this country."[24]

The desire to add a botanic garden to South Park seems to have originated with local citizens. Some of them may have recalled, however, that several years before, when Olmsted was beginning to work with Charles Sprague Sargent on Harvard University's Arnold Arboretum, he had suggested to the Buffalo park commissioners that they establish a place where examples of the native trees of western New York might be planted "so that the varying habits of each species can be shown and the whole made ornamental as well as a source of

Fig. 8.12. The South Park landscape was originally planned to resemble an English deer park. Postcard, c. 1910. Courtesy James Mendola.

information."[25] (Around this time he had also proposed to Leland Stanford that he set up an arboretum on the grounds of Stanford University, and to George Washington Vanderbilt that he establish one at his Biltmore estate in Asheville, North Carolina.) Finally, in April 1894, having formally approved the creation of a botanic garden at South Park, the commissioners instructed the Olmsted firm, then operating under the name Olmsted, Olmsted & Eliot, to adapt the park landscape for a botanic garden. This they did under the direction of Warren Manning, who acted as superintendent of planting. The map the firm forwarded to Buffalo in December 1894 indicated areas for various families of trees and shrubs and eliminated "from the park plan heretofore submitted and adopted, all features inconsistent with this special purpose."[26] The athletic ground and baseball diamonds were removed, and the plan for South Park arrived at its final form. To be sure, South Park was to be a place where the work-weary might come to unwind amid pleasant if undersized meadow, woodland, and water scenery. (Fig. 8.12) But making an equal claim on visitors' attention were invitations to seek instruction in the science of botany and to admire showy displays of annuals and rare plants. There would be no beach, no lagoon for leisurely boat rides, no green for balloon ascents, and no views of the inland sea.

In order for the botanic garden to fulfill its global mandate in the climate of western New York, it would be necessary to equip the park with a suitable conservatory. Only there could warm-weather species be safely displayed to a public that might otherwise never see such exotic flora. Consequently, in addition to propagating houses, in 1897 the city commissioned the local architect H. L. Campbell to design a three-hundred-foot-long "glass palace" to be manufactured by Lord & Burnham.[27] The following year, the $108,000 structure went up on top of the ridge in the southeast corner of the grounds, as the firm had indicated on the 1894 plan.[28] (Fig. 8.13) There, the gleaming conservatory faces the main park entrance, dominating the "English deer park" landscape (which long ago was turned into a

Fig. 8.13. Buffalo and Erie County Botanical Gardens conservatory. Photograph by Andy Olenick.

golf course). We can assume that Olmsted himself had diminished enthusiasm for such developments. Writing home to his partners from England during his travels there in 1892, he lamented that "in the newest work, the landscape end is confused with and subordinated to other ends."[29] In any event, the new South Park conservatory (present home of the Buffalo and Erie County Botanical Gardens) was one of the largest in the world. (Fig. 8.14) When it opened in 1898, Buffalo was emerging in advance of other cities from a long period of recession. Many must have seen it as a harbinger of a new era of prosperity.

While he had been engaged in planning today's inland South Park, Olmsted must have been dismayed to learn that the commissioners had bought thirty

acres at Stony Point, the area that would have been the beach in Olmsted's 1888 plan. On a trip to inspect this water's-edge site, a new commissioner who was apparently unfamiliar with Olmsted's thwarted proposal had innocently remarked that a visit to that picturesque spot might "form a pleasant incident of an afternoon drive." Unmoved by their new colleague's enthusiasm or by the dramatic prospect from the shore that day when "the breakers were rolling in and the wind was blowing at a lively rate," the commissioners stated categorically in their annual report that "no general improvement or ornamentation will be attempted" at the site. They had purchased the property solely with the intent of using it for a plant nursery.[30] Even so, the Olmsteds still held out hope that "some way out of the difficulty of connect-

Fig. 8.14. Rotunda of the Buffalo and Erie County Botanical Gardens conservatory . Photograph by Andy Olenick.

ing the Stony Point Park with South Park" might be found, suggesting that a parkway might be run through a nearby neighborhood.[31]

In 1899 John C. Olmsted revisited Stony Point, together with Daniel Burnham and Warren Manning, when the three men were brought in to advise the Pan-American Exposition site selection committee. By then Frederick Law Olmsted had retired from practice; clearly suffering from what we now call Alzheimer's disease, he was confined to a private psychiatric hospital. John must surely have told Burnham about the extraordinary plan that his father and he had envisioned for Stony Point eleven years earlier. Burnham had championed Olmsted's visionary scheme for the grounds of the 1893 World's Columbian Exposition

on the shore of Lake Michigan, a plan that was the legacy of the original South Park design. Looking at Stony Point through his old friend's eyes, with Olmsted's stepson and former assistant at his side, must have been a moving experience for Burnham. He as much as anyone would have felt the power of the site's boundless view of Lake Erie and appreciated its potential for out-of-the-ordinary "marine effects." And by then the breakwater had been finished, making water access to the area feasible. Nonetheless, in the end, the committee also turned away from the lake and recommended that the fair be situated elsewhere. In the early twentieth century, John J. Albright and his associates acquired Stony Point as part of the 1,500-acre property of the Lackawanna Steel Company.[32]

CAZENOVIA PARK

The Olmsteds began working on designs for Cazenovia Park together with those for the new South Park. Progress toward their realization, however, would encounter a number of setbacks. For one thing, the commissioners disliked the name of the park. Their objection was not that it was the same as that of a residential neighborhood which private investors had recently established on property adjacent to the site, but rather that to their Anglo and Germanic ears it had a "foreign sound" and seemed to them "hardly liquid enough for popular use." They conceded, however, that the difficult-to-pronounce name carried historic significance—Theophilus Cazenove (1740–1811), a Dutch citizen, had been the financial agent in America for the Holland Land Company that originally owned most of western part of the state—and was already in common use locally. So in 1892 they agreed to adopt it as the official name of the new park.[33]

The preliminary plans that the Olmsted firm submitted to the board of commissioners in the spring of 1892 called for the creation of a landscape distinctly different from that of nearby South Park. No reference was made to emulating a pretty English deer park. The flat, square site of eighty-three acres was traversed by Cazenovia Creek, an unruly watercourse that each spring would widely overflow its banks, after which the creek presented a less than ideal appearance. "The beauty and attractiveness of the creek," observed the Olmsteds, "is greatly marred by its raw, caving banks and bare, shelving shores, which are fully exposed during the diminished flow in Summer."[34] Working with these conditions, the Olmsteds proposed to tame the creek by damming it to create a twenty-acre, irregularly shaped lake with two large islands. This water feature would take up most of the space of the park. The lake's length and winding shoreline would make it an ideal place for boating, and accordingly they proposed that the one important structure in the park be a boathouse near the northern entrance from Seneca Street. After

the lake, which in the winter could be used for skating, the second major feature was to be a broad meadow specifically intended for baseball and other field sports. Third, a formal tree-shaded concert grove was planned for the area just behind the boathouse. This space would be graded to slope downward toward the bandstand so that, as in an amphitheater, those in the outer rows of seats could see and hear well. Furthermore, positioning the seating area to face north ensured that neither daytime nor evening audiences would be looking into the sun.

Beyond the grove would be a large carriage concourse where occupants might stay in their vehicles to listen to the music. To keep the noise from the horse-and-carriage audience from interfering with the music, the plan inserted a large flower garden between the bandstand and the concourse. Perhaps embellished with a fountain, it could, the firm advised, "be appropriately decorated with pretty flower beds, varying in pattern and colors from year to year."[35] At one side of this formal grouping of elements was to be a long terrace where spectators might watch and cheer games taking place on the playground. The Olmsteds were reluctant to include a circuit drive around the park because it would have to be kept too close to the border, but they agreed to add one if the commissioners decided that it was necessary (which they would). (Fig. 8.15) Moreover, the firm's draft included a thirty-acre area upstream that the commissioners did not yet own but the landscape architects strongly recommended they acquire. They extended the lake into this additional property and looped the drive around it. The new land would also add some meadowland to the otherwise cramped site.

The commissioners' initial reaction to the firm's plan was one of skepticism. They feared that damming the creek to create the lake might cause damaging floods during sudden storms and that it would be difficult to build a structure strong enough to hold back the water at all times. Distrustful of McMillan's advice that the dam be made of wood so that it could be raised or removed entirely during the period of heaviest flooding, they turned to the engineers of the Department of Public Works for their opinion on the matter. Their reply was that a timber barrier would be feasible and safe.

One of the engineers, Richard Johnson, unexpectedly took the opportunity to tender more than advice on damming. Perhaps at the suggestion of one or two of the commissioners, Johnson offered to submit entirely new plans for the park (as well as for South Park). When McMillan got wind of this, he was furious. In April, when Henry Codman came from Brookline to attend the park commissioners' meeting, he found Johnson "cynical and disagreeable and fault finding." The engineer was both unfriendly to McMillan, whom he was "trying to undermine . . . by one means or another, always behind his back," and "almost insulting" to Codman. Most alarming, reported Codman, was that Johnson had "persuaded some of the Commissioners that anybody (himself particularly) can make plans and a day or two is all that is needed." He had promised to present drawings to the board at its next meeting. For this reason, Codman urged that the office send their revisions for Cazenovia and South Parks to Buffalo

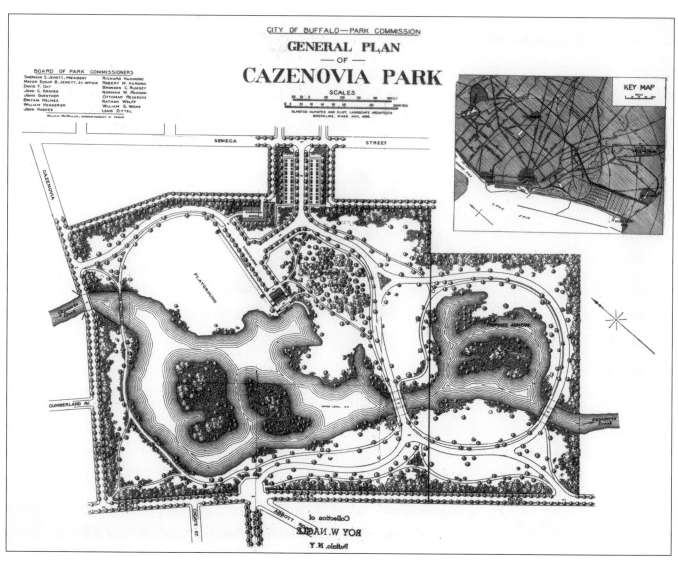

Fig. 8.15. Olmsted, Olmsted & Eliot, general plan of Cazenovia Park, 1894. Author's collection.

THE BEST PLANNED CITY IN THE WORLD

within a week. "Get these plans done for me without fail and I will down him," he pledged.[36]

McMillan had dashed off his own long, angry letters to Brookline. In a reply written under the firm's name but which was probably penned by John C. Olmsted, McMillan was told, "We feel that some of the Park Commissioners have unwittingly put us in an entirely false position by inviting the engineer to present a plan in competition with ours." It isn't clear when Frederick Law Olmsted Sr. got wind of the affair, but surely it must have stirred memories of the early days of Central Park, when Vaux had come to him complaining of the paltry design for the new park that the city had accepted from Egbert Viele, an engineer. Working behind the scenes, Vaux succeeded in having it overturned and a competition held for a new plan, a contest that he and Olmsted won. Somewhat later, when Viele sued, Vaux publicly vindicated both the status of the landscape architect and their work by explaining how it differed significantly from Viele's scheme both aesthetically and practically. Now, all these years later, Olmsted and his colleagues found themselves in a similar situation. "In the case of architecture," they observed, "this distinction between the professions of engineers and architect has come to be very generally understood by the people, and especially by the Commissioners and other representatives of the people, but the public mind is still at sea when it comes to questions of landscape design."[37]

It would fall to McMillan to stand up for them and their profession. Even though the Olmsted firm had sent the commissioners the revised plan for Cazenovia Park in early May, in June the board adopted Johnson's scheme instead. The next month, as the construction season got under way, McMillan addressed the commissioners in a letter that was printed in the *Courier* the following day. "I believe the plan which has been adopted by the Board is wholly unfit and impracticable," he wrote, adding that he refused to begin working on it. "How can I be expected to execute cordially and faithfully all the barbarous features of the landscape design?" he demanded. "How could I suffer the constant viola-

tion of every cherished principle of my profession?" To proceed would be "a crucifixion to me," declared the usually taciturn Scotsman. "I would have to sacrifice all sense of duty, all sentiment of honor, as a servant, and all feeling of self-respect, as a man." If the commissioners wanted to go ahead with this inferior plan, which he condemned for "the awkward shape and outline of the pond, the rigid angular lines of the creek, the long ramparts of expensive masonry guarding its empty channel, the straight lines and street-corner turns of the drive, the absence of necessary walks, play grounds, open greens, shrubbery groups, or border screen, except a few trees stuck in at random like pins in a pincushion," let them "give full charge to the Engineer."[38] He would have none of it. Fortunately Sherman Jewett, who was actually opposed to damming Cazenovia Creek to form a lake, declined to accept his resignation and advised him to "take time for reflection."[39]

Eventually, in early August, after a review by the Board of Public Works found that the Olmsted plan would be just as feasible as its alternative, the commissioners calmed the situation by reversing themselves and unanimously adopting the Olmsted firm's design. The superintendent was then ordered to proceed immediately with the work on Cazenovia Park, together with that already begun on South Park. The decision on how best to provide water for the Cazenovia lake was to be left to McMillan's judgment.[40] "It's a signal triumph for me," McMillan reported to Brookline, "and I have received many cordial congratulations from many citizens."[41]

In the years following the commissioners' approval of the Olmsted design for Cazenovia Park, the landscape slowly took the form the planners envisioned. (Figs. 8.16 and 8.17) The new park was ready for the public by 1896, when band concerts began. The following winter skaters started using the lake. The fertile soil favored the growth of fine trees, of which there are many now. (Fig. 8.18) Yet the designers had had no intention of making it a country park like Delaware Park, or as South Park would have been. Instead, Cazenovia Park

Fig. 8.16. The Cazenovia Park lake in 1857. Courtesy Buffalo and Erie County Historical Society.

THE BEST PLANNED CITY IN THE WORLD

developed into a popular venue for baseball players and their fans. Tennis, football, and softball also brought many to the park over the years, up to the present day. In 1895 the commissioners opened proceedings to

Fig. 8.17. The Cazenovia Park lake, c. 1910. Courtesy James Mendola.

acquire the additional upstream property that the firm had included in its extended plan. The city, however, had no success in this endeavor until 1907, when the Olmsted plans were finally realized. Further expansion of the park upstream took place in 1925, when another eighty acres were acquired for a new golf course. The boathouse, which included a small refectory as well as facilities for storing boats, went up in 1912 to designs by the local architectural firm of Esenwein & Johnson.

Later in the twentieth century, Cazenovia Park underwent numerous changes. A continual source of maintenance problems, the lake and the dam that created it disappeared in the 1970s, and the creek, partly redirected from its original course, now flows once again through the landscape. Today the boathouse sits high and dry on the edge of the spacious lawn that occu-

Fig. 8.18. Cazenovia Park. Photograph by Andy Olenick.

pies the site of the departed lake. In addition, many new buildings have sprung up within the boundaries of the park, including a public library, community center, ice rink, indoor swimming pool, and outdoor wading pool, as well as surface parking lots. Nevertheless, many people living in South Buffalo and neighboring West Seneca are attracted to the 190-acre park for games, sports, exercise, and picnics, making Cazenovia today the most consistently frequented of the city's Olmsted parks.[42]

At the same time that the Olmsted firm provided the dissimilar plans for South Park and Cazenovia Park, it also furnished plans for linking them with new 150-foot-wide parkways.[43] One of these was named in honor of Red Jacket, the name by which Anglos knew Chief Say-goyawatha (1750–1830), the great Native American orator who spoke out for his people's rights, who had lived here in his later years, when the area was Seneca tribal land.[44] But no link between the new South Side parkways and the earlier parkway system on the north side of town was ever established. Neither was Olmsted's ambitious scheme for joining the northern and southern parts of the city by means of a single grand viaduct over the myriad railroad tracks that divided the sectors. Nonetheless, after Olmsted went into retirement the city took bold steps to correct the serious problem created by grade crossings of rail lines along many of its thoroughfares. In 1896 a local journal reported that over the next few years, "thirty-six immense viaducts and subways will be built, and when all are completed Buffalo will have one of the finest systems of elevated and

Fig. 8.19. McKinley Parkway. Photograph by Andy Olenick.

THE BEST PLANNED CITY IN THE WORLD

safe railroad crossings to be found anywhere."[45] Thus, by the early twentieth century, the South Side would be safely joined to the center and the north of the city, though not by parkways.

After this, South Buffalo and West Seneca would rapidly evolve into a desirable place of residence, especially for working-class families. To the local real estate establishment, now attuned to the salubrious effect of public parks on nearby land values, the significance of the South Park botanical garden lay in the fact that "its location in the extreme southern part of the city will greatly enhance the attractiveness and popularity of the new residence district there."[46] In the minds of many of the area's real estate developers in the 1880s and 1890s, however, the laying out of parkways was more important than the creation of parks. (Fig. 8.19) With the evidence of the success of the North Buffalo parkway system before their eyes, many investors thought that parkways would serve as similar trunk lines of progress in South Buffalo. The Olmsteds cautioned that the upscale parkways should be planned in conjunction with other streets in the area, many of which were opened between 1891 and 1895. No records exist, however, to suggest that the firm made plans for new residential neighborhoods as Olmsted had done in North Buffalo.

RIVERSIDE PARK

The last park for Buffalo to come from the drawing boards at Fairsted was Riverside Park. Located on the northwestern border of the city in the Black Rock section of town, twenty-two-acre Riverside Park occupies the site of an earlier fee-for-entry grounds called Germania Park. From the 1870s, this tree-shaded grove, which was located in a still empty section of the city known as the Jones Tract, had been a popular excursion destination for families of all classes and ethnicities and a frequent place of assembly for church groups and political organizations. For fifteen cents (ten cents for children), one could take the steamer *Periwinkle* from

the dock at the foot of Main Street for a voyage to Germania Park, a trip of approximately four miles. From the 1880s, the park was also conveniently accessible by the Belt Line railroad and a new streetcar line. Perhaps because of good transportation, Germania Park became a popular place of assembly for local members of the nascent labor movement. On Labor Day in 1887, a crowd of ten thousand gathered there to hear national union leaders speak, among them Edward McGlynn, the Catholic priest who had been recently excommunicated for his social reformist views and his support for the single-tax proponent Henry George in his unsuccessful run for New York City mayor. The sympathetic crowd listened attentively as McGlynn advocated for the improved education of children, condemned child labor, and denounced the employment of women for "work God did not intend them to do." Other speakers that memorable day were Samuel Gompers and Martin Foran.[47] Four years later on the same holiday, after a pro-labor speech by Governor David B. Hill, the man who had signed the bill creating the Niagara reservation, which allowed families to visit the falls for free, the celebrations concluded with parades of military troops on the green and music and dancing in the dancehall. A local newspaper headlined the event "Workingman Hill," cleverly referring equally to the governor and to the locale.[48]

As residential development began to spread into Riverside, as this neighborhood came to be known, residents expressed the desire, as had those in South Buffalo, for a park in their area. By early 1896 the city was considering the possibility of buying Germania Park for public use. The mayor at the time even suggested that in addition to the Germania Park pier, docks for excursion boats could be built at the Front and at Stony Point, "thus supplementing the splendid system of boulevards with which it is proposed to encircle the city and rounding out by a water route, the communication between the various parts of the city."[49] In April, members of the Common Council went to inspect the site with an eye to its purchase, but they apparently found the price being asked by the proprietor, Oscar Stollmeyer, too high. In May of that year a well-attended meeting of area citizens urged the city to acquire Germania Park, together with a smaller neighboring private grove known as Union Park. Germania was "remarkably well suited for a park," according to the *Express,* which editorialized that the city would regret passing up the opportunity to buy it.[50] Finally, in March of the following year, the council voted to purchase the twenty-two acres and rename the site Riverside Park.[51] The city now possessed within its boundaries a superb piece of land with mature forest trees on the elevated banks of the Niagara River, its other scenic water's edge.

In 1898 the commissioners contacted Olmsted Brothers—now working without their father's guidance or the local assistance of the now-dismissed McMillan—for plans to convert venerable Germania Park into modern Riverside Park. (Fig. 8.20) The drawings were done by August. "By far the most important and valuable circumstance connected with Riverside Park," the Olmsteds told John Hughes, the president of the park commission, "is its situation on the Niagara River, thus enabling visitors to command extensive views across and up and down the river." They would be vigilant in doing everything possible to "avoid injury to the views." This included not planting more trees than already existed on the western side of the grounds that bordered Niagara Street, forgoing the setting out of shrubbery on that side of the park, and stipulating the removal of telegraph poles and electric wires that marred the prospect.[52] (Fig. 8.21) On the bank that sloped down to the Erie Canal across Niagara Street from the main part of the park, a long vine-covered pergola would be built, reminiscent of the vine-clad arbor that Olmsted

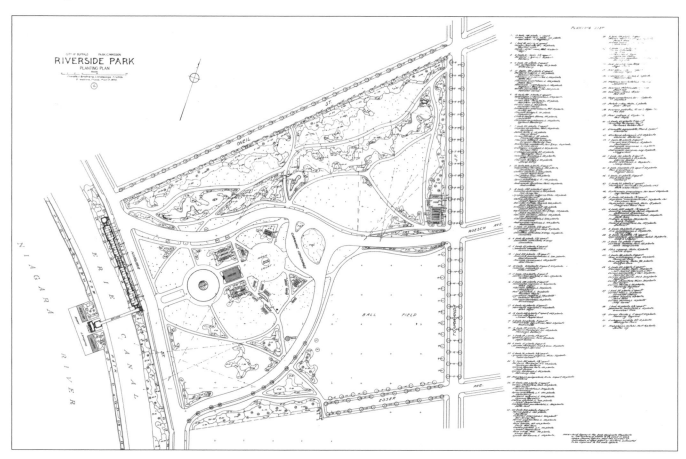

Fig. 8.20. Olmsted Brothers, Riverside Park planting plan, 1899. Courtesy National Park Service, Frederick Law Olmsted National Historic Site.

THE BEST PLANNED CITY IN THE WORLD

Fig. 8.21. Riverside Park, looking toward the Niagara River from the western edge of the park. Postcard, c. 1910. Courtesy James Mendola.

and Vaux had created in Central Park overlooking the Mall. Visitors might descend to this riparian balcony to contemplate the view undisturbed by carriages passing along the roadway. Moreover, the design, the Olmsteds explained, "requires the floor of this pergola to be set at a low enough elevation to keep the trellis for carrying vines overhead no higher than the adjoining sidewalk in Niagara Street, thus the pergola will in no way obstruct the view of the river from any portion of the Park, while the vines upon it will afford an interesting foreground to the views from the adjoining sidewalk."[53] Commenting on the plans, the *Express* gratefully acknowledged that, in the tradition of their esteemed predecessor, the current Olmsteds had capitalized on the view of the river to fashion a "great public outlook over the beautiful scene."[54]

Visitors might reach this new beauty spot by a variety of means. Riverside Park would inherit the former

bond to the river by remaining an excursion destination. The Olmsted firm's plans provided that the old dock and rickety bridge across the Erie Canal would be rebuilt in more substantial form to accommodate passengers arriving and departing by water. Plans for Riverside were also accompanied by plans for parkway approaches, for the creation of the new park was seen, as had been the case in South Buffalo, as a neighborhood-building project.[55] For those in carriages, a one-hundred-foot-wide tree-lined avenue was proposed to connect the new park with Delaware Park via Roesch Street, which terminated at the main entrance on the eastern side of the park. A streetcar line along the eastern border of the park ensured that less well-to-do visitors could enjoy the park as well. With the magnificent prospect across the island-studded river, with the docking facilities at its doorstep, and with public transportation in place, brand-new Riverside Park was one of the

Fig. 8.22. Pools in Riverside Park were constructed among existing trees to recall a brook winding through a forest. Postcard, c. 1910. Courtesy James Mendola.

sites that, in 1899, John C. Olmsted, Warren Manning, and Daniel Burnham seriously considered for the site of the 1901 Pan-American Exposition.

Although the scenery may have been the dominant motif of the Olmsteds' design for Riverside Park, they introduced a number of features into the plan, in the manner of other parks of the time. They considered each of three sections defined by the wishbone drive in a distinctly different way. The wooded northern section would be treated "in a somewhat secluded woodland style." The western section of the park, the triangular area between the two drives, would be laid out in a formal manner as a music grove. The southern portion of the park would be

left open as an athletic field, "with a few shade trees on the margin, but without shrubbery or other decorations liable to be in the way of ball playing."[56] Moreover, for the sake of economy, some of the structures that remained on the site from Germania Park days would be moved and reused in the new scheme.

The existing north woods would fulfill the need for tranquil recreation. To enhance the sense of pleasurable isolation, the border would be thickly planted with shade-tolerant shrubs, and twisty walks would encourage the casual stroll. The most novel component, however, was "a long, narrow meandering pool, intended to be suggestive of a forest brook." (Fig. 8.22) In reality,

THE BEST PLANNED CITY IN THE WORLD

Fig. 8.23. Children enjoyed wading in the tree-shaded pools of Riverside Park. Postcard, c. 1910. Courtesy James Mendola.

this was a series of connected ponds only one to two feet deep, with cement-lined bottoms hidden beneath a bed of gravel. The firm also referred to this water feature as a "minnow pool" and suggested that in place of footbridges, stepping-stones be placed in the water for people to cross.[57] Whether this fictive rivulet, which was excavated by the end of 1899, was ever stocked with tiny fish is unknown, but it did become particularly popular with children, who enjoyed wading there.[58] (Fig. 8.23)

The more formal music grove area on the western edge of the park ensured that the long-standing tradition of summer concerts would continue. On an axis with the footbridge across the canal were a bandstand for afternoon and evening concerts, a shelter "which will be especially valuable in case of sudden showers," a raised fountain basin "which will make a pleasing dis-

play of water," and a formal garden "for the gratification of those who particularly enjoy this style of decoration." (The condescending tone of the last remark suggests that Olmsted's successors shared his distaste for carpet bedding and formal flower gardens in public parks, especially where they might be a distraction from the natural scenery.) Recognizing that more people would come here, especially during the concerts, than to any other part of the park, they proposed to lay out "various radiating walks" to receive and disperse them. Finally, the designers also squeezed in "apparatus for simple forms of children's amusements."[59]

Perhaps to old-style activists, the Olmsteds' remaking of Germania Park seemed like gentrification, and they may have wondered if the commissioners, most of whom were businessmen, had premeditated the upgrading to discourage mass political gatherings. Be that as it may, Riverside Park, which was eventually enlarged by the addition of seventeen acres on the south (including a small cemetery), preserved its earlier role as a pleasant destination for a boat ride from downtown, while it also became a treasured neighborhood amenity. Unfortunately, like so many urban parks from the golden age of the American park movement, Riverside Park in the latter half of the twentieth century suffered from both neglect and alteration. Now, little remains of the concert grove, and sizable modern recreational buildings occupy what was formerly open space.

Epilogue

Twenty-three years after Anthony Trollope remarked that apart from grain elevators there was "nothing specially worthy of remark at Buffalo," the writer Charles Burr Todd told readers of *Lippincott's Magazine* that "the most admirable feature" of the city was "its system of parks, park-ways and avenues." Buffalo was certainly on Olmsted's mind when, late in his career, he wrote that the many large and small parks he had planned around the country were "a hundred years ahead of any spontaneous public demand, or of the demand of any notable cultivated part of the people. And they are having an educative effect perfectly manifest to me—a manifest civilizing effect." In 1937 the urban planner Walter Curt Behrendt contended that the city could find no better way to express its gratitude for what Olmsted and those early citizens who supported him had achieved in Buffalo "than by a strong and never-ceasing vigilance assuring that this most valuable inheritance will never be impaired or destroyed."[1]

The efficient and beautiful city that embodied the wisdom of Olmsted's theories and vision, however, did not survive the postwar shift from public transit to the private automobile as the predominant mode of transportation and from city to suburban living as the preferred way of life. "It would take the automobile, urban renewal, and a less sensitive generation of planners to undo Olmsted and Vaux's achievement," the urban historian Witold Rybczynski writes of Buffalo.[2] Construction of new roads and highways accelerated the extension of the earlier residential character of areas like North Buffalo, which today is referred to as an "urban" neighborhood, farther and farther from the center of town, a center that itself has lost its role as the hub of commerce. Furthermore, as in cities elsewhere in America, steady waning of business and industry has reduced the quality of life in Buffalo, a phenomenon poignantly portrayed by Verlyn Klinkenborg in his book *The Last Fine Time* (1991).

"During the thirty years following the Second World War the Olmsted firm's design legacy suffered," the Olmsted scholar Charles Beveridge notes. "Neglect and the intrusion of incompatible uses beset many of the parks and public spaces designed by the firm."[3] Buffalo proved no exception to this sad decline, and its historic parks and parkways suffered greatly from lack of means and appreciation. In addition, the outbreak of Dutch elm disease, which began to appear in the area in the 1950s, eventually devastated the magnificent monoculture for-

Aerial view of the former water park section of Delaware Park showing the high-speed divided highway (N.Y. State Route 198) that replaced the original carriage drive and the Scajaquada Parkway, 1961. The former farmlands of the Buffalo State Hospital, which in the 1920s became the campus of what is now Buffalo State College, are visible near the upper left. Courtesy Buffalo State College.

est that had grown up along parkways and avenues. In the 1970s a group of park advocates set out to revive the city's memory of its neglected heritage. Reflecting a national reawakening to the Olmsted legacy encouraged by the reissuing of F. L. Olmsted Jr. and Theodora Kimball's *Forty Years of Landscape Architecture* (1970), the presentation in 1972 of a major exhibition on Olmsted at the National Gallery of Art and the inauguration of the Frederick Law Olmsted Papers Project, and

the publication in 1973 of Laura Wood Roper's *FLO: A Biography,* the Buffalo Friends of Olmsted Parks came into being in 1978 with the goal of preserving what remained of Buffalo's Olmsted parks and parkways. The Friends became a voice for the city's outstanding tradition of park and urban planning.

To achieve their aims, the Friends and their allies adopted procedures that historic preservationists had used to protect notable buildings. In 1979 the Friends

THE BEST PLANNED CITY IN THE WORLD

Humboldt Parkway under construction as the Kensington Expressway, part of a limited access state highway (N.Y. State Route 33), c. 1962. Courtesy Buffalo State College.

initiated a survey of the park and parkway system and compiled historical documentation. This effort led in 1981 to listing what remained of these sites in the National Register of Historic Places. The administration of Forest Lawn Cemetery achieved listing of the venerable burial ground in 1990. The buildings and grounds of the Buffalo State Hospital (later known as the Buffalo Psychiatric Center) had already been listed in 1973, but local preservationists succeeded in 1986 in having them elevated to National Historic Landmark status. That same year the Parkside Community Association, a neighborhood improvement organization which had been formed in 1963 during the darkest days of anti-urbanism to combat destructive redlining practices, secured listing of the Parkside neighborhood in the National Register both for its importance in the history of community planning and for its fine collection of domestic architecture. Thus by the mid-1980s the entire landscape of North Buffalo with which Olmsted and Vaux had been associated enjoyed national recognition of its significance and possessed some degree of state and federal protection from further erosion of its historic character.

In addition to advocating for Buffalo's historic parks, the Friends were instrumental in promoting a national revival of interest in Olmsted and his works. In 1980 they invited representatives from other cites with Olmsted landscapes to Buffalo for a meeting to discuss matters of mutual concern. Guest speaker Charles Capen McLaughlin, editor-in-chief of the Olmsted Papers Project, inspired those present to take concerted action on behalf of Olmsted's illustrious design heritage. Out of this meeting grew the National Association for Olmsted Parks, which the following year held the first of many national conferences in Boston. Since then the NAOP has grown into a broadly based organization with offices in Washington, D.C., that advocates for the Olmsted legacy around the United States.

Ever since 2000, the volunteer effort begun in Buffalo by the Friends has been carried on with expanded resources by the Buffalo Olmsted Parks Conservancy. Modeled on the Central Park Conservancy, it aims to "promote, preserve, restore, enhance, and maintain" the

Nighttime lighting of the towers of Richardson's Buffalo State Hospital, 2007. Photograph by Paul Pasquarello.

Buffalo park and parkway system. In 2004, under an agreement with public officials, it assumed responsibility for administering and operating the city's historic park and parkway system. It was the first nonprofit organization to have the opportunity to undertake such an extensive mission. Building on its success, in 2008 the conservancy developed its *Plan for the Twenty-first Century*. The document outlines ambitious plans for restoring the parks as closely as possible to their golden age, for rebuilding destroyed elements, including Humboldt Parkway (lost in the 1960s to an expressway), and for adding new parkland and boulevards to the original system. Mindful of the spirit of Olmsted, Vaux, and McMillan, and observing their efforts, a staff of professionals and a larger company of volunteers have achieved remarkable results in restoring the ailing lungs of the city to health.

Together with the recovery of the Olmsted park system, other efforts on behalf of the Olmsted heritage are under way. In 1979 the Buffalo and Erie County Botanical Gardens Society was formed to rescue the deteriorating conservatory in South Park. After twenty-five years of struggle and growth, the society assumed management of the publicly owned facility in 2004. It is once again a major cultural asset. One of the most difficult local preservation challenges has been to save the remaining buildings and grounds of H. H. Richardson's Buffalo State Hospital, which in the late 1960s the state declared surplus property. After many attempts to come up with an adaptive reuse plan, the Richardson Center Corporation was formed in 2006, with a substantial appropriation of funds from the state. In addition to conserving the buildings, the RCC seeks to reestablish as much as possible of the historic landscape. Having contracted for a cultural landscape report, the RCC, in tandem with the conservancy, has undertaken the re-greening of a significant portion of the south lawn area, the institution's former "pastured pleasure grounds."

Another state-aided project is the Niagara River Greenways Commission. Established in 2004, the commission traces its origins to a 1990 study sponsored by the Friends to find ways to append modern green space to the Olmsted park system. Restating Olmsted and Vaux's dream of linking Buffalo, Niagara Falls, and Lewiston in a regional park and scenic landscape system, the commission aids plans for parks and conservation areas along the American shore of Lake Erie and the Niagara River. (Since 1931 the Niagara Parkway, which Winston Churchill called "the prettiest Sunday afternoon drive in the world," has followed most of the Canadian side of the river.) As in the days of Dorsheimer, Pratt, Rogers, and other pioneer park advocates, enlightened citizens have once again come forward to champion the cause of comprehensive planning that was at the heart of Olmsted and Vaux's philosophy of park design.

"Buffalo was fortunate in Mr. Olmsted's work," stated the *Express* in 1893. What he had done there over a period of twenty-five years, the paper predicted, would surely endure because it had been based on "a foresight of what the city was to become."[4] Despite grievous losses, that great legacy continues to exert its presence in the modern-day metropolis. More than any other city in which Frederick Law Olmsted worked, Buffalo was shaped by what his biographer Laura Roper has called his "double-edged genius" as a landscape designer and a social theorist. "In Olmsted," she writes, "the artistic and the social impulse were equally strong and indissolubly joined; he could not conceive of the first functioning independently of the second."[5] Having encountered on his initial visit a population that generally ignored the waterfront, complained of nowhere to go for pleasure drives or outdoor relaxation, and worried that headlong development would lead to a crowded and chaotic cityscape, Olmsted cultivated a sympathetic audience for his progressive ideas. He also had the extraordinary good fortune of having William McMillan on the scene to make sure that the parks were not "more or less barbarously treated," as so often happened elsewhere once he left town.[6]

To the novelist Lauren Belfer's observation that "if

Delaware Park from Forest Lawn Cemetery. Photograph by Andy Olenick.

Olmsted had been a painter, Buffalo would have been his canvas," I would answer that Olmsted was indeed an artist who, in the words of his friend Daniel H. Burnham, succeeded "with lakes and wooded slopes; with lawns and banks and forest-covered hills; with mountain-sides and ocean views," in creating landscape compositions that can be as life-enhancing as a fine piece of music or an exquisite painting.[7] And like all great masters, he required sympathetic patrons. In the realm of public parks, I would maintain, Buffalo (including Niagara) was the client for which Olmsted exercised the fullest measure of his genius.

Notes

ABBREVIATIONS AND SOURCES

All correspondence between Olmsted and others, unless otherwise noted, is located in the Frederick Law Olmsted Papers, Manuscript Division, Library of Congress, Washington, D.C.

All newspapers cited, unless otherwise indicated, were published in Buffalo.

ARBPC	*Annual Report of the Buffalo Parks Commissioners* (cited by volume and year)
Forty Years	*Forty Years of Landscape Architecture: Being the Professional Papers of Frederick Law Olmsted,* ed. Frederick Law Olmsted Jr. and Theodora Kimball (1922), reprinted in one volume as *Frederick Law Olmsted: Landscape Architect, 1822–1903* (New York: Blom, 1970)
PCC	*Proceedings of the Common Council of the City of Buffalo* (cited by year)

The following volumes of *The Papers of Frederick Law Olmsted,* under the general editorship of Charles Capen McLaughlin and Charles E. Beveridge and published by Johns Hopkins University Press, are cited in the notes as *Papers of FLO* followed by the volume number and page:

Vol. 5. *The California Frontier, 1863–1865,* ed. Charles E. Beveridge and Victoria Post Ranney (1990)

Vol. 6. *The Years of Olmsted, Vaux & Co., 1865–1874,* ed. David Schuyler and Jane Turner Censer (1992)

Vol. 7. *Parks, Politics, and Patronage, 1874–1882,* ed. Charles E. Beveridge, Carolyn F. Hoffman, and Kenneth Hawkins (2007)

Supp. ser., vol. 1. *The Writings on Public Parks, Parkways, and Park Systems,* ed. Charles E. Beveridge and Carolyn F. Hoffman (1997)

INTRODUCTION

1. Anthony Trollope, *North America* (New York: Harper & Brothers, 1862), 160.

2. George M. Bailey, "Ten Years in Buffalo," *Express,* January 12, 1890.

3. Olmsted to George Waring Jr., April 13, 1876.

4. All quotations are from Olmsted, Vaux & Co., "Report of the Landscape Architects," in Board of Commissioners of Prospect Park, *Sixth Annual Report* (Buffalo, 1866), 14.

5. Calvert Vaux, "Letters from the People: A National Park at Niagara," *New-York Daily Tribune,* October 5, 1878.

6. Malcolm Andrews, *Landscape and Western Art* (New York: Oxford University Press, 1999), 67.

7. "Wayfarer" [Frederick Law Olmsted], "The People's Park at Birkenhead, Near Liverpool," *Horticulturist* 6 (May 1851): 224–28, reprinted in *Papers of FLO,* supp. ser., 1:69–78; Frederick Law Olmsted, *Walks and Talks of an American Farmer in England* (1852; repr., Amherst: University of Massachusetts Press in association with Library of American Landscape History, 2002), 93.

8. Olmsted, *Walks and Talks of an American Farmer,* 95.

9. Andrew Jackson Downing, "A Talk about Public Parks and Gardens," *Horticulturist* 3 (October 1848): 153–58; Downing, "The New-York Park," *Horticulturist* 6 (August 1851): 345–49.

10. Andrew Jackson Downing, "The New Park" (1851), reprinted in *Rural Essays,* ed. G. W. Curtis (New York: John Wiley, 1853), 152; and Downing, "A Talk about Public Parks and Gardens," both quoted in Joanna Merwood-Salisbury, "Patriotism and Protest: Union Square as Public Space, 1832–1932," *Journal of the Society of Architectural Historians* 68 (December 2009): 540.

11. The quotation is from *Forty Years,* 1:90–91. When Olmsted displayed a map of the Buffalo park system at the Centennial Exhibition in Philadelphia in 1876, he hung over it an excerpt from Downing's 1851 essay calling for a public park in New York. See "About Buffalo," *Courier,* April 1, 1879.

12. Olmsted to Downing, November 23, 1850, in *Forty Years,* 1:90.

13. Quotations in this and the following paragraph are from F. L. Olmsted, "Public Parks and the Enlargement of Towns," paper read before the American Social Science Association at the Lowell Institute, Boston, February 25, 1870, reprinted in *Papers of FLO,* supp. ser., 1:186.

14. "The Central Park," *Courier,* July 21, 1860.

15. Mariana Van Rensselaer, "Landscape Gardening III," *American Architect and Building News* 23 (January 7, 1888): 4.

1. THE CREATION OF THE PARK SYSTEM

1. David A. Gerber, "The Germans Take Care of Our Celebrations," in *Hard at Play: Leisure in America, 1840–1940,* ed. Kathryn Grover (Amherst: University of Massachusetts Press, 1992), 45; Frances Milton Trollope, *Domestic Manners of the Americans* (1832), 2 vols. (New York: Dodd, Mead, 1901), 1:272–73; Anthony Trollope, *North America* (New York: Harper & Brothers, 1862), 162.

2. "Off the Pavement," *Courier,* July 2, 1851. The references to Bowery boys and target practice may have been an allusion to a picnic grove called Clinton Forest. Located on the Niagara River just north of town, it featured target practice as one of its attractions.

3. *PCC* (1851), 270. The council had at first considered a parcel bounded by Batavia (now Broadway), Milnor, William, and Potter streets, but it was deemed too small. Then Philander Bennett offered two parcels, one bounded by Clinton, Cedar, Eagle, and Pine streets, and the other the 7.5-acre site the council choose, which was bounded by William, Cedar, Clinton, and Pine streets.

4. "Corporation Proceedings," *Commercial Advertiser,* August 27, 1851.

5. *PCC* (1851).

6. *PCC* (1854), 132, 134, 139; 1855, 178; and 1857, 87; "Ought We to Recreate," *Courier,* June 29, 1855. The park was proposed for the area between Main, Michigan, and Ferry streets. See *Index to Records of Streets, Public Grounds, Waterways . . . etc.* (Buffalo, 1896), 502. Another attempt in June 1856 to create a park in the as yet undeveloped Cold Spring district also met with local opposition.

7. This letter from "Civis," prefaced by comments from the paper's editors, ran under the title "A Public Park," *Commercial Advertiser,* July 16, 1856.

8. "Public Grounds," *Daily Republic,* July 19, 1856.

9. Ibid. The Andrew Jackson Downing article was "Public Cemeteries and Public Gardens," *Horticulturist* 4 (July 1849): 12.

10. "A Public Park."

11. Gerber, "The Germans Take Care of Our Celebrations," 46; "Public Ground—Private Buildings," *Courier,* August 7, 1851.

12. Downing, "Public Cemeteries and Public Gardens," 1–2.

13. Warren Granger's artist wife, Mary, and their friend William H. Beard had found subjects for their canvases there.

14. "Forest Lawn Cemetery," *Express,* August 23, 1851, quoted in Bette A. Rupp, "Forest Lawn: Buffalo's Rural Cemetery" (M.A. thesis, University at Buffalo, 1994), 8.

15. F. L. Olmsted, "Public Parks," *Garden,* March 25, 1876, 299.

16. Allen quoted in *Forest Lawn: Its History, Dedications, Progress, and Regulations* (Buffalo: Thomas, Howard & Johnson, 1867), 116. New cemetery regulations would also follow those at Spring Grove. No fences would be allowed around individual plots, and large monuments would be permitted only singly in each plot where smaller family markers might surround them.

17. Ibid., 129, 122.

18. "A Public Park," *Commercial Advertiser,* July 16, 1856.

19. William F. Rogers, *Comptroller's Report: Containing the Annual Statement of the Fiscal Affairs of the City of Buffalo for the Year 1866* (Buffalo: City of Buffalo, 1867), 42.

20. "The Buffalo Exhibition," *New York Times,* October 7, 1869.

21. "Opening of Fine Arts Academy," *Courier,* February 17, 1865.

22. This quotation and those in the next four paragraphs are from Rogers, *Comptroller's Report,* 39–41.

23. The other stream was Cornelius Creek, which is now buried and forms part of the municipal sewer system.

24. Somewhat earlier the men in this group had joined Dorsheimer in a failed stock venture to establish a "driving park" or "trotting course" in the hope that it would eventually evolve into a large public park. See "The Park," *Courier & Republic,* June 25, 1874.

25. Dorsheimer's recounting of Olmsted's 1868 visit was reported in "Local Department: The New Park," *Courier & Republic,* November 26, 1869; all quotations in the next four paragraphs are from this source.

26. Although the general public was unaware of Olmsted's visit, it was informed by the local press that park issues so dear to the

heart of Mayor Rogers were "attracting more than usual attention, at the present time," and that "some steps will be taken at an early day to present the project to the public, and, if possible, to secure the co-operation of the Common Council and the municipal authorities." "Shall Buffalo Have a Park," *Courier & Republic,* August 21, 1868.

27. F. L. Olmsted, "Late Additions to the Plan of Buffalo," in "About Buffalo," *Courier,* April 1, 1879.

28. The quotation is from Olmsted to Mary Perkins Olmsted, August 23, 1868, in *Papers of FLO,* 6:266.

29. Olmsted to Mary Perkins Olmsted, August 25, 1868, in *Papers of FLO,* 6:268.

30. Ibid.

31. "Local Department: The New Park," *Courier & Republic,* November 26, 1869.

32. "The Buffalo Park Project," *Courier & Republic,* August 26, 1868. All quotations in the discussion are from this source. Since Joseph Warren was both the newspaper's owner and the secretary at the meeting, it is fair to assume that he was responsible for the article.

33. Olmsted and Vaux had proposed similar towers for Central Park and Prospect Park.

34. An article in the local press appeared somewhat later explaining in detail how Brooklyn's success in financing Prospect Park might be repeated in Buffalo. See "The Buffalo Park Project," *Courier & Republic,* September 25, 1868.

35. Olmsted to Mary Perkins Olmsted, August 26, 1868, in *Papers of FLO,* 6:269; Olmsted to Vaux, August 29, 1868. Olmsted told Vaux that he had returned to New York on the twenty-eighth. He and Bogart must have spent the twenty-seventh further investigating park sites.

36. Sherman's house stood at 256 Delaware. The stable still exists at 243 South Elmwood.

37. "S. S. Jewett Dead," *Commercial Advertiser,* March 1, 1897.

38. "Off the Roll," *Evening Republic,* October 14, 1884.

39. William Dorsheimer, *The Life and Public Service of the Honorable Grover Cleveland* (Philadelphia: Hubbard Brothers, 1884), 36.

40. "The Buffalo Park Project," *Courier & Republic,* September 25, 1868.

41. J. N. Larned, "Biographical Memoir," in *Letters, Poems, and Selected Prose Writings of David Gray,* 2 vols. (Buffalo: Courier Company, 1888), 1:134.

42. David Gray, "Switzerland," ibid., 2:287–88.

43. "The Park," *Courier,* September 11, 1869.

44. See Joseph B. McCullough and Janice McIntyre-Strasburg, eds., *Mark Twain at the Express: Articles and Sketches by America's Favorite Humorist* (DeKalb: Northern Illinois University Press, 1999). One reason for Mark Twain's silence on the subject of Buffalo's nascent park system may have been that Twain was away from the city on the lecture circuit from October 1869 to January 1870, when the Common Council was debating whether or not to approve Olmsted and Vaux's scheme.

45. The report, sent under the name of Olmsted, Vaux & Co., was subsequently published in the pamphlet *Preliminary Report Respecting a Public Park in Buffalo and a Copy of the Act of the Legislature Authorizing Its Establishment* (Buffalo: Matthews and Warren, 1869), and it is reprinted in *Papers of FLO,* supp. series, 1:158–70. Unless other noted, all quotations in this section are from this source.

46. F. L. Olmsted, "Proposed Extension of the Park System," *ARBPC* 18 (1887), 35. What he had merely sketched out during his talk he now presented in more concrete detail. From the waterfront park at Fort Porter, a parkway would proceed eastward to preexisting Prospect Park and then to Rogers Street (presumably along the route of the present Porter Avenue, the former York Street). The route would then turn ninety degrees northward to the main park along Rogers Street (the present Richmond Avenue), which then ended about a mile farther on at Ferry Street. Extended beyond that point, Rogers Street (to be renamed The Avenue) would eventually "take a more picturesque character than would be desirable nearer the town" (presumably assuming a curving course) to "open fully into the park" near the lake to be created by damming Scajaquada Creek, about half a mile west of Forest Lawn Cemetery. On the East Side, the existing Jefferson Street would become a parkway running in a straight line northward from the High Street park site, along the western edge of the Buffalo Driving Park (the local race course) to "near Main Street, and soon after crossing the latter begin to expand into the crescent ends of the park itself."

47. "A Public Park for Buffalo," *Courier & Republic,* November 23, 1868.

48. "The Parks of Chicago," *Courier,* December 15, 1868; "Parks in Albany and Buffalo," *Courier & Republic,* December 30, 1868.

49. *PCC* (1868), 80.

50. "Parks in Albany and Buffalo." See also "Corporation Proceedings," *Courier & Republic,* December 24, 1868.

51. "Asher P. Nichols," *Courier,* June 2, 1880.

52. *Journal of the Senate of the State of New York at Their Ninety-second Session* (Albany, 1869), 119.

53. The other seven members were Dennis Bowen, Lewis P. Dayton, Dexter Rumsey, John Cronin, John Greiner, Edwin T. Evans, and James Mooney. Several councilmen objected to what they felt was inadequate representation of the German community. The commission functioned throughout the nineteenth century with twelve members; in 1902, the number was reduced to five.

54. "Primary Meeting of the Park Commissioners," *Courier,* May 3, 1869.

55. "Local Department: The New Park," *Courier & Republic,* May 5, 1869.

56. Richardson had received the commission for the Dorsheimer house at 434 Delaware Street in October 1868. It was apparently under construction during the building season of 1869.

57. Olmsted later recounted his stay at Niagara in a letter to C. K. Remington, May 28, 1888.

58. "Local Department: The Park," *Courier & Republic,* September 11, 1869. All quotations are from this source. The *Express* also devoted a long article to describing the parks in its September 11, 1868, edition.

59. The provision in the legislation that required one hundred acres of parkland to be located in this part of town had actually caused the planners considerable difficulty. Limited to a total of five hundred acres for all the parks, they had to reduce the original size planned for the Park. Therefore Olmsted and Vaux pinched the ground north of the lake and gave up on acquiring ten acres of valuable woodland on the water's southern edge. ("There is no other ground in or near any of your parks or places which for twenty years to come will be equally well adapted for large picnic parties," Olmsted noted.) Olmsted to the Buffalo Park Commissioners, in "Communication from Fred Law Olmsted, Esq.," *ARBPC* 5 (1875), 12.

60. Justin Martin, *Genius of Place: The Life of Frederick Law Olmsted* (New York: Da Capo, 2011), 293.

61. "These names are simple, expressive and in good taste," remarked the *Express* of the park names Olmsted and Vaux had provided. "We are disposed to favor their adoption, and to insist upon the same simplicity in the naming of all the places and avenues to be distinguished." "The Park," *Express,* September 11, 1869.

62. The park was bordered by York Street on the south and Vermont Street on the north.

63. At Ferry Street it would give access to the eastern entrance of the Buffalo Driving Park, a privately financed racetrack (now demolished) that had been built a few years before.

64. Gray's reference to Jefferson Street being the western border of this new park may have been incorrect.

65. The New York Central's Belt Line would be accomplished by laying double tracks around the eastern and southern suburbs to join the mainline to Niagara Falls on the West Side. Stations were contemplated at Genesee Street and at Walden Street to accommodate passengers going to the Parade. Another would be built near the Driving Park a bit farther along. Those going to the Park might alight at either Main Street or Delaware Street. The Erie Railroad line would follow virtually the same route.

66. *PCC* (1869), 680. See also "Local Department," *Courier & Republic,* October 12, 1869. Unperturbed by the eruption of anti-park sentiment, the park commissioners met later that evening to discuss a proposal by General Albert J. Myer, father of the U.S. Weather Bureau, that he would donate land of his own for a parkway to extend from the eastern edge of the Parade to the site of a proposed station on the yet to be built Belt Line railroad. Olmsted and Vaux responded favorably to the proposal, but it may never have gone beyond this stage. See "New Park Project," *Courier,* October 12, 1869.

67. On October 7, 1869, the council had voted $50,000 for the purchase of land for the proposed state asylum.

68. *PCC* (1869), 711.

69. "Local Department: Report of the Park Commissioners," *Courier & Republic,* November 9, 1869. The lands were in Wards 7 through 12.

70. And to the fiscal conservatives he reaffirmed his conviction that "the work will not be an expense to the City; but that by its influences upon the valuation of property, it will be found to be a source of revenue." The report also listed the titles by which the parks and parkways were to be known. "In selecting names for the parks, streets, and approaches," Rogers explained, "the Commissioners have had it in mind to choose those which would be simple and appropriate." Descriptive names that Olmsted and Vaux had proposed—they used the word "park" only once—were adopted for the Front (the present Front Park), the Bank (the former circle at Massachusetts and Sixth), the Circle (the present Symphony Circle), The Avenue (the present Richmond Avenue), the Park (the present Delaware Park), and the Parade (the present Martin Luther King Jr. Park). To other locations, the commissioners gave proper names that honored individuals. Chapin Place (the present Gates Circle), Chapin Parkway, Bidwell Place (the present Colonial Circle), and Bidwell Parkway "recalled citizens who fell in battle during the late war," Rogers explained. "'The Soldier's Place' is so designated under the expectation that the Soldier's Monument will be placed there." Thus, the parkways and circles that made up the West Side Park Approaches constituted a tribute to the recently victorious Union and the city's contribution to its preservation. As for Porter Avenue, Lincoln Parkway, and Humboldt Parkway (the central section of this thoroughfare is now occupied by the Kensington Expressway), these names "need no explanation," said Rogers. "Local Department: Report of the Park Commissioners." (Surely the parkway honoring the famous Prussian geographer Alexander von Humboldt was chosen to please the East Side German population.)

71. [David Gray], "Local Department: The New Park," *Courier & Republic,* November 26, 1869. Unless otherwise noted, my account of the Common Council proceedings is based on this article.

72. He also remarked that the citizens of Brooklyn were belatedly considering creating a series of small parks joined by parkways.

73. In the 1870s Limestone Hill became the site of an orphanage and a reform school.

74. "The Park," *Express,* November 26, 1869. In later years Olmsted would take up Orr's call for a South Side park and parkway system.

75. Even after Olmsted and Vaux's park system came into existence, these German-oriented private parks prospered. The Orpheus Festival held in August 1880 at Westphal's Garden was indicative of the enduring popularity of such places among the German population. "The Orpheus Festival," *Evening Republic,* August 24, 1880. In 1891 the *Express* described long-vanished Teutonia Park, which was "only a few steps from the Parade House," as "quite a pretty spot" that featured "swings, small lattice-enclosed pavilions, a dance hall, horizontal bars," and "toy mechanisms which have water for their motive power." *Express,* July 4, 1891. Spring Abbey in the predominately German Cold Spring area and Moffat's, nearer the center of town on Washington Street, were also popular picnic groves.

76. "Local Department: The New Park," *Courier & Republic,* November 26, 1869.

77. Radford completed his work for the commissioners on March 15, 1873. See "Meeting of the Park Commissioners," *Courier & Republic,* March 4, 1873. He might well be considered Buffalo's Haussmann for the proficient manner in which he completed the daunting task of laying down the framework of Olmsted and Vaux's scheme.

78. "Father of the Parks," *Express,* August 3, 1900.

79. Ibid.

80. See the introduction to *Papers of FLO,* 6:28.

81. F. L. and J. C. Olmsted, *Plan for a Public Park on the Flats South of Buffalo* (1888), in *Papers of FLO,* supp. ser., 1:591.

82. "Pascal P. Pratt," *Courier,* June 10, 1905.

83. "Pascal Paoli Pratt," *National Cyclopedia of American Biography,* vol. 8 (New York: James T. White), 414. When a local newspaper published an accusation that membership in the Democratic Party was more important than merit for anyone seeking employment on the parks (where preference was given to Civil War veterans), it was pointed out that Pratt himself was a Republican. "The Workmen on the Park" and "The 'Little Tammany' Commissions," *Courier & Republic,* November 3, 1871.

84. After Radford's services were no longer needed, McMillan would assume responsibility for overseeing future landscape and architectural projects. In June 1873 Vaux came to town for several days to discuss his plans for the superintendent's house and other buildings in the Park, construction of which would begin soon, and the grand refectory envisioned for the Parade.

85. Olmsted to Frederick Kingsbury, January 28, 1873.

86. The historic tour was recounted in several articles in local newspapers, including "The Park," *Courier & Republic,* June 25, 1874; "Local Matters: The Park," *Commercial Advertiser,* June 25, 1874; and "Our Public Park," *Express,* June 25, 1874. Three weeks earlier the commissioners had made a similar park inspection tour of their own. See "The Park," *Courier,* June 6, 1874.

87. The route of observation, reported the *Courier & Republic,* "was down Batavia street [the present Broadway] to its intersection with Fillmore Parkway, up Fillmore Parkway to the Parade; around the Parade to Humboldt Parkway; down Humboldt Parkway to the Park; around the Meadow to the Lake; from the Lake by Lincoln Parkway to Soldiers Place; down Bidwell Parkway to Bidwell Place [the present Colonial Circle]; thence by the 'Avenue' [the present Richmond Avenue] to 'The Front;'—thus making the circle of the Park and its approaches so far as they are open to the public." "The Park," *Courier & Republic,* June 25, 1874.

88. Ibid. Olmsted stayed on the next day and met with the park commissioners to recommend to them what to do next. His advice was: (1) to construct the refectory (Parade House) in the Parade; (2) to finish the Circle (the present Symphony Circle); (3) to complete and separate the walks and drives at the Front; (4) to construct the superintendent's house and other structures in the Park; (5) to erect the boathouse in the Park; and (6) to acquire six to eight acres of land adjoining the picnic grove on the south side of the lake in the Park. He also suggested some names for places in the Park and promised to report more fully on them at a later date. "The Park," *Courier & Republic,* June 26, 1874.

2. THE MAKING OF THE PARK

1. After Radford received a very general plan from Olmsted and Vaux, he broke ground for operations on September 19, 1870.

2. In the 1980s Gala Water was renamed to honor the memory of William Hoyt, a state legislator who championed restoration of the lake and the park.

3. Olmsted to Buffalo Park Commission, undated letter (summer 1870).

4. The tour of the park grounds with Radford is recounted in "Local Department: The New Park," *Courier & Republic,* June 2, 1871.

5. Indeed, maintaining the healthy condition of the new lake would prove a persistent problem. As the city and its suburbs grew, the quality of the water flowing through the creek deteriorated. By the 1920s, residents along the creek beyond the borders of the park regularly used the waterway as a dumping ground for garbage and sewage. By the following decade, the park lake had become a health risk. In 1938 the city constructed a huge conduit to divert most of the sewage to a treatment plant, although storm surges continued to bring some noxious waste into the system. In the 1950s the situation became so dire that

the county health department declared the park lake a health hazard and prohibited public use of it. Construction of a highway through the park in the early 1960s did not help. In the late 1970s engineers constructed a channel and culvert system that allowed creek waters to bypass the lake. Levels have since then been maintained by springs and wells, and water quality has improved. This work, however, together with road construction, has exacted a heavy toll on the physical appearance of the lake's shoreline and the North Bay lagoon, neither of which any longer resembles Olmsted and Vaux's picturesque ideal. In 2002 the Scajaquada Creek Watershed Advisory Council completed a plan to further improve the water quality of the creek and the lake. More recently, in 2009, Forest Lawn Cemetery proposed its own plan for remediation of the creek flow.

6. The roundabout lane, however, remained exclusively a way to get in and out of town; it offered travelers no entrance into the park it traversed. When the new route of Delaware Street was opened, it gave people the false impression that it was another entrance to the park. "Ever since it has been opened," McMillan complained, "a large proportion of the Park visitors have taken this route and forced their way in or out of the Park by rough, devious, and forbidden tracks." "Meeting of the Park Commissioners," *Courier*, August 17, 1873. In October, Olmsted told McMillan that he was "strongly against" any new entrance to the park being opened at this point, as some commissioners had suggested. He feared that the cemetery would then open an entrance across from it, causing congestion and other problems. Olmsted, McMillan informed the board, "thought that the idea of an entrance from Delaware street ought to be abandoned, and the present miscellaneous Park travel by that way strictly prohibited." *ARBPC* 4 (1874), 15.

7. "General Superintendent's Report," *ARBPC* 5 (1875), 18.

8. Olmsted to William McMillan, April 25, 1874.

9. Charles W. Eliot, *Charles Eliot: Landscape Architect* (1902; repr., Amherst: University of Massachusetts Press/Library of American Landscape History, 1999), 36.

10. Olmsted to McMillan, September 11, 1876.

11. *ARBPC* 7 (1877), 20.

12. Olmsted to McMillan, September 11, 1876.

13. Olmsted to Dennis Bowen, September 10, 1876.

14. Olmsted to Dennis Bowen, September 11, 1876.

15. *ARBPC* 7 (1877), 20. North Bay is today known as Mirror Lake.

16. Olmsted to McMillan, April 25, 1874.

17. Olmsted and Vaux had introduced this principle of "separation of ways" in their design for Central Park, and it guided their thinking when they laid out their subsequent parks. It addressed their concern for the safety and comfort of those on foot by making it possible for them to stroll throughout the park grounds free from the worry of colliding with carriages or horseback riders.

18. In 1876 McMillan reported that the park contained three miles and 1,200 feet of finished carriage road and 20,950 feet of walks in various states of completion. See *ARBPC* 7 (1877), 19.

19. The presence of fountains (introduced in 1874 but no longer present) at various points along the paths added to the pleasure of a summer stroll in the new park.

20. The quotation is from Olmsted to McMillan, September 3, 1876.

21. Rowboat rentals commenced with the opening of the boathouse in the summer of 1875.

22. Olmsted to John Rogers, May 7, 1874.

23. McMillan to the Board of Park Commissioners, October 4, 1873, copy in Olmsted Papers, Library of Congress.

24. "The Park: Sixth Annual Report of the Park Commissioners," *Evening Republic,* January 26, 1876.

25. *PCC* (1884), 41.

26. "The Park: Sixth Annual Report of the Park Commissioners."

27. "In the Park," *Evening Republic,* January 26, 1876. It had not been easy to erect the boathouse in this discreet, out-of-the-way location. Because of the steeply sloping shore in this vicinity, it had been necessary to build a massive retaining wall into the bank behind the building. Extraordinary care was taken in building this barrier, McMillan reported, so that it would blend in with the natural environment. Large rough-cut blocks of stone taken from the flint ledges of the park quarry were used in its construction. These stones were laid without mortar in the manner of certain structures in the Ramble in Central Park, and, McMillan said, they had been laid with their "irregular rustic face showing conspicuously the curious flinty modules, and clinker-like condition of the flinty rock." Capped with a wooden railing to guard a footpath on top, the retaining wall was intended to be planted with vines so that it would eventually assume the "aspect of a broken ledge of rock overgrown with ivy." McMillan quoted in "The Park: Sixth Annual Report of the Park Commissioners." The great wall was one of the principal manmade objects within the park.

28. Beginning in 1875 the Union Cornet Band gave summer performances here, and it and other bands attracted large audiences who came both on foot and in carriages. At times the drive and the concourse within earshot of the music were "uncomfortably crowded by vehicles," McMillan complained. Anyone who had doubted that the park and its pleasures had not been worth the expense, observed a local journal a few years later, "may become convinced at once by a jaunt to the park, and strolling along to its lake on any pleasant Sunday afternoon . . . and noticing the crowds of old and young enjoying the bright sunshine and inhaling the vigor and health-imparting balmy air." "A Needed Improvement," *Real Estate and Builders' Monthly* 1 (August 1885): 6.

29. "Skating on Gala Water," *Express,* December 16, 1906.

30. In May 1875 the local press reported that the "exquisite little piece of ornamental architecture" was nearly finished. "The Park," *Courier & Republic,* May 19, 1875. Olmsted recommended planting Austrian and Scotch pines with spreading juniper at the site. For the design of Spire Head House, Vaux may well have drawn freely upon H. A. Daryshire's Moorish style Victoria Fountain of 1862 in London's Victoria Park.

31. When Vaux sent the plans for Spire Head House to Buffalo, a local newspaper printed a detailed description of the unusual structure, which was identified as the Shelter on the Lake. The method of construction was of particular interest to the reporter, who had seen Vaux's now lost plans. "The building," wrote the journalist, "is to be of wood upon stone foundation piers under the center and each angle. An iron bolt of one inch will be built in the masonry of each pier, with ten inch projection about the foundation level to which the sills are to be secured." Vaux predicted that it would take only two months to erect. "Park Improvements," *Courier & Republic,* September 5, 1874. Spire Head House likely influenced the design of the locally famous Blocher tomb (c. 1884) in Forest Lawn Cemetery.

32. F. L. Olmsted, "Public Parks and the Enlargement of Towns," paper read before the American Social Science Association at the Lowell Institute, Boston, February 25, 1870, in *Papers of FLO,* supp. ser., 1:189.

33. "The Park," *Courier & Republic,* June 26, 1874; "The City's Parks," *Courier,* May 4, 1887.

34. *ARBPC* 16 (1886), 31. Golf appears to have been first played informally on the meadow in 1898, and in 1914 the eighteen-hole course was built.

35. According to this original plan, those who chose the latter would follow the bending roadway toward the Concourse, a spacious plaza at the Ledges Gate entrance in the southeast corner of the grounds. This entrance, which opened in 1874, got its name from the nearby quarry, which on park maps was renamed the Ledges. A small wooded area nearby was labeled Ledgewood on the plans. Midway along the route, carriages might have paused together with pedestrians at the Promenade, an area set aside for all to take in the view of the tree-studded meadow. (This area may never have been constructed.) Horseback riders following the South Meadow route were to have had access to a separate bridle road that paralleled the carriage drive until rejoining it at the Ledges Gate Concourse. From that point the East Drive conveyed equestrian traffic along the eastern border northward to the Deer Paddock in the northeast corner of the grounds. There, the East Drive melded into the sinuous North Meadow Drive.

36. "A Needed Improvement," *Real Estate and Builders' Monthly* 1 (August 1885): 6.

37. Olmsted, "Public Parks," 295.

38. *ARBPC* 4 (1874), 10. In 1886 the herd increased to 182 sheep. Unfortunately, a year later all of the sheep had to be sent to the slaughterhouse because of sickness. A new herd later replaced them.

39. *ARBPC* 11 (1882), 8. The difference in appearance between mowed and pastured meadowland was indeed striking, McMillan maintained. "The neat-looking, smoothly-shaven surface," he wrote, "so appropriate to the uses of a door-yard grass-plot, or a garden lawn, or a play-green, is not in good taste or fit keeping with the rural and pastoral character of all the scenery and surroundings of the Meadow Park." "Superintendent's Report," *ARBPC* 9 (1879), 35.

40. *ARBPC* 23 (1893), 15.

41. "The Park," *Courier & Republic,* June 26, 1874. Olmsted also advised the commissioners to erect inconspicuous places of refreshment: "Here families desiring to spend the day in the Park would find a resting place and obtain light refreshments, such as bread, milk, etc." According to early park plans, simple structures were to have been located in the area of the Deer Paddock. But he cautioned that all of the structures should be "comfortable, but not conspicuous." Olmsted also suggested that the commissioners erect a building near the Farmstead to be known as the dairy. Here, park visitors might enjoy light refreshments while drinking in "a broad view over the meadow to the west boundary of the Park" (ibid.). The dairy, however, never got built. The Parkside Lodge, erected in 1914 from designs by James Walker for the convenience of golfers using the new eighteen-hole course installed that year on the meadow, partially fulfills this purpose.

42. "The Park: Sixth Annual Report of the Park Commissioners."

43. Together with H. H. Richardson's Watts Sherman house in Newport, Rhode Island, it was an early example of the Queen Anne style, which was then making its debut in American architecture.

44. Perhaps somewhere here they might have been able to read the lines by the Scottish poet Alexander Smith that McMillan was said to have adopted as his motto:

> Great duties are before me and great songs,
> And whether crowned or crownless when I fall,
> It matters not, so as God's work is done.
> I've learned to prize the quiet lightning deed,
> Not the applauding thunder at its heels,
> Which men call fame.

Quoted in John Emslie, *In Memoriam: The Late William McMillan, Tribute of a Friend* (Buffalo, 1905), 3.

45. Ibid.

46. William McMillan, "Superintendent's Report," *Evening Republic,* January 26, 1876. As a result, two earlier entrances

on Amherst Street in the northeast corner of the park were closed. A new way in was located farther east on the northern border at Colvin Street, and a third entry was planned farther west on the north side of the lake near the West Bluff Concourse. Because of these changes, the Farmstead was relocated from the place where Olmsted and Vaux had originally suggested—opposite Colvin Street—to just north of the new East Meadow entrance.

47. *ARBPC* 7 (1877), 16.

48. McMillan to the Board of Commissioners, October 4, 1873, Olmsted Papers, Library of Congress; *ARBPC* 7 (1877), 9–10.

49. *ARBPC* 10 (1880), 42.

50. *Daily Courier,* August 1, 1880.

51. *ARBPC* 14 (1884), 21.

52. To encourage dispersal from the crowded Beech Bank, he had tables placed in the East Wood, the forested area in the northeast corner of the park near the Colvin entrance. In McMillan's estimation, this locale possessed several advantages over the south bank. "The adjacent open meadow affords ample scope for every kind of athletic sport for which there is no room elsewhere in the Park," he observed. *ARBPC* 14 (1884), 31.

53. F. L. and J. C. Olmsted, *Plans for a Public Park on the Flats South of Buffalo* (1888), in *Papers of FLO,* supp. ser., 1:577.

54. Quoted in *Papers of FLO,* supp. ser., 1:593n4.

55. F. L. and J. C. Olmsted, *Plan for a Public Park on the Flats South of Buffalo,* 1:577.

56. *ARBPC* 17 (1887), 26, and *ARBPC* 18 (1888), 20.

57. In 1907 the Rumsey family donated an additional strip of wooded land on the southern border of the park.

58. *ARBPC* 20 (1890), 35. Flower devotees eventually had their demand satisfied. In 1912, long after McMillan was gone, the city laid out the formal Rose Garden, which included a classical-style pergola, in the area behind the boathouse. Another problem affecting the appearance of the parks was what many saw as inadequate maintenance. Olmsted himself chided the city for not doing all it could by its parks. "There are, in my opinion, some serious shortcomings in the care of your parks," he told the *Express* in 1893, "but I believe that they chiefly betray an effort to keep the expense of maintenance within excessively narrow limits." "Buffalo's Pride," *Express,* October 1, 1893.

59. "Buffalo's Pride."

60. Some of the more significant changes involved alterations to paths and roadways, including the upgrading of walks and drives, the addition of minor new footpaths, the transformation of the little-used footpath on the northern border of the Water Park into a bridle path (1885), the opening in 1893 of a drive from near the Farmstead to a point near the Colvin entrance, the laying out of a twenty-foot-wide bridle path around the meadow averaging two hundred feet from the park boundary, and the construction of a new bridle path around North Bay (1886). In 1888 a five-foot-tall iron picket fence went up along the southern park boundary. (Originally the entire park was surrounded by fencing of one sort or another.)

61. "Olmsted Will Be Here," *Express,* April 29, 1896. For the change of the park's name, see *ARBPC* 27 (1897), 12.

62. Olmsted Brothers to William Hengerer, President of the Buffalo Park Commission, February 8, 1898, "Minutes No. 82," in *Minutes: Park Department, 1898* (Buffalo: Park Commission, 1898), 353–54.

63. See also "Rapped M'Millan," *Express,* September 8, 1897.

64. "Notes," *Garden and Forest* 10 (December 22, 1897): 508.

65. McMillan's talk was printed as "The Care of Urban Parks," *Garden and Forest* 8 (February 27, 1895): 82–83.

66. It was enlarged with wings at either side in 1929. Despite his objections to the new building, John C. Olmsted undertook to prepare landscape plans for the area around it.

67. John J. Albright, the benefactor of the art gallery, was one of a number of private clients who commissioned the Olmsted firm to design grounds around their homes. Others included Robert Livingston Fryer, Frank Goodyear, Edmund Hayes, Spencer Kellogg, Robert Pomeroy, and William A. Rogers. In 1892 the Depew Land Company hired the firm to plan Depew, a railroad town east of Buffalo.

68. "Where Buffalo May Skate," *Express,* December 26, 1897.

69. F. L. Olmsted, "Public Parks," *Garden,* March 25, 1876, 295. During its national meeting in Buffalo in the summer of 1903, the American Park and Outdoor Art Association condemned the plan to place the statue in Delaware Park, declaring that "statues in parks were inartistic." See "Statue of David in Delaware Park," *Commercial Advertiser,* August 25, 1903. In 1894 a German singing society had placed a small bust of Mozart in an inconspicuous location in the park. It was the first piece of sculpture located in the park, which has few such embellishments outside the precincts of the modern zoo. In 1896 a granite boulder was placed on the meadow commemorating the spot where soldiers who died during the War of 1812 are buried (cannons were added to the site in 1913), and in 1929 a bronze casting of John Quincy Adams Ward's *Indian Hunter* (1860) was placed near the southeast entrance to the meadow.

70. "Statues Out of Place in Park," *Courier,* May 6, 1904.

71. Dick Hirsch, "Old Delaware Park Is Due for Facelifting," *Courier-Express,* June 18, 1960.

3. THE FRONT AND PROSPECT PLACE

1. [David Gray], "The Park," *Courier,* September 11, 1869.

2. Unfortunately, the future of the Bank proved less promising than first envisioned. The view of the river that the Bank was intended to command had been seriously compromised by the

construction of a large new pumping station for the nearby waterworks.

3. "The Park and Drive," *Courier & Republic,* June 2, 1871.

4. In his sketch Vaux drew two rectangles at the word "Road," indicating the presence of buildings in the path of the proposed route.

5. "Park Report," *Courier & Republic,* January 14, 1873.

6. "The Park," *Courier,* June 6, 1874.

7. *ARBPC* 3 (1873), 21.

8. Olmsted to Dorsheimer, 1868, in *Papers of FLO,* supp. ser., 1:162; Frederick Law Olmsted, "A Healthy Change in the Tone of the Human Heart (Suggestions for Cities)," *Century Illustrated Monthly Magazine* 32 (1886): 965.

9. Olmsted, "A Healthy Change," 965. Olmsted mistakenly identified the city as Montreal. (He had also visited Quebec City in 1847 on a trip with his father and brother.) Durham Terrace is now known as Dufferin Terrace.

10. Olmsted, "A Healthy Change," 965.

11. Ibid., 964.

12. *ARBPC* 14 (1884), 21.

13. *ARBPC* 15 (1885), 19.

14. *ARBPC* 20 (1890), 22. In 1897 the Front was transformed into Camp Jewett, the site of the Grand Army of the Republic's thirty-first annual reunion of Civil War veterans from around the country.

15. "Superintendent's Report," *ARBPC* 11 (1881), 65.

16. "Park Commissioners' Report," *ARBPC* 14 (1884), 19–20.

17. "The Park System," *Courier,* September 8, 1886.

18. *ARBPC* 17 (1887), 21.

19. "Park Commissioners' Report," *ARBPC* 22 (1892), 10–11. A triangular section of land along the extension of Porter Avenue beyond the railroad tracks was eventually developed for park use, but not according to the Olmsted plan. In 1913 the park superintendent reported that "the concourse in front of the home of the Buffalo Yacht Club [had been] filled in with soil" and planted with trees. The work, he believed, "added greatly to the beauty of the place." *ARBPC* 46 (1913), 9.

20. See G. R. Stange, "The Buffalo Yacht Club: 150 Years of Boating," *Western New York Heritage* 13 (Summer 2010): 30–41.

21. Olmsted Brothers to Buffalo Park Commissioners, September 15, 1898, in *Minutes: Proceedings of the Buffalo Park Commission,* October 4, 1898, 472–73.

22. "Rumsey Site," *Express,* May 14, 1899. See also "Two Will Decide," *Express,* April 4, 1899.

23. Arleyn Levee, "The Olmsted Firm in Buffalo: The Next Generation," in *The Best Planned City: The Olmsted Legacy in Buffalo,* ed. Francis Kowsky (Buffalo: Burchfield Art Center, 1992), 34.

24. The cannons came from Lafayette Square in downtown and were put in place in 1913.

25. The statue, by the artist Charles Niehaus, was commissioned by the New York State Perry Victory Centennial Committee.

26. "Once-Magnificent Front Park Being Whittled Down Anew," *Buffalo Evening News,* April 4, 1957.

27. Despite the bleak situation, the Olmsted Parks Conservancy has fought valiantly for the preservation and restoration of Front Park.

28. The two-city-block parcel is bounded on the west by Columbus Parkway, on the east by Prospect Avenue, on the north by Connecticut Street, and on the south by Porter Avenue (part of the parkway system).

29. "Buffalo and Lake Erie," *Courier,* October 19, 1886.

30. *ARBPC* 6 (1876), 36.

31. *ARBPC* 11 (1881), 12.

32. *ARBPC* 18 (1888), 25.

4. THE PARADE

1. *ARBPC* 7 (1877), 28.

2. The New York State militia bore the title National Guard long before the name became universal throughout the United States.

3. Olmsted to John G. Graves, February 7, 1893.

4. The building was constructed under the direction of Joseph Churchyard, a local builder. Around this time, the firm proposed a similar pavilion for Walnut Hill Park in New Britain, Connecticut, that was never built.

5. "The Park Refectory," *Courier,* March 5, 1876, reprinted in the *Evening Republic,* March 6, 1876.

6. *ARBPC* 7 (1877), 25.

7. "The Park Refectory."

8. The description of the Parade House is drawn from "Parade," *Buffalo Sunday Morning News,* August 27, 1876; ARBPC 7 (1877), 22–23; and "The Park Refectory."

9. "The Park Refectory"; James Fergusson, *A History of Architecture in All Countries from the Earliest Times to the Present Day,* vol. 3 (London: John Murray, 1862), 422.

10. "The Park Refectory," *Courier,* March 5, 1876. This article was written in advance of the Refectory's opening, as the building was nearing completion.

11. *ARBPC* 7 (1877), 27. Among the crowd were surely some of the several hundred unemployed laborers whom the city's Overseer of the Poor had hired to complete the park's drives and paths.

12. "Parade," *Buffalo Sunday Morning News,* August 27, 1876.

13. F. L. Olmsted, "Parks," in *New American Cyclopedia,* vol. 3 (New York: D. Appleton & Company, 1861), 352.

14. McMillan to Olmsted, June 22, 1878.

15. "The Park," *Courier,* May 7, 1879. The next year, the area at the rear of the structure that had not been rebuilt was roofed over

to form a sizable veranda more than one hundred feet long, supported on four rows of columns. Gas lamps were installed in the Grove, which became a favored summer nighttime rendezvous for both couples and families.

16. "A New Police Station," *Courier,* April 19, 1890; "Breathing Places," *Express,* July 5, 1891; "Parade House as Popular Resort," *Express,* July 25, 1892.

17. George M. Bailey, *Buffalo Illustrated: The Queen City of the Lakes* (New York: Acme Publishing, 1890), 211.

18. See "Political," *Evening Republic,* August 19, 1880; "The Military," *Express,* June 17, 1881; and "Jumped to Death," *Express,* May 31, 1893.

19. "Meg's Meditations," *Express,* November 1, 1885.

20. "Not Wanted," *Express,* March 8, 1878.

21. "Our Beery Aldermen," *Express,* July 1, 1879.

22. "Obstruction That Is Good," *Express,* October 29, 1907.

23. Also gone are several local buildings that took inspiration from Vaux's Parade House, including the Oakfield Club and Falconwood Club on Grand Island and the Lake View House at the Front.

24. "No Bath-House," *Express,* July 12, 1896. It was also at this time that Fillmore Avenue became a north–south route across the park.

25. *ARBPC* 25 (1895), 19.

26. In most instances, he wrote, "the simplest and best obstruction" would be a number of light stake-and-rail hurdles about four feet long, with sharpened uprights to secure them in the ground. If park staff was vigilant about shifting these barriers to block incipient short cuts, "the people who do the mischief" would soon realize that "the commissioners and their servants were really serious to preserve the turf." Olmsted to John G. Graves, February 7, 1893.

27. Ibid.

28. Ibid.

29. "No Bath-House."

30. H. L. Malchow, "Public Gardens and Social Action in Late Victorian London," *Victorian Studies* 7 (1985): 121.

31. *ARBPC* 27 (1897), 15.

32. John C. Olmsted to Sophia White Olmsted, October 10, 1903.

33. The building's impressive main entrance facing the parkway has been abandoned for a modern one facing the side parking lot.

34. Patricia M. O'Donnell, "Survey of Buffalo's Olmsted Parks: National Register of Historic Places Nomination" (1979; Register no. 90NR01217), 48, available at http://nysparks.com/shpo/online-tools.

5. PARKWAYS, CIRCLES, AND SQUARES

1. Olmsted to Rogers, April 13, 1876. The quotes from Olmsted in this paragraph come from his "Late Additions to the Plan of Buffalo," reprinted in "About Buffalo: A Map Worth Looking At—A Souvenir of Two Great Exhibitions," *Courier,* April 1, 1879. Olmsted had donated his actual framed display to the city in 1879 after having shown it at the Exposition Universelle in Paris the year before. It is now lost, but a photograph of it survives in the collection of the Frederick Law Olmsted National Historic Site, Brookline, Mass.

2. Buffalo Morning Express, *The Buffalo Park System* (Buffalo, 1881). The newspaper suggested that two missing connections be added to the system (and showed them on the map in green): Broadway could be upgraded to an avenue linking the center city to the Parade, and Sixth Street (now Busti Avenue) could be made to join Niagara Square to the Front. The *Express* text and map were reprinted in *ARBPC* 11 (1881), 70–78.

3. Compared to the Telford method of road construction, calling for a deep stone foundation and a sloping asphalt surface, the system invented by John L. MacAdam in the early nineteenth century dispensed with the foundation and required a rise of only eleven centimeters from the edge of the road to the center. It was suitable for park drives which would be used only by light vehicles. McMillan described the paving methods in use in Buffalo, including a new system by the German Rock Asphalt and Cement Company employed at the Bank, in *ARBPC* 20 (1890), 25–28.

4. Buffalo Morning Express, *The Buffalo Park System,* 10.

5. William H. Dolan, comp., *Our Police and Our City: The Official History of the Buffalo Police Department from the Earliest Days . . . and a History of the City of Buffalo* (Buffalo: Bensler & Wesley, 1893), 307.

6. This "well nigh perfect system of street paving," as the *American Architect and Building News* called it, was laid by the Barber Asphalt Paving Company, at first based in Washington, D.C., and later in New York City, whose president, Amzi L. Barber, was related to two prominent Buffalonians, John J. Albright and Andrew Langdon. Barber's firm did much to popularize the use of asphalt paving in the United States. Buffalo, which in 1890 had more than a million square yards of blacktop covering over 130 streets, remained at the forefront of this trend; a decade later, the city had laid down over thirteen million square yards of asphalt, well ahead of Chicago, which had installed only one million square yards, and New York, which had two million square yards. Quotations and statistics here and in the text are from "Parkways and Boulevards in American Cities," *American Architect and Building News* 62 (1898): 35; "The Ideal Convention City," *Greater Buffalo* 1 (August 20, 1897): 8–9; *Buffalo Illustrated* (Buffalo: Courier Company, 1890), 103; and Otis H. Williams, *Buffalo—Old and New* (Buffalo: The Buffalo Courier, 1901), 89.

7. "Hatmaker Investment Company," *Greater Buffalo* 3 (April 1900): 13.

8. "The Ideal Convention City."

9. Dolan, *Our Police and Our City*, 308.

10. George Bailey, "Ten Years in Buffalo," *Express*, January 12, 1890.

11. "The Parkside District," *Greater Buffalo* 1 (December 1897): 9.

12. Mabel Dodge Luhan, *Intimate Memories* (New York: Harcourt, Brace, 1933), 11.

13. F. L. Olmsted, "History of Streets," paper read to the Brookline Club, ca. 1888, typescript, Frederick Law Olmsted Papers, Manuscript Division, Library of Congress.

14. Dolan, *Our Police and Our City*, 307.

15. Ibid.

16. Buffalo Morning Express, *The Buffalo Park System*, 11. "Where the general travel and traffic is heaviest," the *Express* noted, "a good 'Telford-macadam' road has been constructed. On the other portions a smooth, temporary road-bed, sufficient for light travel, has for the present been formed."

17. Olmsted, "Late Additions to the Plan of Buffalo."

18. William McMillan, "The Park," in Allen. G. Bigelow and J. N. Larned, *The City of Buffalo: Its History and Institutions, with Illustrated Sketches of Its Industries and Commerce and Some of Its Citizens* (Buffalo: Matthews Northrop, 1888), 23.

19. *ARBPC* 14 (1884), in *PCC* (1884), 42.

20. One hundred feet wide and a bit over one mile long, Bidwell Parkway was opened to the Circle (now Symphony Circle) in the summer of 1873.

21. Lincoln Parkway, 1,700 feet in length, was completed as far as Forest Avenue in 1874. Chapin Parkway was 1,900 feet long.

22. The tulip tree required extra care when being transplanted, however, because of its soft roots. Young trees also needed protection from frosts when planted in clay soil such as that of Buffalo. The quotation is from William B. McMillan, "Shade Trees in City Streets," chap. 5 of E. C. Powell and W. B. McMillan, *Street and Shade Trees* (New York: Rural Publishing Company, 1893), 37.

23. Olmsted received a copy from André in June 1879. See Olmsted to André, June 6, 1879. Olmsted may have been shown in advance pages devoted to his work when he visited André in Paris in 1878.

24. Édouard André, *L'Art des jardins: traité general de la composition des parcs et jardins* (Paris: G. Masson, 1879), 634. In 1892 Humboldt Parkway was altered so that the central green space extended its entire length.

25. W. C. Behrendt, "City Fails to Follow Its Noble Plan," *Buffalo News*, December 4, 1937.

26. *ARBPC* 5 (1875), 19. McMillan also reported that by 1874 many of the new tulips on Humboldt Parkway were sickly and some had died.

27. Powell and McMillan, *Street and Shade Trees*, 4.

28. André, *L'Art des jardins*, 633.

29. McMillan called for a permanent macadam surface as soon as possible, for the street was seeing ever-increasing traffic. The following year, conditions had only worsened. During the last three months of 1881, McMillan complained, the carriageway was unfit for travel and for half that time "has been nearly impassable for traffic of any kind." As a result, the Park had been "virtually inaccessible from this portion of the city." *ARBPC* 12 (1882), 18. In 1884 McMillan again remonstrated with his superiors. "The city on each side [of Richmond Avenue]," he argued, "is being rapidly built up, and nearly all the streets intersecting it are already paved. The travel on these paved streets is at times, to some extent, obstructed by the difficulty of even crossing the avenue." *ARBPC* 15 (1885), 29.

30. *ARBPC* 15 (1885), 18.

31. Quoted in Roland Palmer, "Buffalo's Bandwagon," *Courier Express*, January 12, 1951.

32. Olmsted, "Late Additions to the Plan of Buffalo."

33. A. Conger Goodyear, "Delaware Avenue—1877–1927," *Niagara Frontier* 15 (Summer 1968): 11.

34. North of Forest Avenue, the eastern service lane and sidewalk were never built, presumably at the request of the Larkin family, owners of a large soap manufactory, whose property bordered the parkway there.

35. "Fine Growth of Buffalo's Parkways," *Courier*, October 23, 1904.

36. "The East Side Boulevard," *Courier*, April 14, 1873.

37. Below William Street, arrangements were being pursued to remove buildings in the line of the street so it might be extended southward the next year. In 1876 it was carried another three-quarters of a mile south to Seneca Street.

38. "The East Side Boulevard," *Courier*, April 11, 1873.

39. "The City of Buffalo," *Harper's Monthly Magazine* 51 (July 1885): 215.

40. F. L. Olmsted, "Proposed Extension of the Park System," in *ARBPC* 18 (1887), 35.

41. *ARBPC* 13 (1883), 18.

42. *ARBPC* 25 (1895) 18.

43. Ibid.

44. In the summer of 1896 the commissioners held a meeting at the western end of the new roadway (at Grant Street) to show the city council members what had been accomplished and to make a pitch for continuing the work. Commissioner John Graves, who served as spokesman and guide that afternoon, called the councilmen's attention to a new boulevard being built by private investors along the crest of the hill on the north bank of the stream. (This was probably part of a scheme to create a new neighborhood in the area.) The owners, including Bronson C. Rumsey, the former park commissioner, had recently offered to give the commissioners land adjacent to the creek so that the water level could be raised five feet and a continuous lake from the cemetery grounds to Grant Street could

be created. And if a bridge were to connect the parkway on the south side of the creek with the boulevard being built on the north side, Buffalo would have a new three-mile parkway. Born at the dawn of the automobile age, Scajaquada Parkway was transformed in 1961 into the Scajaquada Expressway, a major element of the city's high-speed freeway system.

45. "The Park," *Courier & Republic,* September 11, 1869.

46. *ARBPC* 14 (1884), 11.

47. Ibid.

48. Olmsted to William Rogers, undated letter transmitted with the 1874 plans for the North Street Circle.

49. In the mid-1890s there were only three homes on Soldiers Place. In 1904 William Heath, an executive with the Larkin Soap Company, commissioned Frank Lloyd Wright to design for him an impressive Prairie style dwelling for a property with a splendid view of Soldiers Place. In the 1930s Kneeland Wilkes, a longtime president of the Common Council, paid for the creation of a low-rise foliage island, the remnants of which still occupy the midpoint of Soldiers Place.

50. "Gift to the City," *Express,* February 19, 1902.

51. Olmsted to William Rogers, undated letter transmitted with the plans for the North Street Circle.

52. Jane Mead Welch, "The City of Buffalo," *Harper's New Monthly Magazine* 71 (July 1885): 196.

53. *ARBPC* 5 (1875), 14.

54. Both quotes by Olmsted come from an undated letter (presumably written in 1876) from Olmsted to the Buffalo Park Commissioners. On November 9, 1874, Stanford White wrote to Olmsted on behalf of Richardson telling him that "the arch is almost done." Despite the great respect that Olmsted enjoyed in Buffalo and Maria Love's high standing in society, some in town were upset by the decision to ignore local talent for the design of the arch. "It is alleged that this was engineered by Lieutenant Governor Dorsheimer, who recommended Richardson to the Committee as being an architect of great reputation and therefore the person to whom this matter should be entrusted," complained a local Republican newspaper a few days before the groundbreaking. "That Mr. Richardson is not an architect of extraordinary ability it is only necessary in order to be convinced to look at the design furnished by him, which resembles more the entrance to a fortress of the middle ages than a monument representing modern architecture such as this monument should be." "Ignoring Home Talent," *Buffalo Sunday Morning News,* July 2, 1876. The inflammation of professional tempers in Buffalo was surely aggravated by the heated national controversy that had raged over Dorsheimer's successful campaign to have Richardson and Olmsted, together with New York architect Leopold Eidlitz, replace Thomas Fuller as architect of the ongoing capitol project at Albany.

55. Olmsted to Mrs. William Dwight Whitney, December 16, 1890, quoted in Laura Wood Roper, *FLO: A Biography of Frederick Law Olmsted* (Baltimore: Johns Hopkins University Press, 1973), 421.

56. "The Soldiers' Monument," *Courier,* June 23, 1876.

57. For quotations, see Olmsted's letter to the Buffalo park commissioners, December 15, 1874, in *ARBPC* 5 (1875): 13–16.

58. "A Picture in the City's Heart," *Express,* June 9, 1885.

59. Bowen's protégé Grover Cleveland would begin his meteoric political career in this building in 1882 when he became mayor.

60. Olmsted to Sprague, Gorham & Basom, December 17, 1878.

61. Olmsted to Dennis Bowen, January 1, 1876, in *Papers of FLO,* 7:170; see also 6:174n4 for a summary of other correspondence relating to this project and 172–73 for an illustration of Olmsted's preliminary plan.

62. Ibid., 7:170.

63. Wisedell to Mary Perkins Olmsted, January 19, 1878. These walls may have been designed by Thomas Wisedell, the man who had drawn the plans for the walls around the U.S. Capitol grounds and who came to Buffalo to explain Olmsted's plans and to inspect the work.

64. Olmsted to Mrs. William Dwight Whitney, December 16, 1890, quoted in Roper, *FLO,* 420.

65. Olmsted to Sprague, Gorham & Basom, December 17, 1878.

6. PARKSIDE, BUFFALO STATE HOSPITAL, AND SMALLER PARKS

1. "Park Commissioners' Report," in *ARBPC* 3 (1873), 11.

2. Calvert Vaux, *Villas and Cottages* (New York: Harper and Brothers, 1857), 115.

3. F. L. Olmsted, "The Little Parks" (letter to the editor), *Express,* October 17, 1886.

4. Laura Wood Roper, *FLO: A Biography of Frederick Law Olmsted* (Baltimore: Johns Hopkins University Press, 1973), 318.

5. F. L. Olmsted, "Public Parks and the Enlargement of Towns," paper read before the American Social Science Association at the Lowell Institute, Boston, February 25, 1870, reprinted in *Papers of FLO,* supp. ser., 1:178.

6. Olmsted, Vaux & Co., *Preliminary Report upon the Proposed Suburban Village at Riverside Near Chicago* (New York, 1868), reprinted in *Papers of FLO,* 6:278.

7. Another victim of the Long Depression was the similar residential community of Tarrytown Heights in Westchester County, N.Y., the plans for which Olmsted and Vaux had drawn in 1871–72.

8. Olmsted, "Public Parks and the Enlargement of Towns," 189.

9. Dorsheimer to Olmsted, June 15, 1874.

10. F. L. Olmsted, *Preliminary Report in Regard to a Plan of Public Pleasure Grounds for the City of San Francisco, March 31, 1866,* in *Papers of FLO,* 5:543.

11. In 1875 Olmsted would apply the same thinking to his plan for the western New York community of Point Chautauqua, located across Lake Erie from the more conventionally arranged Chautauqua Institution. See Edgar C. Conkling, *Frederick Law Olmsted's Point Chautauqua* (Buffalo: Buffalo Heritage Unlimited, 2001).

12. F. L. Olmsted and Calvert Vaux, "Preliminary Suggestions for the Grounds of the Buffalo State Hospital for the Insane," in *Papers of FLO*, 6:452.

13. This map is one of several undated plans for Parkside at Fairsted, the Frederick Law Olmsted National Historic Site in Brookline, Mass.

14. It also shows a large blank area representing land owned by a Mr. Russell. Dorsheimer had written Olmsted in June 1874 that Russell was refusing to go along with the scheme, but they might be able to force the "necessary roads" through his property.

15. Olmsted, "Public Parks and the Enlargement of Towns," 154.

16. See *Papers of FLO*, 5:483.

17. "A Residence Park," *Express*, May 2, 1886.

18. The district was created in 1982 and is bounded by the park on the west, Amherst Street on the north, Main Street on the east, and Humboldt Parkway on the south.

19. "A Suburban Elysium," *Express*, November 2, 1890.

20. See Jack Quinan, *Frank Lloyd Wright's Martin House: Architecture as Portraiture* (New York: Princeton Architectural Press, 2004).

21. B. C. Rumsey to Olmsted, January 8, 1885.

22. *Courier*, September 8, 1886.

23. "The Little Parks," *Express*, October 17, 1886.

24. John H. Smith to Olmsted, December 31, 1886.

25. "Real Estate Items," *Real Estate and Builders' Monthly* 3 (May 1887): 5. The venture was to include the Hyde Park, Delaware Park, and Villa Park land companies. The announcement also noted that Rumsey would lay out lands "on the Erie tracks to the northwest" in harmony with this project. The success of the undertaking was dependent on the construction of a new sewer system.

26. F. L. Olmsted & J. C. Olmsted to J. D. Larkin, February 20, 1888.

27. J. B. Stafford to F. L. & J. C. Olmsted, March 18, 1887.

28. Part of this area would become the present-day Central Park neighborhood.

29. "A New Residence Park," *Express*, July 7, 1889.

30. Norton to Olmsted, October 23, 1881, quoted in Roper, *FLO*, 394.

31. It appears that the present-day Parkside Avenue was extended north from Amherst Street at this time. One of the new streets bore Tillinghast's name.

32. "Buffalo Residential Property," *Greater Buffalo* 3 (October 1899): 1. This area today is the Parkside West National Register Historic District.

33. "The New Insane Asylum," *Courier & Republic,* October 14, 1865.

34. "This location was decided upon after mature deliberation," declared the managers, "and is believed to be the most eligible one that could be selected in view of the surroundings. The building will, when completed, present a fine architectural perspective from the avenues and approaches to the Park which the City of Buffalo has recently laid out and is now improving, the west line of which bounds the Asylum grounds." *Proceedings in Connection with the Ceremony of Laying the Corner Stone of the Buffalo State Asylum for the Insane in the City of Buffalo, September 18, 1872* (Buffalo: State of New York, 1872), 9–10.

35. The state commissioners voted on October 16, 1869, to locate the hospital in Buffalo, and on November 8 the Common Council formally donated the land to the state. A part of the land came from the Clinton Forest picnic grove, the rest of which was eventually laid out in building lots.

36. "Joseph Warren," *New York Times,* October 2, 1876.

37. During the first half of 1870, Richardson, who apparently was consulted on the building as early as December 1869, was at work on developing the general plan, which had been established by Gray. On the August 25, 1870, the board adopted Richardson's ground plan. Richardson also presented elevation drawings to the board of managers.

38. The site is now occupied by Columbia University.

39. "The Buffalo Medical Journal of This Month," *Buffalo Express,* July 1, 1870.

40. Quotations in this and the following paragraph are from *Preliminary Suggestions for the Grounds of the Buffalo State Hospital for the Insane* (July 7, 1871), reprinted in *Papers of FLO*, 6:452. For a detailed modern analysis of the asylum grounds, see *Cultural Landscape Report: The Richardson Complex, Buffalo, NY,* prepared by Heritage Landscapes (Buffalo, 2008).

41. The twin-towered administration building and the five (eastern) pavilions for male patients opened late in 1880.

42. In 1884 the present iron fence replaced an earlier picket fence.

43. The historic structure report and master plan for adaptive reuse that the Richardson Center Corporation commissioned can be viewed at www.richardson-olmsted.com.

44. "Late Additions to the Plan of Buffalo," reprinted in "About Buffalo: A Map Worth Looking At—A Souvenir of Two Great Exhibitions," *Courier,* April 1, 1879.

45. Quoted in "The Park System," *Courier,* September 8, 1886.

46. Samuel M. Welch, *Home History: Recollections of Buffalo during the Decade from 1830 to 1840, or Fifty Years Since* (Buffalo: Peter Paul & Brother, 1891), 13.

47. *ARBPC* 18 (1888), 4.

48. By the early twentieth century, the Johnson Park area began

to experience change. Today the section of the tree-lined mall that extended east of Elmwood Avenue to Delaware Avenue no longer exists. Early twentieth-century urbanization also spelled the end of the adjacent Rumsey Park, the elaborately landscaped estate of Bronson C. Rumsey, Olmsted's patron in the Villa Park Land Company and onetime park commissioner. The fenced-in grounds, which Olmsted probably found too much in the gardenesque style to please him, had been laid out in the early 1860s by Henry and Edward Rose, two little-known British architects. They had also designed the Second Empire style mansion (demolished in 1915) for Rumsey fronting on Delaware Avenue.

49. The historic Bennett house was taken down in the fall of 1887.
50. In a letter to McMillan, John C. Olmsted also stressed that it was "a general rule" with him and his father "that all public places and grounds should be separated from private buildings and land by public ways." Thus parks would escape being overlooked by untidy rear premises of houses or businesses. J. C. Olmsted to McMillan, April 21, 1887.
51. "From the Park Commissioners," *Express,* January 21, 1890.
52. "The Park System," *Courier,* September 8, 1886.
53. *ARBPC* 20 (1890), 29.
54. There is no record of the Olmsted firm's having furnished plans for the additional land.
55. J. C. Olmsted to McMillan, November 30, 1894.
56. "Buffalo Parks," *Buffalo Express,* January 9, 1895.
57. The building was later rebuilt after a fire. This second structure was preserved from threatened demolition in the 1970s and is today City Honors High School.

7. THE EMANCIPATION OF NIAGARA

1. F. L. Olmsted, "Notes," in James T. Gardner, *Special Report of the New York State Survey on the Preservation of the Scenery of Niagara Falls* (Albany: State of New York, 1880), 28.
2. "Information for Visitors to Prospect Park, Niagara Falls," *Daily Gazette* (Niagara Falls, N.Y.), June 17, 1883. At the time, each waterfall was referred to in the singular.
3. Olmsted, "Notes," 29.
4. Louis Hennepin, *Nouvelle découverte d'un très grand pays situé dans l'Amérique entre le Nouveau Mexique, et la Mer Glaciale* (Utrecht: Guillaume Broedelet, 1697). The translation is from www.niagara-falls.name.
5. J. W. Orr, *Pictorial Guide to the Falls of Niagara* (Buffalo, 1842), 155; John Douglas Sutherland Campbell, "Niagara," in *Memories of Canada and Scotland: Speeches and Verses* (Montreal: Dawson Brothers, 1884), 60.
6. Timothy Dwight, *Travels in New-England and New-York* (New Haven, 1822), 94.
7. Olmsted to C. K. Remington, May 28, 1888.

8. This bridge, which was for carriage traffic only, was located some three hundred yards beyond the American Falls at the site of the present Rainbow Bridge. Another larger suspension bridge, the Railway Suspension Bridge, constructed by John A. Roebling in 1855, was two miles downstream (near the site of the present Whirlpool Bridge) at the community of Suspension Bridge.
9. Olmsted, "Notes," 29.
10. Olmsted to Charles Eliot Norton, January 22, 1880; Olmsted, "Notes," 29.
11. Calvert Vaux, "Letters from the People: A Natural Park at Niagara," *New-York Daily Tribune,* October 5, 1878.
12. David F. Day, *Catalogue of the Niagara Flora* (Troy, N.Y., 1888), 6.
13. Olmsted, "Notes," 29.
14. Quoted in Charles Mason Dow, *The State Reservation at Niagara: A History* (Albany: J. B. Lyon, 1914), 201.
15. The quotation is from William Howard Russell, *Canada: Its Defences, Condition, and Resources* (London, 1865), quoted in Dow, *Anthology,* 1:328.
16. Henry James, "Niagara," *Nation* 13 (1871), excerpted in Charles Mason Dow, *Anthology and Bibliography of Niagara Falls,* 2 vols. (Albany: State of New York, 1921), 2:1099.
17. William Morris, *Letters Sent Home* (London, 1875), quoted in Dow, *Anthology,* 2:1111.
18. "Earl Dufferin's Farewell Speech," *New York Herald,* September 28, 1878.
19. Calvert Vaux, "Letters from the People."
20. [Henry Miller Alden], "Editor's Easy Chair," *Harper's New Monthly Magazine* 71 (1885), 801.
21. *Journal of the Assembly of the State of New York, 102nd Session* (Albany, 1879), 29, quoted in Dow, *Anthology,* 2:1123.
22. Gardner, *Special Report,* 22.
23. *ARBPC* 11 (1881), 57.
24. Andrew H. Green, "Last Public Address by the Late Hon. Andrew H. Green, Concerning the State Reservation at Niagara: Read before the Convention of the American Park and Outdoor Art Association at Niagara Falls, July 7, 1903," in *Sixteenth Annual Report of the Commissioners of the State Reservation at Niagara* (Albany, 1903), 101.
25. Dow, *State Reservation at Niagara,* 20.
26. Richardson to Olmsted, February 6, 1883.
27. Olmsted to John Bigelow, February 9, 1861.
28. *Report of the Niagara Falls Association Executive Committee* (New York, 1885), 14.
29. All details and quotations in this paragraph are from "The Niagara Falls Park," *Niagara Falls Gazette,* July 10, 1883. In 1897 the present Whirlpool Rapids Bridge (also called the First Steel Arched Bridge) was built upstream from the whirlpool, where it joins the two communities of Niagara Falls, New

York, and Niagara Falls, Ontario. It was not located below the whirlpool, where Vaux had proposed that his bridge span the river.

30. Ibid. Dorsheimer's mention of a railroad bridge refers to the planned renovation of the 1855 Railway Suspension Bridge two miles downriver from the falls.

31. Harrison's letter to the *Sun,* dated August 3, 1883, was reprinted as part of "Preservation of Niagara," *Niagara Falls Gazette,* August 15, 1883.

32. Evershed's map was published as *Map of the Land Proposed to Be Taken by the Commissioners of the State Reservation at Niagara for Preserving the Scenery of the Falls* (Albany, 1883).

33. Olmsted to Charles Eliot Norton, June 21, 1883, quoted in *Papers of FLO,* supp. ser., 1:51.

34. *The State Reservation at Niagara: Speeches of the Hon. Thomas V. Welch of Niagara* (Niagara Falls, N.Y.: privately printed, 1885), 6.

35. It was, nonetheless, a cliffhanger, as Green, who was a close witness to the struggle, vividly remembered: "Few persons realize the powerful concentration of effort made at that time by the devoted friends of Niagara; the terrific strain which they sustained for weeks and up to the last minute of grace allowed by law for the signature of the bill; or the narrow escape of the great and glorious project from defeat. The bill passed the legislature April 16, 1885, and went to Governor Hill. He had until April 30 to sign it, otherwise, according to the two-year limit in the Niagara law of 1883, all proceedings would be void and of no effect. It is said that he had a veto prepared. . . . As the clock was ticking away the precious minutes of the last hour allowed for the signature of the bill, and while some of the friends of the measure, including Mr. Welch, were almost holding their breath with anxiety in the office of the Secretary of State, the Governor's messenger entered with the signed bill, and the great victory was won. Niagara was saved, and a precedent of vast and far-reaching importance established which other State Governments and the Federal Government have freely followed." Green, "Last Public Address," 102.

36. Quoted in Laura Wood Roper, *FLO: A Biography of Frederick Law Olmsted* (Baltimore: Johns Hopkins University Press, 1973), 396.

37. During the course of the campaign to create the reservation, Olmsted had followed up on Lord Dufferin's initiative and visited Canadian officials in Ottawa to gain their support for a corresponding public facility in Ontario. In 1885 the Dominion of Canada established the Niagara Falls Park Commission, with national hero Colonel Casimir Stanislaus Gzowski at its head. In 1887 Olmsted wrote to Gzowski explaining parts of the *General Plan* and offering advice on matters related to the Canadian landscape. Canada would open Queen Victoria Park, as the public grounds on the other side of the border were

called, in the spring of 1888. Olmsted to Gzowski, August 15, 1887.

38. E. B. Perry, "Topics of the Times," *Century* 4 (August 1887): 631.

39. T. V. Welch, "Annual Report of the Superintendent," in *Report of the Commissioners of the State Reservation at Niagara for the Year 1885* (Albany, 1886), 2.

40. See "The Niagara Drive," *Niagara Falls Gazette,* June 2, 1885; "A Needed Improvement," *Real Estate and Builders Monthly* 1 (August 1885): 6; "Governor Hill's Best Day," *Utica Daily Press,* May 24, 1888; and "Batavia Doesn't Get the $30,000," *Batavia Daily News,* June 18, 1889.

41. Olmsted to C. E. Norton, August 4, 1885.

42. Green to Dorsheimer, July 21, 1886, copy in Frederick Law Olmsted Papers, Library of Congress. For his part, Olmsted had threatened to resign from the Niagara Falls Association— "to escape from my interest in it as fast and as far as I can"— when, in 1883, he learned that Green had been appointed to the original Niagara Commission. (Olmsted to Howard Potter, May 9, 1883.)

43. Olmsted to Lucius Robinson, July 21, 1886.

44. "Niagara Falls To-Day," *New York Times,* August 11, 1887.

45. Quoted in *Papers of FLO,* supp. ser., 1:52.

46. John C. Olmsted to Vaux, [February] 22, 1887, quoted ibid.

47. Reprinted in the *Niagara Falls Gazette,* August 10, 1887.

48. Frederick Law Olmsted and Calvert Vaux, *General Plan for the Improvement of the Niagara Reservation* (New York, 1887). The forty-five-page report is reprinted in *Papers of FLO,* supp. ser., 1:535–75. I have used this source in my discussion of the plan, and all quotations unless otherwise indicated are drawn from it.

49. *Minute Books of the Commissioners,* vol. 2 (July 21, 1899), 214, quoted in Dow, *State Reservation at Niagara,* 43.

50. Because the grounds were to be open to the public free of charge, the commissioners were expecting a dramatic increase in tourists from previous years. Crowd management was a serious consideration for Olmsted and Vaux when they created their *General Plan.* They even proposed a turnstile system at the entrance to the grounds. "Under ordinary circumstances," they explained, "the gate would be open and passage to the place unobstructed, but, upon needful occasions, the gate would be closed and visitors let in and let out by turnstiles at each end of the gate, the turnstiles for admission not opening after a certain number had entered except as room was made by those leaving." A plan of the reservation from 1902 shows that the area of Prospect Point was not to be laid out exactly as Olmsted and Vaux had suggested. An administration building was erected there, but not the reception building.

51. In 1910 an elevator shaft excavated through the rock allowed for the removal of the inclined railway.

52. The *General Plan* also included a number of miscellaneous recommendations for other parts of the reservation aimed at improving its appearance and facilitating viewing the scenery. The dilapidated wooden staircase that gave access to the Cave of the Winds behind the American Falls was a particular eyesore that could be seen from both the New York and Ontario sides of the river. It was, the authors declared, a "large artificial object, crossing from top to bottom one of the grandest features of the natural scenery of the Falls." They proposed that it be removed and an elevator shaft sunk to the base of the cliff, some distance back from the brink. Nevertheless, not wishing to see funds diverted from more pressing projects to do this, they conceded that for the time being, the staircase should be repaired. In the 1920s a shaft was dug to take an elevator down to the Cave of the Winds walk.

53. This was the upper end of the former portage route around the falls which early French traders had used as a river haven.

54. Building the benches of stone would not only make them cheap and durable but also "reduce to a minimum the opportunities for penciling and cutting them so irresistible to a certain class." Olmsted and Vaux indicated with arrows what views could be enjoyed from each of these delightful spots.

55. The 360-foot-long structure was said to have been the nation's largest privately owned bridge.

56. Welch had also suggested this be done. Although they maintained that the pedestrian should be king on Goat Island, Olmsted and Vaux also made limited provisions for carriage access to the island. They would revise the existing drive that circumnavigated the shoreline of the island, with the equivalent of a twenty-foot-wide country lane laid out fifty to one hundred feet back from the river's edge. The narrow width, they explained, was necessary to preserve as many forest trees as possible when the path was constructed. Olmsted and Vaux also pointed out that the wider the opening through the forest, "the more havoc will storms make with trees left standing nearby." Carriages would be allowed to pass in only one direction around the circuit and could stop at numerous "harbor points" to wait while passengers explored the nearby area on foot. With one-way traffic, places to pull out, and a six-mile-an-hour speed limit, carriages "will be less crowded on a road of twenty feet than on one of forty feet, as roads are ordinarily used." The partners hoped that the construction of the proposed carriageway on Goat Island would be one of the first projects the commissioners would undertake, not only because the increasing public would soon demand improved vehicle access to the island, but also, more important, because the "healing process of natural restoration by fresh growth" that would take place after the road had been cut through the virgin woodland could begin as soon as possible.

57. F.-A.-R. Chateaubriand, *Recollections of Italy, England and America,* vol. 1 (London: Colburn, 1815), 185.

58. Robinson quoted by Olmsted in "Notes," 29.

59. Duke of Argyll, "First Impressions of the New World," *Living Age* 144 (January 1880): 38, reprinted from *Fraser's Magazine.* Olmsted quoted this passage as well in his "Notes" to the *Special Report,* 30. The duke's celebrated visit to America received considerable attention in the New York press. The quoted passage was printed in the *New York Herald,* December 16, 1879. Olmsted may actually have met the duke, for after his visit to Niagara, the British nobleman was a guest at the home of Olmsted's close friend Charles Eliot Norton in Cambridge, where the Olmsteds spent much of that summer with Norton's neighbor E. L. Godkin.

60. In March 1887 the board presented the *General Plan* to the Ways and Means Committee in the hope that it would approve at least half of the initial $100,000 installment on the estimated $365,000 needed to implement it. Although no money was forthcoming during that legislative session, funds began to flow from Albany the following year. According to the commissioners' annual report for 1888, Olmsted and Vaux received payment on October 5, 1888.

61. Dow, *State Reservation at Niagara,* 177.

62. The board of commissioners appointed Samuel Parsons Jr. landscape architect in 1890. See *Seventh Annual Report of the Commissioners of the State Reservation at Niagara* (Albany, 1894), 16. In 1888 Downing Vaux made a map of the reservation indicating all place-names.

63. The bridge was completed by Downing Vaux in November 1898, three years after Calvert Vaux's death. The quotation is from "Now at Niagara," *Express,* November 13, 1898.

64. Charles Beveridge, "Planning the Niagara Reservation," in Charles Beveridge and Francis R. Kowsky, *The Distinctive Charms of Niagara Scenery: Frederick Law Olmsted and the Niagara Reservation* (Niagara Falls, N.Y.: Buscaglia-Castellani Art Gallery of Niagara University, 1985), 24. Not all of Olmsted and Vaux's recommendations in the *General Plan* became reality. At Welch's suggestion, on Goat Island the carriage drive was brought closer to the water at some places than Olmsted and Vaux preferred, fewer footpaths were laid out than the Olmsted and Vaux plan indicated, and stone seats at the water's edge were omitted. On the mainland, the old millrace was kept, the riverside path followed a straighter course and had no side trails to secluded seats, and carriages were given more space at Prospect Point. Moreover, the viewing areas planned with stone benches surrounded by heavy plantings were not constructed, and carriages were given access to many points that Olmsted and Vaux had reserved for pedestrians. Nonetheless, in 1914 Dow acknowledged the significant contribution of Olmsted and Vaux's analysis of the problems and the suggestions for meeting them which they had made to the management of the reservation. "Comparison of this plan with

what has actually been accomplished," noted Dow, "shows conclusively on what large lines the Reservation was conceived, how sane was the policy adopted, and how accurately it forecast the future." Dow, *State Reservation at Niagara,* 43.

65. Green, "Last Public Address," 96.

66. Patrick McGreevy, "Imaging the Future at Niagara Falls," *Annals of the Association of American Geographers* 77 (1987): 50.

67. Ginger Strand, *Inventing Niagara: Beauty, Power, and Lies* (New York: Simon & Schuster, 2008), 157.

68. *Master List of Design Projects of the Olmsted Firm, 1857–1979* (Washington, D.C.: National Association for Olmsted Parks, 2008), 272.

69. On the early legislation and treaties see Gail E. Evans, "Storm over Niagara: A Catalyst in Reshaping Government in the United States and Canada during the Progressive Era," *Natural Resources Journal* 32 (1992): 27.

70. Green, "Last Public Address," 96.

71. Perry, "Topics of the Times," 362.

8. SOUTH PARK, CAZENOVIA PARK, AND RIVERSIDE PARK

1. Unless otherwise noted, all quotations are from F. L. Olmsted, "Proposed Extension of the Park System," *ARBPC* 19 (1889), 32–39.

2. "Late Additions to the Plan of Buffalo," reprinted in "About Buffalo: A Map Worth Looking At—A Souvenir of Two Great Exhibitions," *Courier,* April 1, 1879.

3. "That South Park," *Express,* July 11, 1888.

4. F. L. Olmsted to Buffalo Park Commissioners, January 26, 1889.

5. The commissioners printed the two documents as a pamphlet titled *The Projected Park and Parkways on the South Side of Buffalo: Two Reports by the Landscape Architects, 1888* (Buffalo: Buffalo Park Commission, 1888). Unless otherwise indicated, all quotations are from this source.

6. By the time the full reports were submitted, the state legislature had passed a bill giving the Buffalo park commissioners authority to select land in South Buffalo and the adjacent town of West Seneca for a new park and parkways.

7. The route from town they advocated was to follow the streets known today as Abbot Road, Triangle Street, South Park Avenue, and Ridge Road. In 1891 the commissioners gave up the notion of linking the new South Park then being planned to Fillmore Avenue, even though the legislature had approved creation of such a route through the area to the north of the park. "No available route can be found through this section that is not beset with difficulties and disadvantages which seem almost insurmountable," the commissioners admitted. "It is all being rapidly built up and also grid ironed with railroad yards and tracks. The leading streets are only four rods wide, and

occupied with double tracked street car lines. All of these are also crossed on grade by about half a dozen steam railroads." *ARBPC* 22 (1892), 14.

8. "The South Park," *Express,* October 21, 1888.

9. [Charles Sprague Sargent], "A Novel Project for a Public Park," *Garden and Forest* 1 (November 21, 1888): 458.

10. "Opposing Interests," *Express,* December 13, 1888.

11. "Proposed South Park," in *ARBPC* 19 (1888), 11.

12. Olmsted to McMillan, January 21, 1889.

13. At the beginning of January 1889, the *Express* had headlined an article "What Will Mr. Olmsted's South-Side Plans Cost? Some People Think the Amount Will Reach $10,000." On January 5, Olmsted submitted his bill for the preparation of the South Park plan; see "Bills to Come: What Will Mr. Olmsted's South Side Plans Cost?" *Express,* January 6, 1889. Olmsted told McMillan (in his letter of January 21, 1889) that he and Vaux had been paid $5,000 for the original park and parkway plans. In fact the Olmsted firm received slightly less than that amount for the South Park plans; the payment of $4,905.51 is recorded in *ARBPC* 20 (1890), 44.

14. Olmsted to the Buffalo Park Commissioners, January 26, 1889. In 1931 the city established Centennial Park (the present LaSalle Park) on filled-in waterfront land near the beginning of the Niagara River, far from the site discussed in 1888.

15. "Something for All," *Express,* May 27, 1889.

16. "Ho for the Lake," *Express,* June 10, 1889.

17. Olmsted to Albert Wright, February 1, 1889.

18. "Proposed South Park Sites," *ARBPC* 20 (1890), 19, 20.

19. Olmsted to J. C. Olmsted, December 5, 1891.

20. Unless otherwise indicated, all quotations are from F. L. Olmsted & Co. to the Park Commissioners of the City of Buffalo, May 7, 1892.

21. Codman to J. C. Olmsted, April 28, 1892.

22. J. C. Olmsted to McMillan, May 7, 1892, and August 10, 1892.

23. *ARBPC* 23 (1893), 14.

24. *ARBPC* 29 (1899), 27.

25. "The Little Parks," *Express,* October 17, 1886.

26. *ARBPC* 25 (1895), 11.

27. "Advanced Rumors," *American Architect and Building News* 58 (November 6, 1897): xiii. The greenhouse was extensively restored in the 1930s and again in the early twenty-first century.

28. There would also be a large formal flower garden laid out behind it. The two elements together resembled similar features Olmsted had introduced into the gardens at Biltmore.

29. Olmsted to Partners, July 1892, quoted in Laura Wood Roper, *FLO: A Biography of Frederick Law Olmsted* (Baltimore: Johns Hopkins University Press, 1973), 441.

30. The first quotation is from "Looking for Sites," *Express,* May 18, 1890; the second is from *ARBPC* 28 (1898), 8.

31. F. L. Olmsted & Co. to McMillan, December 15, 1891.

32. For Stony Point as a site for the Pan-American Exposition, see "Report on Sites," *Express,* April 7, 1899.

33. *ARBPC* 23 (1893), 10.

34. F. L. Olmsted & Company to Buffalo Park Commissioners, May 7, 1892.

35. *ARBPC* 23 (1893), 10.

36. Codman to J. C. Olmsted, April 28, 1892.

37. F. L. Olmsted & Co. to McMillan, May 28, 1892.

38. McMillan submitted this letter, addressed to the Buffalo Park Commissioners, at the commissioners' meeting of July 5, 1892; it was printed in the *Courier* on July 6.

39. "Settled at Last," *Express,* August 3, 1892.

40. "Settled Forever," *Express,* August 3, 1892.

41. McMillan to F. L. Olmsted & Co., August 8, 1892. Johnson had evidently proposed creating a lake without damming Cazenovia Creek. Another area of dispute with Johnson's plan for the lake had been the depth of the water, Johnson apparently arguing for a shallower lake than McMillan and the Olmsteds thought appropriate. McMillan concluded his letter to the firm with this statement: "Another difficulty inherent in the Johnson plan may be mentioned before leaving the subject. It is the liability of the shallow pond to choke up with eel grass and other weeds. With clear water at all times permitting the full action of light on the loamy bottom soil, water-weeds could not have more favorable conditions. At a depth of 3.5 feet weeds need not be rank to tangle an oar in the hands of an amateur. In the Olmsted pond, the midwinter freezing when the ice lies solid on the bottom, and the scouring of spring freshets would prevent any growth of weeds. In the North park weeds would make the Lake useless for boating, and a nuisance instead of an ornament, but for the fact that the water is never clear enough to permit the sunlight to reach the bottom muck."

42. For a complete catalog of changes and addition to Cazenovia Park, see www.olmstedinbuffalo.org/CazenoviaPark.htm. Future plans for the restoration of the Olmsted plan can be seen at www.bfloparks.org/images/uploads/masterplan.pdf.

43. Beginning at Heacock Place, McKinley Parkway (formerly South Side Parkway) runs southwest to McClellan Circle (formerly Woodside Circle), where it meets Red Jacket Parkway coming from Cazenovia Park to the northeast. From McClellan Circle, McKinley Parkway curves in a southeasterly direction to South Park.

44. Before the 1838 Treaty of Buffalo Creek, two other prominent Senecas, Chief Silverheels and Chief Pollard, had made their homes on what is now Cazenovia Park.

45. "Public Improvements," *Greater Buffalo* 1 (July 20, 1897): 7.

46. "South Park Conservatory," *Greater Buffalo* 2 (June 15, 1898): 9.

47. "Labor Day," *Niagara Gazette,* September 6, 1887.

48. "Workingman Hill," *Express,* September 8, 1891.

49. "Park Board Favors It," *Express,* February 12, 1896.

50. "Riverside Park," *Express,* May 14, 1896.

51. "Kennedy Weakened," *Express,* March 16, 1897.

52. Olmsted Brothers to John Hughes, July 26, 1898. The lines were to be placed in underground conduits.

53. Ibid. Presumably, they intended to exempt the Niagara Street border of the park from their recommendation that in order to facilitate maintenance the park grounds be fenced, "with gateways only at the points where walks and drives are shown entering the grounds."

54. "Report on Parks," *Express,* March 18, 1899.

55. Plans were discussed but never realized to connect Riverside Park to Delaware Park by means of an extension of Scajaquada Parkway.

56. Olmsted Brothers to Hughes, July 26, 1898.

57. "Meandering pool" comes from Olmsted Brothers to Hughes, July 26, 1898; "minnow pool" from Olmsted Brothers to John C. Graves, July 20, 1898.

58. The pools were filled with earth in 1931. The Buffalo Olmsted Parks Conservancy hopes soon to restore them.

59. Olmsted Brothers to Hughes, July 26, 1898.

EPILOGUE

1. Anthony Trollope, *North America* (New York: Harper & Brothers, 1862), 162; Charles Burr Todd, "Studies in a Lake Port," *Lippincott's Magazine* 35 (April 1885): 388; F. L. Olmsted to Mrs. William Dwight Whitney, December 16, 1890, quoted in Laura Wood Roper, *FLO: A Biography of Frederick Law Olmsted* (Baltimore: Johns Hopkins University Press, 1973), 420; Walter Curt Behrendt, "City Fails to Follow Its Noble Plan," *Buffalo News,* December 4, 1937.

2. Witold Rybczynski, *A Clearing in the Distance: Frederick Law Olmsted and America in the Nineteenth Century* (New York: Simon & Schuster, 1999), 198. See also Scott Carson, "Frederick Law Olmsted and the Buffalo Park and Parkway System: A Study of the Planning and Design Responses to Nineteenth-Century Urban Growth and Changing Needs and Values of the Twentieth Century" (master's thesis, SUNY College of Environmental Science and Forestry, 1993).

3. Charles Beveridge, *Frederick Law Olmsted: Designing the American Landscape* (New York: Rizzoli, 1995), 270.

4. "Buffalo's Pride," *Express,* October 1, 1893.

5. Laura Wood Roper, *FLO: A Biography of Frederick Law Olmsted* (Baltimore: Johns Hopkins University Press, 1973), 435.

6. Olmsted to Mrs. William Dwight Whitney, December 16, 1890, quoted ibid., 420.

7. Lauren Belfer, *City of Light* (New York: Dial, 1999), 48; Burnham quoted in *Forty Years,* 37.

Acknowledgments

The origins of this book go back forty years, to the time when I was a doctoral student preparing my dissertation on the nineteenth-century architect Frederick Clarke Withers, an associate of Frederick Law Olmsted and Calvert Vaux. In the course of my research, I met Charles Capen McLaughlin and Charles Beveridge, who together were beginning the publication of the Olmsted Papers in the Library of Congress. I can remember telling them over lunch in a Capitol Hill restaurant that I had accepted a position teaching art history at Buffalo State College. They both responded by saying that the plans Olmsted made for Buffalo were his proudest accomplishment. As a youngster, I had come many times to Buffalo with my parents to spend time with relatives who made visiting their hometown a great pleasure. I was unaware, however, of the Olmsted legacy of parks, streets, and neighborhoods that the city possessed.

When I became a resident, I found that most natives were also unfamiliar with the extensive influence that Olmsted, together with Vaux and Olmsted's sons and associates, had had in shaping the city. Nor were many people there aware of the progressive-minded civic leaders who in the late nineteenth century had endorsed the designers' plans. Over the course of my career, I came to know and admire the achievement of which Olmsted had been so proud. Historic photographs revealed to me a city that was once as renowned for its parks and residential neighborhoods as for its industry and commerce. In addition, from time to time I would come upon towering American elms which reminded me that at Olmsted and Vaux's command, thousands of that now depleted species once sheltered Buffalo's thoroughfares. Certainly the investment that Buffalo's Gilded Age generation made in parks and boulevards ranked among the earliest instances in America of large-scale civic improvement. Later generations ignored much of that investment, but important elements of it remain.

This book commemorates my personal journey through the early history of the Olmsted cityscape. I hope that it will convey to both my fellow citizens and those who have yet to visit what an exemplary model of well-arranged urban life Olmsted's Buffalo represented. I second what the playwright A. R. Gurney has said about his native city: "If you walk around town . . . you can get a sense of a century and a half of a particular kind of American life. Buffalo was, and still is, both a small town and a big city, and if you want to know what Booth Tarkington was trying to write about, or what

Charles Ives was trying to make music about, or what Fitzgerald sometimes dreamed of getting back to, go to Buffalo, because it's all still there."

I owe many people a debt of gratitude for the generous assistance they gave me in the preparation of this book. It is with pleasure that I extend special thanks to Charles E. Beveridge, series editor of *The Papers of Frederick Law Olmsted;* Marie Bogner, visual resource curator, Buffalo State College; Joan K. Bozer, longtime advocate for Buffalo's parks; Stanton Broderick, creator of the Olmsted in Buffalo website; Daniel Dilandro, college archivist, Butler Library, Buffalo State College; Brian Dold, associate landscape architect, Buffalo Olmsted Parks Conservancy; Anne Dykstra, photographer, Niagara Power Project; Monica Pellegrino Faix, executive director, Richardson Center Corporation; Margaret Hatfield, librarian, Butler Library, Buffalo State College; Thomas Herrera-Mishler, executive director, Buffalo Olmsted Parks Conservancy; Susan Joffe, director of public information, Buffalo Psychiatric Center; Patrick Kavanaugh, historian, Forest Lawn Cemetery; Arleyn Levee, landscape historian and preservation consultant specializing in the work of the Olmsted firm; James Mendola, MLS, collector of postcard views of Buffalo parks; Martha Neri, MLS, archives manager, Buffalo Olmsted Parks Conservancy; Patricia O'Donnell, principal, Heritage Landscapes; Paul Pasquarello, supervisor, photographic operations, New York Power Authority; Thomas J. Riegstad, professor of English emeritus, Buffalo State College; Greg Robinson, landscape architect, Buffalo Olmsted Parks Conservancy; Dale Rossi, collector of stereo views of Buffalo and an authority on the photographers who made them; David P. Schuyler, Arthur and Katherine Shadek Professor of the Humanities and professor of American studies at Franklin & Marshall College; Catherine Schweitzer, executive director, Baird Foundation; Cynthia Van Ness, librarian, Buffalo and Erie County Historical Society; Martin Wachadlo, the leading authority on Buffalo's historic architecture; and Terry Lasher Winslow, associate librarian, local history department, Niagara Falls, N.Y., Public Library. I am particularly grateful to Andy Olenick for the diligence and meticulousness he brought to the task of providing modern photographs. His eloquently evocative images allow us to contemplate through the lens of the present enduring elements of Olmsted and Vaux's vision of a green and graceful metropolis.

It gives me special pleasure to thank the Library of American Landscape History for making this book a reality. Robin Karson, executive director, has been supportive and helpful throughout the process of preparing the manuscript and bringing to book to fruition, and to her I am most grateful. To Ethan Carr, I owe my appreciation for his confidence in my work and his decision to ask me to write the first book in the LALH series *Designing the American Park.* With Sarah Allaback, project manager, I feel I have formed a bond of friendship as a result of the many phone calls and e-mails we exchanged during the process of gathering images, preparing captions, and generally coordinating the work of production. She overcame many hurdles and generally kept things on track with diligence, persistence, and humor. Jessica Dawson, coordinator of special projects, offered cheerful assistance throughout. I regard myself also extremely fortunate to have had the assistance of two able editors, Amanda Heller and Mary Bellino; Carol Betsch of the University of Massachusetts Press proofread the final pages with vigilant eyes. Martin L. White capably carried out the task of indexing the volume. Jonathan Lippincott, the book's designer, merged text and images with great sensitivity. I am sure that Olmsted and Vaux would be pleased to see their work presented in such a handsome format.

Finally, this book benefited from support given to LALH by the Viburnum Trilobum Fund of the New York Community Trust; Furthermore: a program of the J. M. Kaplan Fund; the Baird Foundation, the Cameron and Jane Baird Foundation, and The Margaret L. Wendt Foundation of Buffalo, NY, all of which contributed significantly to its publication. To all who helped make this book possible, I extend my sincere thanks.

Index

parkways: in Albany, 41; in Buffalo, 6, 17, 37–38, 45, 107–19, 188, 195, 210–11; between Buffalo and Niagara Falls, 159, 168; economic growth and development due to, 118; fit in with Ellicott's original design, 107; Olmsted and Vaux introduce, 3, 17; Olmsted and Vaux's plan for Buffalo squares and, *119;* Parisian, 17; paving, 109; property values increased by, 111; trees planted along, 113. *See also* Humboldt Parkway; Lincoln Parkway; *and others by name*

Parsons, Samuel, Jr., 148, 178, 238n62

Paxton, Joseph, *8,* 8–9

Peace Bridge, 88, 89

Perry, Edward B., 168, 183

Perry, Oliver Hazard, 88

Pierce, Ray Vaughn, 91

Pierce's Palace Hotel, 91, *91*

Place de l'Étoile (Paris), 9, 46, 120, 127

"Plan for Additions to the Front" (Olmsted), 87, *87*

Plan for a Public Park on the Flats South of Buffalo (F. L. and J. C. Olmsted), 189

Plan for the Twenty-first Century (Olmsted Parks Conservancy), 220

Porter, Augustus, 156, 157

Porter, Cyrus K., 98

Porter, Peter Buell, 79, 156

Porter's Field, 145

Potter, Howard, 164

Pratt, Hiram, 89, 90, *90*

Pratt, Pascal Paoli, 38, 51–52; on committee to advocate for parks, 38; in initial construction of Buffalo parks, 51, 227n83; on park commission, 42, 52; photograph, *51*

Price, Uvedale, 11

Progressives, 87

property values, 111

Prospect Hill neighborhood, 79–80, 89

Prospect Park (Brooklyn), 6, 14, *16,* 17, 32, 43, 51, 169, 225n34

Prospect Park (Buffalo), 89, *90*

Prospect Park (Niagara Falls), 153, 154, 163, 167

Prospect Place, 89–91; as heart of Prospect Hill neighborhood, 80; in mid-nineteenth-century Buffalo, 23; in Olmsted's plan for Buffalo parks, 45; photograph around 1910, *90;* reservoir on north side, 80; trees transplanted to the Front from, 82

Prospect Point (Niagara Falls), 153, 154, *154,* 157, 171–72, 178, 238n64

Pückler-Muskau, Hermann von, 27

Putnam's Monthly, 12

Quebec City (Canada), 83, *83*

Radford, George Kent, 50; initial construction of Buffalo parks, 50, 227n77; making of Delaware Park (the Park), 55–56, 57, 70; making of Front Park (the Front), 80; making of Parkside community, 135, 136, *136;* making of the Parade (Martin Luther King Jr. Park; Humboldt Park), 93

railroads: Belt Line, 68, 87, 109–10, 134–40, 189, 226n65; Buffalo as rail center, 29; Olmsted's plan for viaduct over, 188, 194, 195, 210; on *Olmsted's Sketch Map of Buffalo,* 109; street railways, 46, 88, 109, 110, 211, 213; suburban systems, 46–47, 68

Rankine, William B., 180

Red Jacket Park, 197

Red Jacket Parkway, 210, 240n43

Report on the South Parkway Question (F. L. and J. C. Olmsted), 194, 196

Repton, Humphry, 11

reservoir, 80

residential squares and circles, 119–29

Richardson, Henry Hobson, 18; Buffalo State Hospital, 17, 19, 43, 141, 144, 180, 219, 220, 235n37; collaboration with Olmsted, 18, 19; death, 177; Dorsheimer house, 18–19, *19,* 127; and establishment of Niagara Reservation, 164; Gratwick house, 116, *116;* on his creative process, 197; moves to Boston, 53; New York state capitol, 20, 162, 234n54; Niagara Square memorial project, 126–28, *128,* 145; photograph, *18;* Shingle style used, 148; visits Niagara Falls with Olmsted, 158, 161; Watts Sherman house, 229n43

Richardson Center Corporation, 220

Richardson Complex Corporation, 145

Richardsonian Romanesque, 18, 141, 180

Richmond, Dean, 114

Richmond, Henry, 159

Richmond Avenue (The Avenue): The Circle at end of, 123; in Olmsted's plan for Buffalo parks, 45; Olmsted visits in 1868, 33; as park approach, 111, 113–14; photographs, *110, 114, 115*

Riverside (Illinois), 17, 32, 34, 134

Riverside Park, 211–15; expansion, 215; as last Olmsted park, 18; music grove, 215; pools, *214,* 214–15, *215;* Scajaquada Parkway links Delaware Park with, 118; wishbone drive, 214

Riverway (Niagara Falls), 173

Robb, J. Hampden, 164

Robinson, Charles Mulford, 181

Robinson, Lucius, 161, 162

Robinson, William, 176

Roebling, John A., 157, 236n8

Rogers, Sherman S., 164, 168, 169